Lectures on Government and Binding

The Pisa Lectures

Studies in Generative Grammar

The goal of this series is to publish those texts that are representative of recent advances in the theory of formal grammar. Too many studies do not reach the public they deserve because of the depth and detail that make them unsuitable for publication in article form.
We hope that the present series will make these studies available to a wider audience than has hitherto been possible.

Jan Koster
Henk van Riemsdijk
editors

Noam Chomsky

Lectures on Government and Binding

The Pisa Lectures

1982
FORIS PUBLICATIONS
Dordrecht - Holland/Cinnaminson - U.S.A.

Published by:
Foris Publications Holland
P.O. Box 509
3300 AM Dordrecht, The Netherlands

Sole distributor for the U.S.A. and Canada:
Foris Publications U.S.A.
P.O. Box C-50
Cinnaminson N.J. 08077
U.S.A.

First edition 1981
Second revised edition 1982

The editors would like to thank Reineke Bok-Bennema for compiling the index.

ISBN 90 70176 28 9 (Cloth)
ISBN 90 70176 13 0 (Paper)

Printed in the Netherlands by Intercontinental Graphics, H.I. Ambacht.

Table of Contents

Preface

The text that follows is based on lectures I gave at the GLOW conference and workshop held at the Scuola Normale Superiore in Pisa in April 1979. The material was then reworked in the course of lectures at MIT in 1979–80, where I was fortunate to have the participation of a number of visitors from other institutions in the U.S. and Europe. Since the Pisa meetings, there has been considerable research by a number of linguists within more or less the framework developed in the Pisa discussions, or bearing on this framework of ideas and assumptions. I will not attempt a systematic or comprehensive review of this work, much of which seems to me extremely promising, though there are some allusions to it and some is incorporated directly in the main line of presentation, as will be indicated.

The delay in the preparation of these lectures for publication may lead to some confusion in literature citations. There are in current literature references to the Pisa lectures, often using this term, referring naturally to the actual material presented and discussed at the April 1979 meetings. In a rapidly developing field, in which papers are often partly outdated – sometimes, by work in part based on them – by the time they appear, it is inevitable that passage of over a year will lead to changes and modifications, so that this book, though subtitled "the Pisa lectures," is actually different in certain respects from the original. In an effort to help clarify citations in other works, I will occasionally add footnote comment on differences between this text and the April 1979 lectures.

The material presented here borrows extensively from recent and current work in ways that will not be adequately indicated; specifically, from the work of linguists of the GLOW circle who have created research centers of such remarkable vitality and productivity in France, the Netherlands, Italy and elsewhere. The outstanding contributions of Richard Kayne, both in his own work and in stimulating research of others, deserve special mention.

Preparation of the lectures for publication was greatly facilitated by a transcript of the lectures and discussion prepared by Jean-Yves Pollock and Hans-Georg Obenauer, as well as by critical notes by Jan Koster. I am particularly grateful to the participants in the GLOW conference and workshop for their suggestions and criticism, and also to those who took part in a seminar at the Scuola Normale Superiore in March 1979, where much of the material presented in the April lectures was developed. The seminar began with study of an unpublished paper by Tarald Taraldsen (1978b). Though he was not present, his ideas stimulated much of the investigation of binding theory and the nature of variables that was carried out in the seminar. I owe a special debt to Luigi Rizzi for his original ideas and incisive criticism. Students, colleagues and visitors at MIT are also responsible for many improvements and modifications, only partially indicated. Among many others, Henk van Riemsdijk has been particularly helpful with many ideas and suggestions. I am also much indebted to Joseph Aoun and Dominique Sportiche for very helpful comments on the issues, and on the text, and to Jean-Roger Vergnaud for some essential ideas.

I would like to express my gratitude to the Scuola Normale Superiore for having provided me with such excellent conditions for research, and more generally, for the kindness and hospitality accorded both to me and my family during our stay in Pisa in the spring of 1979. I am also grateful to the National Endowment for the Humanities (USA) for their support during this period, when most of this research was completed.

The Pisa lectures were highly "theory internal," in that a certain general theoretical framework was presupposed and options within it were considered and some developed, with scant attention to alternative points of view or the critical literature dealing with the presupposed framework. I have kept to the same format in preparing these lectures for publication. Many criticisms of the general point of view I am adopting are discussed in Chomsky (1980b) and in references cited there, though the discussion is far from exhaustive. See also Piattelli-Palmarini (1980) for discussion and commentary on the general approach rather than on technical developments. An interesting perspective on the backgrounds of recent work is presented in Newmeyer (1980). I have also discussed this topic, less comprehensively and from a more personal point of view, in the introduction to Chomsky (1955).

The text that follows is divided into six chapters with subsections. While material from the original Pisa lectures is scattered throughout, it is concentrated in chapters 3 and 4. My paper at the GLOW conference (Chomsky, 1979a) is a brief outline of material presented in chapter 3 – though again, this material has been subsequently modified and developed, so that references in that paper to the original Pisa lectures do not invariably refer accurately to this text. Some of the material in chapters 3 and 4 is outlined briefly in Chomsky (1979b), and some of the contents of chapters 1 and 2 is presented rather informally in Chomsky (1980c).

Examples are separately numbered in each subsection. I will refer to them simply by number within the subsection in which they appear, and by subsection and number elsewhere. For example, the notation "2.4.1.(7)" refers to example (7) of chapter 2, section 4, subsection 1; the notation "2.4.1" refers to that subsection. Otherwise, notations, conventions and terminology are fairly standard, except where indicated. Specifically, I will often present syntactic structures in much reduced form so as to focus on the question at hand.

Noam Chomsky
Cambridge Mass.
Dec. 1980

Chapter 1

Outline of the theory of core grammar

I would like to begin with a few observations about some problems that arise in the study of language, and then to turn to an approach to these questions that has been gradually emerging from work of the past few years and that seems to me to show considerable promise. I will assume the general framework presented in Chomsky (1975; 1977a,b; 1980b) and work cited there. A more extensive discussion of certain of the more technical notions appears in my paper "On Binding" (Chomsky, 1980a; henceforth, OB). The discussion here is considerably more comprehensive in scope and focuses on somewhat different problems. It is based on certain principles that were in part implicit in this earlier work, but that were not given in the form that I will develop here. In the course of this discussion, I will consider a number of conceptual and empirical problems that arise in a theory of the OB type and will suggest a somewhat different approach that assigns a more central role to the notion of government; let us call the alternative approach that will be developed here a "government-binding (GB) theory" for expository purposes. I will then assume that the GB theory is correct in essence and will explore some of its properties more carefully, examining several possible variants and considering their advantages and defects. The ideas developed and explored in various forms in chapters 2–5 will be reformulated from a somewhat more abstract point of view in chapter 6.

In pursuing this course, it is worthwhile to make a distinction between certain leading ideas and the execution of these ideas. Existing languages are a small and in part accidental sample of possible human languages, and of this sample, only a few have been extensively investigated in ways that bear directly on the questions that concern me here. On a more personal note, there are only parts of this work that I am sufficiently familiar with so as to be able to draw upon it. Furthermore, theoretical innovations commonly suggest new ways of looking at comparatively well-studied languages that present them in a different light, or that bring out phenomena that were previously unexamined, or observed but unexplained. In applying these leading ideas, it is always necessary to make a number of empirical assumptions that are only partially motivated, at best. The leading ideas admit of quite a range of possibilities of execution. The discussion that follows is based on certain leading ideas, some of which are only beginning to be investigated seriously in a theoretical framework of the sort considered here: notions of government, abstract Case,[1] binding, and others. Often I will make some decision for concreteness in order to proceed, though leading ideas may not be crucially at stake in such decisions. The distinction between leading ideas and mode of execution is a rough but nevertheless useful one. In work subsequent to the lectures on which this text is based, other variants of the same or related leading ideas have been pursued, or significant modifications proposed and examined, in important work in progress that I will not be able to discuss adequately here.[2]

The point is, I think, important, sufficiently so that I would like to repeat some remarks published elsewhere on the topic (Chomsky, 1977a, p. 207):

"The pure study of language, based solely on evidence of the sort reviewed here, can carry us only to the understanding of abstract conditions on grammatical systems. No particular realization of these conditions has any privileged status. From a more abstract point of view, if it can be attained, we may see in retrospect that we moved towards the understanding of the abstract general conditions on linguistic structures by the detailed investigation of one or another 'concrete' realization: for example, transformational grammar, a particular instance of a system with these general properties. The abstract conditions may relate to transformational grammar rather in the way that modern algebra relates to the number system.

We should be concerned to abstract from successful grammars and successful theories those more general properties that account for their success, and to develop [universal grammar] as a theory of these abstract properties, which might be realized in a variety of different ways. To choose among such realizations, it will be necessary to move to a much broader domain of evidence. What linguistics should try to provide is an abstract characterization of particular and universal grammar that will serve as a guide and framework for this more general inquiry. This is not to say that the study of highly specific mechanisms (e.g., phonological rules, conditions on transformations, etc.) should be abandoned. On the contrary, it is only through the detailed investigation of these particular systems that we have any hope of advancing towards a grasp of the abstract structures, conditions and properties that should, some day, constitute the subject matter of general linguistic theory. The goal may be remote, but it is well to keep it in mind as we develop intricate specific theories and try to refine and sharpen them in detailed empirical inquiry.

It is this point of view that lies behind the rough distinction between leading ideas and execution, and that motivates much of what follows. I think that we are, in fact, beginning to approach a grasp of certain basic principles of grammar at what may be the appropriate level of abstraction.

At the same time, it is necessary to investigate them and determine their empirical adequacy by developing quite specific mechanisms. We should, then, try to distinguish as clearly as we can between discussion that bears on leading ideas and discussion that bears on the choice of specific realizations of them. Much of the debate in the field is, in my opinion, misleading and perhaps even pointless, in that it concerns the choice among specific mechanisms but uses evidence that only bears on leading ideas which the alternative realizations being considered may all share. The search for the appropriate level of abstraction is a difficult one. It is only quite recently that questions of this nature can even be raised in a serious way. My own suspicion is that as research progresses, it will show that many of the most productive ideas are in fact shared by what appear to be quite different approaches. Some of the subsequent discussion relates directly to this question, as does much current work, for example, Burzio (1981), Marantz (1981).

In work of the past several years, quite a broad range of empirical phenomena that appear to have a direct bearing on the theories of government and binding considered here have been examined in a few comparatively well-studied languages. Several theories have been proposed that are fairly intricate in their internal structure, so that when a small change is introduced there are often consequences throughout this range of phenomena, not to speak of others. This property of the theories I will investigate is a desirable one; there is good reason to suppose that the correct theory of universal grammar in the sense of this discussion (henceforth: UG) will be of this sort. Of course, it raises difficulties in research, in that consequences are often unforeseen and what appear to be improvements in one area may turn out to raise problems elsewhere. The path that I will tentatively select through the maze of possibilities, sometimes rather arbitrarily, is likely to prove the wrong one, in which case I will try to unravel the effects and take a different turning as we proceed. I will be concerned here primarily to explore a number of possibilities within a certain system of leading ideas, rather than to present a specific realization of them in a systematic manner as an explicit theory of UG.

Let us recall the basic character of the problem we face. The theory of UG must meet two obvious conditions. On the one hand, it must be compatible with the diversity of existing (indeed, possible) grammars. At the same time, UG must be sufficiently constrained and restrictive in the options it permits so as to account for the fact that each of these grammars develops in the mind on the basis of quite limited evidence. In many cases that have been carefully studied in recent work, it is a near certainty that fundamental properties of the attained grammars are radically underdetermined by evidence available to the language learner and must therefore be attributed to UG itself.

These are the basic conditions of the problem. What we expect to find, then, is a highly structured theory of UG based on a number of fundamental principles that sharply restrict the class of attainable grammars and narrowly constrain their form, but with parameters that have to be fixed by experience. If these parameters are embedded in a theory of UG that is sufficiently rich in structure, then the languages that are determined by fixing their values one way or another will appear to be quite diverse, since the consequences of one set of choices may be very different from the consequences of another set; yet at the same time, limited evidence, just sufficient to fix the parameters of UG, will determine a grammar that may be very intricate and will in general lack grounding in experience in the sense of an inductive basis. Each such grammar will underlie judgments and understanding and will enter into behavior. But the grammar – a certain system of knowledge – is only indirectly related to presented experience, the relation being mediated by UG.

What seems to me particularly exciting about the present period in linguistic research is that we can begin to see the glimmerings of what such a theory might be like. For the first time, there are several theories of UG that seem to have the right general properties over an interesting domain of fairly complex linguistic phenomena that is expanding as inquiry into these systems proceeds. That is something relatively new and quite important, even though surely no one expects that any of these current proposals are correct as they stand or perhaps even in general conception.

The approaches to UG that seem to me most promising fall within the general framework of the so-called "Extended Standard Theory." Each such approach assumes that the syntactic component of the grammar generates an infinite set of abstract structures – call them "S-structures" – that are assigned a representation in phonetic form (PF) and in LF (read: "logical form," but with familiar provisos[3]). The theory of UG must therefore specify the properties of (at least) three systems of representation – S-structure, PF, LF – and of three systems of rules: the rules of the syntactic component generating S-structures, the rules of the PF-component mapping S-structures to PF, and the rules of the LF-component mapping S-structure to LF. Each expression of the language determined by the grammar is assigned representations at these three levels, among others.

Note that the central concept throughout is "grammar," not "language." The latter is derivative, at a higher level of abstraction from actual neural mechanisms; correspondingly, it raises new problems. It is not clear how important these are, or whether it is worthwhile to try to settle them in some principled way.[4]

The empirical considerations that enter into the choice of a theory of PF and LF fall into two categories: grammar-internal and grammar-external. In the first category, we ask how particular assumptions about PF and LF relate to the rules and principles of grammar; in the second, we ask how such assumptions bear on the problem of determining physical form, perceptual interpretation, truth conditions, and other properties of utterances, through interaction of PF, LF and other cognitive systems.

I will have little to say about PF here. Assume it to be some standard form of phonetic representation[5] with labelled bracketing, what I will refer to as "surface structure," adopting one of the several uses of this term. The nature of S-structure and LF, and the rules of grammar determining and relating them, will be the central focus of my concerns here.

UG consists of interacting subsystems, which can be considered from various points of view. From one point of view, these are the various subcomponents of the rule system of grammar. From another point of view, which has become increasingly important in recent years, we can isolate subsystems of principles. I will assume that the subcomponents of the rule system are the following:

(1)   (i) lexicon
        (ii) syntax
            (a) categorial component
            (b) transformational component
        (iii) PF-component
        (iv) LF-component

The lexicon specifies the abstract morpho-phonological structure of each lexical item and its syntactic features, including its categorial features and its contextual features. The rules of the categorial component meet some variety of X-bar theory. Systems (i) and (iia) constitute the base. Base rules generate D-structures (deep structures) through insertion of lexical items into structures generated by (iia), in accordance with their feature structure. These are mapped to S-structure by the rule Move-α, leaving traces coindexed with their antecedents; this rule constitutes the transformational component (iib), and may also appear in the PF- and LF-components. Thus the syntax generates S-structures which are assigned PF- and LF-representations by components (iii) and (iv) of (1), respectively. Some properties of these systems and some alternative approaches will be considered below, but a good deal will be presupposed from the published literature.

The subsystems of principles include the following:

(2)   (i) bounding theory
        (ii) government theory
        (iii) θ-theory
        (iv) binding theory
        (v) Case theory
        (vi) control theory

Bounding theory poses locality conditions on certain processes and related items. The central notion of government theory is the relation between the head of a construction and categories dependent on it. θ-theory is concerned with the assignment of thematic roles such as agent-of-action, etc. (henceforth: θ-roles). Binding theory is concerned with relations of anaphors, pronouns, names and variables to possible antecedents. Case theory deals with assignment of abstract Case and its morphological realization. Control theory determines the potential for reference of the abstract pronominal element PRO. Properties of these systems will be developed as we proceed.

These subsystems are closely related in a variety of ways. I will suggest that binding and Case theory can be developed within the framework of government theory, and that Case and θ-theory are closely interconnected. Certain notions, such as c-command, seem to be central to several of these theories. Furthermore, the subsystems of (1) and (2) interact: e.g., bounding theory holds of the rule Move-α (i.e., of antecedent-trace relations) but not of other antecedent-anaphor relations of binding and control theory. Each of the systems of (1) and (2) is based on principles with certain possibilities of parametric variation. Through the interaction of these systems, many properties of particular languages can be accounted for. We will see that there are certain complexes of properties typical of particular types of language; such collections of properties should be explained in terms of the choice of parameters in one or another subsystem. In a tightly integrated theory with fairly rich internal structure, change in a single parameter may have complex effects, with proliferating consequences in various parts of the grammar. Ideally, we hope to find that complexes of properties differentiating otherwise similar languages are reducible to a single parameter, fixed in one or another way. For analogous considerations concerning language change, see Lightfoot (1979).

A valid observation that has frequently been made (and often, irrationally denied) is that a great deal can be learned about UG from the study of a single language, if such study achieves sufficient depth to put forth rules or principles that have explanatory force but are underdetermined by evidence available to the language learner. Then it is reasonable to attribute to UG those aspects of these rules or principles that are uniformly attained but underdetermined by evidence. Similarly, study of closely related languages that differ in some clustering of properties is particularly valuable for the opportunities it affords to identify and clarify parameters of UG that permit a range of variation in the proposed principles. Work of the past several years on the Romance languages, some of which will be discussed below, has exploited these possibilities quite effectively. Ultimately, one hopes of course that it will be possible to subject proposals concerning UG to a much broader test so as to determine both their validity and their range of parametric variation, insofar as they are valid. Since these proposals concern properties of grammars – apart from empirical generalizations, which should be regarded as facts to be explained rather than part of a system of explanatory principles of UG – it is possible to put them to the test only to the extent that we have grammatical descriptions that are reasonably compelling in some domain, a point of logic that some find distasteful, so the literature indicates.

In early work in generative grammar it was assumed, as in traditional grammar, that there are rules such as "passive," "relativization," "question-formation," etc. These rules were considered to be decomposable into more fundamental elements: elementary transformations that can compound in various ways, and structural conditions (in the technical sense of transformational grammar) that are themselves formed from more elementary constituents. In subsequent work, in accordance with the sound methodological principle of reducing the range and variety of possible grammars to the minimum, these possibilities of compounding were gradually reduced, approaching the rule Move-α as a limit. But the idea of decomposing rules such as "passive," etc., remained, though now interpreted in a rather different way. These "rules" are decomposed into the more fundamental elements of the subsystems of rules and principles (1) and (2). This development, largely in work of the past ten years, represents a substantial break from earlier generative grammar, or from the traditional grammar on which it was in part modelled. It is reminiscent of the move from phonemes to features in the phonology of the Prague school, though in the present case the "features" (e.g., the principles of Case, government and binding theory) are considerably more abstract and their properties and interaction much more intricate. The notions "passive," "relativization," etc., can be reconstructed as processes of a more general nature, with a functional role in grammar, but they are not "rules of grammar."

We need not expect, in general, to find a close correlation between the functional role of such general processes and their formal properties, though there will naturally be some correlation. Languages may select from among the devices of UG, setting the parameters in one or another way, to provide for such general processes as those that were considered to be specific rules in earlier work. At the same time, phenomena that appear to be related may prove to arise from the interaction of several components, some shared, accounting for the similarity. The full range of properties of some construction may often result from interaction of several components, its apparent complexity reducible to simple principles of separate subsystems. This modular character of grammar will be repeatedly illustrated as we proceed.

When the parameters of UG are fixed in one of the permitted ways, a particular grammar is determined, what I will call a "core grammar." In a highly idealized picture of language acquisition, UG is taken to be a characterization of the child's pre-linguistic initial state. Experience –in part, a construct based on internal state given or already attained –serves to fix the parameters of UG, providing a core grammar, guided perhaps by a structure of preferences and implicational relations among the parameters of the core theory. If so, then considerations of markedness enter into the theory of core grammar.

But it is hardly to be expected that what are called "languages" or "dialects" or even "idiolects" will conform precisely or perhaps even very closely to the systems determined by fixing the parameters of UG. This could only happen under idealized conditions that are never realized in fact in the real world of heterogeneous speech communities. Furthermore, each actual "language" will incorporate a periphery of borrowings, historical residues, inventions, and so on, which we can hardly expect to – and indeed would not want to – incorporate within a principled theory of UG. For such reasons as these, it is reasonable to suppose that UG determines a set of core grammars and that what is actually represented in the mind of an individual even under the idealization to a homogeneous speech community would be a core grammar with a periphery of marked elements and constructions.[6]

Viewed against the reality of what a particular person may have inside his head, core grammar is an idealization. From another point of view, what a particular person has inside his head is an artifact resulting from the interplay of many idiosyncratic factors, as contrasted with the more significant reality of UG (an element of shared biological endowment) and core grammar (one of the systems derived by fixing the parameters of UG in one of the permitted ways).

We would expect the individually-represented artifact to depart from core grammar in two basic respects: (1) because of the heterogeneous character of actual experience in real speech communities; (2) because of the distinction between core and periphery. The two respects are related, but distinguishable. Putting aside the first factor – i.e., assuming the idealization to a homogeneous speech community[7] – outside the domain of core grammar we do not expect to find chaos. Marked structures have to be learned on the basis of slender evidence too, so there should be further structure to the system outside of core grammar. We might expect that the structure of these further systems relates to the theory of core grammar by such devices as relaxing certain conditions of core grammar, processes of analogy in some sense to be made precise, and so on, though there will presumably be independent structure as well: hierarchies of accessibility, etc. Some examples will be discussed below; see also the references of note 6, and much additional work. These should be fruitful areas of research, increasingly so, as theories of core grammar are refined and elaborated.

Returning to our idealized – but not unrealistic – theory of language acquisition, we assume that the child approaches the task equipped with UG and an associated theory of markedness that serves two functions: it imposes a preference structure on the parameters of UG, and it permits the extension of core grammar to a marked periphery. Experience is necessary to fix the values of parameters of core grammar. In the absence of evidence to the contrary, unmarked options are selected. Evidence to the contrary or evidence to fix parameters may in principle be of three types: (1) positive evidence (SVO order, fixing a parameter of core grammar; irregular verbs, adding a marked periphery); (2) direct negative evidence (corrections by the speech community); (3) indirect negative evidence – a not unreasonable acquisition system can be devised with the operative principle that if certain structures or rules fail to be exemplified in relatively simple expressions, where they would be expected to be found, then a (possibly marked) option is selected excluding them in the grammar, so that a kind of "negative evidence" can be available even without corrections, adverse reactions, etc. There is good reason to believe that direct negative evidence is not necessary for language acquisition,[8] but indirect negative evidence may be relevant.[9] We would expect the order of appearance of structures in language acquisition to reflect the structure of markedness in some respects, but there are many complicating factors: e.g., processes of maturation may be such as to permit certain unmarked structures to be manifested only relatively late in language acquisition, frequency effects may intervene, etc.

It is necessary to exercise some care in interpreting order of appearance. For example, it has been observed that children acquire such structures as "John wants to go" before "John wants Bill to go," and that they do not make such errors as *"John tries Bill to win" (cf. "John tries to win"). It has sometimes been argued that such facts support the conclusion that there is a multiple lexical categorization for such verbs as *want*, namely, as taking either a VP or a clausal complement, the latter subcategorization perhaps more marked. In fact, there is evidence that the V-VP alternative is the unmarked case for surface structure, but this does not bear on the question of multiple subcategorization. Rather, it relates to a very different question: namely, the correct analysis of the surface structure V-VP at D-structure, S-structure and LF. I will argue later that this is a structure of the form V-clause at D- and S-structure and at LF, where the clause is invariably of the form NP-VP, with NP = PRO (the empty pronominal element) as an unmarked option in these cases. If so, then the order of acquisition is quite compatible with the preferable assumption that there is only a single categorization: *want*-clause.[10]

How do we delimit the domain of core grammar as distinct from marked periphery? In principle, one would hope that evidence from language acquisition would be useful with regard to determining the nature of the boundary or the propriety of the distinction in the first place, since it is predicted that the systems develop in quite different ways. Similarly, such evidence, along with evidence derived from psycholinguistic experimentation, the study of language use (e.g., processing), language deficit, and other sources should be relevant, in principle, to determining the properties of UG and of particular grammars. But such evidence is, for the time being, insufficient to provide much insight concerning these problems. We are therefore compelled to rely heavily on grammar-internal considerations and comparative evidence, that is, on the possibilities for constructing a reasonable theory of UG and considering its explanatory power in a variety of language types, with an eye open to the eventual possibility of adducing evidence of other kinds.

Any theory – in particular, a theory of UG – may be regarded ideally as a set of concepts and a set of theorems stated in terms of these concepts. We may select a primitive basis of concepts in terms of which the others are definable, and an axiom system from which the theorems are derivable. While it is, needless to say, much too early to hope for a realistic proposal of this sort in the case of UG,[11] nevertheless it is perhaps useful to take note of some of the conditions that such a theory should satisfy.

In the general case of theory construction, the primitive basis can be selected in any number of ways, so long as the condition of definability is met, perhaps subject to conditions of simplicity of some sort.[12] But in the case of UG, other considerations enter. The primitive basis must meet a condition of epistemological priority. That is, still assuming the idealization to instantaneous language acquisition, we want the primitives to be concepts that can plausibly be assumed to provide a preliminary, pre-linguistic analysis of a reasonable selection of presented data, that is, to provide the primary linguistic data that are mapped by the language faculty to a grammar; relaxing the idealization to permit transitional stages, similar considerations still hold.[13] It would, for example, be reasonable to suppose that such concepts as "precedes" or "is voiced" enter into the primitive basis, and perhaps such notions as "agent-of-action" if one believes, say, that the human conceptual system permits analysis of events in these terms independently of acquired language. But it would be unreasonable to incorporate, for example, such notions as "subject of a sentence" or other grammatical relations within the class of primitive notions, since it is unreasonable to suppose that these notions can be directly applied to linguistically unanalyzed data. Rather, we would expect that such notions would be defined in UG in terms of a primitive basis that meets the condition of epistemological priority. The definition might be complex. For example, it might involve some interaction of syntactic configurations, morphology, and θ-roles (e.g., the grammatical subject is the (usual) agent of an action and the direct object the (usual) patient), where the terms that enter into these factors are themselves reducible to an acceptable primitive basis.[14] Again, an effort to develop a principled theory of UG is surely premature, but considerations of this sort are nevertheless not out of place. They indicate that we should, for example be wary of hypotheses that appear to assign to grammatical relations too much of an independent status in the functioning of rule systems. I will return to some examples.

Since virtually the origins of contemporary work on generative grammar, a major concern has been to restrict the class of grammars made accessible in principle by UG, an obvious desideratum if UG is to attain explanatory adequacy, or, to put the same point differently, if UG is to account for the fact that knowledge of language is acquired on the basis of the evidence available. The problem can be viewed in a slightly different light when we distinguish between core grammar and marked periphery. Consider the theory of core grammar, assuming it to be decomposable into the subsystems of rules of (1). It is reasonable to suppose that the rules (iv) of the LF-component do not vary substantially from language to language, and that such variety as may exist is determined by other elements of the grammar; the language learner, after all, has little direct evidence bearing on the character of these rules. While there is variety among the systems associating S-structure and phonetic form (iii), it is plausible to assume that this variety falls within finite bounds. X-bar theory permits only a finite class of possible base systems (ib), and the transformational component, consisting of the single rule Move-α, admits at most a finite degree of parametric variation (perhaps, choice of α, or specification of landing sites in the sense of Baltin (1978, 1979)). The lexicon allows for infinite variety only in the trivial sense that there may be no finite bound on the length of words and morphemes; subcategorization frames and the like are narrowly limited in variety.

If these assumptions are correct, then UG will make available only a finite class of possible core grammars, in principle. That is, UG will provide a finite set of parameters, each with a finite number of values, apart from the trivial matter of the morpheme or word list, which must surely be learned by direct exposure for the most part. Depending on the nature of the theory of markedness, there may or may not be an infinite class of possible grammars, but this is an essentially uninteresting question in this connection, since marked constructions will be added by direct evidence (or indirect negative evidence), and can thus proliferate only slowly, raising no questions of principle.

The conclusion that only a finite number of core grammars are available in principle has consequences for the mathematical investigation of generative power and of learnability.[15] In certain respects, the conclusion trivializes these investigations. This is evident in the case of the major questions of mathematical linguistics, but it is also true of certain problems of the mathematic theory of learnability, under certain reasonable additional assumptions. Suppose that UG permits exactly n grammars. No matter how "wild" the languages characterized by these grammars may be, it is quite possible that there exists a finite set of sentences S such that systematic investigation of S will suffice to distinguish the n possible grammars. For example, let S be the set of all sentences of less than 100 words in length (a well-defined notion of UG, if the set of possible words is characterized). Then it might be that for each of the n possible grammars there is a decision procedure for these "short" sentences (even if the grammars lack decision procedures in general) that enables the n grammars to be differentiated in S. The grammars may generate non-recursive sets, perhaps quite "crazy" sets, but the craziness will not show up for short sentences, which suffice to select among these grammars. Under this assumption, so-called "language learning" – i.e., selection of a grammar on the basis of finite data – will be possible even if the languages characterized by the grammars have very strange properties.

Note that the assumption is not unrealistic, surely no more unrealistic than others standard in the theory of learnability. Thus, contrary to what has often been alleged, there is no conceptual connection between recursiveness and "learnability" (in any empirically significant sense of the latter term) – which is not to deny that one might construct some set of conditions under which a connection could be established, a different matter.[16] Hence certain questions of the mathematical theory of learnability are trivialized by the assumption that UG permits only a finite set of grammars, under plausible additional assumptions, such as those just mentioned. Note also that one should be very wary of arguments purporting to favor one linguistic theory over another on grounds of alleged problems concerning learnability. On fairly reasonable assumptions, these questions simply do not arise.

But even if correct, the finiteness assumption for UG does not show that investigations in mathematical linguistics or the theory of learnability for infinite classes of grammars are pointless. Rather, it indicates that they proceed at a certain level of idealization, eliminating from consideration the properties of UG that guarantee finiteness of the system of core grammar. One may then ask whether the infinite set of core grammars available under this abstraction from UG is learnable in some technical sense of the word, or what the properties may be of the class of generated languages. Work conducted at this level of idealization might prove to have empirical consequences in an indirect but perhaps significant way. For example, abstracting from properties of UG that guarantee finiteness, the set of possible grammars and languages, now infinite, might be unlearnable in some technical sense. If, on the contrary, the set turns out to be learnable under this idealization, then this is a possibly interesting though rather abstract empirical discovery about the properties of UG. Furthermore, even for finite classes of grammars that are learnable for a reasonable finite potential data base, significant questions arise in the theory of learnability, specifically, questions relating to the bounds on complexity of sentences that suffice for selection of grammar.[17]

Similar observations hold of the study of the power of various theories. There have been many allusions in the literature to this topic since the appearance of the badly-misunderstood work of Peters and Ritchie (1973) on the generative power of the theory of transformational grammar. In essence, they showed that in a highly unconstrained theory of transformational grammar, a particular condition on rule application (the survivor property, which, Peters independently argued, was empirically well-motivated; cf. Peters (1973)) guarantees that only recursive sets are generated, whereas without this condition any recursively enumerable set can be generated by some grammar. The common misunderstanding is that "anything goes," since without the survivor property or some comparable constraint all recursively enumerable languages have transformational grammars. In fact, the questions do not even arise except under the idealization just noted if UG permits only a finite class of grammars. It might, for example, turn out that these grammars characterize languages that are not recursive or even not recursively enumerable, or even that they do not generate languages at all without supplementation from other faculties of mind, but nothing of much import would necessarily follow, contrary to what has often been assumed.[18]

It is worth asking whether the correct theory of UG does in fact permit only a finite number of core grammars. The theories that are being studied along the general lines I will be discussing here do have that property, and I think that it probably is the right property. It may also be worthwhile to investigate the properties of UG under an idealization that would permit an infinite class of grammars, but care must be exercised in considering the implications of results attained in such investigation.

One must guard against other fallacies. Early work in transformational grammar permitted a very wide choice of base grammars and of transformations. Subsequent work attempted to reduce the class of permissible grammars by formulating general conditons on rule type, rule application, or output that would guarantee that much simpler rule systems, lacking detailed specification to indicate how and when rules apply, would nevertheless generate required structures properly. For example, X-bar theory radically reduces the class of possible base components, various conditions on rules permit a reduction in the category of permitted movement rules, and conditions on surface structure, S-structure and LF allow still further simplification of rules and their organization. Such reductions in the variety of possible systems are obviously welcome, as contributions to explanatory adequacy. But it is evident that a reduction in the variety of systems in one part of the grammar is no contribution to these ends if it is matched or exceeded by proliferation elsewhere. Thus, considering base rules, transformations, interpretive rules mapping the output of these systems to phonetic and logical form, and output conditions on PF and LF, it is no doubt possible to eliminate entirely the category of base systems by allowing a proliferation in the other components, or to eliminate entirely the category of transformations by enriching the class of base systems and interpretive rules.[19] Shifting the variety of devices from one to another component of grammar is no contribution to explanatory adequacy. It is only when a reduction in one component is not matched or exceeded elsewhere that we have reason to believe that a better approximation to the actual structure of mentally-represented grammar is achieved.

The objective of reducing the class of grammars compatible with primary linguistic data has served as a guiding principle in the study of generative grammar since virtually the outset, as it should, given the nature of the fundamental empirical problem to be faced – namely, accounting for the attainment of knowledge of grammar – and the closely related goal of enhancing explanatory power. Other guiding ideas, while plausible in my view, are less obviously valid. It has, for example, proven quite fruitful to explore redundancies in grammatical theory, that is, cases in which phenomena are "overdetermined" by a given theory in the sense that distinct principles (or systems of principles) suffice to account for them. To mention one example that I will consider below, the theories of Case and binding exhibit a degree of redundancy in the OB-framework in that each suffices independently to determine a substantial part of the distribution of the empty pronominal element PRO: PRO appears in positions that are not Case-marked, and from an independent point of view, in positions that are transparent (non-opaque) in the sense of binding theory; but see chapter 4, for some qualifications. In OB, this is mentioned as a problem (cf. OB, note 30); in chapter 3, I will suggest that it is to be resolved by reduction of both Case and binding theory to the more fundamental concepts of the theory of government.

To mention another case, I will suggest that the *[*that*-trace] filter of Chomsky and Lasnik (1977) is too "strange" to be an appropriate candidate for UG and should be reduced to other more natural and more general principles (cf. Taraldsen (1978b), Kayne (1980a), Pesetsky (1978b)). Similarly, I will suggest that the two binding principles of the OB-system – the (Specified) Subject Condition SSC and the Nominative Island Condition NIC – are implausible because of their form, and should be reduced to more reasonable principles. Much recent work is motivated by similar concerns.

This approach, which has often proven fruitful in the past and is, I believe, in the cases just mentioned as well, is based on a guiding intuition about the structure of grammar that might well be questioned: namely, that the theory of core grammar, at least, is based on fundamental principles that are natural and simple, and that our task is to discover them, clearing away the debris that faces us when we explore the varied phenomena of language and reducing the apparent complexity to a system that goes well beyond empirical generalization and that satisfies intellectual or even esthetic standards. These notions are very vague, but not incomprehensible, or even unfamiliar: the search for symmetry in the study of particle physics is a recent example; the classical work of the natural sciences provides many others.

But it might be that this guiding intuition is mistaken. Biological systems – and the faculty of language is surely one – often exhibit redundancy and other forms of complexity for quite intelligible reasons, relating both to functional utility and evolutionary accident. To the extent that this proves true of the faculty of language, then the correct theory of UG simply is not in itself an intellectually interesting theory, however empirically successful it may be, and the effort to prove otherwise will fail. Much research on language has been guided by the belief that the system is fairly chaotic, or that language is so intertwined with other aspects of knowledge and belief that it is a mistake even to try to isolate a faculty of language for separate study. Qualitative considerations based on "poverty of the stimulus" arguments, such as those mentioned above and considered in more detail elsewhere, strongly suggest that this picture is not generally correct, but it might prove to be correct for large areas of what we think of as phenomena of language. In the cases just mentioned, for example, it could turn out to be the case that the redundancies simply exist, that odd and very special properties such as the *[*that*-trace] filter or the two binding conditions of the OB system are simply irreducible and must be stipulated with UG, or that these principles are already too abstract and that we must be satisfied with superficial empirical generalizations.

It is pointless to adopt *a priori* assumptions concerning these matters, though one's intuitive judgments will, of course, guide the course of inquiry and the choice of topics that one thinks merit careful investigation. The approach I will pursue here can be justified only in terms of its success in unearthing a more "elegant" system of principles that achieves a measure of explanatory success. To the extent that this aim is achieved, it is reasonable to suppose that the principles are true, that they in fact characterize the language faculty, since it is difficult to imagine that such principles should merely hold by accident of a system that is differently constituted. Considerations of this sort are taken for granted, generally implicitly, in rational inquiry (for example, in the more advanced sciences), and there is little reason to question them in the present context, though it is quite appropriate to do so elsewhere; specifically, in the context of general epistemology and metaphysics.[20] But it is worth bearing in mind that this class of rather vague methodological guidelines has a rather different status, and much less obvious validity, than the search for more restrictive theories of UG, which is dictated by the very nature of the problem faced in the study of UG. It is quite possible to distinguish between these concerns. For example, a theory of UG with redundancies and inelegant stipulations may be no less restrictive than one that overcomes these conceptual defects.

Insofar as we succeed in finding unifying principles that are deeper, simpler and more natural, we can expect that the complexity of argument explaining why the facts are such-and-such will increase, as valid (or, in the real world, partially valid) generalizations and observations are reduced to more abstract principles. But this form of complexity is a positive merit of an explanatory theory, one to be valued and not to be regarded as a defect in it. It is a concomitant of what Moravcsik (1980) calls "deep" as opposed to "shallow" theories of mind, and is an indication of success in developing such theories. It is important to distinguish clearly between complexity of theory and complexity of argument, the latter tending to increase as theory becomes less complex in the intuitive sense.

There is little point in dwelling on these matters, though I think it is perhaps useful to bear them in mind, particularly, if one hopes to make sense of current tendencies in the study of language. It is not difficult, I think, to detect the basic difference in attitude just sketched in work of the past years, and my personal feeling is that it may become still more evident in the future, as questions of the sort just briefly mentioned come more to the fore, as I expect they will.

Notes

1.   Henceforth, I will capitalize the word "Case" when used in its technical sense, along lines suggested originally by Jean-Roger Vergnaud. Cf. OB, Rouveret and Vergnaud (1980), and Vergnaud (forthcoming). See also Babby (1980), van Riemsdijk (1980).
2.   See, for example, the references in chapters 4, 5, below.
3.   See Chomsky (1980b,c) for some discussion.
4.   See Chomsky (1980b,c) for further discussion. See also the final remarks of chapter 1, Chomsky (1965).
5.   For some intriguing recent ideas on this subject, see Halle and Vergnaud (1980).
6.   Cf. Kean (1975), van Riemsdijk (1978b), George (1980); also many papers in Belletti, Brandi and Rizzi (forthcoming).
7.   On the legitimacy of this idealization and the implausible consequences of rejecting it, see Chomsky (1980b, chapter 1).
8.   On this matter, see Wexler and Culicover (1980). See also Baker (1979), Lasnik (1979).
9.   For a concrete example illustrating this possibility, involving stylistic inversion and the so-called "pro-drop parameter," see Rizzi (1980b).
10.   For discussion, see Rizzi, *ibid.*
11.   Cf. Chomsky (1955) for an early, and no doubt premature effort in this direction. For further discussion of the issue, see Chomsky (1965, chapter 1) and (1977a, chapter 1); also Baker (1979), Wexler and Culicover (1980), and other related work.
12.   See Goodman (1951).
13.   On this matter, see Chomsky (1975, chapter 3).
14.   Cf. Marantz (1981), where it is suggested that broader considerations (including developmental factors) are involved.
    One might, perhaps, take a different tack, and suppose that these or other notions are primitives, linked to notions that meet the condition of epistemological priority by postulates that do not suffice to guarantee definability. The consequence is indeterminacy of the choice of grammar when the extension of each of the primitives meeting the condition of epistemological priority is fixed. The less fully such notions as those of the theory of grammatical relations, for example, are reducible to primitives meeting this condition, the greater the indeterminacy of grammars selected on the basis of primary linguistic data. There is, however, little reason to suppose that such indeterminacy exists beyond narrow bounds. Insofar as this is true, we should be skeptical about theories with a primitive basis containing concepts that cannot plausibly be assumed to enter into the determination of the primary linguistic data, or about unrealistic assumptions concerning such data (cf. references of note 8). Again, more complex versions of these considerations apply if we turn to accounts of language acquisition that proceed beyond the idealization to instantaneous acquisition, say, along the lines discussed in Chomsky (1975, chapter 3), Marantz (*op.cit.*).
15.   On the latter topic, see Wexler and Culicover (1980) and material reviewed there. Also Pinker (1979).
16.   On the question of recursiveness and learnability, see Levelt (1974), Lasnik (1979, 1980), R. Matthews (1979). Also Chomsky (1980b, chapter 3).
17.   See Wexler and Culicover, *op.cit.*, for interesting work on this topic.
18.   See Chomsky (1965, p. 62), and the references of note 16.
19.   As was done, for example, in the earliest generative grammar in the modern sense, which had as its syntactic component a phrase structure grammar (which could perfectly well have been presented as a context-free grammar) with indices to express interrelations among scattered parts of syntactic structures (Chomsky, 1951). The class of such grammars (which generate context-free languages, a fact of minimal significance) is extremely rich in descriptive power and quite uninteresting for this among other reasons. It was an advance when subsequent work showed that these powerful, but clumsy and unrevealing systems, could be factored into two components (base and transformational), each with quite natural properties.
20.   See the references cited in the preface for further discussion.

Chapter 2

Subsystems of core grammar

Let us now turn to the theory of UG, concentrating on core grammar. In chapter 1, several subsystems of rules and of principles were identified (cf. 1.(1), 1.(2)). We now turn to some properties of these. Since the subsystems interact so closely and are so interdependent, perhaps the most satisfactory procedure will be to develop them more or less in parallel, beginning with a first approximation to each and then turning to further refinements, even at the cost of some redundancy and some internal conflict as early approximations are modified.

2.1. Levels of representation

Consider first the subsystems of rules 1.(1). At the most general level, assume UG to have three fundamental components, organized as in (1):

(1)

$$
\begin{array}{c}
\text{syntax} \\
\downarrow \\
\text{S-structure} \\
\swarrow \qquad \searrow \\
\text{PF} \qquad\qquad \text{LF}
\end{array}
$$

The rules of the syntax generate S-structures. One system of interpretive rules, those of the PF- component, associates S-structures with representations in phonetic form (PF); another system, the rules of the LF-component, associates S-structures with representations in "logical form" (LF), where it is understood that the properties of LF are to be determined empirically and not by some extrinsic concern such as the task of determining ontological commitment or formalizing inference; the term "LF" is intended to suggest – no more –that in fact, the representations at this level have some of the properties of what is commonly called "logical form" from other points of view.[1]

At the most general level of description, the goal of a grammar is to express the association between representations of form and representations of meaning. The system (1) embodies certain assumptions about the nature of this association: namely, that it is mediated by a more abstract S-structure and that the mappings of S-structure onto PF and LF are independent of one another.

The system (1), when its elements are specified, will be a theory of UG, of the language faculty in a narrow sense of this term. It is reasonable to suppose that the representations PF and LF stand at the interface of grammatical competence, one mentally represented system, and other systems: the conceptual system, systems of belief, of pragmatic competence, of speech production and analysis, and so on. Any particular theory of UG, say, a specification of (1), involves empirical assumptions of a somewhat abstract sort concerning legitimacy of idealization, assumptions that may prove incorrect but are unavoidable if we hope to gain some understanding of a system as complex as the language faculty, and more generally, the human mind. I will put these questions aside, and continue with the investigation of (1) in a way that embodies and sharpens one system of assumptions about these questions.[2]

I assume further that each of the components of (1)–the syntax, the PF-rules and the LF-rules – include rules of the form Move-α, where α is some category, their exact nature and properties to be determined. Thus, among the PF-rules there may be rules of movement, rearrangement, etc., which are sometimes called "stylistic rules"; among the LF-rules is the rule of quantifier movement QR (quantifier rule)[3]; and in the syntax there is the single rule Move-α that constitutes the transformational component 1.(liib). For reasons already noted, it is reasonable to suppose that the LF-rules are subject to very little variation among languages, but the option of employing Move-α may or may not be taken in each of the three subsystems, and if taken, may be subject to some parametric variation.

Turning first to the syntax, apart from the rule Move-α, which is a potential element of each of the three components, it consists of a base which in turn consists of a categorial component and a lexicon. The base generates D-structures (deep structures) which are associated with S-structure by the rule Move-α. To clarify terminology, I will use the term "surface structure" in something like its original sense, referring to the actual labelled bracketing of an expression at the level PF. Changing usage over the years has given rise to a fair degree of confusion. The term "surface structure" has been used in much recent work to refer to a more abstract representation than the actual labelled bracketing of an expression, the earlier sense of "surface structure," to which I return here.

Let us consider now some properties of representations at the levels of surface structure (PF), LF and S-structure. Consider first the sentences (2):

(2)   (i) the students prefer for Bill to visit Paris
        (ii) the students prefer that Bill visit Paris

The verb *prefer*, as an inherent lexical property, takes a clausal complement which has a subject NP and a predicate VP (*Bill* and *visit Paris*, respectively, in (2)), and an element (call it "INFL," suggesting "inflection") indicating in particular whether the clause is finite or infinitival. Suppressing the distinction between indicative and subjunctive, we will say that

INFL has the values $[\pm\text{Tense}]$, where $[+\text{Tense}]$ stands for finite and $[-\text{Tense}]$ for infinitival. Following Bresnan (1970, 1972), we assume that a clause ($\bar{S}$) consists of a complementizer COMP and a propositional component (S); the latter is analyzed as NP-INFL-VP at LF. Thus at the LF-level, the sentences (2) are represented as in (3), where in the case of (2i), COMP = *for* and INFL = $[-\text{Tense}]$; and in the case of (2ii), COMP = *that* and INFL = $[+\text{Tense}]$:

(3)   the students $[_{VP}$ prefer $[_{\bar{S}}$ COMP $[_S$ Bill INFL $[_{VP}$ visit Paris $]]]]$

The S-structure underlying (3) may be assumed to be identical with (3) in this case, so that the mapping of S-structure to LF is trivial. Similarly, the mapping of S-structure to surface structure is quite straightforward in this case.

Consider next the sentences of (4):

(4)   (i) the students want to visit Paris
        (ii) the students wanna visit Paris
       (iii) the students want Bill to visit Paris
        (iv) the students want that Bill visit Paris

Sentence (4iv) is not idiomatic English, but we may assume this to be an accidental gap reflecting properties that are not part of core grammar; thus assume (4iv) to be fully grammatical at the relevant level of abstraction, as in the analogous case of (2ii) and as in languages otherwise similar to English. At the level of LF, then, (4iv) is again of the form (3), with *want* in place of *prefer*.

Turning to (4iii), it is analogous to (2i) except that it lacks the COMP *for*. Consideration of such examples as (5) reveals that this reflects an idiosyncratic property of the verb *want* in these dialects of English:

(5)   (i) the students want very much for Bill to visit Paris
        (ii) what the students want is for Bill to visit Paris

Let us tentatively assume (subject to later discussion) that a rule of the PF-component deletes *for* directly after *want* in these dialects, as is also possible directly after *prefer*, subject to idiosyncratic variation. Then the LF-representation of (4iii) is, again, of the form (3), with *want* in place of *prefer*. Examples (4iii) and (4iv) differ at the LF-level in exactly the way that (2i) differs from (2ii), with the choice of COMP = *for* and INFL = $[-\text{Tense}]$ in one case, and COMP = *that* and INFL = $[+\text{Tense}]$ in the other, the regular association of these elements. The underlying S-structures are again identical to the LF-representations. Surface structures are derived by *for*-deletion in the case of (4iii) and other details that we need not consider.

Now consider the examples (4i) and (4ii). At the level of surface structure, assume these to be represented with the categorial structure of (6i, ii), just as (4iii) is represented with the categorial structure of (6iii): [4]

(6)   (i) the students $[_\alpha$ want $[_\beta$ to $[_\gamma$ visit Paris$]]]$
       (ii) the students $[_\alpha$ wanna $[_\gamma$ visit Paris$]]$
       (iii) the students $[_{VP}$ want $[_{\bar{S}}[_S$ Bill to $[_{VP}$ visit Paris$]]]]$

Recall that (iii) derives from the underlying S-structure by deletion of the COMP *for*. Since surface structures observe (phonological) word boundaries, (6i) and (6ii) differ as indicated. But they are surely the same at the LF-level and indeed are of the same general form as (6iii) at this level. Thus all the sentences of (6) are of the form (7) (analogous to (3)) at the level of LF-representation:

(7)   the students $[_{VP}$ want $[_{\bar{S}}$ COMP $[_S$ NP INFL $[_{VP}$ visit Paris$]]]]$

COMP in (7) is *for* and INFL, correspondingly, is $[-\text{Tense}] = to$, exactly as before, in minimal contrast to (4iv) with COMP = *that* and INFL = $[+\text{Tense}]$.

The choice of the embedded subject of the clausal complement of *want* in (7) differs, however, for (6i,ii) on the one hand and (6iii) on the other. In the case of (6iii), the embedded subject NP is *Bill*. In the case of (6i,ii) it is a pronominal element marked in some way to indicate that its reference is that of the phrase *the students*, the matrix subject; it is something like "they (the students)," as in (8), the common LF-representation for (6i,ii):

(8)   the students $[_{VP}$ want $[_{\bar{S}}$ for $[_S$ they (the students) to $[_{VP}$ visit Paris$]]]]$

How shall we analyze the informal notation "they (the students)"? We will use the device of coindexing to indicate intended reference in the relevant sense, assuming that each noun phrase is assigned a numerical index; for the moment, let us assume this assignment of index to be free. Then assuming that the noun phrase *the students* has been assigned the index i, the phrase "they (the students)" of (8) becomes P_i, where P is some kind of pronominal element. The pronominal element P has no properties beyond those of a minimal pronominal element: namely, the features person, number and gender, which must of course match those of the coindexed antecedent in a well-formed LF-representation. We will use the notation "PRO" for the collection of these features, with some choice of values. Thus the LF-representation (8) becomes (9):

(9) $[_{NP_i}$ the students$]$ $[_{VP}$ want $[_{\bar{S}}$ for $[_S$ PRO$_i$ to $[_{VP}$ visit Paris$]]]]$

The element PRO in the LF-representation (9) has exactly the same θ-role as *Bill* in (3) or in the corresponding LF-representation for (4iii,iv); PRO differs from *Bill* in that (in this case) its reference is determined by its co-indexed antecedent, rather than being "inherent" through an independently assigned index, a matter dealt with in the theory of control.

Consider next the S-structure underlying the surface structures (6i,ii) and the LF-representation (9). The simplest assumption, once again, is to assume that the S-structure is virtually identical with the LF-representation in this case. Let us tentatively assume, then, that the S-structure associated with (4i) and (4ii) is identical to (9) apart from the indexing of PRO, the latter being determined by the rule of control in the LF-component. Then the underlying S-structure is (10):

(10) $[_{NP}$ the students$][_{VP}$ want $[_{\bar{s}}$ for $[_S$ PRO to $[_{VP}$ visit Paris$]]]]$

Alternatively, we might assume that PRO too receives its index at S-structure, taking the rule of control to be a rule of index-checking rather than index-assignment; then the S-structure too is (9). Throughout, we have suppressed the INFL of the matrix sentence and other details irrelevant to the discussion.[5] The surface structures (6i) and (6ii) are derived from (10) or (9) in a perfectly straightforward way, differing by application (in(6ii)) or nonapplication (in (6i)) of the optional rule (11) of the PF-component:

(11)   want + to → wanna

The phonological rules of the PF-component do not "see" the abstract features of PRO, which are relevant only to the LF-component, or to morphology.

Summarizing, the verbs *want* and *prefer* take clausal complements as a lexical property. The clauses are of the form (12), where either COMP = *for* and INFL = $[-\text{Tense}]$ or COMP = *that* and INFL = $[+\text{Tense}]$:

(12) $[_{\bar{s}}$ COMP $[_S$ NP INFL VP$]]$

The mapping of S-structure to LF is trivial, involving only the coindexing of PRO in the examples so far discussed. The mapping of S-structure to PF is also straightforward, involving only the idiosyncratic rule of *for*-deletion and the optional contraction rule (11). As for the choice of α, β, γ in the surface structures (6), clearly $\alpha = \gamma = $ VP, and while little if anything turns on the matter of categorial representation in surface structure in this case, the simplest assumption is that $\beta = [_{\bar{s}}[_S$, exactly as in the parallel example (6iii).

In these examples, the approach to the central problem of grammar – namely, the association of PF- and LF-representations – that is represented in (1) appears to be quite well-motivated. Notations and irrelevant details aside, the PF- and LF-representations that we have assumed are relatively uncontroversial and seem to be the simplest possible, with uniform lexical entries for such verbs as *want, prefer,* expressing exactly their role in LF-representation. The assumptions that should be considered more carefully are (i) those embedded in (12), the analysis of the notion "clause"; and (ii) those relating to S-structure and its role in mediating the association between PF- and LF-representation. In the cases so far considered, these assumptions seem optimal.

Let us now apply a similar analysis to some slightly more complicated examples. Consider first the sentences (13) :

(13)   it is unclear $\Big\}$ that Bill saw Mary

    John knows

The matrix predicates *unclear, know* take clausal complements, so the LF-representations of (13) are (14), where we will use *M* ambiguously for the matrix element of (13):

(14) $M - [_{\bar{S}} \text{that} [_S \text{Bill} [+\text{Tense}] [_{VP} \text{see Mary}]]]$

The S-structure underlying (14) may once again be taken to be identical to the LF-representation, so that the mapping from S-structure to LF is trivial. The surface structures corresponding to (13) derive by a rule of the PF-component assigning the element $[+\text{Tense}]$ (here further specified as *past*) to the verb *see*.

In (13), *M* takes a declarative complement, but it may also take an interrogative complement as in the surface structure (15):

(15) $M - \text{who Bill saw}$

The embedded complement corresponding to (15) is represented at LF as something like (16):

(16)   for which person x, Bill saw x

For empirical evidence bearing on the LF-representation (16), see the references of note 10.

Still pursuing the natural assumption that the mapping from S-structure to LF be reduced to the minimum, the optimal S-structure underlying (15), (16) will be (17):

(17) $M - [_{\bar{S}} \text{who} [_S \text{Bill} [+\text{Tense}] [_{VP} \text{see } \alpha]]]$

Here α has the following properties: (i) it has the θ-role of the direct object of *see*, exactly as does *Mary* in (14); (ii) it is associated with *who*, as a representation of the variable bound by the quasi-quantifier *who* which is interpreted as "for which person x" at LF; (iii) it disappears at PF. Given (i), α is an NP. Given (ii), it is coindexed with *who* (adapting the indexing device already proposed). Given (iii), it lacks phonetic properties. Therefore, we take $\alpha = [_{NP_i} e]$, where e is the identity element and i is the index of *who*. We will refer to α in such cases as this as the "trace" of *who*, and will often use the notation t in place of α. The S-structure underlying (15), (16) is therefore (18):

(18) $M - [_{\bar{S}} who_i[_S Bill [+ Tense][_{VP} see\ t_i]]]$

Note that we are distinguishing trace from PRO, the empty pronominal; while it is not obvious that they are distinct, reasons for distinguishing them will appear in subsequent discussion, and we will maintain this distinction throughout, recasting it in somewhat more abstract terms in chapter 6. Note also that the rules associating antecedent and trace are distinct from the rules associating antecedent and PRO, whether the antecedent of trace is a *wh*-phrase, as in the case we are now considering, or a phrase of a different type, as in cases to which we return. The association of antecedent and PRO is determined by a rule of control which either assigns to PRO the index of an antecedent or checks the indices of PRO and antecedent in accordance with the theory of control, which belongs to the LF-component. We will see that the properties of this rule are quite different from those of the rule determining the association of antecedent and trace, which does not fall under the theory of control. I will assume, in fact, that the latter coindexing is a property of the rule Move-α. In the present case, the D-structure underlying (18) is (19); application of the rule Move-α, assigning identical indices to *who* and its trace, maps (19) into (18) within the syntax:

(19) $M - [_{\bar{S}} COMP [_S Bill [+Tense] [_{VP} see\ who]]]$

The D-structure underlying (13) differs from the D-structure underlying (15) in two respects: (i) the object of the embedded clause is *Mary* in the case of (13) and is *who* in the case of (15); the COMP is *that* in the case of (13) and is something different in the case of (15). I will assume that COMP may be one of the following in D-structure:

(20) $COMP \rightarrow \left\{ \begin{array}{l} [\pm WH] \\ for \end{array} \right\}$

The element $[+WH]$ heads an interrogative complement and is selected by certain matrix predicates, e.g., M but not "John said." The element $[-WH]$ is spelled out as *that* in English (it may also be null) and equivalents in other languages. The element *for* is the *for*-complementizer already discussed. In the case of (13), the D-structure is identical with the S-structure and the LF-representation (14). In the case of (15), the D-structure (19) becomes the S-structure (18) by application of Move-α in the syntax, and the corresponding LF-representation is formed by spelling out the *wh*-phrase *who$_i$* as "for which person *x*," where t_i is taken as the variable *x*. Apart from these differences, the structures (13) and (15) correspond point-by-point, as desired.

In these cases, once again, the approach represented in (1) is empirically well-motivated, yielding a very simple rule system for associating PF- and LF-representations, with properties that seem optimal.

In examples (13) and (15), *M* takes a finite ($[+$Tense$]$) complement. We would expect, then, that such matrices should also take infinitival ($[-$Tense$]$) complements, and in fact they do, as in (21):

(21)   M – who to see

Because of lexical properties of the particular predicates in *M*, the infinitival complement happens to be interrogative in this case, but in general it may be interrogative or declarative and $[\pm$Tense$]$. Consider now the various representations of (21).

At LF, the representation is clearly (22):

(22)   M – $[_{\bar{S}}$ for which person x $[_S$ α to see $x]$

That is, the LF-representation of (21) is exactly the same as that of (15) (namely, (16)), apart from the choice of INFL in the embedded clause and the choice of the subject of that clause: *Bill* in (15) and α in (22). The element α has the same θ-role as *Bill* in (15) but lacks independent specific reference. The optimal assumption is that α = PRO, the minimal pronominal, which is coindexed with *John* by the theory of control when *M* = *John knows* and is arbitrary in reference, there being no antecedent, when *M* = *it is unclear*. Assume therefore that this is so.

The S-structure underlying (22) is (23):

(23)   M – $[_\alpha$ who$_i$ $[_\beta$ X to $[_\gamma$ see $t_i]]]$

The pair (*who$_i$*, t_i) is converted to the corresponding LF-forms by rules already established. Clearly γ = VP, and α = $\bar{S}$ since it has the distribution of $\bar{S}$ and converts to it at LF, and, like $\bar{S}$, dominates COMP.... What is β? β is a category with the following properties: (i) it is the domain of *wh*-movement; (ii) $\bar{S} \rightarrow$ COMP β; (iii) it dominates *to*-VP; (iv) it converts to S in LF-representation. Clearly β = S, the sole category having exactly these properties.

Turning now to the internal structure of the embedded S in (23), we have to determine the nature of X. There are two plausible possibilities: (i) X is null, i.e., no element at all, so that the embedded clause is: $[_S$ to $[_{VP}$ *see* $t_i]]$ (ii) X = PRO. On assumption (i), the basic rules analyzing S are (24);

on assumption (ii), they are (25):

$$(24) \quad S \rightarrow \left\{ \begin{array}{l} \text{(NP) to VP} \\ \\ \text{NP Tense VP} \end{array} \right\}$$

(25) $S \rightarrow$ NP INFL VP

Under (25), INFL may become either $[\pm\text{Tense}]$, freely, subject to lexical idiosyncrasies common to the two alternative analyses. Furthermore, NP in (25) may only be PRO in (23).

Clearly, the analysis (25) is preferable on conceptual grounds. This is particularly clear if there are reasonable principles that determine that the NP is PRO when INFL is $[-\text{Tense}]$ as in (23) but not when INFL = $[+\text{Tense}]$. If so, then (25) expresses exactly the correct generalization, abstracting from properties of language determined by other principles; whereas (24) redundantly expresses some of the content of these other principles. As we shall see, the theories of government, binding and Case do have this consequence; they determine the distribution of PRO in exactly the manner required by adoption of (25), and do so on quite reasonable grounds, with many desirable consequences that are independent of the properties of PRO. Therefore we adopt the analysis (25), taking the S-structure of (21) to be (23) with $X =$ PRO.

The consequence, once again, is that the mapping of S-structure to LF is quite straightforward, as is the mapping of S-structure to PF. The mapping to LF involves the same rules for interpretation of *wh*-phrase and trace that are independently required for finite clauses, and the control rule indexing PRO, just as in the cases discussed earlier. The mapping of S-structure to PF requires no special rules. The configurations (15) and (21) differ in exactly one respect: abstracting from the content of lexical categories, both configurations derive from the S-structure (26), where INFL = $[+\text{Tense}]$ in (15) and INFL = $[-\text{Tense}]$ in (21):

(26) $M - [_{\bar{S}} \text{who}_i [_S \text{NP INFL} [_{VP} \text{see } t_i]]]$

Again, this is the optimal result: configurations that differ minimally differ in exactly one structural property, in this case, $[\pm\text{Tense}]$, chosen freely contingent upon lexical properties of M.

Recall, however, the basic assumption yet to be established: that the distribution of PRO is somehow determined on reasonable grounds.

Suppose that α in (23) were taken as $\overline{\text{VP}}$, where $\overline{\text{VP}} \rightarrow \text{COMP VP}_1$, VP_1 being an infinitival verb phrase, as has occasionally been proposed in one or another variant. This amounts to adopting the analysis (24) in essence, replacing it by the considerably clumsier system of rules (27):

(27)   (i) $\overline{\text{VP}} \rightarrow \text{COMP VP}_1$
         (ii) $\overline{\text{S}} \rightarrow \text{COMP S}$

      (iii) $S \rightarrow$ NP VP$_1$ when COMP $= for$; $S \rightarrow$ NP VP$_2$ otherwise

      (iv) VP$_1$ is *to*-VP and VP$_2$ is Tense-VP

Furthermore, all rules introducing embedded $\overline{S}$ will have to be extended to include $\overline{VP}$, which has the same distribution as $\overline{S}$, lexical idiosyncrasies apart. This rule system can be stated in various ways, but it is clearly no genuine alternative to (24), which is to be rejected in favor of the simpler (25). I will return to variants of (24), which raise still further difficulties, in 2.4.

    Independent and in this case direct evidence in favor of (25) over (24) is provided by the behavior of pleonastic elements such as *there* and impersonal *it*; we return later to their counterparts in other languages (French impersonal *il* and, we will later suggest, impersonal PRO in such languages as Italian and Spanish). There are certain constructions in which these elements must be inserted, as illustrated in (28):

(28)   (i) *there* is a good reason for his refusal
      (ii) I believe *there* to be a good reason for his refusal
      (iii) I'd prefer for *there* to be a better reason for his refusal
      (iv) I'd prefer *there* being a better reason for his refusal
      (v) I believe *it* to have rained (*it* to be clear who won)
      (vi) I'd prefer *its* raining in September (*its* being clear who won)

The italicized category NP cannot be omitted in (28); some NP must appear in these positions. As we shall see, the theory of government excludes PRO from these positions in (i), (ii), (iii), (v); properties of the embedded VP and the gerund exclude PRO from these positions in (iv) and (vi), since if PRO appeared here the theory of control would assign an LF-representation with the sense "I'd prefer my being a better reason for his refusal," "I'd prefer my raining in September," etc. –the same considerations redundantly exclude PRO in (ii), (iii), (v). We will return later to the choice of *there* versus *it*; for the moment, let us simply identify them as an obligatory pleonastic element α, which, clearly, is an NP.

    Obligatory insertion of the NP α follows from the fact that the constructions illustrated require subjects for some structural reason; call it the principle P. Clearly, P does not derive from θ-theory; the italicized elements bear no θ-roles. Nor does P derive from considerations of subcategorization. Verbs do not subcategorize for subjects, which may be freely missing when P is inapplicable, as in (29) and other constructions to which we will return:

(29)   (i) my belief that there will be a good reason for his refusal
      (ii) the belief that there will be a good reason for his refusal

The principle P, plainly, is the structural requirement that certain configurations – infinitivals and gerunds – must have subjects; i.e., the principle P
is simply the rule (25), which incorporates both cases if we take gerunds to
have clausal as well as NP structure (as is well-motivated on other familiar
grounds) and if we continue to assume, as above, that the italicized element
α in (28ii–vi) is not in the matrix clause but is rather the subject of the
embedded clausal unit, exactly as is the case in the LF-representations.
Rule (25) predicts the facts of (28) whereas (24) leaves them unexplained,
an additional and compelling reason for selecting (25) over (24) beyond
those already discussed.

We might approach these questions from a slightly different point of
view. Consider the structure of clauses at LF. Keeping to a reasonable conception of core grammar – thus eliminating from consideration elliptical
expressions, etc. – a clause must at least contain a predicate, which we
take to be of the category VP. The minimal clause, then, will be something
like (30):

(30)   it rains

Here *rain* is the VP predicate and there is no argument. In more complex
cases, the predicate may itself contain an argument (e.g., (31i) with the
VP predicate: *seem*-clause; (31ii) with the VP predicate: *hit-Bill*), and may
contain a subject argument (e.g., (31ii)):

(31)   (i) it seems that John is here
        (ii) John hit Bill

Suppose we assume further, subject to some reconsideration later, that a
clause at LF must contain a "mood-indicator" of some sort, namely, what
we have called INFL, which may be finite or infinitival. Then a clause at
LF will at least contain the structure (32), as in (30):

(32)   INFL VP

We might then tentatively adopt the assumption that obligatory presence
of subject represents a particular choice for a certain parameter of UG.
English and French, for example, make this choice; thus we have such
structures as (28) and the base rule (25). In the case of (25), what must be
specified in the particular grammar of French and English is obligatoriness
of NP and order of the elements. Other languages might not require that
NP is obligatory; the Semitic languages are possible candidates. In such
languages, putting aside questions of order, the base rule would then be
not (25) but (33):

(33) $S \rightarrow$ (NP) INFL VP

The choice between (25) and (33) is a choice with regard to a certain parameter of UG: namely, obligatoriness of subject in syntactic structure. In addition, there are choices with regard to ordering of elements. I will suggest in §2.8 that much the same is true at the level of LF even for non-configurational languages lacking a syntactic phrase VP.

Care must be taken, however, to determine whether (25) or (33) is selected in various languages. Thus consider the Romance languages apart from French. In these, as in Latin, the analogue to (30) lacks an overt subject (cf. Hall (1979)). This fact suggests that these languages select option (33). But the conclusion is questionable. Such languages as Spanish and Italian differ from French and English in a distinct parameter, namely, what has been called the "pro-drop parameter," which entails a variety of consequences, as we shall see; that is, in these languages, not only "weather verbs" such as *rain* but also verbs that have subjects with a definite θ-role may appear at surface structure with no NP subject. In such cases, there is surely a subject at LF, and there is good evidence, as we shall see, that there is an NP subject at S-structure too in cases lacking any subject in surface structure. It may be, then, that the "weather verbs" simply fall under this distinct principle. We will see in chapter 6 that there is good reason to suppose this to be the case. See the discussion of 6.(6), and references cited there.

The argument might cut the other way as well. If Kayne (1972) is correct, then French sentences with subject pronouns have no surface subject, the pronoun being a clitic. As usual, a survey of surface forms is quite uninformative.

Now let us return to the question whether the property [±Tense] should be treated in the manner of (24) or (25). Note that this question is distinct from the question of obligatoriness of subject. The question does not arise in languages that require an obligatory subject in syntactic structure. For such languages as French and English, the rules (24) are not an option at all, as shown by (28). Consider, then, languages that do not require an obligatory subject. In this case, by assumption, NP is optional when the clause is finite. Again, (24) is not an option. The choices in UG are restricted to the question of whether the subject is or is not obligatory; i.e., (25) or (33).

Summarizing, all of the constructions with embedded clauses that we have discussed are of the general form (34), where M is some matrix element:

(34) $M - [_{\bar{S}} \text{COMP} [_S \text{NP INFL VP}]]$

A matrix verb or adjective that takes a clausal complement appears at D- and S-structure in the configuration (34). Non-embedded clauses are also of the form of the embedded clause in (34), with INFL = [+Tense] for other reasons (which, incidentally, are relaxed in certain cases in other languages and also marginally in English). For reasons yet to be discussed, when INFL = $[-\text{Tense}]$ and COMP $\neq$ *for* in syntactic representations, then the NP subject of the embedded clause in (34) may be and normally must be PRO; otherwise, it cannot be PRO. We also will return to the case of gerunds, where PRO and lexical subjects contrast. Specifically, with $M = \textit{it is unclear}$ or $M = \textit{John knows}$, as above, the embedded phrase of (35) is clausal, exactly as in the variants (36) or as in (37):

(35)   M – what to do
(36)   what Bill is to do

(37)   M – that Bill is to do that

Let us formulate these observations as a guiding principle for the theory to be developed:

(38)   Representations at each syntactic level (i.e., LF, and D- and S-structure) are projected from the lexicon, in that they observe the subcategorization properties of lexical items.

Let us call this principle and later refinements the "projection principle" for syntactic representations.[6] We will generalize it in the next section, discussing further its relation to the rule (25) analyzing S as NP-INFL-VP. Note that we are for the moment attributing a different status to the projection principle and to rule (25). The former, we are assuming to be a general principle of UG, while rule (25) may be in part a language-particular rule of English. It might be, then, that some language does not satisfy (25) in general, though it will satisfy this rule insofar as the rule follows from the projection principle, as in part it will under a reformulation to be proposed in the next section.

Let us now consider the meaning of the projection principle. Clearly, subcategorization properties of lexical items must be satisfied at LF. This is true by definition; if this condition is violated, the sentence is simply not well-formed, so there is no need to stipulate that the principle holds in some form at LF. If *persuade*, for example, takes an NP object and a clausal complement as a lexical property, then an LF-representation including this verb will be well-formed only if it is assigned an NP object and a clausal complement at this level of representation. Whatever notation we adopt, the sentences (39) will all have LF-representations of roughly the form (40) (in one reading of (i), (ii)):[7]

(39)   (i) we persuaded John that he should finish college
         (ii) John was persuaded that he should finish college
         (iii) we persuaded John to finish college
         (iv) John was persuaded to finish college
(40)   ... $[_{\text{VP}}$ persuade $[_{\text{NP}}$ John$]$ $[_{\bar{\text{S}}}$ that he (John) should finish college$]]$ ...

Naturally, to express the intended interpretation (40) of (i), (ii) we will use the same device that has already been suggested for the case of (iii), (iv), where this interpretation is obligatory; namely, a pronominal co-indexed with *John*, either *he* (as in (i), (ii)) or PRO (as in (iii), (iv)). The fact that coindexing is required in cases (iii), (iv) but not (i), (ii) of (39) follows from the theory of control and other properties of pronominals.

In accordance with the projection principle, the categorial requirements of the verb *persuade* expressed in (40) must be satisfied at D- and S-structure as well. Assuming the rule (25) and the projection principle, the S-structures of (39) must be (41):

(41) (i) we INFL $[_{VP}$ persuade $[_{NP}$ John$]$ $[_\bar{S}$ that he should finish college$]]$

(ii) John INFL be $[_\alpha$ persuade $[_{NP} \beta$ $]$ $[_\bar{S}$ that he should finish college$]]$

(iii) we INFL $[_{VP}$ persuade $[_{NP}$ John$]$ $[_\bar{S}$ PRO to finish college$]]$

(iv) John INFL be $[_\alpha$ persuade $[_{NP}\beta][_\bar{S}$ PRO to finish college$]]$

In (ii) and (iv), α and β are to be determined. The D-structures differ from (41) only in replacement of $[_{NP} \beta]$ by its antecedent, *John*. Thus, the D-structures are mapped to the S-structures by the rule Move-α, which has an effect only in case (ii) and (iv) of (41), leaving the trace $[_{NP} \beta]$, which, as in the case of *wh*-movement discussed earlier, we assume to be co-indexed with its antecedent by the movement rule. We will return to the status of α at the end of the next section and again in §2.7. As for β, there is no apparent reason to take it to be anything other than *e*, as we have assumed in the case of *wh*-movement, though we will reconsider this question in §2.4.6 and in chapter 6.

The projection principle yields some of our earlier conclusions. For example, we assumed that the S-structure underlying (42) is (43), for reasons already discussed:

(42) it is unclear who to see
(43) it is unclear $[_\bar{S}$ who$_i$ $[_S$ PRO to see t$_i]]$

The presence of the trace t_i is determined by the projection principle, given that *see* has a direct object as a lexical property. The presence of PRO is determined by rule (25).

The projection principle requires that an NP appear as object of *persuade* in (41ii, iv) and *see* in (43). θ-theory will clearly require that this NP be associated with *John* in (41) as a device for assigning to *John* its proper θ-role; in our notation, such association will be represented again by co-indexing. As we have seen, independent considerations require that the trace be coindexed with *who* in (43). Thus, the basic rudiments of trace theory follow from the projection principle and certain fairly obvious principles of interpretation. One might say that trace theory in its essentials is nothing other than the minimal way of satisfying these requirements, taking the coindexed NP that satisfies the projection principle to be maximally simple, i.e., to have no unmotivated properties.

On the assumption that the projection principle holds, the role of the categorial component of the base is reduced to a minimum. It will simply express language-particular idiosyncrasies that are not determined by the lexicon. It is unnecessary for base rules to stipulate that structures such as those of (41) are generated, as far as the choice of complements for *persuade* is concerned. If *persuade* is inserted in some different frame, the projection principle will be violated and no well-formed LF-representation will be derived. Exactly what properties of the categorial component must be stipulated in a particular grammar is a question to which we return; perhaps such properties as order of major constituents, insofar as this is not determined by lexical properties and other principles of grammar.

The grammar of a particular language can be regarded as simply a specification of values of parameters of UG, nothing more. Since the projection principle has the consequence of substantially reducing the specification of the categorial component for a particular grammar, it has corresponding implications for the theory of language acquisition. Someone learning English must somehow discover the subcategorization features of *persuade,* one aspect of learning its meaning. Given this knowledge, basic properties of the syntactic structures in which *persuade* appears are determined by the projection principle and need not be learned independently. Similarly, a person who knows the word *persuade* (hence knows its lexical properties, specifically, its subcategorization features) can at once assign an appropriate LF-representation and S- and D- structure when the word is heard in an utterance, or in producing the word, and will recognize the sentence to be deviant if other properties of the utterance conflict with this assignment. Hence languages satisfying the projection principle in their basic design have obvious advantages with respect to acquisition and use.

Consideration of the projection principle illuminates a conceptual deficiency of theories of UG of the type considered in Chomsky (1965). In such theories, the lexicon is a set of lexical entries, each with its specific contextual features (among other properties). The categorial component of the base, quite independently, specifies a certain class of subcategorization frames in which lexical items may appear. Thus information concerning the class of subcategorization frames is in effect given twice in the grammar: once – implicitly – in the lexicon, as a property of the class of lexical items in its totality; and once – this time directly – by the rules of the categorial component. The fact has, of course, not gone unnoticed. The categorial component of the base is sometimes described as a specification of redundancy rules of the lexicon, i.e., as an explicit formulation of the class of subcategorization frames that are found in the lexicon. But this formulation is misleading; as a specification of redundancy rules, the categorial component does no work. Compare, for example, the case of truly effective redundancy rules, such as those that specify that if a lexical item has a certain property P, then it will also have the property P'; e.g., if the item has the feature [human], it will have the feature [animate]; or if it has the property that it begins with three consonants, then it has the property that it begins with /s/. In such cases, the redundancy rules are effective in the sense that once the rule is stated that an item with property P has the property P', then it is unnecessary to include the property P' in the entry of any lexical item with the property P. But the rules of the categorial component do not have this effect; even when these rules are explicitly formulated, each lexical item must still contain a full specification of its subcategorization frames. For example, if the base rules of English state that VP $\rightarrow$ V NP $\bar{S}$, it is still necessary to include in the lexical entry for *persuade* the information that it takes an object and a clausal complement – though their order need not be stipulated, given the rule of the categorial component. Apart from order, the rule of the categorial component serves no function as a redundancy rule; as for order, I will suggest below that this specification too is probably unnecessary in this case, and in quite a few others.

In short, there is an unwanted redundancy between the rules of the categorial component and the lexicon in a grammar of the sort outlined in Chomsky (1965). The information about the class of subcategorization frames that is thus dually represented cannot be eliminated from lexical entries. Therefore, we should attempt to eliminate it from the categorial component. The projection principle in fact accomplishes this, in quite a sweeping way. Given the projection principle and the general properties of X-bar theory, the categorial component for a particular grammar will be quite meager.

While the projection principle is a natural one from several points of view, it is by no means obviously correct. Its empirical consequences are quite far-reaching, as we have already seen and will find again later on. Thus the principle is far from innocuous. It is violated by theories that conform to the general outlines of Chomsky (1965), or by any theory that does not incorporate something similar to trace theory, assuming that it has syntactic representations at all. It is also violated by most approaches that incorporate trace theory, e.g., the OB-theory, with its "structure-building rules." Similarly, a theory that adopts something like (24) as the analysis of S, and, correspondingly assigns to such infinitivals as (44) the structure (45), violates the projection principle:

(44)   I expect it to rain

(45)   I $[_{\text{VP}}$ expect $[_{\text{NP}}$ it$]$ $[_{\alpha}$ to rain$]]$ (α = S or α = VP)

The reason is that at the level of LF-representation, *expect* clearly takes only a clausal complement, but in the structure (45), it has an NP object that does not appear in the LF-representation. For similar reasons, an analysis of (46) as (47) is excluded by the projection principle:

(46)   I consider John intelligent
(47)   I[$_{VP}$ consider [$_{VP}$ John][$_{AP}$ intelligent]]

In general, an approach that analyzes such matrix predicates as *want, per-suade, unclear,* etc., in certain of the ways that we have been led to reject earlier will violate the principle; or to put the same point differently, the reasons that led us to reject these analyses (for example, their failure to predict the behavior of pleonastic elements or to accommodate the principles – yet to be formulated – that determine the distribution of empty categories) lend empirical support to the much more general projection principle by showing that many of its specific consequences are independently justified. I will explore a variety of such consequences below.

Recall that the validity of the projection principle is closely related to the question of whether the theories of government, binding and Case do provide an independently motivated and reasonable account of the properties and distribution of PRO and trace, a matter that will become still clearer when we reformulate the principle in a slightly different way in the next section. If these theories do not provide satisfactory answers to the questions concerning the distribution of empty categories, then the projection principle is dubious, since it would have to be supplemented by stipulations of some sort concerning the empty categories. If these theories do provide principled answers to these questions, then the projection principle receives indirect but significant support, since it reduces the specification of D- and S-structures to exactly what is not determined elsewhere, and does so on quite reasonable general grounds. Let us continue to assume that these questions will be answered appropriately by the theories of government, binding and Case, and continue to explore the consequences of this assumption – to which we return – thus adopting the projection principle.

Reviewing the levels of representation we have considered, for the sentence (48) we have the four representations (49):

(48)   it is unclear who to see
(49)   (i) it is unclear [$_{\bar{S}}$ who [$_{S}$ to see]]
           (ii) it is unclear [$_{\bar{S}}$ who $_i$ [$_{S}$ PRO to see t $_i$]]
           (iii) it is unclear [$_{\bar{S}}$ COMP[$_{S}$ PRO to see who]]
           (iv) it is unclear [$_{\bar{S}}$ for which person x [$_{S}$ PRO to see x]]

Representation (i) is the surface structure and representation (ii) the S-structure, with *who* in the COMP position and *t* its trace. Representation (iii) is the D-structure, while (iv) is the LF-representation. Representations (i) and (iv) are derived (independently) from (ii), which in turn is derived from (iii) by Move-α.

As noted earlier, in recent work within the framework I am assuming here, representation (ii), which is considerably more abstract than (i) with an empty NP subject and an empty object in the embedded infinitival clause, has been called the "surface structure," whereas in earlier usage, to which I return here, the latter term applied to the representation (i) at PF. Use of the term "surface structure" for S-structure has conveyed the erroneous impression that some radical change has been introduced as contrasted with earlier approaches, with a departure from abstract underlying representations; but when terminology is clarified, it is evident that the change is much less radical than has been assumed, and in some respects is in directions opposite to what is sometimes assumed.[8]

In the S-structure representation (49ii), a distinction is made between PRO and trace, each an empty category in the sense that it is assigned no intrinsic phonetic content – though presence of trace may affect phonetic representation, a matter to which we will return. As noted, it is not obvious that PRO and trace should be distinguished; in fact, in the OB-framework and earlier work (e.g., Chomsky (1977b)) they are identified as a category lacking lexical content.[9] I will argue, however, that they are distinct and that they differ in fundamental respects. For the moment, let us simply adopt the distinction tentatively.

Summarizing these remarks, we have formulated the projection principle (38) as a guiding principle, with the consequence that the role of the categorial component for a particular grammar is reduced to the specification of values of such parameters as order of major constituents. We have adopted the analysis (25) for S. Correspondingly, the rules of the LF-component will necessarily be quite simple. In the cases considered so far, they are fairly trivial, as are the rules of the PF-component. We have distinguished two empty categories, PRO and trace, their precise properties to be established. The reference of PRO is determined by the theory of control. The analysis is based on the assumption that the distribution of trace and PRO will follow from the theories of government, binding and Case. If the principles determining the distribution of empty categories are sound, then we have strong evidence for the approach so far outlined, and specifically, for the projection principle.

2.2. *LF-representation and θ-theory (1)*

Let us turn next to what are sometimes called the "interpretive components" of the system outlined in 2.1.(1), namely, the PF- and LF-components, now considering the projection principle and its consequences more carefully.

As noted, I will have little to say about the characteristics of PF, which we may assume to be a surface structure in some standard system of phonetic representation. The properties of LF, however, are central to this discussion. Work has advanced to the point where it is possible to consider some nontrivial questions about the properties of LF, in particular, about the syntax of LF. For example, there is linguistic evidence in support of the hypothesis that quantification in LF uses something like the standard quantifier-variable notation (as in 2.1.(16), (22)) rather than a quantifier-free notation.[10] One might seek evidence to determine whether something like the notation of familiar predicate calculus plays a role in LF, as has sometimes been suggested. Thus consider the following representations of the sentence *John seems to be sad:*

(1)   John$_i$[$_{VP}$ seems [$_S$ t$_i$ to [$_{VP}$ be sad]]]
(2)   seems (sad (John))

In theories of the sort I will be considering here, (1) is the S-structure representation of the sentence, while (2) – understood as indicating that *sad* is predicated of *John* and *seems* of the proposition *sad (John)* – is reminiscent of notations of familiar logics. The null hypothesis, within the theories considered here, is that (1) is also the LF-representation. While it would be simple enough to design an algorithm to convert (1) into (2) or something like it, empirical evidence would be required to support any such move. Informally speaking, there is no *a priori* reason to suppose that the brain uses such notations as (2) in preference to (1), though there might be empirical evidence,[11] as there is now some empirical evidence that it uses quantifier-variable rather than quantifier-free notation. Without such empirical evidence, there would be no motivation for adding rules to the LF-component (the right branch of 2.1.(1)) to map (1) into something like (2). I will tentatively assume that representations such as (1) are indeed appropriate for LF.

It has traditionally been assumed that such notions as "agent-of-action," "goal-of-action," etc., play an important role in semantic description, and there has been important recent work elaborating these ideas. These notions in fact enter into many different theories of semantic description. They are the semantic relations of Jerrold Katz, the thematic relations of Jeffrey Gruber and Ray Jackendoff, the case relations of Charles Fillmore, and the primitive notions of event logics such as that of Donald Davidson, which analyzes, e.g., *John ran quickly* as: there is an event *e* which is a running event with John as its agent, and *e* is quick. Let us assume that LF must be so designed that such expressions as *the man, John, he* are assigned θ-roles, that is, are assigned the status of terms in a thematic relation. Let us call such expressions "arguments,"[12] as distinct from idiom chunks (e.g., *too much* in *too much has been made of this problem*), non-argument *it* (as in *it is certain that John will win*), or existential *there* (as in *there are believed to be unicorns in the garden*), terms which assume no θ-role. Thus, we understand NP arguments to be NPs with some sort of "referential function," including names, variables, anaphors, pronouns; but not idiom chunks or elements inserted to occupy an obligatory position of syntactic structure. Let us refer to a position in LF to which a θ-role is assigned as a "θ-position." Idioms apart, each position satisfying the subcategorization features of the lexical head of a construction is a

θ-position; in the terminology of X-bar theory, each complement position is a θ-position. Furthermore, a θ-role may (though it need not be) assigned in the position of subject, whether of NP or S, a position not associated with a subcategorization feature of a lexical head. The θ-positions are those bracketed in (3): [13]

(3)   (i) [they] persuaded [John] [that [he] should leave]
        (ii) [we] hold [that [these truths] are [self-evident]]
       (iii) [we] hold [[these truths] to be [self-evident]]
        (iv) it is held [that [these truths] are [self-evident]]
         (v) these truths are held [[t] to be [self-evident]]
        (vi) [these truths] are [self-evident]
       (vii) [we] put [the books] [on [the table]]
      (viii) the books were put [t] [on [the table]]
        (ix) advantage was taken t of [Bill]

Some θ-positions are filled by arguments; all complements of a head are θ-positions apart from examples restructured by idiom rules in ways to which we will return; the subject is a θ-position where a θ-role is determined for it.

A reasonable criterion of adequacy for LF is (4): [14]

(4)   Each argument bears one and only one θ-role, and each θ-role is assigned to one and only one argument.

I will refer to (4) as the "θ-criterion." An argument is assigned a θ-role by virtue of the θ-position that it or its trace occupies in LF.

Consideration of the θ-criterion suggests a modification of the projection principle 2.1.(38). The natural intuitive sense of this principle is that every syntactic representation (i.e., LF-representation and S- and D-structure) should be a projection of the thematic structure and the properties of subcategorization of lexical entries, similar but not identical requirements. Only the latter requirement is encompassed in the formulation 2.1.(38). Suppose, then, that we recast the projection principle more generally to incorporate both cases. As a preliminary to doing so, let us identify more closely some of the basic notions that are involved.

Consider structural configurations of the form (5), where α is an immediate constituent of γ:

(5)   (i) $[_{\gamma} \ldots \alpha \ldots \beta \ldots]$
        (ii) $[_{\gamma} \ldots \beta \ldots \alpha \ldots]$

Thus α c-commands β. These are the basic configurations for GB-theory. In particular, α governs β in (5) under additional conditions that we will explore, "government" being the fundamental concept unifying various subtheories.

Consider the special case of (5) in which $\gamma = \bar{\alpha}$ and β too is an immediate constituent of γ. Thus α is the head of γ and β is one of its complements (or an optional interpolated element, e.g., an adverbial, a possibility that we will henceforth ignore, restricting attention to β a complement). This configuration is familiar, of course, from the theory of subcategorization. If α is a 0-level category of X-bar theory, then the category β must satisfy the subcategorization frame of α. In this case, we will say that α *subcategorizes the position occupied by* β.

The same configuration is relevant to determination of θ-role. Given (5) with the further proviso that β is an immediate constituent of γ, then the position occupied by β may be a θ-position with respect to α – i.e., a position for which α determines a θ-role. Whether it is or not depends on properties of α. If it is, we will say that α θ-*marks the position occupied by* β.

To relate these notions to the θ-criterion, let us extend the notion "θ-marking" in the following way. We will say that α θ-*marks the category* β if α θ-marks the position occupied by β or a trace of β.[15] Note that α subcategorizes a position but θ-marks both a position and a category.

This account presupposes that the θ-role of a subject (where it has one) is determined by the VP of S rather than by the verbal head of this VP (analogously, in the case of subject of NP). I will assume this convention throughout. If the assumption is incorrect, then the definition of "θ-marking" will have to be revised in an obvious way.[16]

Clearly, θ-marking is closely related to subcategorization. The two notions are not identical, however. Thus, if α is VP in (5) with $\gamma = $ S, then α may θ-mark the NP subject β but does not subcategorize it. But we must require that if α subcategorizes the position β, then α θ-marks β. Were this condition not to hold, then the definition of "subcategorize" just given would fail to capture the intended sense of this notion. For example, the verb *hit* might appear in the same subcategorization frame as *persuade*, namely, $- \text{NP } \bar{\text{S}}$; or it might appear in a VP of the form $[\text{}_{\text{VP}} \text{V } \alpha\beta\gamma]$, where α and γ are clauses and β is an empty NP; etc. We therefore require that subcategorization entails θ-marking. That is, all complements of a head are θ-marked by the head, as stated above. The sole exception to this requirement is the case of idioms. In the case of the idiom "take advantage of Bill," for example, no actual θ-role is assigned to *advantage*, though we might say that the idiom rule that converts the phrase "take advantage of" into a derived lexical item (cf. note 94) permits this derived item to θ-mark the object *Bill*.

We can bring subcategorization and θ-marking together more closely by inventing a new θ-role, call it $\#$, for non-arguments that are subcategorized by heads, e.g., *advantage* in "take advantage of." Then even in idioms, each subcategorized position is a θ-position. We may now regard, e.g., *advantage* as a kind of argument, call it a *quasi-argument*. We will see in chapter 6 that there is some independent justification for this move, which for the present is simply an artifice. We can now assume that without exception, if α subcategorizes the position β, then

α θ-marks β and θ-marks a category C such that C or a trace of C occupies the position β.

The requirement that subcategorization entails θ-marking has several consequences. Consider, for example, a hypothetical rule R of raising-to-object. If the raised element α is in a θ-position in D-structure, then α will be doubly θ-marked at S-structure and at LF, violating the θ-criterion. The reason is that the position to which α moves is subcategorized and therefore θ-marked. The rule R is, in fact, barred on independent grounds whatever the status of the D-structure position of α; cf. notes 91, 108.

This requirement also restricts the variety of lexical entries. It is minimally necessary that the lexicon provide, for each lexical head, information about θ-marking for this element. We are now assuming that it is also maximally necessary; that is, there is no independent subcategorization information, except, possibly, in the case of idioms, or with regard to the linking of θ-role and category (e.g., is an infinitival complement an NP or only an $\bar{S}$?). Even the latter may well be eliminable either on general grounds or, at worst, in terms of redundancy rules for the lexicon of a particular language.

Recall that θ-marking takes place in the configuration (5), where β as well as α is an immediate constituent of γ, assuming α to have appropriate properties determined ultimately by the lexicon. There are two cases: (i) $\gamma = \bar{\alpha}$; (ii) β is the subject of α. In case (i), α is a lexical element that subcategorizes and hence θ-marks β; let us say that in this case, α *directly θ-marks* β or a category C such that it or its trace occupies the position β. In case (ii), if α θ-marks β (a position or category), let us say that the lexical head of α *indirectly θ-marks* β. Direct or indirect θ-marking are therefore properties of lexical items determined by the lexicon. If α directly or indirectly θ-marks β, we say that α *selects* β. A verb, for example, selects its complements and also selects its subject if it participates in assigning a θ-role to the subject. Note again that if α selects β, then β is either a position or a category C such that C or its trace occupies the position selected by α.

Bringing together these various observations, we can restate the projection principle 2.1. (38) as (6):

(6)   (i) if β is an immediate constituent of γ in (5) at L_i, and $\gamma = \bar{\alpha}$, then α θ-marks β in γ

    (ii) if α selects β in γ as a lexical property, then α selects β in γ at L_i

    (iii) if α selects β in γ at L_i, then α selects β in γ at L_j

The variables L_i, L_j range over what we are considering throughout to be the "syntactic levels": LF, D-structure, S-structure. Case (i) of (6) stipulates that subcategorization in the purely formal sense entails θ-marking, as is required to capture the intended sense of the principle. In case (ii), β is necessarily a position, not a specific category such that it or its trace occupies the selected position; the lexicon states, for example, that *kill* takes an NP object in a VP, but does not specify that this object is, say, *Bill*. Case (ii) expresses the basic intuition that all syntactic representations are projections of the thematic structure (hence the subcategorization) indicated in the lexicon, including both direct and indirect θ-marking. We will give a slightly sharper formulation of (ii) directly, distinguishing between obligatory and optional positions. Case (iii) guarantees that categories and positions must be θ-marked in the same way at all syntactic levels; here β may be a category or a position. Given that the θ-criterion holds at LF, it follows from (iii) that it must hold as well at D- and S-structure. Principle (6) subsumes 2.1 (38), but adds to it a requirement concerning subjects in θ-positions that we will clarify directly.

In a well-designed theory of UG, case (iii) of (6) should follow without stipulation from (i) and (ii); that is, grammars conforming to this theory should simply not provide devices that permit (i) and (ii) to be satisfied but (iii) violated by a derivation. What then is the status of (i) and (ii), now taken to express the essential content of the projection principle? It seems most natural to regard the principle as part of the definition of "well-formed derivation" given in UG. The same is true of the θ-criterion, clearly a closely related principle.

The θ-criterion and the projection principle will play a fairly important role in subsequent discussion. In chapter 6, we will give a somewhat different and more precise version of the θ-criterion, incorporating modifications that will be introduced in the course of this discussion. As for the projection principle, for most of the ensuing discussion it suffices to have clearly in mind the intuitive idea it is intended to express: that representations at each of the three syntactic levels are projections of lexical properties. The preceding comments sketch one way to think about this intuitive idea, but there is plainly much more to be said about the precise character and status of this principle, which I think may prove to be an important one.

In accordance with our general framework 2.1.(1), S-structure is derived from D-structure by the rule Move-α. Actually, a stronger principle is intended: D-structure is derived from S-structure by abstracting from all effects of Move-α. That is, S-structure is factored into two components: D-structure and Move-α. D-structure lacks the antecedent-trace relation entirely. At D-structure, then, each argument occupies a θ-position and each θ-position is occupied by an argument. In this sense, D-structure is a representation of θ-role assignment – though it has other properties as well, specifically, those that follow from X-bar theory and from parameters of the base (e.g., ordering of major constituents) in a particular language.

Given the projection principle in the form (6), it follows that the bracketing indicated in (3) must appear at every syntactic level. It also follows, as before, that the subcategorization frames at every syntactic level must be exactly those that appear at LF and that they correspond to

θ-marking in head-complement constructions, and that when the subject is a θ-position at LF it appears as a θ-position at every syntactic level.

Evidently, the projection principle relates closely to the rule 2.1.(25) that requires that all clauses have subjects at D- and S-structure, as discussed in § 2.1. It entails a subcase of 2.1.(25), namely, the subcase in which the subject bears a θ-role. The projection principle, however, leaves open the possibility that languages may differ as to whether non-θ-positions must be represented at each syntactic level. Thus, if the subject position must be filled in some language, as in English, this fact is determined by the projection principle where the subject is a θ-position, but is determined by some distinct principle whether or not the subject is a θ-position; this distinct principle is the base rule 2.1.(25), we have assumed. Recall that it is the obligatory presence of the NP subject that must crucially be specified in 2.1.(25).

In short, θ-theory requires that clauses with certain verb phrases (e.g., *persuade John to leave* but not *be raining* or *be a good reason for his refusal*) must have subjects at the level of LF-representation. By the projection principle, these clauses must have subjects at D- and S-structure, either PRO, or the trace of an NP, or some phonetically-realized NP. But as we have seen, there is compelling evidence that the subject of a clause is obligatory in English and similar languages. The rule 2.1.(25) embodies the structural principle *P* of § 2.1 that requires that the subject position be filled, a principle that may or may not hold in a particular language, we have so far assumed. But the special case of *P* that falls under the projection principle holds generally, so we are now assuming. We will return in § 2.8 to the projection principle in non-configurational languages.

What about non-clausal (i.e., non-gerund) NPs, which do not require subjects (e.g., 2.1.(29))? Plainly, there is a fundamental difference between $\bar{N}$ and VP in that $\bar{N}$ does not obligatorily θ-mark even if its head N is lexically specified as an element that indirectly θ-marks a subject, whereas VP does obligatorily θ-mark if its head has this property. It is not really accurate, then, to say, as we did a moment ago, that the projection principle entails that subjects must be present when the head indirectly θ-marks a subject. Rather, we must rely on the principle 2.1.(25), guaranteeing that clauses have subjects, to make the required distinction. Given this principle, we may interpret the notion θ-marking in the following way: if a structural position that can be θ-marked is obligatory, then it is obligatorily θ-marked by an element that may θ-mark it; if such a position is only optionally present, then θ-marking of this position is correspondingly optional, and will apply just so as to satisfy the θ-criterion. There are two cases of obligatory positions: those determined by the subcategorization frames of lexical items, and subjects of clauses, as determined by principle 2.1.(25). Since subjects must appear in S by virtue of 2.1.(25), these subjects will necessarily be θ-marked by the VP if it has the appropriate properties (i.e., those of *kill Bill* or *persuade John to leave,* but not *rain* or *seem that John left*). But in NPs, the subject may or may not be present. Suppose that the head N of the NP has the property that it indirectly θ-marks the subject. If an argument appears in subject position at D-structure, then the position is θ-marked at every syntactic level. If no subject appears at D-structure, then the position is not θ-marked at any syntactic level. This convention gives the required distinction, while also permitting NP-movement to the S-structure subject position of an NP, not a θ-position, without violation of the θ-criterion.

Suppose that the rule 2.1.(33) is selected by a grammar in place of 2.1.(25). Then S and NP are not distinguished in the required way; neither requires an NP subject. We thus have no basis for accounting for the distinction just noted between NP and S. It is therefore natural to suppose that rule 2.1.(33) is not an option permitted in UG, contrary to what we tentatively assumed earlier. As we have seen in §2.1, the absence of a subject at surface structure tells us very little about whether the grammar chooses 2.1.(25) or 2.1.(33), i.e., whether or not it requires subjects in S. Specifically, the absence of subject at surface structure might be connected to the pro-drop parameter, quite a different phenomenon. Putting these observations together, let us now adopt the position that 2.1.(25) is the only base rule analyzing S in UG (order aside). If so, then the NP subject is just as much a requirement for S as is INFL and VP. Apparent cases to the contrary will have to be accounted for in some other way. Cf. Aoun (1980c) for evidence supporting rule 2.1.(25) in Arabic. We return to the question in the case of the Romance languages in the subsequent discussion, particularly chapter 4.

There are certain further questions that arise in connection with the projection principle. Consider, for example, the phenomenon of restructuring, either in the case of idiom rules or in other constructions (e.g., restructuring verbs in Romance in the sense of Rizzi (1978a), Rouveret and Vergnaud (1980), Burzio (1981), and much other work; preposition-stranding constructions if analyzed along the lines of Weinberg and Hornstein (1978); etc.). Is the projection principle satisfied in these cases, and if so, how? There are several possible ways to deal with these questions, depending on exactly what mechanisms are adopted for restructuring. Since I will not pursue the restructuring phenomenon in any detail here, I will leave this question open, noting merely that it must be dealt with somehow. Similarly, I will not explore many other relevant questions, for example, the implications of the projection principle for such constructions as relative clauses (free or with heads), topicalization, dislocation, and others that raise obvious and pertinent questions.

The grammar must contain rules determining surface structure, θ-role assignment, and the relation between them. I have been assuming that this relation is mediated by S-structure. Surface structure is (in part) an impoverished form of S-structure, as the examples given above indicate. S-structure is mapped onto LF in a fairly direct manner, given the projection principle. The problem of relating surface structure to θ-role assignment thus reduces to the problem of relating S-structure to θ-role assignment, in essence.

From the earliest work in generative grammar, as in traditional grammar, it has been assumed that what I am now calling "θ-role" is determined in part by a representation in terms of grammatical functions (GFs) such as subject-of, object-of, and so on, where GFs are determined in terms of syntactic configurations for certain types of languages (configurational languages) and by other properties where syntactic configurations do not suffice.[17] In the S-structure (7i), underlying the surface structure (7ii), for example, *they* is the subject of the sentence and *John* is the object of the verb phrase *killed John:*

(7)   (i) $[_S[_{NP}$ they $]$ INFL $[_{VP}[_V$ kill $] [_{NP}$ John $]]]$
       (ii) they killed John

Following a familiar practice,[18] let us use the notation "$[NP,S]$" to express the GF "subject-of-S" and the notation "$[NP,VP]$" to express the GF "object-of-VP." Thus *they* in (7i) bears the grammatical relation $[NP,S]$ to the sentence (7i) and has the GF: $[NP,S]$ of (7i). Particular lexical properties of the verb *kill* assign to its object a specific θ-role; thus *kill* θ-marks the object position. Analogously, properties of the VP in (7i) require that this VP θ-mark the subject of (7i).

In more complex structures, such as (8), representations at various levels may include more than one occurrence of a particular category:

(8)   John was believed to have been killed

In such cases, I will distinguish occurrences by indexing: $S_1, S_2 \ldots$, etc. I will use the notation "$[NP,S_1]$" to express the GF $[NP,S]$ of S_1, i.e., subject of S_1; and so on.

Given the projection principle and other properties of syntactic representation, the S-structure of (8) will be something like (9):

(9) $[_{S_1} [_{NP}$ John$]$ INFL $[_{VP}$ be $[_{\alpha_1}$ believe $[_{S_2}$ t' INFL have been $[_{\alpha_2}$ kill t $]]]]]$

We return to the status of α; each trace is a trace of *John*. Thus *John* is $[NP,S_1]$, t' is $[NP,S_2]$ and t is $[NP, \alpha_2]$ in S-structure (where α is something like VP).

Note that the basic properties of the representation (9) are determined by the projection principle, since *believe* takes a clausal complement as a lexical property. It remains to show that the empty category in (9) is indeed trace, not PRO, assuming the two to be distinct.

We are now assuming, following standard practice, that two factors enter into the determination of θ-role: intrinsic lexical properties of lexical items which are heads of phrase categories (as the verb is the head of VP), and GFs such as subject, object, clausal complement, head, etc. To assign θ-roles properly in the sentences (7), (8), for example, we must know that *they* is $[\text{NP,S}]$ in (7i), underlying (7ii), that *John* is $[\text{NP,VP}]$ in (7) and that its trace is $[\text{NP}, \alpha_2]$ in (9), that *kill* is $[\text{V,VP}]$ in (7) (a special case of the more general notion "head") and is head of α_2 in (9), etc. We have been assuming that S-structures are formed from D-structures by the rule Move-α and are thus in effect factored into two components: the base and the transformational component. On this assumption, D-structure is a level of representation at which the GFs relevant to assignment of θ-role and only these have arguments bearing them; henceforth, let us refer to such a GF as a GF-θ. This is the case trivially in (7), and it is true as well for (8), (9) on the assumption that *John* appears in the position of *t* in the D-structure underlying (9) and is moved successively to the position of *t'* and then to its S-structure position.

To summarize: a property of D-structure, following from the projection principle, is that every θ-role determined obligatorily in the D-structure must be filled by some argument with the appropriate GF, and that each argument must fill exactly one θ-role as determined by its GF. In the D-structures underlying (7) and (8), for example, each NP fills one θ-role and each θ-role is properly filled by an NP with the appropriate GF-θ. Thus, D-structure is a direct representation of GF-θ, among other properties. We may think of this property as constituting the θ-criterion for D-structures, as determined by the projection principle.

It is clear that apart from GF-θ represented at D-structure, other GFs are also relevant to LF. In the sentence (9), the trace of *John* bears the relation object to the abstract predicate *kill t* just as *John* bears this relation to *kill John* in (7), but *John* in (9) bears the relation $[\text{NP,S}_1]$ to the sentence (9) itself. Each of these GFs plays a role in determining properties of LF. The former determines the θ-role of *John* as patient or theme. To illustrate the contribution of the latter to LF, consider the sentences (10):

(10)   (i) it seems to each other that they are happy
       (ii) they seem to each other to be happy

Lexical properties of *seem* indicate that it takes an optional *to*-phrase and a clausal complement, so by the projection principle and the θ-criterion, the D-structure of both sentences of (10) must be (11) (order aside):

(11) $[_{S_1}$ NP* INFL $[_{VP}[_V$ seem$][_{PP}$ to each other$][_{S_2}$ they INFL be happy $]]]$

where INFL in S_2 is finite $([+\text{Tense}])$ in (10i) and infinitival $([-\text{Tense}])$ in (10ii) and NP* is an empty NP assigned no θ-role and ultimately filled by pleonastic *it* or the subject of the embedded clause. In both sentences, the θ-role of *they* is subject of the predicate *be-happy*, as determined by the

GF of *they* as $[NP,S_2]$ in (11). But in (10ii), *they* can serve as antecedent for the reciprocal *each other,* whereas in (10i) it cannot, so that the latter sentence is ungrammatical, with an anaphor lacking an antecedent. The reason, obviously, is that in (10ii), but not (10i), *they* takes on a secondary GF: $[NP,S_1]$ alongside of $[NP,S_2]$. Each of these GFs thus contributes to LF. There are many other kinds of examples illustrating the contribution of such secondary, non-thematic GFs to LF; for example, in many languages, subjects (whether thematic or not) and only subjects serve as antecedents for the reflexive element.

It seems, then, that we have two notions of GF relevant to LF: GF-θ and GF-$\bar{\theta}$, where the former is the notion relevant to assigning θ-role and the latter is relevant to LF (if at all) only in other ways. GF-θ is represented at D-structure; GF-$\bar{\theta}$ at S-structure. As noted earlier, the basic question of how surface structures are related to LF reduces to the question of the relations of S-structure to θ-role assignment. In substantial part, this is the question of how GF-θ representations are related to GF-$\bar{\theta}$ representations. I have been assuming so far that the answer is given by the factoring of S-structure into the two components that generate it: D-structure and Move-α. Of course, the rule Move-α performs a range of other functions in the grammar: it may appear in the PF- and LF-components: and in the syntax, apart from associating GF-θ and GF-$\bar{\theta}$, it also serves to relate the quasi-quantifier in a *wh*-phrase to the abstract variable it binds (as in (12)), to express the fact that in (13) the subject of the predicate *is here* is the abstract phrase *a man whom you know* and that in (14) an idiomatic interpretation must be constructed involving *take advantage of,* along with much else:

(12)   (i) who did you think would win
(ii) for which person x, you thought $[x$ would win$]$
(13)   a man is here whom you know
(14)   advantage was believed to have been taken of John

One central assumption of transformational grammar, adopted here, is that the rules playing the essential role in assigning GF-θ to elements of surface form are rules of the same kind that serve many other functions in grammar – indeed, the very same rule: Move-α – rather than being rules of some new and distinct type, an important generalization if correct, as I think it is.

In the case of sentence (9), we were led by the projection principle to assume that the rule Move-α applies twice, leaving the two traces t and t', successively. The original position of *John* indicated by t is relevant to LF by virtue of the GF-θ that it fills, and the final S-structure position of the antecedent of trace may also be relevant, as shown in (10). The GF-$\bar{\theta}$ filled by medial traces such as t' in (9) may also be relevant to LF; for example in the sentence (15), with a D-structure analogous to (11), where the medial trace serves as the antecedent of *each other,* which requires an antecedent in the same clause in such cases in accordance with binding theory:

(15)   they are likely [t' to appear to each other [t to be happy]]

To put it differently, *they* in (15) serves as antecedent of *each other,* via its trace, though it is neither the D-structure nor the S-structure subject of the clause in which *each other* appears, and thus is not in a position to serve as antecedent in either of these structures.

Note that there is a good sense in which S-structure represents both GF-θ and GF-$\bar{\theta}$. In (9), for example, the antecedent *John* bears the GF [NP,S$_1$] by virtue of its actual position in (9), and bears the relations [NP,S$_2$] and [NP, α_2] by virtue of the positions of its traces t', t, respectively. Suppose we associate with each NP in S-structure a sequence $(p_1, \ldots, p_n)$ which, in an obvious sense, represents the derivational history of this NP by successive applications of Move-α; thus p_1 is the position of the NP itself; p_2 is the position (filled by a trace) from which it was moved to its final position; etc., p_n being the position (filled by a trace) occupied by the NP in D-structure. Correspondingly, let us associate with each NP in S-structure the sequence of GFs (GF$_1, \ldots,$ GF$_n$), where GF$_i$ is the GF of the element filling position p_i in the S-structure configuration: the NP itself for $i = 1$, a trace in each other case. If NP was base-generated, then GF$_n$ is its GF at D-structure, a GF-θ. If NP is a non-argument inserted in the course of a syntactic derivation, then GF$_n$ is the GF associated with the position in which it is inserted, a GF-$\bar{\theta}$. Let us call (GF$_1, \ldots,$ GF$_n$) the "function chain" of the NP filling GF$_1$.

I have defined the function chain in terms of successive applications of Move-α, but it can in fact be recovered from S-structure itself, given other properties of syntactic representations; this is a basic assumption of the Extended Standard Theory (EST) as represented in 2.1.(1), with no direct connection between D-structure and LF. We may therefore think of S-structure as an enriched D-structure incorporating the contribution of D-structure to LF, thinking still of D-structure and the rule Move-α as the two components that interact to yield the full S-structure, D-structure being a representation of GF-θ determined by abstracting from the effects of Move-α.

Returning to example (9), *John* is assigned the function chain (GF$_1$, GF$_2$, GF$_3$), where GF$_1$ is [NP,S$_1$] and GF$_3$ is [NP,α_2]. Thus *John* acquires the θ-role assigned by *kill* to its object, and is the S-structure subject of the full sentence; no θ-role is assigned to the latter position, which can therefore be filled by idiom chunks, as in (14), or by non-arguments, as in (16):

(16)   it was believed that John was killed

Suppose that NP has the function chain (GF$_1, \ldots,$ GF$_n$) in some S-structure. Then we have the following consequences of the θ-criterion and the projection principle:

(17)   (i) if NP is an argument, then GF_n is a GF-θ
        (ii) for $i \neq n$, GF_i is a GF-$\bar{\theta}$

The projection principle yields (i) directly, since it implies that the θ-criterion holds at D-structure, where each chain is of length one. For argument NP, (17ii) follows directly from (17i) by the θ-criterion, for if GF_i is a GF-θ then the NP will be doubly θ-marked. If NP is a non-argument, (17ii) holds by virtue of the θ-criterion, for if GF_i is a GF-θ then this non-argument will be assigned a θ-role by GF_i. We return to some concrete examples in §§ 2.6, 3.2.3.

Under a revision of the notion of θ-role assignment that we will adopt in chapter 3, this derivation of (17ii) from (17i) no longer goes through for the case of NP an argument. But we can reach the same conclusion in a slightly more indirect way, which will stand under later revisions. Suppose GF_i to be a GF-θ, for $i \neq n$. Then by the projection principle, it is assigned an argument at D-structure, and this argument is "erased" by application of Move-α to this position. But any reasonable version of the principle of recoverability of deletion will require that arguments cannot be erased by substitution; in fact, the target of movement can only be $[_\alpha e]$ lacking an index, a non-argument. Hence (17ii) follows from the projection principle and the principle of recoverability of deletion.

It follows that movement must always be to a position to which no θ-role is assigned; and apart from idiom chunks and other expressions that are not "referential" in the appropriate sense and thus do not serve as arguments, movement must be initially from a position in D-structure to which a (genuine) θ-role is assigned. Again, D-structure serves as a representation of θ-role assignment *(inter alia)*. For example, since a θ-role is assigned obligatorily to the complements of a verb in its verb phrase, there can be no movement to a position within VP.[19] But since the position of subject, which is not subcategorized by the verb of VP, may lack a θ-role, as in the examples (9), (10), (14), there can be movement from object or subject to subject, though not to the position of a subject assigned a θ-role by its VP. These are general properties of the rule Move-α, or of its counterpart in non-configurational languages, to which we return in § 2.8.

In § 2.4.6, we will consider the question of choosing between the version of EST expressed in 2.1.(1) and an alternative theory that replaces the rule Move-α by a new class of interpretive rules, with the same properties as Move-α, mapping S-structure to LF. The differences between these variants is quite subtle, and it may turn out (as suggested in the remarks in Chomsky (1977a) quoted in chapter 1, above), that they will ultimately be shown to reduce to the same theory at the appropriate level of abstraction. We have evidence in favor of the variant that assumes the existence of D-structure and the rule Move-α, as in 2.1.(1) (or some mere notational variant of it), whenever we can show that some empirical argument relies on a property of an independent level of D-structure. As we have just seen, the principles (17) rely on such a property; namely, the property that the θ-criterion be satisfied at D-structure. In § 2.6 we will see that the principles (17) have direct empirical consequences (cf. 2.6.(35)–(37)). Therefore, we have an empirical argument supporting 2.1.(1) over an alternative that invokes a new interpretive rule of the LF component in place of the syntactic rule Move-α, relating two levels of syntactic representation. Other examples of a similar sort will appear as we proceed.

It seems to me that the weight of evidence supports 2.1.(1) over the alternative just mentioned, but it will be observed that the arguments supporting this conclusion are highly theory-internal. Of course, all arguments are theory-internal, but there are important differences of degree. Thus, the behavior of non-arguments provides quite direct evidence that the subject position is obligatory in syntactic representation in English, and the distinction between S and NP with regard to obligatoriness of θ-marked subjects provides indirect evidence, more theory-bound, that the same is true quite generally. It is inevitable that empirical arguments bearing on the choice between theories that are very close in conceptual structure, as in the case we are now considering, will be highly theory-internal. To the extent that questions of this sort can be raised at all and confronted with evidence, we have indication of progress in theoretical understanding.

The GFs discussed in the preceding remarks are those that belong to the thematic complex associated with the head of a construction, in the sense of Rouveret and Vergnaud (1980); namely, subject-of-S and complements of $\overline{X}$ (X = N, V, A, P). The positions in which these GFs are assigned are sometimes called "argument positions" (cf. note 12), but since I am using the term "argument" in a slightly different way, I will avoid this terminology, referring to them rather as "A-positions" and to the GFs determined in them as "A-GFs." An A-position is one in which an argument such as a name or a variable may appear in D-structure; it is a potential θ-position. The position of subject may or may not be a θ-position, depending on properties of the associated VP. Complements of $\overline{X}$ are always θ-positions, with the possible exception of idioms. In addition, I have mentioned the GF "head of α," not a θ-position, obviously. Another non-A-position ($\overline{A}$-position) is that of an adjunct of one sort or another.

Consider, for example, *wh*-movement, which we may assume to be adjunction to COMP in the sense of OB (Chomsky, 1980a). The function chain (GF$_1$, GF$_2$) produced by a single application of *wh*-movement contains GF$_2$, necessarily an A-GF, and GF$_1$, a non-A-GF ($\overline{A}$-GF) that we may denote "adjunct of COMP." Assume that there are two types of movement rules: substitution and adjunction, the latter always forming a structure of the form $\left[_\beta\, \alpha\, \beta \right]$ or $\left[_\beta\, \beta\, \alpha \right]$, where α is adjoined to β by Move-α. Then the only GFs are heads, complements, adjuncts and subject.[20] A principled approach to the theory of GFs, which I will not undertake here, will begin by defining such general notions as "head," etc., then defining particular GFs in terms of them. Cf. Chomsky (1955) for an outline of such a theory. In such a theory, we should also express the fact that $[\text{NP}, \bar{X}]$ is the GF direct object whether X is N, V or A; and that $[\text{NP}, \text{NP}]$ and $[\text{NP}, \text{S}]$ both express the GF subject.

Note that the notation does not suffice for the case in which more than one term of category α appears as a complement, as in double-NP constructions V-NP-NP (*give-John-a book*). In this case, let us simply use the notation $[\text{NP}^1, \text{VP}]$, $[\text{NP}^2, \text{VP}]$ (primary and secondary object); similarly, in other cases. As in the outline of θ-theory, I am omitting discussion of many other relevant questions: e.g., the status of predicate nominals, topics, heads of relatives. Note also an ambiguity of the notation in the case of adjuncts: thus the notation "$[\text{NP}, \text{VP}_1]$" does not distinguish between (18i) and (18ii), the former being a case of adjunction, the latter, direct object:

(18)   (i) $[_{\text{VP}_1} \text{VP}_2 \text{NP}]$
        (ii) $[_{\text{VP}_1} \text{V NP}]$

The problem can easily be resolved by means of a more careful development of theory and notations in terms of heads, complements and adjuncts. No problems arise within the restricted class of constructions that I will be considering here, so I will simply put these matters aside, for consideration elsewhere.

In § 2.8. I will turn to the question of how these notions can be appropriately generalized to languages in which GFs are not represented configurationally, as they are in English.

2.3. The categorial component and the theories of case and government

A number of assumptions have been made in the foregoing discussion about the categorial component of the base. Let us now review and extend these somewhat. Assume that the rules of the categorial component meet the conditions of some version of X-bar theory. Specifically, let us assume a variant based on two categories of traditional grammar: substantive $([+\text{N}])$, including nouns and adjectives, and predicate $([+\text{V}])$, including verbs and adjectives. Let us refer to substantives and predicates as the "lexical categories." So we have a system based on the features $[\pm\text{N}]$, $[\pm\text{V}]$, where $[+\text{N}, -\text{V}]$ is noun, $[-\text{N}, +\text{V}]$ is verb, $[+\text{N}, +\text{V}]$ is adjective, and $[-\text{N}, -\text{V}]$ is preposition, the first three being lexical categories. The basic rule for lexical categories is (1), where . . . is fixed for all lexical categories in the unmarked case:

(1) $\bar{X} \rightarrow \ldots \underline{X} \ldots (X = [+\text{N}, \pm\text{V}] \text{ or } [+\text{V}, \pm\text{N}])$

That is, I am assuming that in the unmarked case, nouns, verbs and adjectives have the same complement structures. Thus (2i) and (2ii) have the same form in the base, apart from lexical content, as do (3i) and (3ii); and

I assume that (4ii) is derived from (4i), a "transitive adjective," by the same rule of *of*-insertion that gives the surface forms of (2ii), (3ii), so that adjectives have close to the full range of verbal and nominal complement structures:[21]

(2)   (i) destroy the city
        (ii) destruction of the city
(3)   (i) write the book
        (ii) writer (author) of the book
(4)   (i) proud John
        (ii) proud of John

Of course, in surface structure, verbal constructions differ from nominal and adjectival constructions in form. I assume that the reasons derive from Case theory.[22] The crucial idea is that every noun with a phonetic matrix must have Case; i.e., we assume the principle (5):

(5) $*[_N \alpha]$, where α includes a phonetic matrix, if N has no Case

Assuming that Case is assigned to NPs by virtue of the configurations in which they appear and percolates to their heads, (5) follows from the *Case Filter* (6), which I will assume to be a filter in the PF-component:

(6)   *NP if NP has phonetic content and has no Case

Only the empty categories trace and PRO may escape the Case Filter, appearing with no Case.

Note that the Case Filter (6) is somewhat more general than (5), since it holds also for NPs that have no lexical N as head, for example, gerunds or clauses (if these are NPs[23]). Thus in positions in which no Case is assigned, say the subject of an infinitive in the unmarked case, neither gerunds nor NPs with lexical heads can appear, as illustrated in (7), where *t* is the trace of *who:*

(7)   (i) *it is unclear $[_{\bar{S}}$ who $[_S[_{NP}$ reading books$]$ to interest t $]]$
        (ii) *it is unclear $[_{\bar{S}}$ who $[_S[_{NP}$ John$]$ to visit t $]]$

In the embedded subject position of (7), we may only have an empty category, either trace or PRO, by virtue of the Case Filter; other considerations to which we return restrict the choice to PRO. Note that the Case Filter gives a partial answer to the question raised earlier of where PRO may or must appear, since it excludes categories with phonetic content from such positions as embedded subject of (7). The Case Filter is much wider in application, however; cf. OB.

In English, only the $[-N]$ categories verb and preposition are Case-assigners. In OB, it is assumed that verbs assign objective Case and that prepositions assign oblique Case, apart from marked properties. Let us tentatively assume, following a suggestion of Kayne's, that in English both verbs and prepositions assign objective Case, the richer Case systems having been lost (cf. § 5.2). Furthermore, nominative Case is assigned to the subject of a tensed sentence and genitive Case is assigned in the context $[_{NP} - \bar{X}]$, as in "John's book," "his reading the book." In other languages, categories other than $[-N]$ are Case-assigners, and there are other Cases and other conditions under which Case is assigned, a matter to which we return in § 3.2.2, though not in any comprehensive way.

Case-assignment is closely related to government, a crucial notion to which we will return in chapter 3. Normally, Case is assigned to an NP by a category that governs it. As for the notion "government," for the moment let us simply assume that the potential governors are the categories $[\pm N, \pm V]$ and INFL, that a category governs its complements in a construction of which it is the head (e.g., V governs its complements in VP, etc.), and that INFL governs the sentence subject when it is tensed.[24] To illustrate, consider the example (8):

(8)   John $[_{INFL} [+\text{Tense}]]$ $[_{VP}[_{V} \text{think}][_{\bar{S}} \text{that} [_{S} \text{he} [_{INFL}$
        $[+\text{Tense}]][_{VP}[_{V}\text{leave}]$ $[_{NP}\text{his book}][_{PP}[_{P}\text{on}]$
        $[_{NP}\text{the table}]]]]]]$
        ("John thought that he left his book on the table")

The matrix verb *think* governs its complement $\bar{S}$, but not any element (e.g., *he*) inside $\bar{S}$. The embedded verb governs its complements *his book* and *on the table*, but does not govern any element (e.g., *his* or *the table*) within these categories. Thus, *his book* and *book* receive objective Case (the latter, by percolation). The two occurrences of INFL govern *John* and *he*, assigning them nominative Case. The preposition *on* governs and assigns objective Case to its complement *the table*. The genitive rule assigns genitive Case to the ungoverned element *his*.

Returning to (7), the embedded subjects are ungoverned and therefore receive no Case. Some languages have marked rules that permit Case to be assigned to the subject of an infinitive in such structures.[25] I will not pursue these and other such topics here, though they raise many interesting questions.

Let us now return to the examples (2)–(4). Since only the $[-N]$ categories verb and preposition are Case-assigners, it follows that in the complement ... of X in (1), Case will not be assigned by X for $X \neq [-N]$. Then the language requires some other device if it is to allow these complement structures to surface. One device, typical of English-like languages that use prepositions instead of inflectional Case systems, is to insert an empty preposition devoid of semantic content as a kind of Case-marker to permit nominal complements, as in (2ii), (3ii), (4ii). Thus we have the rule (9):

(9)   NP → $[_{P}\text{of}]$ NP in env.: $[+N]$ –

We leave open the exact formulation of this rule (e.g., does it adjoin *of* to NP forming [NP *of* NP]?); (cf. note 21). M. Anderson (1977) shows that assuming *of*-insertion, the rule Move-α (under constraints that she discusses) will then yield such expressions as *the city's destruction* from *destruction – the city*, but not, say, *John's gift* from *gift to John* or *John's belief to be a fool* from *belief – John to be a fool* (cf. *John is believed to be a fool*); see also Fiengo (1979), Kayne (1980b). Thus, the nominal corresponding to (2i) can surface in one of two forms: as (2ii), with *of*-insertion, or under Move-α followed by genitive Case-assignment. In either case, the Case Filter is satisfied, but one or the other option must be taken or the filter is violated.[26]

Such examples as (2)–(4) raise some technical questions concerning the projection principle. At D-structure, *destruction* (or, perhaps, its head *destroy*) subcategorizes and θ-marks the NP object *the city* in (2i). If the projection principle is valid, this must also be true at S-structure and LF. There is no problem if the *of*-insertion rule is an adjunction rule forming the NP [NP *of* NP], as in one of the options we have just considered, or if the *of*-phrase is base-generated as a PP (cf. note 21). If the *of*-insertion rule creates a PP, however, we must continue to hold that *destruction* subcategorizes its NP object at S-structure and LF. Note that still another possibility would be to assume that the *of*-insertion rule forms a neutralized NP-PP of the form [$-V$], in which case, again, no problem arises and this category will share properties of both NP and PP. Little seems to be at stake beyond terminology, so I will drop the matter.

The examples (2)–(4) shed some light on the relations among the notions "subcategorize," "θ-mark," "govern" and "Case-assign." Generally these coincide, but not always; we have already noted the possible dissociation of subcategorization and θ-marking (cf. §2.2). In such examples as (2ii), the NP *the city* is subcategorized by *destruction* or its verbal head, θ-marked by this element, governed by the inserted preposition *of*, and assigned Case by *of*. As the example indicates, government rather than subcategorization is the relevant notion for Case-assignment – in this case, at S-structure. But government is also the relevant notion for subcategorization in D-structure in case (2i), and generally. Thus the theories of subcategorization, θ-marking and Case all fall within the general theory of government, at least in their essentials.

There has been much recent discussion of further projections of the basic categories to higher bar structures. I will not enter into these issues here, but will simply assume that there are maximal projections with the appropriate number of bars for each category. I will use the notation X^i for X with i bars, and will continue to use NP for the maximal projection of [$+N, -V$], AP for the maximal projection of [$+N, +V$], and PP for the maximal projection of [$-N, -V$].

One debated question is whether the S, $\bar{S}$ system[27] should be regarded as a projection of V, with verbs taken to be heads of clauses, or whether this is a separate system, perhaps with INFL as head. I will assume here that the S, $\bar{S}$ system is separate and will use the symbol VP for the maximal projection of V, a constituent of S. Some considerations bearing on this decision will arise later on.

I have been assuming the expansion (10) for S in English (cf. § 2.1):

(10)   S → NP INFL VP

The "inflectional" element INFL may, in turn, be $[\pm\text{Tense}]$, i.e., finite ($[+\text{Tense}]$) or infinitival ($[-\text{Tense}]$). If finite, it will, furthermore, have the features person, gender and number; call this complex AGR ("agreement"). The element AGR is basically nominal in character; we might consider it to be identical with PRO and thus to have the features $[+N, -V]$. If so, then we may revise the theory of government, taking AGR to be the governing element which assigns Case in INFL. Since $[+N, -V]$ is not generally a Case-assigner, we must extend the theory of Case so that $[+N, -V, +\text{INFL}]$ is a Case-assigner along with $[-N]$, regarding $[+\text{INFL}]$ as basically "verbal," if we take AGR to be nominal. INFL governs the subject if it contains AGR, then assigning nominative Case by virtue of the feature $[+\text{INFL}]$. It now follows that the only governors are categories of the form X^0 in the X-bar system (where $X = [\pm N, \pm V]$). Subjects are nominative when they agree with the matrix verb – technically, with its inflection. In some languages, e.g., Portuguese, AGR may also appear with infinitives, and the subject is indeed nominative in this case. The question of whether it is AGR or $[+\text{Tense}]$ (or perhaps some other property, either a configurational property or one involving features of the verb) that governs and assigns nominative Case is an important one with many consequences. We will return to this topic.

Avoiding questions of markedness, let us assume that INFL may in principle be the collection of features $[[\pm\text{Tense}], (\text{AGR})]$.[28] In surface structure, INFL may appear phonetically as part of a verbal affix system, but I will assume here that in S-structure the representation is as in (10). If the S-bar system is a separate system, it might be regarded as a projection of INFL.

Let me stress again that many important questions are begged or simply omitted in the preceding account, some of which will be considered in more detail below. I present these assumptions here as a concrete basis on which to proceed, pending later modifications.

I have also been assuming that there is a rule (11) introducing S, where COMP may be the specifier of S, or perhaps, as some have argued, the head of $\bar{\text{S}}$:

(11) $\bar{\text{S}}$ → COMP S

What about the structure of COMP? I have been assuming – largely as a matter of execution – a theory such as that of OB and earlier work that postulates two positions in COMP, one that may be filled with a *wh*-phrase or other category (e.g., PRO) that has been moved to COMP, and one that is

$[\pm WH]$, where $[-WH] = that$ (and analogues in other languages) and
$[+WH]$ is the abstract element that appears in direct or indirect questions,
and might be base-generated with lexical content in the case of such
elements as *whether*. In English there is also the complementizer *for* in
infinitivals.[29] So we have something like (12), where X is a phrase moved
to COMP (cf. 2.1.(20)):

$$(12) \qquad \left[_{\text{COMP}} X \left\{ \begin{array}{c} [\pm WH] \\ \\ for \end{array} \right\} \right]$$

The order is not very well-motivated empirically. If (12) is adopted, we
might think of it as arising from a rule of adjunction to COMP as suggested
in OB, giving the more detailed structure (13) for COMP:

$$(13) \qquad \left[_{\text{COMP}} X \left[_{\text{COMP}} \left\{ \begin{array}{c} \pm WH \\ \\ for \end{array} \right\} \right] \right]$$

If we now assume that c-command is a necessary requirement for the antecedent-trace relation, it follows that the internal COMP must be deleted
if a *wh*-phrase is moved to COMP. Thus the doubly-filled COMP filter of
Chomsky and Lasnik (1977) follows without stipulation, as noted by Luigi
Rizzi. What of languages that appear to have doubly-filled COMP? It
would now be necessary to assume that the overt complementizer is not in
COMP, but rather in a pre-S position within S, as suggested by Reinhart
(1979b), where a theory of bounding is developed in these terms. Further
consequences of these ideas are developed by Rizzi in work in progress.[30]
   In the theory outlined in Chomsky and Lasnik (1977), there was good
reason to suppose that the *wh*-phrase in COMP was subject to a rule of free
deletion in COMP applying to *that* and *for* as well. The latter rule was closely connected to the $*[\text{NP-}to\text{-VP}]$ filter, which is now largely eliminated in
terms of the Case Filter, following a suggestion by J. -R. Vergnaud. In the
OB theory, it was proposed that the *wh*-phrase in infinitives is deleted up
to recoverability, along lines suggested by Kayne for French, and it was
observed that one might eliminate the residue of the $*[\text{NP-}to\text{-VP}]$ filter
in this way.[31] This approach has consequences with regard to the rule of
free deletion in COMP; namely, the motivation for it is weakened once
there is a different source for the deletion of *wh*-phrases in infinitivals.[32]
We might therefore turn to a different approach to the structure of COMP
that was unacceptable in the framework of Chomsky and Lasnik (1977)
but is compatible with the OB approach, namely, that the rule that expands
COMP is optional; if it does not apply, then COMP will simply lack a
complementizer in declaratives. This has the effect of free deletion of
that and *for*. There are many consequences to this assumption, among
them, weakening of the motivation for taking *wh*-phrases to be in COMP.[33]

I will tentatively adopt the assumption that the rule expanding COMP is optional, continuing to assume that *wh*-movement is to COMP. Thus, tensed clauses may have *that* or no complementizer in D-structure, and infinitives may have *for* or no complementizer. We now have no need for a rule of deletion in COMP apart from the *wh*-phrase of relatives ("the man (who) you saw"), some residual problems concerning *for* in English, and the trace of *wh*-phrases in COMP. As for the first of these, assume this to be a marked property of English, perhaps governed by a filter as outlined in Chomsky and Lasnik (1977) or in the different manner developed in Peset-sky (1978b). We return to the other cases.

This approach to COMP bears on the formulation of selectional restrictions between matrix verbs and embedded clauses. There are evidently relations between COMP and INFL (*that*-tense, *for-to*), and matrix verbs differ with regard to the complements they take (declarative or interroga-tive, finite or infinitival).[34] If COMP may be empty, we might permit direct relations between matrix verbs and INFL of the embedded clause, where the verb accepts one but not the other of $[\pm\text{Tense}]$ in its clausal comple-ment – presumably a marked property. Again, this perhaps suggests think-ing of INFL as the head of S.

In discussing passives, I left open the question of the category to which the passive phrase belongs. To take the simplest case, consider the expres-sion (14) with the S-structure (15) and the D-structure (16), where *kill** is a form of *kill*, *t* is the trace of *John*, and $[_{NP} e]$ is a base-generated empty category:

(14)   John was $[_\alpha \text{killed}]$
(15)   John INFL be $[_\alpha \text{kill}^* \text{ t}]$
(16) $[_{NP} \text{e}]$ INFL be $[_\alpha \text{kill}^* \text{ John}]$

These, recall, are the S- and D-structures required by the θ-criterion and the projection principle. What is the proper choice of α in these struc-tures?

Since the sentence is copular in structure, it is reasonable to assume that $\alpha = \text{AP}$, as in *John was sad*. This conclusion is appropriate for pas-sive participles that are generated in the lexicon, e.g., the "unpassives" such as *untaught, unlettered, uneducated*; etc. But the case of syntactic passives such as (14) is different. In some constructions that allow APs, syntactic passives are excluded; and syntactic passives appear in some verbal constructions that do not permit adjectives; e.g., (17), (18):

(17)   John seems old (sad, tired, troubled, untaught, *taught by Bill, *believed to be a fool, *killed)
(18)   John had Bill leave (killed, taught French, *sad, *troubled, *untaught)

These and similar facts indicate that syntactic passive participles differ in some respect from their lexical counterparts (which are sometimes homophonous : *tired, closed, frightened,* etc.).[35] The minimal assumption is that they differ in one feature. A natural decision would be that syntactic passive participles are not adjectives ($[+N, +V]$) but rather neutralized verb-adjectives with the feature structure $[+V]$. Then α in (14)–(16) will be $[\overline{+V}]$. The property of *seems* in (17) is that it requires adjective complements, as distinct from *be*, which takes $[+V]$ complements. And the property of *have* in (18) is that it rejects $[+N]$ complements, permitting $[+V]$ but not $[+N, +V]$.[36] Thus syntactic passive participles are sometimes treated as adjectival and sometimes as verbal. In the case of such forms as *frightened*, which appear in both (17) and (18), we therefore expect, and find, ambiguity, depending on whether the participle is lexically generated or a syntactic passive. We return to passives in §§ 2.7–8, noting that the clustering of properties of lexical and syntactic passives follows directly: passives that must be lexical by virtue of their morphology (e.g., "unpassives," or passives with other prefixes such as *pseudo-, semi-,* etc.) have one complex of properties, while the syntactic passives have a different complex, and some ambiguously have both complexes. Note that this discussion leaves open the question of how *kill** appears or is generated in (15), (16). We assume here only that it has the categorial feature $[+V]$; the morphological shape may be determined by Affix-movement, a lexical rule, or a morphological rule of the PF-component. The differences are of some interest, and have been much discussed, but I will not pursue the matter here.[37]

2.4. Empty categories

2.4.1. Trace and PRO
So far, we have simply stipulated that the empty categories trace and PRO are distinct. Let us now turn to a closer examination of this question, inquiring into the properties of these elements, and more generally, into the properties of the rule Move-α – i.e., the properties of the antecedent-trace relation – as compared to those of other rules relating antecedents and anaphors, what are often called "rules of construal."[38]

The question of the nature of empty categories is a particularly interesting one for a number of reasons. In the first place, the study of such elements, along with the related investigation of anaphors and pronouns, has proven to be an excellent probe for determining properties of syntactic and semantic representations and the rules that form them. But apart from this, there is an intrinsic fascination in the study of properties of empty elements. These properties can hardly be determined inductively from observed overt phenomena, and therefore presumably reflect inner resources of the mind. If our goal is to discover the nature of the human language faculty, abstracting from the effects of experience, then these elements offer particularly valuable insights.

The examples discussed so far involve the pronominal element PRO and three types of antecedent-trace relation, which we may identify by the descriptive terms in (1):

(1)   (i) John $_i$ seems (to us) $[$ t $_i$ to like ice cream $]$ (NP-movement)
       (ii) John knows $[$ what $_i$ we like t $_i]$ (movement-to-COMP)
       (iii) $[$ NP a man t $_i$ $]$ was here $[$ $_i$ who John knows $]$ (extraposition)

Each of these descriptive categories includes a range of possibilities, which we will illustrate as we proceed. In case (i), the antecedent is an NP with a GF; in case (ii), it is a phrase (here, a *wh*-phrase) in COMP; in case (iii), it is a phrase (here, a relative clause) adjoined to VP.[39]

One property of the rule Move-α, illustrated by these examples, is that the antecedent is not in a θ-position. This fact follows from the θ-criterion and the projection principle, as we have seen in § 2.2. In case (i), the antecedent *John* is in an A-position but one that is not a θ-position, and in (ii) and (iii) it is clear that the position of the antecedent (*what, who John knows,* respectively) is one that is assigned no θ-role.

A second general property of the rule Move-α is that it observes the subjacency condition, and thus falls under the theory of bounding 1.(2i). A third property, still more theory-dependent, is that the trace must be governed in some sense, a matter to which we will return in chapter 4 and that we will simply assume now. Summarizing, we have the following properties of trace:

(2)   (i) trace is governed
       (ii) the antecedent of trace is not in a θ-position
       (iii) the antecedent-trace relation satisfies the subjacency condition

PRO lacks all of these properties: it is ungoverned; its antecedent (if there is one) has an independent θ-role, as does PRO; the antecedent-PRO relation (where PRO has an antecedent) need not satisfy the subjacency condition. Furthermore, PRO need have no antecedent, as in (3), while trace always has an antecedent:

(3)   it is unclear $[$ what PRO to do t $]$

In (3), the trace is governed by the verb *do* (satisfying (2i)) while PRO is ungoverned; the antecedent of the trace (*what*) is assigned no θ-role (satisfying (2ii)) while PRO, lacking an antecedent in this case, has an independent θ-role; and the antecedent-trace relation (*what-t*) satisfies subjacency (condition (2iii)). The same properties are illustrated if we replace the matrix *it is unclear* in (3) by *I told (asked) you:*

(4)   (i) I told you $[$ what PRO to feed yourself (*myself) t $]$
       (ii) I asked you $[$ what PRO to feed myself (*yourself) t $]$

The theory of control determines the choice of antecedent for PRO in (4), differently in the two cases, as we see from the choice of reflexive with PRO as antecedent. In each case, the antecedent has an independent θ-role, as does PRO, though *what*, the antecedent of trace, has none.

We will modify these observations slightly as we proceed, but they are close enough to accurate so that we can accept them now as a very good first approximation, and an adequate basis for exploring the properties of the empty categories.

That antecedent-PRO relations (relations of control, one subcase of relations of construal) may violate the subjacency condition is illustrated in (5), where the brackets are bounding categories (NP and clause):

(5)　　(i) John thinks [that it will be difficult [PRO to feed himself]]

$$\text{(ii) John thinks } [\text{that } \left\{ \begin{array}{l} [\text{PRO to feed himself}] \\ [\text{PRO feeding himself}] \end{array} \right\} \text{ will be difficult}]$$

　　　(iii) [any attempt [PRO to help himself]] will be difficult for John

Other relations of construal may also violate subjacency, as illustrated by the antecedent-anaphor relation in (6) and other more complex examples to which we will return in chapter 3:

(6)　　(i) they think [that [pictures of each other] will be on sale]
　　　(ii) they expected [that [each other's pictures] would be on sale]

Suppose that we replace *thinks* by *seems* in (5), giving (7):

(7)　　(i) John seems [that it will be difficult [t to feed himself]]

$$\text{(ii) John seems } [\text{that } \left\{ \begin{array}{l} [\text{t to feed himself}] \\ [\text{t feeding himself}] \end{array} \right\} \text{ will be difficult}]$$

In the sentence (7), the antecedent is in a position lacking a θ-role (cf. (8)) so that the empty category must be trace, not PRO:

(8)　　it seems that John feeds himself

But the trace in (7), while satisfying condition (2ii), violates conditions (2i) and (2iii). The trace is ungoverned (violating (2i)) and the antecedent-trace relation does not satisfy subjacency (violating (2iii)). Therefore the examples are ungrammatical.

Comparison of (5) and (7) illustrates the contrasting behavior of PRO and trace. Example (7) also illustrates the fact that condition (2ii) does not suffice to characterize the rule Move-α, i.e., the antecedent-trace relation. Either (2i) or (2iii) must be satisfied for the rule to be applicable. In (7), while (2ii) is satisfied, both (2i) and (2iii) are violated, so the sentences are ungrammatical. In fact, (2i) and (2iii) must each be satisfied for the rule Move-α to be applicable. Let us now look into this question.

Note that (2ii) need not be stipulated; it follows from the θ-criterion and the projection principle, as we have seen. Suppose that (2i) holds in addition to (2ii). Consider the set of examples (9):

(9)   (i) it is certain [that John likes ice cream]
          (ii) John is certain [t to like ice cream]
        (iii) it seems [that John likes ice cream]
        (iv) John seems [t to like ice cream]
         (v) it seems [that it is certain [that John likes ice cream]]
        (vi) it seems [that John is certain [t to like ice cream]]
      (vii) *John seems [that it is certain [t to like ice cream]]

From (9i), we see that *is certain* assigns no θ-role to its subject, so that (9ii) satisfies property (2ii). Since (9ii) also satisfies (2i) (assuming that *certain* governs the trace, as does *seems* in (9iv), for reasons to which we return) and (2iii), the sentence is grammatical. The same is true of (9iii,iv). Example (9v) illustrates again the fact that the subjects of *seem* and *be certain* are not θ-positions, so that (9vi) satisfies property (2ii). It also satisfies (2i) and (2iii), and is therefore grammatical. Turning to (9vii), the trace satisfies (2i) and its antecedent is not in a θ-position (compare (9vi)). Therefore it must be that (9vii) is ungrammatical because it violates some other condition C. Assuming C to be the subjacency requirement (2iii), we see that the latter is independent of the other two properties of (2).

It might be argued that the relevant condition C in this case is not the subjacency requirement but rather a requirement of the binding theory, namely, the (Specified) Subject Condition of the OB-framework, which we will reinterpret in a different way in chapter 3. But this seems incorrect. While there are, as we shall see, binding theory violations of a structural form similar to (9vii), they seem very different in level of acceptability from the completely ungrammatical (9vii), indicating that (9vii) is not a binding theory violation. Direct evidence that it cannot be a binding theory violation that accounts for the status of (9vii) is presented in Longobardi (forthcoming). We therefore conclude that it is the subjacency requirement that is the relevant condition C in this case. The conclusion requires a sharpening of the theory of bounding, to which we return in §5.4.

To illustrate the independence of property (2i), consider the examples (10):

(10)   (i) John knows [how [NP to solve this problem]]
         (ii) *there knows [how [NP to be a unicorn in the garden]]
       (iii) *Bill is known [how [t to solve this problem]]
       (iv) it is (well-)known [how [NP to solve this problem]]
        (v) it is (well-)known [how [Bill solved this problem]]
       (vi) it is possible [for [John to win]]
      (vii) it is possible [[PRO to win]]
     (viii) *John is possible [[t to win]]

In (10i), *John* occupies a θ-position, as is obvious from the sense and from the ungrammaticality of (10ii) (compare "there seems to be a unicorn in the garden," "there is certain to be a unicorn in the garden tomorrow").[40] Therefore, the embedded subject in (i) (similarly, (iv)) must be PRO, not trace, by (2ii). In example (10iii), however, the antecedent *Bill* is not in a θ-position as indicated by (iv), (v), so that (2ii) is satisfied, as is the subjacency condition (2iii).[41] But the ungrammatical status of (iii) follows from the property (2i). The participle *known* does not govern the subject of the embedded infinitival complement, nor is it internally governed, so that PRO is permitted in (10iv) but trace is barred in (10iii). Examples (10vi-viii) illustrate the same facts: it is only property (2i) that bars (viii), where the two brackets are categorized $\bar{S}$ and S, blocking government of the embedded subject and thus permitting PRO in (vii) but not trace in (viii). See note 41.

Properties (2i) and (2iii) must each hold, then, independently of the other properties of (2), for the rule Move-α and the antecedent-trace relation. While property (2ii) follows from the projection principle and the θ-criterion, properties (2i) and (2iii) must be stipulated in some fashion for trace. The requirement that trace must be governed turns out to have wide ramifications, apart from the examples considered here; see chapter 4. The theory of bounding, based on the principle (2iii), holds just of the rule Move-α.

We may think of the rule Move-α a bit more abstractly as expressing the configuration (11):

(11) α locally binds β and is not in a θ-position

To say that α locally binds β is to say that α and β are coindexed, α c-commands β, and there is no γ coindexed with α that is c-commanded by α and c-commands β (cf. § 3.2.3). In this configuration, β is trace, and if α is an argument, it is assigned its θ-role by β. Condition (2i) states that in (11), β must be governed (later, in chapter 4, we will see that in fact a narrower condition is required). As far as I can see, this requirement, which has many consequences, must be stipulated as a principle of the theory of government; cf. chapter 4. Condition (2iii) states that the condition of subjacency holds of the pair (α, β) in (11). There is strong evidence that this condition holds of movement-to-COMP, extraposition, and inversion of subject to post-verbal position (cf. §2.4.4). The simplest assumption, then, is that subjacency simply holds of the configuration (11), that is, of the rule Move-α and the antecedent-trace relation. In the absence of explicit evidence to the contrary, we would naturally conclude that condition (2iii) holds of NP-trace. If there were evidence to the contrary, we would be compelled to replace the simple theory (12i) by (12ii):

(12)   (i) Subjacency holds of (11)
         (ii) Subjacency holds of (11), except when α is in subject position

It was therefore somewhat misleading to say, as I did above, that condition (2iii) has to be stipulated for NP-trace. It has to be stipulated for trace, as in (12), but it comes "free" for NP-trace. Patterns such as (9) illustrate that we have to appeal to the fact that NP-trace meets condition (2iii) to account for certain facts; thus (9) offers independent confirmation for (12i), as opposed to (12ii). But even without such independent confirmation, we would surely adopt (12i) over (12ii). To put the same point differently, we see, once again, that the rules that assign θ-roles to arguments and that associate non-arguments with the configurations in which their basic properties are determined (i.e., that determine the interpretation of idiom chunks or of impersonal *it*, etc.) are not some new kind of rule, but are rather rules of the same kind that are involved in many other processes, for example, extraposition, movement-to-COMP, NP-inversion, etc. In fact, the single rule Move-α (possibly with some further specification as to landing sites) accounts for all of these phenomena. We turn to a further generalization in § 2.8.

Turning to PRO, the fact that it does not satisfy the analogue of condition (2ii) but requires an antecedent with an independent θ-role, while assuming an independent θ-role itself, indicates that PRO behaves in the manner of a pronoun; other properties of PRO also support this conclusion, specifically, the fact that it need not satisfy the subjacency condition (cf. (2iii)), that it need not have an antecedent, and that if it has an antecedent that binds it, then the antecedent will be "remote" – i.e., not within the same clause or NP. Let us therefore continue to regard PRO as a pronoun lacking a phonetic matrix, i.e., as an NP with the grammatical features person, number and gender, and perhaps others (e.g., perhaps Case in some instances), but not phonetic features or the features of a reflexive element, etc. See chapter 6 for a more careful and improved account.

If it is true that trace must be governed (namely, (2i)) and that PRO must be ungoverned, then we have the principle (13), given that an empty category – one lacking phonetic features – is either trace or PRO:

(13)   If α is an empty category, then α is PRO if and only if α is ungoverned (equivalently, α is trace if and only if α is governed)

We will see, however, that things do not seem to be quite that simple, since trace must meet a slightly more stringent condition than government, what we will call the condition of "proper government." See chapter 4. We will therefore keep the two parts of principle (13) separate: (I) trace must be governed (i.e., (2i)); (II) PRO must be ungoverned. We will return to (13) in § 4.5, after having discussed the various concepts of the theory of government more fully. In discussing the theory of binding in chapter 3, we will see that (II) follows from the principles of this theory under minimal assumptions. Pending these clarifications, we can adopt (13) tentatively as a central principle of the theory of government.

Adapting to our purposes terms used in American Indian linguistics, we will call a pronoun or PRO "proximate" when it is coindexed with an antecedent and "obviative" when it is not. Proximate PRO is controlled, as in (4); obviative PRO is arbitary in reference, as in (3), though we will sharpen and slightly modify this notion in chapter 4. When PRO is proximate, it must agree in features with its antecedent, exactly as in the case of pronouns. The features of PRO when obviative are subject to some parametric variation: thus PRO is singular in Spanish, English and French, but plural in Italian; e.g., (14) is Italian:[42]

(14)   non è chiaro come essere allegri
        ("it is unclear how to be happy (plural)")

The fact that PRO manifests the property $[\pm\text{plural}]$ in the obviative use again suggests that it is similar to pronouns.

PRO differs from pronouns, then, in that it does not satisfy the Case Filter 2.3.(6). I will use the term "pronominal" to refer to elements with just the grammatical features indicated above, whether or not they have a phonetic realization: thus, PRO and pronouns. Note that the term "pronominal" is purely descriptive; it does not refer to a feature, apart from the grammatical features person, number, gender. PRO is a pronominal, while trace is an empty category $[_\alpha e]$, coindexed with its antecedent in the manner of an anaphor such as reciprocal or reflexive. The referential properties of PRO are determined by the theory of control 1. (2vi); cf. §2.4.3.

As noted earlier, it is not obvious that PRO and trace are distinct, and in earlier work I assumed them to be the same element. But a deeper analysis indicates that they are quite different in their properties. I return to a more abstract consideration of their status in chapter 6, recasting the fundamental distinction between trace and PRO in different terms.

There are many other examples illustrating the difference between PRO and trace. To illustrate with a different kind of case, consider the following examples (noted by Luigi Burzio):

(15)   (i) they assigned one interpreter each to the visiting diplomats
        (ii) one interpreter each was assigned t to the visiting diplomats
        (iii) one interpreter each seems [t to have been assigned t to the visiting diplomats]
(16)   *one interpreter each tried [PRO to be assigned t to the visiting diplomats]

Throughout, *t* is the trace of a moved element: *one interpreter each* in (15), PRO in (16). Example (16) is ungrammatical though it differs from (15iii), which is grammatical, only in replacement of trace by PRO. The distinction cannot be accounted for in terms of the properties (2); these are satisfied for trace in (15iii) and for PRO in (16). Evidently, the D-structure position of *one interpreter each* must be "close enough" to the phrase *the visiting diplomats* for *each* to be interpreted appropriately as a quantifier related to the latter phrase. Perhaps the association is established prior to movement of the phrase *one interpreter each,* perhaps by a rule of each-movement, also leaving trace. Or perhaps the correct approach is to consider the function chains associated with the phrase *one interpreter each.* In (16), the function chain is just ([NP,S]), where S is the matrix clause, while PRO has a two-member function chain with the GF of the trace as its final member. But in (15), the GF of the most-deeply-embedded trace is the final member of the function chain of *one interpreter each.* Crucially, PRO in (16) breaks the function chain into two, while trace in the corresponding position in (15ii,iii) does not, again reflecting the fundamental difference in status between PRO and trace. The chain might then serve as the basis for a reconstruction rule of the sort discussed in Chomsky (1977b). Still another possibility is an interpretation of movement in terms of copying and deletion as discussed in §2.4.6. But whatever the exact mechanisms may be, clearly PRO and trace again differ in fundamental respects. Cf. Burzio (1981) for extensive discussion of the issues raised by this and many similar questions.

Other differences between trace and PRO are discussed in Rizzi (1980b). He observes that there are certain configurations in which control complements (with PRO subject) can appear in Italian, but not raising complements (with trace subject); and there are others in which raising complements can appear but not control complements:

(17)   (i) Gianni vuole tornare a casa
          ("Gianni wants to come back home")
        (ii) è tornare a casa che Gianni vuole
          ("it is to come back home that Gianni wants")
       (iii) Gianni sembra tornare a casa
          ("Gianni seems to come back home")
        (iv) *è tornare a casa che Gianni sembra
          ("it is to come back home that Gianni seems")

(18)   (i) i colpevoli sembrano essere stati puniti duramente
          ("the guilty seem to have been punished severely")
        (ii) i colpevoli dichiarano di essere stati puniti duramente
          ("the guilty assert that they have been (to have been) punished
          severely")
       (iii) i colpevoli si sono puniti duramente
          ("the guilty have been punished severely")
        (iv) i colpevoli sembrano essersi puniti duramente
          ("the guilty seem to have been punished severely")
        (v) *i colpevoli dichiarano di essersi puniti duramente
          ("the guilty assert that they have been (to have been) punished
          severely")

Here again we have direct contrasts between PRO and trace, with PRO in (17ii) versus trace in (17iv), and trace in (18iv) versus PRO in (18v).

Rizzi suggests that the explanation for the PRO-trace contrast in (17)-(18) lies in the theory of government. Consider first (17). Examples (i) and (iii) are control and raising complements, respectively, with PRO and trace as the respective subjects of the embedded complements. As (ii) and (iv) indicate, the control complement but not the raising complement can appear in the focus position of a cleft sentence; while the English example (ii) is perhaps not fully acceptable, the distinction between (ii) and (iv) is clear in English, and is a straightforward grammatical-ungrammatical distinction in Italian. The distinction can be explained in terms of the condition (13), which requires that trace be governed and PRO ungoverned. In (17iv), the trace subject of *tornare* is ungoverned, as contrasted with (17iii), where it is governed by *sembra*, so that (17iv) is ungrammatical by virtue of condition (2i). But PRO is permitted in this ungoverned position, so that (17ii) is grammatical.

The examples (18) are more complex. Examples (18i) and (18ii) illustrate respectively a passive embedded infinitival in a raising context with trace subject, and a control configuration with PRO subject. Example (18iii) illustrates the impersonal construction with the clitic *si*, which Rizzi assumes (following Belletti (1980b)) to be in the INFL position in the NP-INFL-VP structure. Thus the S-structures of the raising configuration (18iv) and the control configuration (18v) are (19i), (19ii), respectively.

(19)   (i) i colpevoli sembrano [t si [$_{VP}$ essere puniti duramente]]
        (ii) i colpevoli dichiarano di [PRO si [$_{VP}$ essere puniti duramente]]

On the status of *di*, see §5.2. A rule of the PF-component (analogous to affix-movement) attaches the clitic *si* to the right of the infinitival verb *essere* to yield the forms (18iv), (18v). We have assumed that INFL (or at least, "nominal" elements in INFL) govern the subject. Therefore the trace is governed in (19i) and PRO is governed in (19ii). By property (2i), trace must be governed, so that (19i), hence (18iv), is grammatical. But as we have seen, PRO must be ungoverned, so that (19ii), hence (18v), is ungrammatical. The passives (18i) and (18ii) are both grammatical, since there is no governing element within the embedded clause, so that trace may appear (governed by the matrix verb) and PRO may appear in the corresponding ungoverned position in the control structure (18ii).

Considerations to which we return in chapter 4 suggest a different approach to explaining the contrast between trace and PRO illustrated by (18iv), (18v). Note that the trace subject of the embedded construction in (19i) is governed by the matrix verb in any event, so (19i) (hence (18iv)) meets the condition (2i) irrespective of the status of *si*. As for (19ii), it may be that *si* is actually a subject clitic and that the PRO is in effect an impersonal pronominal associated with *si* and not subject to control in this case for other reasons, thus blocking (19ii). This account, to which we return in more detail, still reduces the distinction between (18iv) and (18v) to the theory of government, but in a somewhat more intricate way.[43]

Note that in these examples, property (2ii) is satisfied throughout. In the raising structures, the matrix subject is not in a θ-position, while it does receive an independent θ-role in the control structures. Property (2iii) is also satisfied. Whatever the explanation may be for examples (15)-(18) – perhaps those just indicated – they illustrate again the contrasting behavior of PRO and trace.

While PRO and trace differ in important respects, they are alike in others. For example, both PRO and NP-trace behave as anaphors with respect to the binding theory and are thus excluded from positions that are opaque in the sense of OB. Other traces, while satisfying the conditions (2), have somewhat different properties. The theory of grammar must explain why empty categories of various kinds have these specific properties and how languages may vary in these respects.

2.4.2. Further properties of PRO

Let us now consider the behavior of empty categories more closely, beginning with PRO. In the case of PRO, we have to consider three conditions: those under which PRO may appear (the gap is permitted), under which it must appear (the gap is obligatory), and under which it may not appear (the gap is impermissible).

Principle 2.4.1(13) stipulates that PRO is ungoverned. If so, it will be excluded from the complement positions governed by the head of some construction and from the position of subject of a tensed clause. PRO may appear, then, in the position of subject of an infinitive, specifier (subject) of an NP, or COMP, as in (1):[44]

(1)   (i) it is unclear $[_{\bar{S}}$ what $[_S$ PRO to do t $]]$
         (ii) I'd much prefer $[_{NP}$ PRO going to a movie $]$
         (iii) I bought a book $[_{\bar{S}}[_{COMP}$ PRO $[_S$ PRO to give t to Mary $]]]$

Case (i) we have already discussed. Here, PRO is permissible since the position is ungoverned, and obligatory since the position is not Case-marked (unless the language has marked devices to assign Case; cf. note 25). We return to case (iii) directly. In case (ii), PRO is permissible since the position is ungoverned, but is not obligatory, since genitive Case can be assigned in this position, as in (2):

(2)   I'd much prefer $[_{NP}$ his going to the movie $]$

We might assume that genitive Case-assignment is optional, with a phonetically-realized NP subject as in (2) when it is assigned; or that genitive Case-assignment is obligatory but not phonetically realized when PRO is selected as the option, so that PRO is Case-marked but ungoverned in (1ii). Let us leave this as a question of execution.

Note that in (3), PRO is barred:

(3) (i) *I like $[_{NP}$ PRO book $]$
     (ii) I like $[_{NP}$ his book $]$

In § 3.2.1, I will return to the question of why gerunds differ in this way from NPs with a nominal head.

The structures (1ii), (2) differ from (3) in another respect, apart from the fact that the specifier of the NP may be either PRO or a phonetically-realized NP in the former but only a phonetically-realized NP in the latter. Compare the examples of (4):

(4) (i) John would much prefer [his going to the movie]
     (ii) John would much prefer [his (own) book]

In case (ii), the pronoun *he* of *his book* may or may not refer to John. In case (i), there is at least a strong preference for taking it to be someone other than John, particularly when it is unstressed. As (4ii) indicates, this is not a position of disjoint reference. I think that the choice of reference for *he* in (i) is dictated not by the disjoint reference principle but rather by a principle that we may state in the most general terms as (5), interpreted as imposing a choice of PRO over an overt pronoun where possible:

(5) Avoid Pronoun

Thus in (4i), where PRO may appear, the overt pronoun is taken as distinct in reference from *John*; but in (4ii), where PRO may not appear, the overt pronoun is free in reference. Principle (5) might be regarded as a subcase of a conversational principle of not saying more than is required, or might be related to a principle of deletion-up-to-recoverability, but there is some reason to believe that it functions as a principle of grammar.[45]

Consider finally case (iii) of (1). Here PRO appears as subject of the purposive infinitival, as in (1i). Following the analysis in OB (Chomsky, 1980a, Appendix; 1980b), it also appears in the (ungoverned) COMP position as antecedent of the trace, an instance of movement-to-COMP (cf. 2.4.(1ii)). It was assumed in OB that the movement of PRO to COMP, where it is controlled by an element of the matrix clause, is an instance of Move-α in the syntax, but it is possible that it is an instance of Move-α in the LF-component analogous to the rule postulated in Chomsky (1977a, chapter 3) to account for the range of interpretation of sentences with embedded *wh*-phrases such as (6):[46]

(6) I don't know who remembers who put the book where

We will see in § 3.2.3 that there is good reason to suppose that movement-to-COMP in this case is indeed syntactic movement, rather than movement in the LF-component. The range of examples discussed in Chomsky (1977b) under the rubric of "*wh*-movement" may also be regarded as instances of movement of PRO to COMP, where PRO perhaps has the feature [*wh-*] (cf. 2.6.(45)). This eliminates the need for a rule deleting the *wh*-phrase in COMP and also explains the absence of PP-movement in many of these cases, PRO being excluded as object of a preposition, a governed position. See also note 32.

As we have seen, PRO is in general obligatory as the subject of an infinitive by virtue of the Case Filter, but phonetically-realized NP may appear as subject if the infinitive is in the context V– or P–, as in (7):

(7)   (i) [for [John to leave]] would be a mistake
       (ii) I expect [him to leave]; I believe [him to be incompetent]
       (iii) I'm eager [for [you to take part]]
       (iv) I V [(for) [him to take part]]   (V = *want, prefer,* etc.)

The exception is quite natural, under the assumptions of Case theory; in exactly these two contexts, Case can be assigned by the governing verb or prepositional complementizer, presumably marked options in English. Normally, PRO is obligatory as the subject of an infinitival complement to a verb, as in (8):

(8)   John tried [PRO to win]

I assume (8) to be the unmarked case. By the projection principle, verbs with infinitival complements appear with clausal complements, as indicated by their lexical features. Clausal complements are of the category $\bar{S}$, which we have assumed to be an absolute barrier to government, thus requiring PRO as subject of the embedded clause since the subject is not governed clause-internally. English *for*-infinitivals, with a prepositional complementizer, escape this requirement since *for* may govern and assign Case to the subject, excluding PRO and permitting a phonetically-realized NP.[47] In languages similar to English, the verbs of (7ii) require PRO subjects for the infinitival complement. A reasonable assumption, then, is that English has a marked rule of $\bar{S}$-deletion for complements of verbs of the *believe*-category, permitting the verb to govern the subject of the embedded complement, thus excluding PRO and permitting phonetically-realized NP in (7ii). This move requires a slight modification of the notion "government" given informally in § 2.3; we return to this question in §§ 3.2.1 and 5.2.

On the same assumption, the trace is governed by *believed* in such examples as (9), satisfying requirement 2.4.1.(2i) for trace (namely, that trace be governed) and overcoming a problem that would otherwise arise for such examples:

(9)   John was believed [t to be incompetent]

Example (9) derives from the D-structure (10), where INFL = [− Tense]

(10)   [$_{NP}$ e] was believed [COMP John INFL [$_{VP}$ be incompetent]]

If INFL = [+ Tense] in (10), we derive (11) by *it*-insertion:

(11)   it was believed [that John is incompetent]

Thus (9) and (11) derive from D-structures differing only in the value of INFL in (10) and the corresponding value of the embedded COMP. The complement of *believe* is clausal at LF as a lexical property, and the clausal complement may be finite or infinitival, the simplest case. By the projection principle, we expect (10) at D-structure and (9) or (11) at S-structure. Derivation of (11) is straightforward. Application of Move-α is blocked by principles of binding theory if INFL = [+ Tense] in (10); thus *it*-insertion yielding (11) is obligatory. Application of Move-α is permitted in the derivation of (9) because of the rule of $\bar{S}$-deletion which ensures that the trace is governed. *John* receives no Case from within the embedded clause in (10) with INFL = [− Tense], and is not Case-marked by *believed*, which is not a Case-assigner since it has the categorial structure [+ V] (it is not [− N]).[48] Therefore for (10) to surface in this case some rule must apply to assign Case to *John*. The *of*-insertion rule 2.3.(9) is inapplicable since *believed* is not [+ N].[49] Therefore, Move-α is obligatory, placing *John* in a position in which it can receive Case in (9), which satisfies all of the requirements for the antecedent-trace relation (cf. §2.4.1.(2)).

Note that the situation with respect to (9)–(11) is quite analogous to that of the nominal and adjectival constructions 2.3.(2) – (4), repeated as (12):

(12)   (i) destruction – the city
         (ii) author – the book
         (iii) proud – John

In (12), the Case Filter is violated so that either *of*-insertion or Move-α must apply, only the former being applicable in case (iii) while either may apply in cases (i) and (ii).

The same ideas extend to raising predicates such as (13):

(13)   (i) John seems [t to be a nice fellow]
         (ii) John is likely [t to be a nice fellow]

The D-structures are (14), exactly as in (15), with empty NP becoming *it* in (15):

(14) (i) NP seems [John to be a nice fellow]
   (ii) NP is likely [John to be a nice fellow]
(15) (i) it seems [that John is a nice fellow]
   (ii) it is likely [that John is a nice fellow]

As (15) indicates, a lexical property of *seem* and *likely* is that they take clausal complements and assign no θ-role to their subjects. Therefore, by the projection principle, the D-structures for the sentences corresponding to (13) must be (14). Again, the embedded clause may be [$\pm$Tense], the unmarked case. If it is finite ([+Tense]), we derive (15). If it is infinitival ([−Tense]) as in (14), the embedded subject receives no Case, so to satisfy the Case Filter, application of Move-α is obligatory (the *of*-insertion rule 2.3.(9) being inapplicable) yielding (13). As for the conditions 2.4.1.(2) on trace, condition (i) is satisfied if we assume that the predicates *seem, likely* – like *believe* – delete $\bar{S}$, so that the trace in (13) is governed; condition (ii) is satisfied since the subject lacks a θ-role; and condition (iii) (subjacency) is satisfied in (13) though it would not be in the derivation of (16ii) from the D-structure (16i), as we have seen in 2.4.1.(9):

(16) (i) NP seems [NP is likely [John to win]]
   (ii) John seems [it is likely [t to win]]

The option of deleting $\bar{S}$ is in part a lexical idiosyncrasy; thus, it is a property of *likely* but not of its near-synonym *probable*. It is the property that characterizes "raising predicates." Note that there is no sense, in our framework, to the question whether (9) is an example of passive or raising. These are simply descriptive categories, not rules; (9) is an instance of the application of Move-α, which covers both categories. See the comments on decomposition of rules in chapter 1.

In general, then, the subject of an infinitival is PRO in the unmarked case. English permits two marked exceptions, exactly the two we expect given that the Case-assigners are the categories [−N]: *for*-infinitivals and verbs with $\bar{S}$-deletion. In both instances, Case is assigned over the S boundary and the trace is governed, as required, when it appears after a predicate such as *believed, seem, likely* that deletes $\bar{S}$.

As these examples illustrate, "raising predicates" that delete $\bar{S}$ and thus govern a trace in the subject position of an infinitival complement are not Case-assigners; that is, the trace left by NP-movement is governed but not Case-marked. The same is true of monoclausal passives. We return to these properties in a more general setting in §2.6.-8. In contrast, the trace left by movement-to-COMP (whether *wh*-movement or PRO-movement) is Case-marked. The latter is interpreted as a variable in LF and shares properties of names in the theory of binding, as in the cases of (strong) crossover; while the trace of NP-movement, in contrast, behaves as an anaphor under the binding theory. We return to these matters, which are familiar in part from earlier literature. We therefore have the following observation:

(17)   a trace is a variable if and only if it is Case-marked

I will return to the question of whether (17) holds without exception, and if so, whether it must be stipulated in whole or in part or whether it follows from other principles. In the examples so far discussed the observation holds but need not be stipulated. Tentatively, let us assume that (17) is true: variables are Case-marked traces.

We have reviewed the properties of examples (7i-iii). Consider now (7iv), verbs of the *want*-type that take *for*-infinitivals as complements. As is well-known, there is some variability, in part dialectal, as to whether the *for* is deleted in immediate post-verbal position. Thus we have such examples as (18):

(18)   (i) John wants very much [for Bill to win]
          (ii) what John wants is [for Bill to win]
          (iii) John wants [Bill to win]
          (iv) John would like [(for) Bill to win]

These are the structures implied by the projection principle, with the bracketed expression a clausal complement; *that*-clauses are often an optional variant, the unmarked case. The complementizer *for* is undeletable in (i), (ii) as required by the Case Filter.[50] Why is it deletable in (iii), (iv)? One possibility is that these verbs sometimes permit S̄-deletion, so that when *for* does not appear the subject of the infinitival complement can receive Case from the matrix verb, as in the case of *believe*-type verbs; a second possibility is that there is a rule of *for*-deletion in immediate post-verbal position for these verbs in the PF-component (with idiosyncratic variation, in either case). The second option appears to be the correct one. If these verbs permitted S̄-deletion, we would expect to find passive forms such as (19), analogous to (9):

(19)   *John was wanted (liked, preferred, ...) [t to win]

But such examples are uniformly excluded, exactly as in the unmarked case of verbs with infinitival complements:

(20)   *John was known [how [t to solve the problem]]
          (= (2.4.1.(10ii)))

It seems, then, that *want*-type verbs do not permit S̄-deletion as a marked option.[51]

Some verbs (e.g., *expect*) permit either of the two marked options. Thus we have (21) :

(21)   (i) John was expected [t to win] (with S̄-deletion)
        (ii) what John expected was [for Bill to win] (with *for*-com-
        plementizer)

But in general, certain verbs take one or the other but not both of the two
marked options permitted in English.[52]
   Another well-known fact about verbs of the *want, prefer* category supports the same conclusion. These verbs are much more resistant to heavy
NP-shift than those of the *believe*-category:[53]

(22)   (i) they'd believe to be foolish any candidate who would take the
        trouble to run in every primary
        (ii) *they'd want to win any candidate who would take the trouble
        to run in every primary

The exact status of the rule in question need not concern us here. Perhaps
it is a stylistic rule of the PF-component that does not cross S̄-boundaries,
or perhaps, as Tim Stowell suggests, it is a syntactic rule leaving trace
which must be governed by virtue of 2.4.1.(i), so that it can apply only
in cases of S̄-deletion. In either case, the rule is applicable in structures
that have undergone S̄-deletion as in (22i) while in the corresponding
cases with *want*-type verbs it is not, indicating again that they do not
permit Exceptional Case-marking by S̄-deletion but rather invariably
have S̄-complements at S-structure. Similarly, in such examples as (23),
which we must also assume to involve S̄-deletion, heavy NP-shift is acceptable, as in (24):

(23)   I consider [John intelligent]
(24)   I would consider intelligent anyone capable of understanding
        Gödel's completeness proof

   As noted in chapter 1, we do not expect to find chaos in the marked
periphery of language. The examples just reviewed illustrate a more
plausible expectation. Since the Case-assigners are the [−N] categories
V and P, we have two marked options for escaping the Case Filter which
prevents phonetically-realized subjects in infinitival complements: Exceptional Case-marking by verbs of the *believe*-type, and a prepositional
complementizer *for*, the latter device also permitting infinitives with
phonetically-realized subjects in other positions as well.
   When an infinitival complement is not in the context [−N]−, PRO is
obligatory as subject, as in (25), and there are no marked exceptions:

(25)   (i) V NP [PRO to VP] ("I persuaded Bill [PRO to leave],"
        *"I persuaded Bill [Tom to leave]")

    (ii) V AP [PRO to VP] ("I was sorry [PRO to leave],"
      *"I was sorry [Bill to leave]")

   (iii) V PP[PRO to VP] ("I appealed to Bill [PRO to leave],"
      *"I appealed to Bill [Tom to leave]")

   (iv) V ... [*wh*-phrase [PRO to VP]] ("I asked (Bill) [what PRO
      to do]," *"I asked (Bill) [what Tom to do]")

In these cases too there are tensed counterparts. By the projection principle, the embedded construction in each case is $\overline{S}$, declarative or interrogative, and if declarative, finite or infinitival,[54] depending on properties of the matrix verb.

Since PRO is a pronominal, it must assume a θ-role; thus it is either in a θ-position itself or binds a trace that is in a θ-position. PRO is excluded from governed θ-positions as in (26):[55]

(26)   (i) *it is unclear [how PRO solved the problem]
      (ii) *it is unclear [how to solve PRO]
     (iii) *I'd much prefer [his going to PRO]
     (iv) *it is unclear [what to give t to PRO]
      (v) *it is unclear [who to give PRO to t]

The positions from which PRO is excluded are opaque, in the sense of binding theory, an important property of this element to which we return in chapter 3. PRO is also excluded as subject of an infinitive after a prepositional complementizer or an Exceptional Case-marking verb such as *believe*, or as the subject of an NP with a nominal head, as in (3i); the latter property is still to be explained and there are also some questions concerning *for*-complementizers to which we will return. PRO may appear otherwise as subject of infinitive, subject of NP, in COMP, or in INFL (as AGR).

These properties of PRO are not mere idiosyncrasies. We would like to reduce them, as far as possible, to general principles, even if these prove ultimately to be subject to some parametric variation, as in Exceptional Case-marking. As we have seen, straightforward explanations are forthcoming for all of these properties of PRO (with some exceptions, as noted, to which we will return) if we assume the projection principle and the analysis of S as NP-INFL-VP, assumptions which seem to be near optimal. The obligatoriness of PRO follows from Case theory. Otherwise, its distribution follows from the projection principle and the θ-criterion and the principle that PRO is ungoverned, the latter still to be grounded in the GB-theory in such a way as to account for the properties that PRO shares with overt anaphors such as *each other* and with pronouns; specifically, that it is excluded from opaque contexts. It will be the task of the binding theory 1.(2iv) to show in what manner PRO is subject to the conditions which, for example, permit overt anaphors as subject of an infinitive but not elsewhere in a clause, and which require disjoint reference for pronouns under the same circumstances, while guaranteeing that PRO is ungoverned. The fact that PRO shares basic properties with overt anaphors and pronouns (while differing from them in some respects as a consequence of its lack of phonetic content, given the Case Filter) and that it shares certain fundamental properties of trace (while differing from it by virtue of the conditions of 2.4.1.(2) and 2.4.1.(13)) is an important one; it provides significant independent support for the projection principle and the rule 2.1.(25) analyzing S as NP-INFL-VP, in that this complex of similarities and differences follows from independently-motivated and reasonable principles: the binding principles for anaphors and pronouns; the θ-criterion, which is virtually a definition of well-formedness at LF; the projection principle, which has a wide range of consequences quite independent of empty categories, some grammar-internal, some beyond; the general principle 2.4.1.(13) concerning government of empty categories, in part reducible to the binding theory, and with a wide range of consequences as we shall see in chapter 4; the Case Filter, which partially supplants the *[NP-*to*-VP] filter of Chomsky and Lasnik (1977) (cf. OB) and has a variety of consequences, e.g., with regard to obligatoriness of rules of NP-movement, the impossibility of such structures as "John to have won is widely believed," "what he expects is John to win," etc. We will see further in chapter 6 that the Case Filter is closely related to the θ-criterion.

Note that the distribution of the empty categories, the differences among them and their similarities to and differences from overt elements are determined through the interaction of quite simple principles that belong to several different subtheories, in accordance with the modular approach to grammar that we are pursuing throughout. Note also that there is no need to stipulate that certain configurations are "control structures." The current discussion is a continuation of efforts initiated in Chomsky and Lasnik (1977) to eliminate this notion, except as a descriptive category. The situation is more complex, as we shall see when we consider pro-drop languages in chapter 4, but the conclusion nevertheless stands. See chapter 6 for summary and further extensions.

Continuing with these assumptions, we will account for the ungrammatical status of (27) and (28) in the same way:

(27)   they wanted [me to feed each other]
(28)   they told me [what PRO to feed each other]

Tentatively assuming the binding theory of the OB-framework, to be improved later, the (Specified) Subject Condition prevents *each other* from taking *they* as antecedent in (27) because the anaphor is in the c-command domain of a subject, *me*; in (28), the same is true in the domain of the subject PRO, which is controlled by *me*, not *they*, because of properties of the matrix verb *tell* (compare "they asked me what to feed each other"). Thus at the level at which the binding theory applies, we want to have PRO in (28) in the position occupied by *me* in (27). If the binding theory applies at S-structure, as we will conclude in chapter 3, then PRO must be present in (28) at S-structure. If the binding theory applies at LF, then the simplest assumption again – and the only one consistent with the projection principle – is that PRO is present at S-structure; then no LF-rule is required to give the LF-representation from S-structure.

It might be thought that these phenomena could be described somehow in terms of properties of control verbs directly, but that would be a mistake, because the same phenomena appear when there are no control verbs at all. Consider the sentences (29), (30):

(29)   they thought NP said $\left[\text{that} \left[\left\{ \begin{matrix} \text{to feed} \\ \text{feeding} \end{matrix} \right\} \text{each other (themselves)} \right] \right.$
        would be difficult $\left. \vphantom{} \right]$

(30)   (i) they thought NP said [that [pictures of each other (them-
            selves)] would be on sale]
            (ii) they thought NP wanted [[each other's candidates] to win]
            (iii) they thought NP wanted [each other to win]

In example (29), whatever the choice of NP, the matrix subject *they* can be taken as antecedent of the anaphor *each other* (*themselves*).[56] Thus if NP = *Bill*, the sentences can be taken as meaning that each of them thought Bill said that to feed the others would be difficult (etc.); and if NP = *we*, the sentences are ambiguous as to choice of antecedent. In examples (30), however, the matrix subject *they* cannot be taken as antecedent. If NP = *Bill*, the sentences are not well-formed; if NP = *we*, then it is necessarily the antecedent. The properties of (30) follow directly from the binding theory for the anaphors (reciprocal, reflexive) in (30); namely, the (Specified) Subject Condition in the OB-framework. But evidently this does not hold for the anaphors in (29), though they are embedded in the same way in relevant respects. The correct conclusions follow, again, if we assume that the embedded phrase in (29) is (31) at LF:

(31) $\left[\text{PRO} \left\{ \begin{matrix} \text{to feed} \\ \text{feeding} \end{matrix} \right\} \text{each other (themselves)} \right]$

Then the antecedent of the overt anaphor (reciprocal, reflexive) is PRO, which need not be locally controlled in contrast to trace; cf. 2.4.1.(2iii), 2.4.1.(5),(7). By the projection principle, the same must be true at D- and S-structure.

As these examples again illustrate, the theory of control permits the controller of PRO to be remote as in the case of other anaphors apart from trace, which alone is subject to the theory of bounding. As we have seen, PRO is like other anaphors and overt pronouns with respect to the theory of binding as well, in that it may appear only in transparent (non-opaque) constructions. But the examples (29), (30) also illustrate some differences between PRO and overt anaphors. The binding theory must account for the fact that PRO shares with other anaphors the property that it may appear only in transparent contexts, but it must also explain why PRO in (29) (incorporating (31)) may take the remote antecedent *they*, while the anaphors of (30) may not. The binding theory of OB yields the wrong prediction in this case, requiring that neither PRO nor other anaphors may have remote antecedents in such examples, where the NP of (29), (30) is a lexical argument. This is a problem to which we will return in reformulating the theory of binding in chapter 3.

The examples (29), (30) provide evidence for a PRO analysis of EQUI constructions as against a *self*-deletion analysis (cf. Fodor (1975), Chomsky (1975, 1977a), Chomsky and Lasnik (1977), OB and other work). If we were to assume that the embedded phrase is (32) instead of (31) at S-structure, with *for-self* deleted by rules of the PF-component, then the anaphor *self* should be assigned NP rather than *they* as antecedent in (29), as in (30), by the binding theory (whether in the OB-framework or the GB-framework to which we turn in chapter 3):

(32)   [for self to feed each other (themselves)]

Note that *for*-NP, with phonetically-realized NP, can appear in the embedded phrase of (29), as in (33):

(33)   they thought Bill said [that [for us to feed each other] would be difficult]

We therefore have two options for choice of NP in the embedded phrase: PRO or phonetically-realized NP. The same was true in (lii), (2), the subject position of a gerund. If the Case-marking element *for* is selected as complementizer, then we may have a phonetically-realized NP; if it is not, we must have PRO. This follows from the Case Filter.[57]

2.4.3. Control theory

Recall that there are three basic questions that arise in connection with the element PRO: (i) where may it appear?; (ii) where must it appear?; (iii) how is its reference determined? The first question falls under general principles of the theories of government and binding, the second under the projection principle and Case theory, and the third under control theory. The first two questions we have discussed in a preliminary way: PRO is restricted to ungoverned positions that are non-opaque in the sense of the theory of binding; and it must appear in positions where an NP is required but no Case is assigned (excluding phonetically-realized NP) and the position is ungoverned (excluding trace). The OB-framework provides partial answers to question (i) in terms of the binding theory it contains, though there are problems, some noted, to which we return in chapter 3. The answer to question (ii) in the OB-framework seems to me to be essentially correct as far as it goes, though it becomes more principled in the light of the projection principle and is now extended to trace by 2.4.1.(13). There is also a partial theory of control presented in OB. It seems to me on the right track, though as noted there, it is too restricted. Inadequacies in this approach are discussed in Manzini (1980), where an improved account is proposed. I will not attempt a comprehensive theory of control here, but will simply indicate some of its properties.

Consider first structures of the form (1), where $\bar{S}$ is a clause containing PRO with an A-GF (cf. §2.2), which, by principles of binding theory, must be that of subject:

(1) $\quad NP[_{VP}V \begin{Bmatrix} NP \\ PP \end{Bmatrix} \bar{S}]$

The embedded clause $\bar{S}$ with PRO subject may be declarative or interrogative, as in (2), (3), respectively:

(2)   (i) John persuaded Bill [PRO to feed himself]
            (ii) John promised Bill [PRO to feed himself]
            (iii) John appealed to Bill [PRO to feed himself]
            (iv) John pleaded with Bill [PRO to feed himself]

(3)   (i) John asked Bill [how PRO to feed himself]
            (ii) John told Bill [how PRO to feed himself]
            (iii) it is unclear [how PRO to feed oneself]

Depending on the nature of the verb, PRO is controlled either by the complement of the verb (as in (2i,iii,iv); (3ii)) or by its subject (as in (2ii), (3i)). The reflexive in these examples takes as its (ultimate) antecedent the controlling NP.[58] Arbitrary reference is impossible in (2), though it is possible in (3), with interrogative complements, as illustrated in (3iii). As noted in OB, it is perhaps marginally possible in cases (i) and (ii) of (3), with *oneself* replacing *himself*, or as in (4):

(4)   (i) John asked Bill how to prove the theorem without using the axiom of choice
            (ii) John asked Bill how to behave oneself under such circumstances

We might say that arbitrary reference is always possible with interrogative complement, but that control properties of the verb establish a strong preference relation for NP-control, with the choice of NP determined by properties of the verb. Given the possibility of arbitrary reference with interrogative complement but not declarative complement, we have such examples as (5) but not (6):[59]

(5)   John was asked t [what PRO to do]
(6)   *John was promised t [PRO to win]

In (5) and (6) the passivized verb has no subject, so subject control is impossible as required by these verbs; arbitrary reference is possible in (5) but not in (6).

Other examples suggest that something more general is involved in these cases. Consider (7):

(7)   (i) John asked Bill his plans
         (ii) John told Bill his plans
         (iii) John promised Bill his consent
         (iv) John promised Bill his admission to the university

If not free, the reference of *he* (in *his*) is to Bill in (i), John in (ii) and (iii), and Bill in (iv). Note that the NP-antecedent in (i), (ii), (iv) reverses the normal properties of the verbs in the control structures (2), (3). These are at least strong preferences, perhaps requirements.

The normal control properties illustrated in (2) and (3) can sometimes be reversed. Thus (8) is ambiguous as to controller, and in (9), subject control is preferred to object control:

(8)   John asked the teacher to leave early
(9)   John asked (begged, pleaded with, . . .) the teacher to be allowed to leave early

With *persuade* as the main verb, reversal of control as in (9) seems much more difficult. Another familiar case, violating the descriptive observations just reviewed, is (10):

(10)   John was promised to be allowed to leave

In (10), as distinct from (6), *John* may be the controller.

A natural suggestion is that choice of controller is determined by θ-roles or other semantic properties of the verb, or perhaps pragmatic conditions of some sort. If so, we would expect to find subject control in (11) (analogous to (9)) and control by the surface subject in (12) (analogous to (10)):

(11)   John asked Bill to get (receive) permission to leave early
(12)   John was promised to get (receive) permission to leave early

Example (11) seems to me to behave as expected on this assumption, while (12) does not.

Arbitrary reference is also possible in complements to adjectives that take *for*-clauses as in (13); cf. (14):

(13)   it is important (difficult, etc.) [PRO to get an A in math]
(14)   it is important for us [for you to get an A in math]

In OB, the fact is related to the presence of an overt complementizer, as in (3), but comparative evidence indicates that this is the wrong idea; as Manzini notes, the same is true, say, in Italian, where there is no overt complementizer.

In purposive infinitivals, reference of the subject PRO may be arbitrary as in (15)[60] or determined by properties of the matrix verb, as in (16):

(15)   the books were sold [PRO to help the refugees]
(16)   (i) I sold the book [PRO to help the refugees]
           (ii) I bought Bill a book [PRO [PRO to give t to Mary]]
           (iii) I got a book from Bill [PRO [PRO to give t to Mary]]
           (iv) I bought a book from Bill [PRO [PRO to give t to Mary]]

In (i), *I* is the controller. In (ii)-(iv), *book* controls the PRO in COMP which is the antecedent of the trace *t*, a variable in LF; PRO in the subject position is controlled by *Bill* in (ii) and by *I* in (iii), (iv), again suggesting that semantic or pragmatic considerations are operative.

Note that c-command is not required for control, as illustrated in (2iii,iv) or more clearly in (17), in which there is no possibility of some kind of reanalysis:

(17)   (i) [PRO to clear myself of the charges] is important to me
           (ii) [PRO finishing my work on time] is important to me

Other anaphors are marginally possible with c-command violations, as in (18):[61]

(18)   the rumors about each other irritated the men (were annoying to the men)

In the case of PRO, and marginally in the case of other anaphors, it suffices for the antecedent to be an element of the argument structure of the clause. Note that in the case of PRO, the binding theory imposes no requirement on choice of antecedent as is already evident from the case of long-distance control, a matter to which we return. Thus, PRO behaves in this respect like other pronominals. In the case of trace, the antecedent must always c-command, so it appears, as required by the binding theory.

While PRO may have a non-c-commanding antecedent, the latter may not be contained within an NP that is a possible controller:

(19)   (i) PRO finishing his work on time is important to John
           (ii) PRO finishing his work on time is important to John's friends
           (iii) PRO finishing his work on time is important to John's development

In (i) and (iii), *John* is the controller, but in (ii) only *John's friends* may serve as controller, so that *he* (in *his*) refers to someone other than the referent of PRO.

As we have seen, PRO may be controlled by a remote antecedent though trace may not, as in (20):

(20) (i) they thought (that I said) that $\left[\begin{array}{l}\text{PRO feeding each other}\\\text{PRO to feed each other}\end{array}\right\}$ $]$

   would be difficult

  (ii) *they seemed (that I said) that $\left[\begin{array}{l}\text{t feeding each other}\\\text{t to feed each other}\end{array}\right\}$ $]$

   would be difficult

Cf. 2.4.1.(9vii). There are some subject–object asymmetries, at least in preference, in such long-distance control, as illustrated in (21):

(21) (i) they thought I had suggested [PRO feeding each other]
   (ii) they thought I had suggested that [PRO feeding each other] would be difficult
   (iii) they told John that [PRO feeding himself] was impossible
   (iv) John told them that [PRO feeding himself] was impossible

Many speakers seem to find (ii) and (20i) more natural than (i), and prefer (iv) to (iii).[62] Very loosely, it appears that PRO searches for a possible antecedent within its own clause, and if it can't find one there, looks outside. In (21i), *I* is a possible controller within the clause, yielding an ungrammatical embedded clause since *each other* has an improper antecedent; whereas in (ii), there being no controller in the same clause, any outside controller is permitted. If there is a real distinction between (iii) and (iv), it indicates that PRO prefers a subject to a complement antecedent,[63] a familiar phenomenon in the case of anaphor in many languages. But these appear to be fairly loose requirements. Thus (22) seems to be ambiguous, with PRO taking either *they* (within its clause, but not c-commanding it) or *we* (outside its clause) as antecedent:

(22) we feel that $\left[\begin{array}{l}\text{PRO learning to cooperate}\\\text{PRO helping each other}\end{array}\right\}$ $]$ is important for

  their development

The phenomena are reminiscent of those studied by Hale and his colleagues in languages where various rules of construal play a fundamental role.[64]

These are among the properties that will have to be accounted for by the theory of control. They suffice to indicate that this theory involves a number of different factors: structural configurations, intrinsic properties of verbs, other semantic and pragmatic considerations. Sorting these factors out and explaining the cross-linguistic differences and similarities remains an open problem.[65] The formulation in OB is at best a first approximation. I will adopt it here as a rough guide, with the modifications informally reviewed here, knowing of no substantial improvement.

2.4.4. Trace and bounding theory

So far, we have been considering one type of NP-gap, namely, the type with the properties of PRO. The basic properties of the second category, NP-trace, have already been illustrated in the course of the discussion. To review briefly, consider the sentences (1):

(1) (i) it is certain [that John is here]
     (ii) John is certain [X to be here]
     (iii) it seems [that John is here]
     (iv) John seems [X to be here]
     (v) it is believed [that John is here]
     (vi) John is believed [X to be here]

As (i), (iii), (v) indicate, the predicates *certain, seem, believe(d)* take clausal complements. By the projection principle and the θ-criterion, $X = $ NP in the bracketed constructions, which are of the category S, filling the gaps in the paradigm; thus INFL in the embedded clauses may be [$\pm$Tense]. The matrix predicates of (1) are not Case-assigners, so X cannot be phonetically-realized in S-structure. θ-theory requires that X be the trace of the matrix subject *John,* assigning to *John* its θ-role, and that in D-structure (where GF-θ is represented) the position is filled by the NP *John,* mapped to S-structure by Move-α, obligatorily, by virtue of the Case Filter. The trace is governed and meets the subjacency condition, and its antecedent is not in a θ-position, so the conditions of 2.4.1.(2) are satisfied. Still assuming that the binding theory provides an independent explanation applying as well to overt anaphors, PRO and pronouns for the fact that the subject of an infinitive may be an empty category, and that Case and binding theory provide an independent explanation for the fact that a subject of an infinitive must be an empty category in (1), we can maintain the theory of syntax in its simplest form: clauses are finite or infinitival, with no further stipulations to express their general properties, formal or semantic.

In general, then, we expect to find that infinitival and tensed clauses appear in approximately the same positions. In the unmarked case, we expect to find such pairs as "I promise that I will be there," "I promise to be there"; "I persuaded him that he should leave," "I persuaded him to leave"; etc. If a verb (similarly, a noun or adjective) takes a clausal complement as a lexical property, then in the unmarked case it should take either type of clausal complement. By the projection principle, the same expectation holds at every level of syntactic representation (LF and S-

and D-structure). There will, of course, be lexical idiosyncrasies, but in general, the assumption appears to be reasonably well borne out.

To complete this review of properties of empty elements, let us turn to the second and third type of trace noted in 2.4.1.(1): the trace left by movement-to-COMP and by extraposition; for example, (2):

(2)   (i) John knows $[_{\bar{S}}$ what$_i$ we like t$_i]$
        (ii) I bought a book $[_{\bar{S}}[_{COMP}$ PRO$_i]$ $[_S$ PRO to give t$_i$ to Mary$]$
        (iii) $[_{NP}$ a man t$_i]$ was here $[_{\bar{S}_i}$ who John knows$]$

In each case, the trace is governed,[66] its antecedent is not in a θ-position, and the subjacency condition is met; thus the conditions on trace in 2.4.1.(2) are satisfied. We have also noted that the trace left by movement-to-COMP, unlike NP-trace or the trace left by extraposition, is Case-marked (see 2.4.2.(17)).

We have seen that bounding theory holds of trace but not of PRO or other anaphors, and that the subjacency requirement of bounding theory does not follow from other properties of trace but must be independently stipulated. The examples given so far involve NP-trace, specifically, raising. But the same is true for other traces, so it appears.[67] The subjacency condition for movement-to-COMP has considerable explanatory power and permits a unified development of substantial parts of the theory of islands in the sense of Ross (1967); cf. Chomsky (1977b), van Riemsdijk (1978a), Rizzi (1978b), Taraldsen (1978a), Reinhart (1979b), Sportiche (1979), and the references of note 67, among much other work relevant to this topic. It also figures crucially in other discussions, among them, the account of stylistic inversion in French in Kayne and Pollock (1978) and the explanation of some properties of Case-assignment in *wh*-constructions to which we return, along with other questions (cf. Milner (1978)). On subjacency as a property of extraposition, see Ross (1967), Akmajian (1975), Guéron (1978), Baltin (1978, 1979), among others.

The distinction between antecedent-trace relations and other construal relations with regard to subjacency, illustrated above in the case of anaphors, can be seen as well in the case of extraposition.[68] Compare the examples (3):

(3)   (i) pictures of several people are for sale which I like
        (ii) *pictures of several people are for sale who I like

The S-structure representations of the NP subjects are (4i,ii), respectively,[69] with *t* the trace of the extraposed relative clause:

(4)   (i) $[_{NP}[_{NP}$ pictures of several people$]$ t$]$
        (ii) $[_{NP}$ pictures of $[_{NP}[_{NP}$ several people$]$ t$]]$

In case (i), extraposition crosses only one bounding category (namely, NP), observing subjacency, so that (i) is grammatical. But in case (ii), it crosses two NP boundaries so that subjacency is violated and (ii) is ungrammatical. This is the general pattern.

Consider now the following examples:

(5) (i) pictures of [so many people] are for sale – that I decided to go to the show
    (ii) pictures of [more people] are for sale – than I expected
    (iii) *pictures of [more people] are for sale – than I met yesterday
    (iv) *pictures of [several people] are for sale – who I like (= (3ii))

In each case, the extraposed clause is associated with the bracketed NP, which is within another NP so that extraposition by Move-α is blocked by subjacency. This explains the ungrammatical status of (iii), (iv). But cases (i), (ii), which are similar in configurational structure to (iii), (iv) in relevant respects, are nevertheless grammatical. This fact would lead us to suspect that examples (i) and (ii) are not formed by extraposition, but rather that a rule of construal in the LF component associates the extraposed phrase with the bracketed NP;[70] as we have seen throughout, rules of construal, including control, are not subject to subjacency, a property of Move-α.

There is independent evidence justifying this conclusion. Consider the following examples:

(6) (i) [so many people] like [so many pictures] – that the show will go on for a week
    (ii) [more silly lectures] have been given by [more boring professors] – than I would have expected
    (iii) *[more silly lectures] have been given by [more boring professors] – than I met yesterday
    (iv) [several men] met [several women] – who I like

The examples (i)-(iv) correspond, respectively, to (5i-iv). Examples (i) and (ii) are grammatical in both (5) and (6), and (iii) is ungrammatical in both cases. Similarly, (iv) is ungrammatical in (5) and the interpretation in which the extraposed phrase is associated with both bracketed NPs is excluded in (6iv).[71] The point illustrated is that the extraposed clauses of (i) and (ii) may be associated with "split antecedents," namely, both of the bracketed expressions of (6i,ii), and so cannot have been derived by Move-α.[72] In contrast, (6iii,iv), where such an association is impossible, indicate that the extraposed clauses of (iii), (iv) are derived by Move-α, leaving a trace in the NP from which the clause is moved. Correspondingly, (5i,ii), which involve a rule of construal not observing subjacency, are grammatical, but not (5iii,iv), in which application of Move-α would violate subjacency. The examples are rightward movement analogues to the leftward movement cases that we have already discussed, for example, (7), where a rule of construal (in this case, control) violating subjacency associates PRO with its antecedent *they*, but the rule of movement relating trace and *they* in (ii) is blocked; or (8), where a rule of construal relates *they* and *each other* but Move-α relates *who* and its trace:[73]

(7)   (i) they thought that [PRO to feed each other] would be difficult
      (ii) *they seem that [t feed each other] would be difficult
(8)   (i) they heard [NP stories about [NP pictures of each other]]
      (ii) *who did they hear [NP stories about [NP pictures of t]]

The paradigm (5) is quite general, as illustrated by such sets of examples as the following:

(9)   (i) pictures that $\begin{Bmatrix} \text{were admired by [so many excellent critics]} \\ \text{[so many excellent critics] admired} \end{Bmatrix}$ were for sale – that I decided to attend the show

      (ii) pictures that $\begin{Bmatrix} \text{were admired by [more critics]} \\ \text{[more critics] admired} \end{Bmatrix}$ were for sale – than I expected

      (iii) *pictures that $\begin{Bmatrix} \text{were admired by [more critics]} \\ \text{[more critics] admired} \end{Bmatrix}$ were for sale – than I met

      (iv) *pictures that were admired by [several critics] were for sale – who I met

(10) (i) the construction of [so many bridges] is necessary – that we'll have to raise taxes
      (ii) the construction of [more bridges] is necessary – than we expected (meaning: "more bridge construction is necessary than we expected")
      (iii) *the construction of [more bridges] is necessary – than we saw
      (iv) *the construction of [a bridge] is necessary – that will span the river
(11) (i) the design of [so many houses] is pleasing to the eye –that I've decided to become an architect
      (ii) the design of [more houses] is pleasing to the eye – than I expected
      (iii) *the design of [more houses] is pleasing to the eye –than Tom builds
      (iv) *the design of [houses] is pleasing to the eye – that Tom builds

(12) (i) composers of [so many songs] won prizes – that the award ceremony went on for hours
  (ii) composers of [more songs] won prizes – than I expected
  (iii) *composers of [more songs] won prizes – than John wrote
  (iv) *composers of [songs] won prizes – that John liked

(13) (i) a speech about the construction of [so many bridges] was announced – that I decided to skip the meeting
  (ii) a speech about the construction of [more bridges] was announced – than I expected
  (iii) *a speech about the construction of [more bridges] was announced – than Tom designed
  (iv) *a speech about the construction of [bridges] was announced – that are to span the river

These examples illustrate two kinds of comparative construction: those involving construal with possibly split antecedents, such as (ii), and those involving movement, such as (iii). There is another type of comparative with *than*-NP rather than a clause, e.g., (14):

(14) John likes more people than Bill

It appears that these fall into the category of examples (ii), with construal, rather than examples (iii), with movement; compare (15):

(15) (i) no airline saves you more money in more ways than Delta[74]
  (ii) no one saw pictures that were admired by [more excellent critics] at the exhibit – than John
  (iii) *no one saw pictures that were admired by [excellent critics] at the exhibit – who he respected

Example (i) illustrates the possibility of split antecedents, and (ii), correspondingly, the case of construal violating subjacency, which holds, however, in the Move-α case (iii).

Leftward construal violating subjacency is standard in other constructions as well, e.g., (16):[75]

(16) (i) I told him that [she] should have come last week, that woman you met
  (ii) je leur ai dit qu'[elle] aurait dû venir la semaine dernière, Marie

Quite generally, then, the pattern seems to be that rules of construal (including control) may violate subjacency whereas the rule Move-α observes it regularly: NP-movement, movement-to-COMP, extraposition and others not considered here. That is, the antecedent-trace relation observes the condition 2.4.1. (2iii), while other rules associating elements do not.

The considerations reviewed in this section give a strong reason to suppose that there is a unitary process underlying extraposition, the association of an operator such as a *wh*-phrase with the variable it binds, the association of GF-$\bar{\theta}$ with GF-θ (as in raising and passive), the interpretation of idiom chunks (as in raising and passive), and a number of other processes, e.g., PP-cliticization in the Romance languages. These constructions all observe the conditions of 2.4.1.(2). Furthermore, GF-θ gaps (similarly, the positions in which remote idiom chunks or pleonastic elements are interpreted) share a crucial property with overt anaphors, as has been noted: they appear only in positions that are transparent in the sense of binding theory. Consider (17):

(17)   (i) they seem [t to be competent]
        (ii) they are believed [t to be competent]
        (iii) *they seem [t are competent]
        (iv) *they are believed [t are competent]
        (v) *they seem [Bill likes t] (cf. "it seems Bill likes them")
        (vi) *they are believed [Bill likes t] (cf. "it is believed [Bill them]")

The position of the GF-θ gap – that is, the position in which the θ-role of the displaced antecedent is determined – is structurally parallel to that of an overt anaphor, abstracting from the effects of the Case Filter and the requirements of the theory of government, as illustrated in (18):

(18)   (i) (a) John was killed t
            (b) they killed each other
        (ii) (a) they were believed [t to have been killed]
             (b) they believed [each other to be competent]
             (c) they wanted [each other to win]
             (d) they'd prefer [for each other to win]
             (e) they tried [PRO to win]

The parallel illustrated in (i) also extends to antecedent-PRO relations, if we assume that clitics "absorb" Case and government in such structures as (19), a matter to which we return in chapter 4:

(19)   je l'ai vu PRO
        ("I saw him")

As we have seen, the rule that associates GF-θ and GF-$\bar{\theta}$ –i.e., that assigns a θ-role to a "displaced argument" in a non-θ-position as in (17), (18)–also serves to assign the proper idiomatic interpretation to displaced elements that bear no genuine θ-role, as in (20), and to relate a non-argument to its base position, as in (21):

(20)   (i) advantage was taken t of John
       (ii) too much has been made t of his failure
       (iii) excellent care seems [t to have been taken t of the orphans]

(21)   (i) there seems [t to be considerable support for this conclu-
            sion]
       (ii) it is believed [t to have been snowing all day]

Furthermore, such displaced non-arguments may be assigned certain properties in terms of their D-structure position, as in the case of inserted
there in English or the empty subject pronominal of Italian, which agree
with the matrix verb in a raising construction while receiving their features
on the basis of their position as embedded subject. Cf. §§ 2.4.5, 4.5.

There are, then, compelling reasons to assume that the rule that assigns
a θ-role to a displaced argument that is not in a θ-position is a case of
Move-α in the languages we have been considering; for a generalization to
other language types, see § 2.8. We have also seen that there are strong
reasons to assume that PRO – which is crucially distinct from trace – is an
empty pronominal filling a gap in D- and S-structure. In brief, the projection principle is well-motivated; it expresses exactly the properties that
are not determined by the several subsystems of principles 1.(2). The range
of phenomena – by no means exhausted in the preceding discussion – is
fairly complex, but it follows, assuming the projection principle, from quite
simple and for the most part independently-motivated principles of the
interacting theories of bounding, government, binding, Case and control,
a fact of some significance, I believe.

2.4.5. *The evolution of the notion "trace" in transformational generative grammar*

Trace theory has often been understood as a fairly sharp departure from
earlier transformational grammar.[76] This is not really correct, however.
A variant of trace theory is implicit in the earliest work and explicit in the
earliest formalizations (specifically, Chomsky (1955)), and the more recent
versions arise in a rather natural way from the continuing effort from the
early 1960s to reduce the descriptive power and variety of grammatical
rules, that is, to converge on an explanatory theory of UG. We can see how
the concept emerges (conceptually, if not historically) by considering such
examples as (1):

(1)   (i) three men from England arrived last night
       (ii) there arrived last night three men from England

The common D-structure of these sentences, representing GF-θ, is approximately (2):

(2)   [$_{NP}$ three men from England] [$_{VP}$ arrived last night]

That is, *three men from England* bears the GF [NP,S] in (1) and gains its
θ-role thereby. The S-structure of (1ii) is something like (3):

(3)   [$_{NP}$ there][$_{VP}$[$_{VP}$ arrived last night][$_{NP}$ three men from Eng-
       land]]

Thus, the rules forming (3) from (2) first adjoin the subject to the predicate
and then insert *there* in the position of the moved subject.

In the earliest versions of transformational generative grammar, it was
assumed that each grammatical transformation consists of a structural description (SD) and a structural change (SC), where the SD specifies the
domain of the transformation and its analysis into phrases subject to the
SC, and the SC is an operation compounded of elementary abstract operations of substitution, adjunction, deletion, etc. Movement consists of
substitution or adjunction followed by deletion of the moved element;
i.e., copying of one or another sort followed by deletion. In the case of
(3), the rule forming this structure from (2) – call it T – would consist, in
these terms, of an SD of the form (NP, VP) and an SC compounded from
three elementary operations: adjunction, deletion, and substitution of
there in the base position of the adjoined NP, i.e., in the position of the
"gap" vacated by the moved subject. The inserted element *there* is an NP
by virtue of the fact that it is inserted into the NP position of the moved
subject. This abstract position into which *there* is inserted is, in effect, the
trace of the moved NP. The basic assumption, then, was that a movement
rule leaves a trace which can be filled by another element, all of this internal
to the operation of the single transformation T.

One major step towards reducing the class of possible transformations
is to eliminate the possibility of compounding elementary operations. As
one step in this direction, we may replace the compound movement-dele-
tion by a single movement operation, which leaves the empty category
[$_{NP}$ e] as its trace (but see §2.4.6). The operation T, then, consists of an
adjunction rule moving the NP subject and leaving trace, and a rule of
there-insertion placing *there* in the vacated trace position, which retains
its NP category throughout. A second step is to eliminate conditions on
ordering, so that we must now consider the two rules to be separate and
independent. The first of these rules is simply an instance of Move-α,
and the second is a rule of *there*-insertion.

Pursuing the goal of reducing the variety of rules still further, we assume
that Move-α applies freely and that *there*-insertion permits *there* to be
inserted in any position freely, and that these two rules are entirely independent of one another, stipulation of dependencies among rules being
excluded in principle. A major problem now is to discover general principles that exclude unwanted applications of these rules, not an insignificant challenge. Suppose that this challenge can be met. Then the earlier
assumption that movement leaves a trace when it is a component of a more
complex transformation becomes the principle that the rule Move-α always

leaves a trace, namely, an empty category of the type α; i.e., trace theory, in its current sense. The latter theory, then derives in a natural way from the process of reducing the potential descriptive power of grammar, and correspondingly enhancing the explanatory power of linguistic theory, though it is also motivated independently by considerations of the sort discussed earlier: the projection principle and the phenomena reviewed in § 2.4. We then face three basic tasks: meeting the challenge just indicated, determining how the properties of S-structure including trace relate to determination of PF and LF, and determining the properties of trace and their relations to those of other elements such as PRO (which, in turn, evolves from the study of EQUI-NP deletion in earlier work). These are the questions that we have been considering.

Let us examine the possibility of taking *there*-insertion to be a perfectly free and independent rule. We can appeal to the principle of recoverability of deletion to ensure that *there* will only be inserted in the position of an empty category. Why is it obligatory after adjunction of NP to VP in (3)? The reason is that trace, as an anaphor, must be properly bound; furthermore, the empty category trace must be governed (cf. 2.4.1.(2i)), and as we shall see in chapter 4, the AGR element of INFL is not a proper governor for trace. The rule of *there*-insertion, like the rule of *it*-insertion that applies in the D-structure (4), overcomes these problems, permitting a well-formed S-structure to surface:

(4)   (i) $\left[\text{}_{NP} \text{ e}\right]$ is raining
        (ii) $\left[\text{}_{NP} \text{ e}\right]$ is held that these truths are self-evident

It remains to consider the properties of *there*, and to explain why *there* is inserted in (3) and *it* is inserted in (4), not conversely.[77] Suppose that the item *there* has the lexical entry (5):

(5) $\left[\textit{there}, \left[\alpha \text{ number}\right]\right]$

That is, *there* is an element that must receive number. In fact, *there* takes on the number of the NP coindexed with the trace for which it substitutes, as we see in (6):

(6)   (i) there is arriving a man from England
        (ii) there are arriving three men from England
        (iii) there seems to be a man arriving from England
        (iv) there seem to be three men arriving from England

As (iii) and (iv) indicate, the number assigned to *there*, via the NP coindexed with the trace it replaces, is carried over under raising. It follows that *there* must replace an NP, in fact, an empty NP, retaining its index.

Consider the possibility of inserting *there* in a base-generated empty position, as in (7):

(7)   (i) John saw [$_{NP}$ e]
       (ii) [$_{NP}$ e] saw Bill
       (iii) [$_{NP}$ e] is raining

In case (i), *there*-insertion is blocked by the requirement that number be determined and also by the θ-criterion, since *there* is not an expression that can receive a θ-role. In case (ii), the subject position is also a θ-position – hence immune to *there*-insertion – if we assume, as in § 2.2, that θ-marking is obligatory in obligatory positions, a well-motivated assumption as we have seen. Under this assumption, it is not relevant here that the phrase *see Bill* does not necessarily assign a θ-role, as in (8), where *see* requires no subject:

(8)   [the sight of Bill] astonished me

In (7iii), however, the empty category is not in a θ-position, so that θ-theory does not block *there*-insertion. We conclude, then, that the requirement that *there* must receive number from a coindexed NP determines the possibilities for *there*-insertion. If this line of reasoning is correct, then *there*-insertion can be maintained as a free and independent rule, asserting simply (9):

(9)   insert *there* anywhere

The rules Move-α and (9) account for the examples (1)–(3), (6), given the lexical entry (5) for *there*.

In other languages, inserted elements may have properties other than number. Consider for example Italian, where we have such structures as (10):[78]

(10)   sembro essere io
        ("it seems to be me")

In (10), the verb *sembro* is first person singular, agreeing with *io*. A natural assumption, following Luigi Rizzi's suggestion, is that an empty pronominal element of some sort is inserted in the subject position of the embedded clause, agreeing in number and person with the embedded predicate *io* with which it is coindexed, and is then raised to the subject position of the matrix verb which agrees with it in person, number and gender. Note that if this analysis is correct, then Italian, like English, incorporates the condition 2.1.(25) requiring that clauses have subjects, even though no subject need appear in surface structure.

Analysis of such constructions as (1) in terms of (9) and a rule that associates the post-verbal NP and the matrix subject position (Move-α in the case of (1), I have assumed) is optimal. It remains to be seen whether it can be sustained without qualification or not, and whether or not the challenge cited above can be met in full generality. In any case, we see that trace theory is not a radical innovation in the theory that we have been considering here, but is a very natural development as we pursue the questions that arise within transformational generative grammar, attempting to discover and formulate the essential properties of UG.

2.4.6. Some variants and alternatives

I remarked at the outset that I will make no serious effort here to consider alternatives to the assumptions that are being developed that definitely seem worth exploring, or anything remotely approaching this. Perhaps it is worthwhile to stress the point again.

One question that should be considered, however, relates directly to the discussion of movement rules in the last section. Recall that in earlier work, the rule of movement was assumed to be decomposed into two elementary transformations: copying and deletion. Suppose that we were to continue to adopt this idea, rather than taking movement to be a copying rule leaving an empty category as trace. The natural way to work this out in the present framework would be to establish the convention for Move-α that when α is moved it is not deleted but left unchanged, apart from a feature D indicating that it is to be deleted in the PF-component (in fact, D is redundant, determinable from other properties of the grammar). Movement, then, consists of copying of α in a new position, and both occurrences of α enter the LF-component. Consider now such sentences as (1):

(1)   whose brother did he see?

The S-structure will be either (2) or (3), depending on which of the two conventions we adopt for trace theory:

(2) $[_i$ whose brother$]$ he saw $[_{NP_i} e]$
(3) $[_i$ whose brother$]$ he saw $[_{NP_i, D}$ whose brother$]$

It is a reasonable (though not necessary) assumption that the LF-representation for (1) is (4):

(4)   for which x, x a person, he saw x's brother

This representation is derivable directly from (3) but requires a reconstruction rule of the sort discussed in Chomsky (1977b) if the S-structure is (2). The reason for assuming an LF-representation such as (4) rather than one derived directly from (2) is, first of all, the sense, and secondly the possibility of explaining a number of crossover phenomena – e.g., the fact that x in (4) is not coindexable with *he* – in terms of the same properties that exclude such coindexing in *he saw John's brother.* In contrast, consider (5), where the same properties block coindexing of *he* and *John,* though this is permitted in the *wh*-form (6), which presumably has the LF-representation (7) involving no reconstruction rule:

(5)   he read the book that John likes
(6)   which book that John likes did he read
(7)   for which x, x a book that John likes, he read x

There are many problems that arise in this connection, which would take us too far afield.[79] I will therefore drop this issue here, merely noting that the approach to trace that I will continue to adopt – that trace is $[_\alpha e]$ – raises questions for complex *wh*-phrases, and that there is an obvious alternative that might be explored, based on dissociation of movement into copying and deletion. In chapter 6, we will adopt a variant of the idea that movement involves copying.

Some of the assumptions I have been discussing are quite central to the GB-framework; others are considerably more marginal. An example of the latter is the subdivision of the syntax into base rules and Move-α. An obvious alternative to the theory outlined so far would be to suppose that base rules generate S-structures directly with new interpretive rules of the LF-component associating phrases and their traces (now base-generated), in place of the system described so far, in which the base generates D-structures mapped to S-structures by application of the rule Move-α. Let us now consider this question, which has already been discussed briefly in connection with 2.2.(17).

Consider first a theory that I will call "Theory I." In this theory we assume that sentences have the S-structures postulated in the preceding discussion, including trace and PRO. Consider now two variants of Theory I. One variant, call it Ia, assumes as above that Move-α forms these S-structures from base-generated D-structures. A second, call it Ib, assumes that the base generates S-structures directly. Theories Ia and Ib share certain interpretive rules, specifically, the rules of construal relating antecedents to overt anaphors and to certain extraposed phrases (cf. § 2.4.4), and the rules of control determining the referential possibilities for PRO. These shared rules do not observe conditions analogous to 2.4.1.(2), as we have seen. Theories Ia and Ib differ, however, in their treatment of antecedent-trace relations, that is, relations that meet the conditions 2.4.1.(2). In Theory Ia, these relations are established in the syntax by the rule Move-α; in Theory Ib, by new interpretive rules of the LF-component satisfying the conditions 2.4.1.(2), and whatever other conditions may distinguish trace from PRO.

It is not easy to find empirical evidence to distinguish between Theories Ia and Ib. It may be that they are to be understood as two realizations of the same more abstract theory, which captures the essential properties of UG at the level of abstraction appropriate for linguistic theory. See the quoted remarks at the opening of chapter 1, which were motivated by just this question. Perhaps there are empirical differences between the two theories, but they will surely be rather subtle. For example, the theories differ somewhat in the way in which they handle idioms[80] and in their treatment of such examples as 2.4.1.(15)-(18). The theories may also differ in a more subtle respect. Theory Ia posits the existence of D-structure as a representation of GF-θ, a level of representation distinct from S-structure or LF. The assumption has consequences, as we saw in discussing the principles 2.2.(17), which were established on the basis of a property of D-structure. Insofar as these consequences are conceptually or empirically desirable, we have indirect support for Theory Ia. We will come across other examples of this sort as we proceed. But the arguments are restricted and highly theory-internal, as one should expect when we consider alternatives so close in conceptual structure as Theories Ia and Ib. For the purposes of our inquiry here, it is rarely necessary to distinguish the two theories. I will continue to adopt Theory Ia, with the rule Move-α, since it seems to me that the evidence, though hardly overwhelming, supports this decision; thus I assume that the rule Move-α appears uniformly in all three components of grammar, though possibly with somewhat different properties in the three components. Very little turns on this decision in our discussion here, but it does have certain consequences that should be carefully considered.

The virtual interchangeability of Theories Ia and Ib is clear within the framework of trace theory. While it should not be assumed too quickly that the two theories are empirically indistinguishable variants – my suspicion is that they are not – nevertheless the problem of choosing between them (if it exists) is a fairly marginal one, as was recognized in the earliest work on trace theory about 10 years ago (cf. Chomsky (1977a, chapter 3, § 17; chapter 4)).

Similar observations hold of the general question as to whether syntactic theory should involve derivations from D- to S-structure or rather a single level of representation in which all syntactic properties are expressed. So formulated, the question is scarcely meaningful. Thus, the Extended Standard Theory in the form 2.1.(1) can be understood in either way, given the association between a function chain in S-structure and the derivations of which it can be regarded as a projection. The primary question, again is whether the properties of the rule Move-α conceived abstractly as 2.1.(11) are indeed distinct from those of other rules, as we have argued, and whether the scope of this rule has been properly fixed; and a secondary, though not uninteresting question is whether certain arguments turn on the existence of D-structure, a representation of GF-θ, as a separate level.

Suppose it were argued that Theory Ib is preferable to Theory Ia because it reduces the class of transformational devices not merely to the single rule Move-α, but still further, namely, to none at all. This is an example of the fallacy discussed in chapter 1. While Theory Ib eliminates the rule Move-α from the syntax (leaving it, however, as an option in the PF- and LF-components and presumably in the marked periphery outside of core grammar), it does so by adding a new category of LF-rules, with exactly the properties of the rule Move-α. Thus no argument based on conceptual economy applies, at least if the rule Move-α has different properties from the interpretive rules shared by the two theories, as the preceding discussion indicates.

Consider now a different theory, call it "Theory II," which generates different S-structures from those of the two variants of Theory I. Theory II generates S-structures lacking empty categories – trace or PRO. One might imagine other variants of Theory II in which some of the structures with gaps to be interpreted have trace and others do not (perhaps movement-to-COMP might be distinguished from NP-movement in this way, for example). Theory II is rather different in its properties from Theory I. For example, Theory II does not observe the projection principle; furthermore, it assigns θ-roles to arguments that are not in θ-positions by devices quite different from those that are employed to relate operators such as *wh*-phrases to the variables they bind, to associate extraposed phrases with their antecedents, to interpret idioms, to deal with the properties of non-arguments that "inherit" features from their D-structure positions as in the case of English *there* and Italian empty pronominals discussed in § 2.4.5, and to deal with phenomena such as 2.4.1.(15–18), etc., all of these cases involving the rule Move-α in Theory I. Furthermore, it does not relate the properties of interpreted gaps to those of overt anaphors and pronouns with disjoint reference, as does Theory I. In these and other respects, Theories I and II differ substantively.

Much of the preceding discussion can be regarded as an argument that Theory I is preferable to Theory II on conceptual and empirical grounds. But the point to be noted here is that the theories do differ sufficiently so that one might hope to find grounds for choosing between them, whereas in the case of the two variants of Theory I, such choice may be extremely difficult or impossible. Perhaps when variants of Theories I and II are further refined, it will be discovered that they too fall together at some appropriate level of abstraction, or are somehow intertranslateable. But if so, the demonstration will be considerably more complex than a demonstration that variants Ia and Ib are interchangeable (if indeed they are). Theories I and II appear, at least, to be rather different in their conceptual and empirical properties; not so much in their coverage of data – presumably either can be developed in such a way as to deal in some manner with phenomena that are at all well-understood – but in their frameworks of unifying principles and assumptions about the nature of UG.

These remarks relate only to the internal structure of the syntax (namely, 2.1.(1)), not to the organization of modules of 1.(1) and 1.(2), which is, I think, quite well-motivated and is central to the discussion here.

2.5. The Base

Let us now turn to a closer examination of the categorial component and of the lexicon, to which we have assigned a central role in the syntax by virtue of the projection principle. We take the lexicon to be a set of lexical entries, each specified as to category and complement structure, with further idiosyncrasies.[81] The categorial and complement structure determine the possibilities for lexical substitution, which I will assume to be at the base level, largely as a matter of execution.[82]

Let's assume that each lexical element α assigns a θ-role to every NP or clause in its complement (if there are any), including NP in PP linked to α, in which case the θ-role will be determined compositionally by α and the P head of PP.[83] Thus the verb assigns a θ-role to each element of the complement in such structures as (1):

(1)   (i) promise – NP – $\bar{\text{S}}$ (*promise John* $\begin{Bmatrix} that\ S \\ to\ VP \end{Bmatrix}$)

       (ii) promise – NP – NP   (*promise John victory*)
       (iii) promise – NP – PP   (*promise victory to John*)
       (iv) prefer (want, believe) – $\begin{Bmatrix} NP \\ \bar{\text{S}} \end{Bmatrix}$ (*prefer* $\begin{Bmatrix} it \\ for\ you\ to\ leave \end{Bmatrix}$)

In case (iv), the verbs differ in that *prefer* takes a *for*-complementizer while *believe* does not, while *want* takes a *for*-complementizer which deletes in immediate post-verbal position; and in that $\bar{\text{S}}$-deletion takes place after *believe*; cf. § 2.4.2.

Similarly, the adjective assigns a θ-role to its complement in (2):[84]

(2)
       (i) eager – $\bar{\text{S}}$ (*eager* $\begin{Bmatrix} that\ you\ win \\ for\ you\ to\ win \\ to\ win\ (=\ PRO\ to\ win) \end{Bmatrix}$)

       (ii) proud – $\begin{Bmatrix} NP \\ \bar{\text{S}} \end{Bmatrix}$ (*proud* $\begin{Bmatrix} (of)\ John \\ that\ he\ won \end{Bmatrix}$)

The same is true of N and P complements. Quite generally, as these examples illustrate, NP and clause alternate in lexical representations.[85]

These properties of lexical items are relevant at least to the level of LF; they specify the positions in LF in which a lexical head may appear, and the θ-role assigned to its complements. Surveying the full class of lexical entries, we find certain general properties. For example, there are verbs like *promise* with complements of the form – NP $\bar{\text{S}}$, – NP PP, – NP NP, but none with complement structure of the form – $\bar{\text{S}}$ NP, – AP NP, – PP NP. A standard approach is to assume that these properties are stated in the rules of the categorial component, which in this respect serves as a statement of redundancy rules of the lexicon. As we have seen in § 2.1, this is a highly misleading move. Assuming the projection principle, none of this structure (namely, choice of possible complements) need be specified in the base rules, though the problem of determining order remains. We might hope to do still better and to explain this property of the lexicon too on some general grounds rather than stipulating it in any part of the grammar. For the examples cited, an explanation may again lie in Case theory. Suppose that Case-assignment for English observes a condition of adjacency; that is, Case is assigned by V or P to an adjacent NP, and if an adjacent NP has been assigned Case, to the next NP. But Case-assignment never "skips a category" in a string. Then the properties of lexical entries just described follow, as well as the fact that adverbs and particles cannot be interpolated between verb and object in English. We might assume this to be one of the unmarked options for Case theory.[86]

Put as an addition

We assume that Case-marking takes place at S-structure (or in some cases, perhaps, at D-structure; cf. OB and §§ 3.2.2, 5.2). Therefore the notion of "adjacency" that is relevant is that of S-structure, not surface structure. An illustration is provided by Pulleyblank (1980) in Yoruba. At S-structure, the verb assigns objective Case to an adjacent NP following it. Some kind of "topicalization" or "clefting" is normal, with the fronted topicalized element presumably leaving a trace in its base position. Suppose we have a surface form $NP_1 \ldots V\text{-}NP_2$, where NP_1 is interpreted as the topicalized object of V. Then NP_2 is not assigned objective Case, though it is adjacent to V in surface structure; rather, it is assigned an empty element *ni* as Case-marker, where *ni* is analogous to *of* in English *proud of John*, etc. For the purposes of Case-marking in S-structure, NP_2 is not adjacent to V, but rather is separated from V by the trace of NP_1.

Note that we have extended the adjacency condition for the case of double-object verbs such as *give*, if they have the complement structure – $NP_1 \ NP_2$ (*give John a book*), where NP_1 is the primary object with the GF $[NP^1, VP]$ and NP_2 the secondary object with the GF $[NP^2, VP]$.[87] Thus we assume that certain verbs have the property of assigning a secondary Case to their secondary object, given the form of the adjacency condition stated above; the secondary object is "as close as it can be" to the verb, given that it is a secondary object. Thus such structures as "John gave Bill yesterday a book" are ruled out at S-structure (perhaps they can be formed by stylistic rules of the PF-component), along with "John gave yesterday Bill a book," etc., by the adjacency condition.

Assuming this condition as an unmarked option for Case-assignment, it is unnecessary to assign order to the complements in a lexical entry or in the rules of the categorial component of the base. Unwanted orders will violate Case theory, or the form of it that applies in English. Thus *promise*

√ verb

can be listed in the lexicon as having an NP complement along with either an NP, $\bar{S}$ or PP complement, with no order assigned to these. And the basic X-bar rule 2.3.(1) expanding $\bar{X}$ in the categorial component need not specify the order or choice of categories in . . .

Hale (1978) has suggested that languages fall into two types with regard to base structure. Some, like English, have an X-bar grammar with relatively fixed (unmarked) order, while others, like Walbiri, have an unordered base. Perhaps we might account for the difference, in part at least, in terms of parameters of Case theory. Thus, if the adjacency requirement is dropped for Case-assignment, order will be free, at least for complements;

and further extension to other instances of Case-assignment might account for other variations in order. Note that from this point of view, we would not expect *languages* to be of the English-type or the Walbiri-type, but rather aspects of languages. Thus English would share the order-free property for PP complements but not for NP complements. Cf. § 2.8 for further comment.

Returning to the general properties of the full set of lexical entries, some may be explicable on general grounds, as in the example just discussed, but others will be idiosyncratic to the language in question; for example, whether complements follow or precede lexical categories. Insofar as the choices are language-specific, they must be specified in the grammar. Assuming them to be specified at the level of the categorial component, rules such as 2.3.(1) expanding $\bar{X}$ will appear in the particular grammar of English only as a specification that complement follows head; apart from this, the rule belongs to UG rather than the grammar of English. Universals of the sort explored by Joseph Greenberg and others have obvious relevance to determining just which properties of the lexicon have to be specified in this manner in particular grammars – or to put it in other terms, just how much must be learned as grammar develops in the course of language acquisition.

Continuing with these assumptions, we have to explain such facts as the impossibility of a complement structure – α PRO. An explanation in terms of Case will not suffice, since PRO need not be assigned Case, as we have seen. In fact, the impossibility of this complement structure will follow in the GB-framework from the fact that PRO is necessarily ungoverned,[88] as Aoun has observed. There are, needless to say, numerous other questions of the sort that remain open.

Let us assume these further questions to be settled either by resort to general principles such as those of Case theory (the optimal situation) or by specification of parameters of the categorial component with regard to ordering and internal structure of major categories (e.g., the much-debated matter of the internal structure of complex NPs in English). The categorial component of the core grammar for a particular language, then, will be just a specification of these parameters. Given this specification, the class of well-formed base structures for the language is determined by properties of lexical entries under the projection principle, and by general principles such as those of Case theory, perhaps also parametrized. Many potential grammars are excluded by these assumptions, which seem to me to observe as well as possible the general guiding principle of restrictiveness for linguistic theory discussed briefly in chapter 1, and familiar from other work.

Let us now compare these assumptions with some others that come to mind, and that have been discussed in one or another form in recent literature (which, as noted in the preface, I will make no attempt to survey). Consider again the fact that there are no verbs that appear in the structure (3) where NP′ is phonetically-realized, i.e., ≠ PRO:

(3)   NP V NP $[_S$ NP′ to VP$]$

We have suggested an explanation for this fact in terms of Case theory: NP′ cannot be assigned Case within S, and cannot be assigned Case by the verb of the matrix sentence.[89]

Suppose that one were to depart from these assumptions, postulating the rule (4) for the analysis of $\bar{S}$:

(4) $\bar{S} \rightarrow$ $\begin{cases} \text{(that) NP}\,[+\text{Tense}]\,\text{VP} \,(I\ believe\,(that)\,John\ won) \\ \text{(PP)}\,[-\text{Tense}]\,\text{VP, PP} = for\,\text{NP} \,(I'd\ prefer\,(for\ John)\ to\ win) \end{cases}$

Rule (4) would be supplemented by a principle P determining that the infinitival VP is assigned a subject either from the matrix clause in which it is embedded or from the PP *for*-NP, or is arbitrary in reference. The examples of (5) would be base-generated with (essentially) the structures indicated:

(5)   (i) John $[_{VP}$ believed Bill $[_{\bar{S}}$ to $[_{VP}$ be sad$]]]$
          (ii) John $[_{VP}$ persuaded Bill $[_{\bar{S}}$ to $[_{VP}$ leave$]]]$
          (iii) John $[_{VP}$ preferred $[_{\bar{S}}[_{PP}$ for Bill$]$ to $[_{VP}$ leave$]]]$
          (iv) John $[_{VP}$ preferred $[_{\bar{S}}$ to $[_{VP}$ leave$]]]$

The role of subject of the embedded VP is assigned by P to the direct object of the matrix sentence (*Bill*) in (i), (ii); to the object of the embedded PP (*Bill*) in (iii); and to the subject of the matrix sentence (*John*) in (iv). The projection principle is violated. Similarly, the θ-criterion is violated at LF-representation in (ii) and (iv) (since *Bill* and *John*, respectively, have dual θ-roles) and at S-structure in (i) (since *Bill* is not in a θ-position).

Returning to (3), it would be excluded in this system by the stipulation in the categorial component that there are no base-generated structures of the form (6):

(6)   NP V NP NP $\bar{S}$

There are no lexical entries of this form, but one cannot appeal to the projection principle to bar (6) since the principle is not operative in this system. Under this approach, it would be natural to express the stipulation within a theory of grammatical relations, call it GR, where syntactic grammatical functions are now taken as distinct from the thematically relevant grammatical functions of the LF-structures; thus *Bill* is the syntactic direct object of the matrix verb in both (5i,ii), but at the LF-level it is unrelated to *believe* in (5i) while it is the direct object of *persuade* in (5ii). The stipulation excluding (6), then, could be expressed in GR by the requirement that each base-generated NP must be a term of a syntactic grammatical relation, whereas GR provides no grammatical relation for the third NP in (6).

Structures of the form (6) do exist in the syntax, however; e.g., purposive infinitival constructions such as (7):

(7)   [John] gave [Bill] [Moby Dick] – (for Tom) to read

But the theory GR would require that in a structure such as (6)–(7), the grammatical roles of the three bracketed NPs must be: subject, primary object, secondary object, and the theory might preclude the possibility of mapping this formal network into an LF of the form (3) in some manner.

This alternative approach suffers from a number of defects, as compared with the one we have suggested, in particular, the following:

(8)   (i)   it is considerably more complex, requiring a more complex system of base rules, a new interpretive principle P, and a theory GR of grammatical relations that precludes the mapping of (6) to (3) while permitting a syntactic direct object to be dissociated from its governing verb in mapping (5i) (but not (5ii)) to LF

        (ii)   the approach fails to relate properties of subjectless infinitives to independent principles of government, binding and Case theory that determine the behavior of overt anaphors and pronouns, thus replacing an explanation of these properties by a series of stipulations

        (iii) the approach fails to explain the obligatory insertion of pleonastic elements in clausal structures that assign no θ-role to the subject as discussed in § 2.1.

        (iv)   the approach requires reference to independent properties of base structure not derivable from properties of lexical items at LF; in this case, some otherwise unmotivated notion of syntactic grammatical function

Point (i) is straightforward; (ii) and (iii) we have already discussed. Point (iv) relates to the issue now under consideration: the desirability of eliminating reference in the grammar to independent properties of base structures as distinct from those accounted for in terms of properties of lexical items at LF and independent general principles. All these defects are overcome under the approach adopted above, assuming the θ-criterion and the projection principle, the rule analyzing S as NP-INFL-VP, and the base option of selecting PRO or a phonetically-realized NP freely for any occurrence of NP. In this case, then, the restrictive assumptions we have been considering, which reduce the categorial component to a minimum, seem well-justified.

We noted in chapter 1 that a desideratum for linguistic theory is that grammatical relations be reducible to acceptable primitive notions. The considerations just reviewed bear on this point insofar as they argue against developing a theory GR of syntactic grammatical relations independent of the properties of well-formed base structures that are determined (under the projection principle) by the properties of lexical entries at LF and independent principles.

A variant of the GR-theory that seems to me somewhat more plausible – call it GR' – retains the rule analyzing S as NP-INFL-VP (or some similar rule requiring that S has subject) and the option of taking NP as PRO or phonetically-realized, while still taking *Bill* in (5i) to be the direct object of the matrix verb. The sentences of (5) would then appear in the form (9):[90]

(9)   (i)   John $\left[_{VP}\right.$ believed Bill $\left[_{\bar{S}}\right[_S$ PRO to be sad $\left.\right]\left.\right]\left.\right]$
       (ii) John $\left[_{VP}\right.$ persuaded Bill $\left[_{\bar{S}}\right[_S$ PRO to leave $\left.\right]\left.\right]\left.\right]$
       (iii) John $\left[_{VP}\right.$ preferred $\left[_{\bar{S}}\right.$ for $\left[_S$ Bill to leave $\left.\right]\left.\right]\left.\right]$
       (iv) John $\left[_{VP}\right.$ preferred $\left[_{\bar{S}}\right[_S$ PRO to leave $\left.\right]\left.\right]\left.\right]$

This approach is closer to the one we have been considering. In fact, the analyses are identical in the case of (ii)–(iv), differing only in case (i). Recall that we have been assuming the analysis of (i) at S-structure to be (10):

(10)   John $\left[_{VP}\right.$ believed $\left[_S$ Bill to be sad $\left.\right]\left.\right]$

The S-structure (10) conforms to the projection principle; that of GR' does not. The approaches differ in the way in which they interpret the properties of (9i) and (10). Both approaches correctly regard this phenomenon as exceptional. Our approach interprets the marked property of verbs such as *believe* in English to be Exceptional Case-marking, analogous to the marked construction (9iii) and to raising constructions, which require S̄-deletion for trace-government. GR' interprets the marked property of *believe* to be a departure from the projection principle, with *Bill* assigned a GF that is not a GF-θ.[91]

Our approach and GR', while rather close, still differ somewhat in empirical consequences. Consider, for example, such structures as (11) with the S-structure (12):

(11)   John pleaded with Bill to leave
(12)   John $\left[_{VP}\right.$ pleaded $\left[_{PP}\right.$ with Bill $\left]\right[_{\bar{S}}\right[_S$ PRO to leave $\left.\right]\left.\right]\left.\right]$

Evidently, this is a control structure; *Bill* is in a position that permits control of PRO. Assuming that the projection principle permits marked violations in accordance with GR', as in (9i), there might be a verb *PLEAD* such that *PLEAD with* (like *plead with*) means (roughly) "exhort," so that (13) would mean that John exhorted that Bill leave, the matrix verb lacking a thematic object as in (9i):

(13)   John PLEADed with Bill to leave

If we take the contrary position, assuming that the projection principle is inviolable and that the marked property of *believe* is accounted for by Exceptional Case-marking, then no such verb as PLEAD can exist, since the S-structure (and D-structure) of (13) would have to be (14):

(14)　　John $[$ vp PLEADed $[$ pp with $[$ s̄$[$ s Bill to leave$]]]$

But (14) is ruled out in principle, since prepositions do not take clausal complements as a consequence of lexical properties, the θ-criterion, and the projection principle.

There seem to be no such exceptional structures as (13), analogous to the marked verb *believe*. Assuming this to be a fact and not an accidental one – i.e., assuming there to be principled reasons for the fact – it follows that the marked property of *believe* should be interpreted as a case of Exceptional Case-marking analogous to (9iii), the projection principle being inviolable. Independent arguments against assuming *Bill* to be the matrix object in (9i) are presented in Kayne (1980c), to which we return in § 5.2.

I will continue to assume, then, that the projection principle is indeed inviolable so that the categorial component is restricted to the specification of parameters such as those noted earlier, all clauses being of the form NP-INFL-VP and marked infinitivals being cases of Exceptional Case-marking. As a side observation, it is worth noting that certain additional empirical facts support these conclusions, as Mark Baltin has observed (cf. Baltin (1980)). Thus compare (15) to the considerably less acceptable (16):

(15)　　I told (persuaded, promised, asked, . . .) Bill myself to leave the room
(16)　　I expected (believed) Bill myself to be a liar

Similarly if the emphatic reflexive *myself* is replaced by *himself* and the matrix subject is replaced by *John*, (15) is ambiguous while in (16) *himself* refers unambiguously to *Bill* (at least, with a very strong preference, as contrasted with (15)). Suppose that (15) is derived from (17) by Move-α applied to *myself*:

(17)　　I myself told Bill $[$ s̄ PRO to leave the room$]$

Then Move-α can move *myself* either to the left or the right boundary of the embedded clause (or to the right of either the full VP or the "small VP" *told Bill*, perhaps), in accordance with Baltin's landing site theory (Baltin (1978, 1979)). Assuming (16) to derive from (18) rather than (19), this option is impossible and (16) is blocked, as required; assuming (16) to derive from (19i), as in the theory of subjectless infinitives GR, or from (19ii), as in GR′, there is no reason for (16) to have a different status from (15), contrary to fact:

(18)   I myself expected [Bill to be a liar]
(19)   (i) I myself expected Bill [to be a liar]
        (ii) I myself expected Bill [PRO to be a liar]

In short, the difference between (15) and (16) follows from the assumption that *Bill* is in the matrix clause in (15) in S-structure and in the embedded clause of (16), in accordance with the LF-representations and the projection principle. Recall that Case theory prevents movement of *myself* to the immediate post-verbal position in (18), as in (19).

Other examples illustrate the same point. Thus, although insertion of adverbs and other qualifiers is fairly free so that the distinctions are not sharp, there is surely a tendency in the direction of preferring (20) to (21):[92]

(20)   (i) John promised Bill with all his heart (sincerely) $\left\{ \begin{array}{l} \text{that he would} \\ \text{visit him; to} \\ \text{visit him} \\ \text{tomorrow} \end{array} \right\}$

        (ii) John forced Bill angrily to leave
(21)   John expected (believed) Bill sincerely to be more forthcoming

There are other similar examples supporting the same conclusion.[93] But the more fundamental point, I think, is that the alternative approaches assuming subjectless infinitives or violating the projection principle weaken the connection between thematic and grammatical relations, raising the difficulties discussed above. Putting the matter in different terms, I assume that the child acquiring English has principled reasons for adopting the θ-criterion and the projection principle and, correspondingly, the analysis NP-INFL-VP for S rather than the much more complex (4) (on the assumptions of GR) or (9) (on the assumptions of GR'), and therefore knows without evidence that the facts are as illustrated in (15)–(21), rather than making the implausible assumption that the analysis according with the θ-criterion and the projection principle is selected over the alternatives on the basis of such evidence as (15)–(21).

I assume, then, that the θ-criterion and the projection principle are maintained in their strongest forms and that there are, therefore, no subjectless infinitives in D- or S-structure. The device of $\bar{\text{S}}$-deletion is a marked property of such verbs as *believe*, distinguishing them from their counterparts in German, French, and Italian, for example, and from such verbs as *try*, which I assume to represent the unmarked case. In § 5.2. I will turn to a proposal by Kayne that there is no $\bar{\text{S}}$-deletion or other modification of syntactic structure involved in Exceptional Case-marking, and that this phenomenon in English derives from an independent property that distinguishes English from French and Italian, namely, a difference in how prepositions govern. If this proposal can be sustained, then Exceptional Case-marking verbs in English are exactly like their counterparts in similar languages, the apparent differences resulting from other independent properties of these languages, obviously a significant improvement. For the present, however, let us tentatively keep to the device of $\bar{S}$-deletion, thus maintaining the connection between Exceptional Case-marking and raising.

2.6. *LF-representation and θ-theory (2)*

Having sharpened somewhat our theory of the base, let us return to consideration of LF. The fundamental notion is that of θ-role. I have been assuming that a θ-role is determined for each NP and clause in the complement of a head α, including NP in PP in such constructions as *put the book on the table* or *send the book to John.* The sole exception is provided by idiom rules, which we may assume to apply in the base after lexical insertion, excluding the italicized item from a genuine θ-role in such expressions as "take *care* of Bill," "make *much* of Bill," while assigning an idiomatic interpretation.[94]

In discussing LF above, I proposed the θ-criterion, which requires that each argument bear one and only one θ-role and that each θ-role be filled by an argument, as a reasonable criterion of adequacy for LF. Let us now assume that arguments fall into the following categories:

(1)   (i) overt anaphors
            (ii) pronominals
            (iii) R-expressions
            (iv) clauses

Non-arguments include other non-NP categories as well as NPs that are "non-referential": impersonal *it*, existential *there*, perhaps idiom chunks, and analogues in other languages. Since NP-trace transmits its θ-role (if any), I will take trace to be a non-argument if it is not a variable. The intuitive idea is that arguments are the elements that bear a θ-role. Thus each argument or its trace is in a θ-position, hence an A-position (cf. § 2.2). There will be slight revisions as we proceed.

Reviewing briefly the categories of (1), overt anaphors such as *each other* receive θ-roles and are therefore arguments. Possibly they are to be analyzed in terms of variables at LF. Thus we might define $\bar{x}$ as follows:

(2)   In an expression of the form (i), where Q is an operator, x may take any value in α and $\bar{x}$ may take any value in α apart from the value of x:
            (i) Qx, x an α: ... x ... $\bar{x}$ ... (equivalently, ... $\bar{x}$ ... x...)

For example, (3i) will be interpreted as (3ii,iii):

(3)   (i) the men like each other
            (ii) for each x, x one of the men; x likes $\bar{x}$
            (iii) for all y, z ($y \neq z$), y, z one of the men; y likes z

This is only a first approximation, but it will do for present purposes.[95] Then the variable x of $\bar{x}$, being an R-expression, receives a θ-role, but the complex $\bar{x}$ (which we might think of as involving the variable x and an operator "bar") is not a variable and receives no θ-role. A similar analysis is possible for reflexives, though for English we might adopt the analysis of Helke (1971), taking the reflexive to be an NP of the form $[_{NP}$ pronoun $[_N$ self$]]$, with a bound pronoun, so that the questions do not arise.

The second category of arguments, pronominals, includes pronouns and PRO. Pronominals have the features gender, number and person, and perhaps other grammatical features, but not those of overt anaphors or R-expressions. A pronoun in addition has a phonological matrix and therefore must also have Case, by virtue of the Case Filter. PRO is, in effect, a pronoun lacking a phonological matrix so that it is immune to the Case Filter. The term "pronominal," then, simply refers to any element with just the relevant collection of features. Let us identify PRO and AGR, the agreement element of the inflectional element INFL, returning to some considerations relevant to this decision.

R-expressions, the third category of arguments, include noun phrases with heads that are in some intuitive sense "potentially referential" (e.g., *John, wood, sincerity, book,* etc.) and variables, where we tentatively understand the notion "variable" in the following sense, subject to later refinement:

(4) α is a variable if and only if $\alpha = [_{NP} e]$ in S bound by an operator

We will understand operators to include quantifiers, *wh*-phrases, or a binding NP in COMP; or definite or indefinite operators as in relative clauses.[96] Recall that variables appear to have the property that they are Case-marked traces (cf. 2.4.2.(17)). It is well-known from the study of crossover phenomena that variables share certain fundamental properties of names; we return to this matter. As we shall see, there is good reason to believe that variables, like other R-expressions, are not subject to the binding conditions for trace and other anaphors.

We return to the analysis of the notion "variable" and its properties. Note that the treatment of variables as analogous to names is natural if we regard the device of quantification as an idealization of coordination beyond listable domains, that is, to domains of infinite size or unknown membership. For finite domains of known size and known (nameable) membership, quantification can be reduced to coordination (conjunction or disjunction), but not elsewhere, as is well-known. The interpretation of variables as analogous to names, while natural, is not necessary. In earlier work I took variables to be anaphors, but accumulating evidence, to which we return in chapter 3, indicates that this was an error. The crossover phenomena provide one class of cases; others will appear below.

The fourth class of arguments is clauses. We have already seen that clauses and NPs tend to play a parallel role in the complement structure of lexical entries, and it seems reasonable to assume that they bear comparable θ-roles when they appear as complements. We might ask whether in place of the syntactic notion "clause" we should develop some more abstract notion corresponding to "proposition," interpreted perhaps as a "complete θ-system" – a verb with each θ-role assigned to an argument related to the verb. I will tentatively assume that there is no need for this additional conceptual apparatus within the grammar (there may be in a broader theory providing richer interpretations for grammatical structures), and that the notions we need are expressible within the syntax of LF in a narrower sense, discussing the consequences as we proceed.

We have assumed that a complement of α is θ-marked by α. Beyond this, we must fix a way to assign a θ-role to the subject of S. There is a familiar ambiguity in the usage of the term "subject." Sometimes, we speak of the subject of a verb, sometimes of the subject of a predicate (a VP) or a sentence. Let us assume the second sense of the term "subject." Then it is the VP that determines the θ-role of the subject, compositionally. The subject is not governed by the verb as the complements of the verb are governed by it.[97]

This decision, while not necessary, is again rather natural, quite apart from the fact that it subsumes θ-marking in general under government; cf. § 2.2. Verbs require that their complements be appropriately filled, and VPs, as we have seen, require that the subject position be filled in S,[98] whether or not a θ-role is assigned to the subject. But as we have noted in §§ 2.1, 2.2, verbs do not in themselves require subjects. Thus the verb *believe* lacks a subject in such structures as those of (5):

(5)   (i) John is (widely, generally) believed to be a liar
        (ii) the belief that John is a liar is widespread (*belief* = $[_N[_V$ *believe*]–nom])
        (iii) the belief is held by no one

In (i), it is reasonable to take *John* to be the subject not of *believe* but of the copula[99]; if an agent phrase (e.g., *by everyone*) is added, then a θ-role is assigned to its NP by the preposition *by*, and this θ-role is similar to (perhaps identical with) the θ-role assigned to the agent by the VP in the corresponding sentence or to that of the optional adverbial in (i), these being mutually incompatible elements.[100] But it would be a mistake to suppose that in such agentless passives as (i) there is a suppressed phrase *by*-PRO or something of the sort (perhaps a deleted *by*-phrase, as in the earliest versions of transformational grammar).[101] This is clear from such examples as (ii)–(iii), or from (i) with choice of the parenthesized adverbial.

Other constructions illustrate the same fact. Consider, for example, causative constructions in the Romance languages; e.g., (6):

(6)   –faire [manger la pomme par Pierre]
        ("–to have the apple be eaten by Pierre")

As Kayne (1975) observes, the embedded phrase has the properties of passive constructions. As in passives, no subject appears at D- or S-structure. The example (6) differs from (5i) and similar constructions in that it lacks passive morphology and there is no movement. The two facts correlate. Since *manger* maintains its categorial status as a full verb ($[+V, -N]$) in (6), Case is assigned to the object *la pomme* so that movement is unnecessary to satisfy the Case Filter. The example incidentally illustrates the independence of passive interpretation from passive morphology or movement, but it also illustrates, in the present connection, the plausibility of the assumption that the subject is not assigned a θ-role by the verb itself as obligatory complements are, but rather by the construction of which the verb is head, which may or may not have a subject.

To help clarify the issues that arise, consider again the class of nominal constructions such as (7):[102]

(7)   (i) the barbarians' destruction of Rome
        (ii) Rome's destruction (by the barbarians)
        (iii) the destruction of Rome (by the barbarians)
        (iv) *the barbarians' destruction

Example (i) is the nominal expected on the assumptions of X-bar theory, analogous to "the barbarians destroyed Rome." Since *destroy* requires an object (cf. *"the barbarians destroyed"), (iv) is excluded. As (iii) indicates, the verb *destroy* does not require in itself that the subject position be filled, though it can be filled, receiving a θ-role, as in (i). The rule of *of*-insertion saves (i) and (iii) from the Case Filter, the alternative to (iii) being (ii), where Move-α has applied. In (ii), we take *Rome*, with the function chain ($[NP, NP], [NP, \bar{N}]$) (analogous to ($[NP, S], [NP, VP]$)), to have the GF-θ object-of-*destroy*. Again, 'the range of phenomena, which follows from Case theory given lexical properties of *destroy*, illustrates the fact that there is no necessary connection between passive morphology and movement, and that verbs do not require subjects.[103]

Given these properties, it is natural to regard the subject as "subject-of-VP" or "subject-of-S" rather than "subject-of-verb," though it should be stressed that this whole question is more peripheral than many others that we have been considering. If so, then we may assume that the θ-role of the subject (where it exists) is determined compositionally by the VP in general (as may also be the case in quasi-idiomatic constructions such as *take him seriously*). In (8), for example, John is understood to be the agent of the action in (i), though there is another interpretation in which he is taken to be instrument as in *the hammer broke the window*, where we think of the hammer (or John) as being wielded by someone who is the agent; sentence (ii) has these interpretations, but its more normal interpretation takes John to be patient, so that (ii), but not (i) might be the response to *What happened to John?*

(8)   (i) John broke the window
       (ii) John broke his arm

Assuming the θ-role of subject to be determined compositionally by VP, we may continue to associate the grammatical relations closely to obligatory assignment of θ-role.

Continuing to explore these ideas, let us consider how some familiar cases would be analyzed, regarding these remarks more as an outline of a program to be executed than as a set of results.

In the sentence (9), the verb *hit* assigns a θ-role (patient) to *Bill*, and the VP *hit Bill* assigns a θ-role (agent) to *John*:

(9)   John $\left[_{VP} \text{hit Bill} \right]$

In the sentences of (10), the verb *break* assigns the θ-role patient to *window* in (i) and to the trace *t* in (iii), thus derivatively to its antecedent *window*; and the VP $\left[_{VP} \left[_{V} break \right] \right]$ assigns this θ-role to *window* in (ii), so that *break* is, in effect, ergative.[104] The θ-role agent is assigned to *John* by the VP *break the window* in (i) and by *by* in (iii):

(10)   (i)   John broke the window ($=$ (8i))
       (ii) the window broke
       (iii) the window was [broken t] by John
       (iv) the window was broken

Example (iv) is ambiguous, depending on whether *broken* is taken as an adjective or a syntactic (agentless) passive with trace.

Consider next such items as *seem, appear*. The lexicon specifies these as monadic predicates with a propositional argument to which they assign a θ-role. So far we have not introduced a notion corresponding to "proposition," but have kept to notions expressible in the syntax of LF. Let us see what happens if we persist in this vein. Consider the sentences (11):

(11)   (i)   it seems [that John hit Bill]
       (ii) John seems [t to have hit Bill]
       (iii) John seems sad

Suppose we assume (I) that there is a uniform entry for *seem* in the lexicon, while (II) persisting with the assumption that the projection principle holds, so that the categorial component contains no rules relevant to these matters; rather, the properties of well-formed structures generated by the categorial component are determined by properties of the lexicon, "checked" at the LF-level, in the manner already described. Clearly, these are the optimal assumptions.

As (11i) indicates, *seem* takes a clausal argument and thus must have the lexical entry: $-\bar{S}$. By assumption (I), this is its only argument (apart from an optional *to*-phrase, which we may disregard here). Thus in (11ii), *seem* must assign to the embedded infinitival clause the same θ-role that it assigns to the embedded clause in (i). And in (ii), *John* will receive its θ-role derivatively as antecedent of the trace which is assigned a θ-role by *hit Bill* as in (9). All of this seems unproblematic.

Turning to (11iii), by assumptions (I) and (II) the representation at LF must be of the form (12):

(12)   John seems clause

The natural conclusion, then, is that the LF-representation and S-structure is (13), derived from the D-structure (14) by Move-α, where the embedded phrase is clausal, as in (11i,ii):

(13)   John seems $[\text{t sad}]$
(14)   NP seems $[\text{John sad}]$

Thus the embedded phrase is a "small clause" in the sense of Williams (1974, 1975). In this case, assignment of θ-roles is exactly as in (11ii). Intuitively, this analysis takes the representation of (11iii) at LF to be of the form (15), with *sad* a monadic predicate holding of *John* and *seem* a monadic predicate holding of the proposition *sad(John)*, but without introducing any notion of "argument" more abstract than that of syntactic clause:

(15)   seems (sad (John))

We are pretty much led to these conclusions by the decision to keep to minimal assumptions. There seems no obvious problem with them, but they deserve careful attention.

A similar line of reasoning applies in the case of such words as *consider*, which appears in the structures (16):

(16)

$$\text{John considers} \begin{cases} \text{the problem} & \text{(i)} \\ \text{that S} & \text{(ii)} \\ \text{Bill to be foolish} & \text{(iii)} \\ \text{Bill foolish} & \text{(iv)} \\ \text{it impossible that S} & \text{(v)} \end{cases}$$

As usual, *consider* takes NP or clausal arguments, as indicated in (i)–(iii). It is therefore similar to the *believe*-type verbs we have discussed. By the assumption (I) of uniformity of lexical entry – the null hypothesis – (iv) and (v) must also involve clausal arguments; and by the assumption (II) of lack of structure in the categorial component, the underlying D- and S-structures of (iv) and (v), projected from the lexicon, should be *John considers clause*, as in (ii), (iii). We must assume $\bar{S}$-deletion in (iv), (v) as in (iii), so that the embedded subject is governed and Case-marked, as required by the Case Filter.[105] Since the embedded subject is governed, it cannot be PRO, but it can be trace or an overt anaphor. Thus we have (17):

(17)   (i) *John considers [PRO foolish]
         (ii) John is considered [t foolish]
         (iii) they consider [each other foolish]

Again, no obvious difficulties arise.

The complement of *consider* in (16iv,v), (17ii,iii) is again a "small clause" – a clausal structure lacking INFL and the copula. The obligatory presence of *it* in (16v) again illustrates the fact that subject is an obligatory element of clausal structures; cf. § 2.1 and subsequent discussion. Comparison with languages similar to English suggests that $\bar{S}$-deletion is obligatory for small clauses, as contrasted with infinitives, for which $\bar{S}$-deletion is a marked option available in English for certain verb types.[106] Putting this observation in a more general form, we have the principle (18):

(18)   Small clauses are not maximal projections

It is most unlikely that (18) is a stipulated principle of UG. We will assume it for the moment, returning in § 3.2.1 to the question of why it holds. Given (18), PRO is impossible as subject of a small clause since it will be governed, but trace, lexical anaphors, and other phonetically-realized items are permitted, as illustrated in (16) and (17).

Consider again such examples as (19):

(19)   John persuaded Bill – clause

The clausal complement of *persuade* can be finite or infinitival, as in cases already discussed. Can it be a small clause, as in (20)?:

(20)   John persuaded Bill [NP AP]

Evidently not. Small clauses are excluded from postnominal complement position. More generally, $\bar{S}$-deletion is barred in this position; we do not find such expressions as (21), with NP ≠ PRO:

(21)   John persuaded Bill [NP to VP]

There is a rather natural general pattern of explanation for such cases, which we will apply to the case of (18) in § 3.2.1. What we have to show is that if the complement clause in (19) is not a maximal projection (for example, if $\bar{S}$-deletion has taken place in (21)), then every possible choice for the NP subject of the complement clause is barred, so that the construction cannot exist. Therefore, the complement clause in (19) is a maximal projection. In particular, the complement clause remains an $\bar{S}$ in (21) so that the only choice for the NP subject is PRO, and (20) is excluded completely, since the conclusion is incompatible with (18).

Suppose, then, that the complement clause in (19) is not a maximal projection. There are four possible choices for its NP subject: PRO, phonetically-realized NP, variable, or NP-trace. We can at once rule out the possibility of PRO, since the position of the complement subject is governed if the clause is not a maximal projection blocking government. Phonetically-realized NP is also barred, since Case cannot be assigned in this position, as we have seen. Nor can a variable appear in this position, since by 2.4.2.(17) (from left to right), variables must be Case-marked; cf. § 3.2.2. Therefore, the only possible conclusion is that the small clause construction (20) and the infinitival construction (21) are generated solely with NP-trace as subject, hence either in the forms (22i) with raising-to-object, (22ii) with raising-to-subject, or the passive forms (22iii):

(22)   (i)(a) NP persuade NP$_i$ $[\,t_i\,AP\,]$
        (b) NP persuade NP$_i$ $[\,t_i\,\text{to VP}\,]$
    (ii)(a) NP$_i$ persuade NP $[\,t_i\,AP\,]$
        (b) NP$_i$ persuade NP $[\,t_i\,\text{to VP}\,]$
  (iii)(a) NP$_i$ be persuaded α $[\,t_i\,AP\,]$
        (b) NP$_i$ be persuaded α $[\,t_i\,\text{to VP}\,]$

We have to explain, then, why such forms as (22) are excluded.[107] The cases of (i) with raising-to-object are barred at once because movement to a θ-position is impossible, as we have seen. The same is true of (ii); we will see below (cf. (38) and subsequent discussion) that quite generally, transitive verbs assign a θ-role to their subject. This leaves case (iii). Applying again the line of argument just employed, we have to show that there is no possible choice for α in (iii). Passive participles do not assign Case since they are not of the category $[-N]$ but, we have assumed, of the category $[+V]$. Therefore phonetically-realized NP and variable are barred. PRO is excluded since α is governed. The only remaining possibility is that α is NP-trace. This is possible only if the matrix NP is moved successively from the position of t_i to the position of α and then to the matrix subject position. But the first step in this derivation is again barred, as in the case of (22i). Therefore, there is no possible choice for α in (22). Consequently, NP-trace is impossible in the embedded subject position of t_i in (22). Since PRO, phonetically-realized NP and variable are also excluded, the small clause (20) and the infinitive (21) cannot exist if the clausal complement of (19) is not a maximal projection. Therefore it is a maximal projection. Small clauses are therefore excluded by (18), so that (20) is impossible; and (21) must be a control structure with the NP subject of the embedded complement clause taken as PRO.

Other verbs can be analyzed along similar lines, e.g., those of (23):

(23)   I like (want, prefer, . . .) it hot

Here, *it* may be a referential pronominal (as in "I like my coffee hot") or non-argument *it* (as in "I like it better raining than snowing"), analogous to (16v). In these cases, passives are often excluded or marginal; cf. note 51.

Consider next the verb *regard*, as in (24):

(24)   John regards Bill as foolish

A question now arises as to whether we should take the structure to be (25i) or (25ii):

(25)   (i) John regards Bill as [NP foolish]
        (ii) John regards [Bill as foolish]

If (i) is correct, then *regard* is analogous to *persuade*; if (ii) is correct, then it is analogous to *consider*. In (i), the embedded NP subject of the small clause would have to be taken as PRO, but this seems dubious, given (18), since it should then be governed by *as*. If (ii) is correct, then *regard* does not assign a θ-role to *Bill* in (24), and we should expect to find such examples as (26), analogous to (27):

(26)   (i) I regard it as obvious that he will win
        (ii) I regard there as being many reasons to continue with our efforts
        (iii) I regard too much as having been made of his failure
(27)   (i) I consider it obvious that he will win (cf. (16v))
        (ii) I consider there to be many reasons to continue with our efforts
        (iii) I consider too much to have been made of his failure

Example (26i) is clearly grammatical, strongly supporting the analysis of (24) as (25ii), but the relatively unacceptable status of (26ii,iii) is unaccounted for.

Similar analyses are possible – and similar questions arise – in the case of other constructions that have been discussed in the same connection.[108] Consider for example (28):

(28)   (i) John impressed me as intelligent
        (ii) it impressed me as obvious that John would win
        (iii) NP* impressed me clause

Thematic properties of *impress* indicate clearly that the LF-representation must be something like (iii), with the direct object *me* and a clausal *as*-complement. In this respect, *impress* is unlike *regard*, which has only a clausal *as*-complement as in (25ii) if our previous conclusions are accurate. NP* in (28iii) is not a θ-position, as we see from (28ii); cf. (26i). With regard to the *as*-complement of *impress*, the projection principle requires that it be clausal, and the simplest assumption plainly is that it should be structurally identical to the *as*-complement of *regard*, namely, $[_S \text{NP } as \ldots]$, a small clause with $\bar{\text{S}}$-deletion. The NP subject cannot be PRO in this governed position. Nor can it be a phonetically-realized NP at S-structure, since Case cannot be assigned in this position for reasons already discussed (cf. note 89). Therefore, the subject of the small clause can only be trace. That is, (28i,ii) must be raising constructions, with the subject of the clausal complement moved from its non-Case-marked position to the matrix subject position, which is not a θ-position as required.

The conclusions sketched above merit much more careful examination, but they seem *prima facie* plausible. They conform to the thematic structure where this is clear as well as to the projection principle, and they appear to yield the basic facts of surface structure. They also yield the correct binding properties, as we shall see in § 3.2.3. Cf. the discussion of 3.2.3.(37). These conclusions differ from those of OB, where it was suggested that certain "structure building rules" apply to give the clausal representations required for these expressions, as shown by the functioning of the binding principles (opacity).[109] That approach, of course, is inconsistent with the projection principle.

We can extend the analysis in obvious ways to more complex constructions such as those of (29):

(29)   (i)   it seems certain that S (it seems $[_S t \text{ certain } \bar{\text{S}}]$)
        (ii) John seems certain to be sad (John seems $[_S t \text{ certain } [_S t \text{ to be sad}]]$)
        (iii) John seems (to be) certain that S (John seems $[_S t \text{ (to be) certain } \bar{\text{S}}]$)
        (iv) John seems (to be) easy to convince people to like (John seems $[_S t \text{ (to be) easy } \bar{\text{S}}]$)

The parenthesized forms are the associated representations at LF and S-structure. In examples (iii) and (iv), the adjectives (*certain, easy*) are dyadic,[110] and *seem* is monadic throughout.

In such structures as (30), the VP presumably assigns a θ-role to the subject compositionally:

(30)   John looks (feels) sad

Correspondingly, we do not have such forms as "John looks (feels) to be sad," etc.

A problematic class of cases for the θ-criterion is that studied in Williams (1980a), for example, (31):

(31)   (i) John left the room angry
        (ii) John left the room empty

A possibility would be to assume that the S-structure and LF-representations are, respectively, (32i,ii):

(32) (i) John [$_{VP}$ left the room] [PRO angry]
      (ii) John [$_{VP}$ left the room] [PRO empty]

Then the VP will assign a θ-role to *John* and PRO will receive its θ-role in the final clause, which is something like the clausal element in (32):[111]

(33) John left the room while he was angry

The theory of control would then assign control of PRO, in terms of factors that Williams discusses. In languages with overt adjective agreement, the adjective would have the features of PRO – e.g., masculine singular in (32i).

Decisions such as these permit the θ-criterion to be met in a broad class of constructions. It is not obvious that they are the right decisions, and other constructions (e.g., predicate nominals, free relatives, and others) remain to be treated. But the conclusions to which we are led do not seem implausible. Let us continue to assume that they are correct in essence, adopting the projection principle without exception. If this is correct, we are not compelled to construct new and more abstract types of argument (e.g., propositions, in some sense) beyond those that are already expressed in the syntax of S-structure and LF.

The specific analyses proposed here are not the only ones that accord with the projection principle and the θ-criterion. In fact, they raise certain problems that suggest that some modifications might be in order. Consider our use of the notion "small clause" as in the structures (34):

(34) (i) they consider [John stupid]
      (ii) they prefer [it hot]
      (iii) they consider [John the best candidate]
      (iv) *they prefer [John the best candidate]

The examples illustrate the well-known fact that the matrix verb commonly subcategorizes the predicate of the embedded phrase, unexpected if the latter is a clause, in which case INFL is commonly selected but not the embedded VP. A possibly related fact is that these small clauses lack INFL, which we have suggested several times might be the head of S. One might approach both problems along lines suggested by Stowell (1980a); see also Manzini (1980). Suppose that *X*-bar theory is generalized so that all maximal projections may have subjects, PRO or phonetically-realized under the usual conditions. Then (34i), for example, could have the structure (35), with *John* the subject of AP:

(35) they consider [$_{AP}$ John [$_{A}$ stupid]]

The verb *consider*, then, subcategorizes for AP, so that the selection of the complement is (34) is no longer a problem, nor the absence of INFL. The NP subject is the specifier of AP in (35). AP with subject is now regarded as a "proposition" in the sense required at LF, along with S. In the examples (32), however, we continue to assume that the small clause is of the category S rather than AP, since there is no selection of AP by the main verb in this case, presumably. Various adjustments are necessary to preserve the main lines of the argument already outlined, but they do not seem to involve questions of principle beyond those already mentioned. We return to the question of analysis of small clauses in § 3.2.1.

Continuing with the assumption that the θ-criterion and the projection principle hold without exception, let us consider again some of their properties. The θ-criterion states that each θ-position is assigned exactly one argument and that each argument is assigned to exactly one θ-position, where an argument is assigned to a θ-position if it or its trace occupies this position. The θ-criterion was defined in § 2.2 for the level LF, where it holds as a necessary condition for well-formedness (see note 14). But the projection principle implies that it is satisfied as well at the levels of D- and S-structure, within the range of constructions that we are considering, with assignment to a θ-position through the medium of trace irrelevant in the case of D-structure. Thus we have the general condition that the θ-criterion holds at D-structure, S-structure and LF.

The requirement that the θ-criterion hold at D-structure expresses the idea that D-structure is (*inter alia*) a representation of GF-θ; cf. § 2.2. This requirement is stronger than the requirement that the θ-criterion hold at S-structure and LF, and properly so. As we saw in discussing 2.2.(17), the requirement that the θ-criterion hold at D-structure is essential to demonstrating that movement is always to a non-θ-position. Let us now consider some concrete examples.

From the requirement that the θ-criterion hold at S-structure and LF, it follows that movement from a θ-position to a θ-position is blocked, since the element moved would be assigned a dual θ-role: (i) from the position it occupies and (ii) from the position occupied by its trace. But this requirement still incorrectly allows movement from a non-θ-position.[112] Suppose, for example, that English used *Jove* instead of *it* in expressions similar to "it rains," where *Jove* is an R-expression. And suppose further that *SEEM* is a verb exactly like *seem* except that it assigns a θ-role to its subject. Then consider the D-structures (36):

(36)   (i) $[_{NP} e]$ SEEMs $[_S$ John to be intelligent$]$
        (ii) $[_{NP} e]$ SEEMs $[_S$ Jove to rain$]$

Since *SEEM* (like *seem*) is not transitive, (i) violates the Case Filter unless *John* moves to the matrix subject position. If it does, the θ-criterion is violated at S-structure and LF; in any case, it is violated at D-structure. Thus (i) underlies no well-formed sentence. Similarly in (ii), the Case Filter requires that *Jove* move to the matrix subject position, yielding (37):

(37)   Jove SEEMs to rain (meaning: "it seems that it rains")

In (37), the θ-criterion is satisfied at LF and S-structure, since *Jove* is assigned a θ-role by *SEEM*, by assumption. But (36ii), its D-structure source, violates the θ-criterion at D-structure. Therefore, there can be no such verb as *SEEM*. Surely this conclusion is correct: there can be no such verb. Therefore, the θ-criterion holds at D-structure, as implied by the projection principle, which is violated by the verb *SEEM*. Intuitively, D-structure provides a representation of GF-θ. The subject position for a raising verb cannot be a θ-position, and, more generally, movement to a θ-position is always excluded. Cf. 2.2.(17). See also 3.2.3.(44).

There is, then, no verb *SEEM* which is like *seem* in that it induces $\bar{\text{S}}$-deletion and is intransitive, but unlike *seem* in that it assigns a θ-role to its subject. Could there be a verb *SEEM'* which is like *seem* in that it induces $\bar{\text{S}}$-deletion and assigns no θ-role to its subject but unlike *seem* in that it is transitive? Then *SEEM'* permits Exceptional Case-marking to yield (38):

(38)   it SEEMs [John to be sad]   (meaning: "John seems to be sad")

There is no such verb, and presumably the gap is not fortuitous. The reason why no such verb exists may be that transitive verbs tend to have agent subjects, therefore to assign a θ-role to their subject; but *SEEM'* violates this very strong tendency.[113] Insofar as this tendency holds, we have the following observation:

(39)   A verb that assigns Case to its object assigns a θ-role to its subject[114]

Later, we will see that the (virtual) converse holds: a verbal element (specifically, a participle) that does not assign Case to an NP that it governs assigns no θ-role to its subject; cf. § 2.7. Generalizing slightly, we therefore have the following observation:

(40)   A verbal element assigns Case to an NP that it governs if and only if
        it assigns a θ-role to its subject[114]

As it stands, (40) is too strong – similarly, (39) – as is clear from examples that we have already discussed (cf. (28)). Furthermore, insofar as it is accurate, its status is unclear: is it an independent principle, or, as is more likely, does it follow from independent considerations insofar as it is accurate? A number of problems arise as we consider these questions, particularly, problems concerning the analysis of extraposed clauses, constraints on nominalization, possibilities of passivization with extraposed clauses, and so on. I will put these questions aside; pending their resolution, it would be pointless, though straightforward, to reformulate (40) in such a way as to hold of all but the unwanted cases such as (28).

Note that (40) does not block intransitive verbs that assign a θ-role to their subject. Rather, we interpret (40) as holding vacuously from right to left in the case of a verbal element that governs no NP.

In summary, consider the sentences of (41), where the θ-positions are italicized:

(41)　(i) *John* expected $[Bill$ to win$]$
　　　(ii) *John* promised *Bill* $[PRO$ to win$]$
　　　(iii) John is certain $[t$ to win$]$
　　　(iv) John was expected $[t$ to win$]$
　　　(v) John$_i$ was asked $t_i[$what$_j[PRO$ to do $t_j]]$
　　　(vi) John was killed t

In these examples, the θ-criterion is satisfied in the manner already indicated; *John*, for example, either occupies a θ-position or is assigned to a θ-position by a trace which occupies this position. Thus in case (iv), t occupies a θ-position and *John* is assigned to this position, acquiring its θ-role from the VP *win* but occupying no θ-position itself, so that we find such sentences as (42):

(42)　(i) it was expected – that S
　　　(ii) much was expected to be made of John's exploits
　　　(iii) good care was expected to be taken of John
　　　(iv) there was expected to be a hurricane last night
　　　(v) it's expected to snow tomorrow

Similarly, in (41v) *John* is assigned to the θ-position occupied by t_i, while t_j is a variable bound by the coindexed quasi-quantifier *what* (hence is an R-expression and an argument), and is assigned to the θ-position that it occupies.

Notice that the θ-criterion overlaps with the requirements of Case theory, but not completely. Normally, an NP is Case-marked if and only if it is assigned to a θ-position. But there are exceptions in both directions, as illustrated in (43):

(43)　(i) there seems to be some reason to believe him
　　　(ii) I tried $[PRO$ to win$]$

In (i), *there* is Case-marked but lacks a θ-role; neither the phrase nor its trace is in a θ-position. In (ii), PRO is not Case-marked but is in a θ-position and receives a θ-role. We return in § 3.2.2 and chapter 6 to the connections between Case theory and θ-role.

There are certain technical adjustments needed to ensure that the

θ-criterion has the sense we intend. Consider the sentences (44):

(44)   (i) who did John see t
        (ii) John bought a book $\left[_{\bar{S}} \alpha \text{ for } \left[_S \text{ Mary to read t} \right] \right]$
        (iii) John read every book

With respect to (i), the intuitive sense of our proposals is that *t* has a θ-role but that *who* does not. It would, in the first place, make little sense to suppose that the quasi-quantifier in (i) bears a θ-role; furthermore, this would violate the θ-criterion, since clearly the variable it binds would have this very same θ-role. Nevertheless, the element *who* is capable of bearing a θ-role, given that it appears in a θ-position in D-structure. One approach would be to assume that it is only the pronominal content of *who* that appears at D-structure under lexical insertion, the feature $\left[wh\text{-} \right]$ being added in the syntax. We then understand this feature to exempt the element from the class of R-expressions. Then the source of *who* in D-structure bears a θ-role but *who* at S-structure and LF does not. Proceeding in this way, we might adopt the general principle (45):

(45)   Move-α can move α to COMP only if α contains the feature $\left[wh\text{-} \right]$

The principle (45) is in a certain sense implicit in the foregoing in that we have been tacitly assuming that such lexical NPs as *John, the book*, etc., can never move to COMP. Principle (45) makes this assumption explicit. One might construe it as a version of Emonds's structure-preserving hypothesis. Furthermore, operators now form a natural class: $\left[wh\text{-} \right]$-elements and their traces, or quantifier expressions.

Note however that these moves still do not resolve the problem fully, for in multiple *wh*-questions such as (46), *what* appears in a θ-position in S-structure and therefore must be an argument:

(46)   I don't remember who read what

We might pursue the possibility of developing a still more abstract variant of the idea that a $\left[wh\text{-} \right]$ feature is added at some point, excluding the element from the class of R-expressions, but the artificiality is apparent. Since it seems that little if anything is involved beyond terminology, let us simply assume that *wh*-phrases are R-expressions and that elements in COMP are not considered arguments.

Now consider (44ii). Here, α is an NP moved from the position of its trace *t*. Assuming the conventions just discussed, the feature $\left[wh\text{-} \right]$ is added to α to permit it to move to COMP, and when it has so moved it is no longer an argument, so that (44ii) satisfies the θ-criterion with the variable *t* bearing the θ-role assigned in the θ-position it occupies.

Example (44iii) works the same way, essentially. We must now consider quantifier expressions to be R-expressions, since *every book* occupies a θ-position at D- and S-structure. When the quantifier-movement rule applies in the LF-component, and the quantifier phrase is reanalyzed along the lines we have discussed, it no longer counts as an R-expression; rather the variable left behind receives the θ-role assigned in the position it occupies.

The example (44ii) reveals that the θ-criterion must be sharpened in another respect as well. We assumed earlier that an argument is assigned a θ-role when it or its trace occupies a θ-position. But example (44ii) brings to light an ambiguity in the notion "its trace," in this formulation. In (44ii) the NP *a book* c-commands and is coindexed with the variable *t* in the embedded S, though the latter cannot be regarded as "the trace of *a book*" in the sense required for θ-role assignment, or there will be a violation of the θ-criterion once again; *a book* will now be assigned one θ-role in the position it occupies and another by virtue of the position of its trace. Evidently, we must exclude the pair (*t, a book*) from the relation "trace of α" in (44ii), and more generally, whenever the pairing is established not by movement but by construal in the LF-component. The only such situation that can arise, so it appears, is of the type illustrated in (44ii), where an NP is coindexed with an operator and its trace by a rule of control. In this case, the variable bound by the operator is not the trace of the NP in the sense of this notion required for θ-role assignment. We therefore require the following refinement of our earlier notion of "θ-role assignment":

(47) α is assigned the θ-role ϕ if and only if α or a trace *t* coindexed with α occupies a θ-position that is θ-marked ϕ, where *t* is not bound by an operator that fails to bind α

These notions will be developed more carefully in § 3.2.3 and chapter 6. The intuitive sense of (47) is clear: variables do not transmit θ-role.

One might ask whether it is correct to assume, as we have so far been doing, that the operator α in COMP in (44ii) is PRO rather than $[_{NP} e]$. If the latter, we would have a somewhat more unified approach to the structure of COMP: apart from a complementizer, only a lexical *wh*-phrase or trace could appear in COMP, either the trace of successive-cyclic movement or the operator in such constructions as (44ii) – with the feature $[wh-]$, if (45) is valid. We also could overcome a problem noted in OB, namely, that PRO in COMP in purposive constructions (similarly, in other analogous constructions) cannot be arbitrary in reference.[115] The question no longer arises in the same manner under the replacement of PRO by trace. As for $[_{NP} e]$ in COMP or elsewhere, we must require that it be bound, but since this is true uniformly we do not have to distinguish the COMP position from others in this respect. In part, the binding requirement follows from binding theory, but we might suppose it to reflect a more general property of an element $[_{\alpha} e]$, namely, that there is no interpretation at LF for such an element unless it is either bound by an operator or assigned content by an antecedent – an assumption that seems generally plausible in itself and that accommodates quite naturally interpretive accounts of gapping and similar phenomena (cf. Wasow (1972) and much subsequent work). A question would then arise concerning the status of trace in COMP with respect to government; this reduces to the same question in the case of trace in COMP left by successive-cyclic movement; we return to it in § 5.3.

While these considerations give some reason to suppose that the moved element α in (44ii) is $[_{\text{NP}} e]$ rather than PRO, this assumption is inconsistent with the projection principle, which requires that the D-structure position of α be filled by an argument; hence PRO, not $[_{\text{NP}} e]$. We return to this question in chapter 6, concluding finally that it is devoid of content.

Aoun (1979b) notes that there is a certain parallelism between θ-role and Case, the former a property of the LF-component and the latter essentially a property of the PF-component, an idea that he explores further in this paper and in (1980b). Intuitively, NPs are identified by Case in PF-representation and by θ-role in LF-representation. He suggests further that rules of the LF-component disregard items with no θ-role and that rules of the PF-component disregard items with no Case. We return to some similar ideas. More generally, Aoun suggests that features are naturally subdivided into those relevant to the PF-component (e.g., phonological features) and those relevant to the LF-component (e.g., θ-features), and that these features are "visible" only to rules of the components to which they are relevant, an idea well worth exploring. One can imagine how it might be adapted, say, to yield the conclusion that resumptive pronouns are indistinguishable from variables at the level of LF-representation, and that a pronoun or PRO coindexed with a quantifier and in its domain is automatically treated as a variable bound by this quantifier at this level (cf. Higginbotham (1979a)). The potential for such analysis will become clearer in chapter 6. I will not explore these possibilities further here, merely noting that they deserve examination.

2.7. *Some remarks on the passive construction*

We have already briefly discussed passive constructions, as in (1):

(1) (i) John was killed t
     (ii) John is believed [t to have won]
     (iii) John is believed [t to have been killed t']

We have suggested that whereas *t* in (ii) and (iii) is the subject of the embedded S, *t* in (i) and *t'* in (iii) are within phrases of the neutralized category $[+V]$, as is the embedded clause in (ii), (iii). In contrast, lexical passives such as the morphologically complex forms *unexpected, semi-educated*, etc., or the lexical source of the ambiguous *frightened, closed, furnished*, etc., are simply adjectives, monadic predicates that assign to the subject the θ-role of the direct object of a corresponding verb, with considerable idiosyncrasy, as one expects in the lexicon. From these conventional and rather natural assumptions, we derive the well-known properties of syntactic and lexical passives: syntactic passives are not restricted to direct objects of verbs and require no thematic relation between the verbal base and the surface subject, non-arguments appear in the surface subject position, the meaning of the passive is strictly determined by properties of the D- and S-structures with no contribution from the rules forming the construction beyond this, and there are no morphologically complex cases; whereas in contrast the lexical passives are sharply restricted thematically (*John was taught, John was taught French, John was untaught *(French), John was known to be a fool, John was unknown *(to be a fool)*, etc.), assign a θ-role and therefore cannot have non-argument subjects (*much was *(un)made of John*, etc.), have idiosyncratic semantic properties as expected for lexical items, and may be morphologically complex.[116] In short, the clustering of properties of syntactic and lexical passives follows directly from the way they are generated, on the assumption that morphologically complex passives are necessarily lexical; that there is an *en*-VP option in English of the category $[+V]^i$, the VP having its standard internal structure and the complex being post-copular in clauses; that there is a rule Move-α; and that verbs of certain categories (e.g., the *frighten*-class) are generated both in the lexicon as adjectives and under the *en*-VP option, with the expected ambiguity.

Luigi Rizzi notes an interesting distinction between syntactic and lexical passives in Italian. In the relative clause construction (2i), *comunicata* is a syntactic passive, whereas in the parallel form (2ii), the complex form *sconosciuta* (*s-conosciuta* = "unknown") is necessarily lexical:

(2)   (i) la verità che è stata comunicata a Maria
            ("the truth that was communicated to Maria")
       (ii) la verità che è sconosciuta a Maria
            ("the truth that is unknown to Maria")

In either case, the PP (*a Maria*) may be cliticized, as in (3):

(3)   (i) la verità che gli è stata comunicata
       (ii) la verità che gli è sconosciuta

In the corresponding reduced relatives, the PP cliticizes to the syntactic passive from *comunicata*, as in (4i), but not to the lexical passive *sconosciuta*:

(4)   (i) la verità comunicatagli
       (ii) *la verità sconosciutagli

The reason is that adjectives do not take clitics, and the morphologically complex form *sconosciuta* can only be base-generated as an adjective. The contrast shows the at most semi-adjectival character of the syntactic passive and the necessarily lexical (hence fully adjectival) character of the morphologically complex "unpassive."

Other distinctions between syntactic and lexical passives are discussed by Burzio (1981). He cites the French examples (5):

(5)   (i) il a été achevé plusieurs constructions cette annéé
        (ii) plusieurs constructions ont été achevées cette année
        ("many buildings were finished")

Example (i) is essentially the base-generated form, with *plusieurs constructions* in the direct object position and *il*-insertion corresponding to *there*-insertion in the (quite marginal) English analogue: "there were finished several buildings." Example (ii) derives from the same base-generated form by application of Move-α. But the corresponding morphologically complex "unpassives" differ:

(6)   (i) *il est inachevé plusieurs constructions
        (ii) plusieurs constructions sont inachevées

Since the morphologically complex "unpassives" are necessarily base-generated as adjectives, (6ii) is possible as an NP-copula-adjective construction. But there is no source for (6i), which therefore contrasts as expected with (5i). We return to properties of such structures as (5i).

Burzio observes that the same pattern can be observed in Italian in connection with *ne*-cliticization. For reasons to which we will return in chapter 4, *ne*-cliticization is possible from the object position but not from pre-verbal position or from the post-verbal position that results from adjunction of the inverted subject. Thus we have (7) but not (8):

(7)   (i) ne furono riconosciuti molti
            ("of-them were recognized many" – "many of them were
            recognized")
        (ii) ne sono stati limitati troppi
            ("of-them were limited too many" – "too many of them were
            limited")
(8)   (i) *ne furono sconosciuti molti
            ("of-them were unknown many" – "many of them were
            unknown")
        (ii) *ne sono stati illimitati troppi
            ("of-them were unlimited too many" – "too many of them
            were unlimited")

In (7), the source of the clitic *ne* is the NP *molti-ne, troppi-ne*, in the direct object position; therefore, *ne*-cliticization is possible. Apart from movement of the clitic *ne*, the examples of (7) are in base-generated form, which is permitted for syntactic passives in Italian for reasons to which we return.

But the examples (8) derive from base-generated structures of the form NP-copula-adjective, with a morphologically complex adjective. The subject *molti-ne, troppi-ne* is moved to post-verbal position by an inversion rule that adjoins the subject to the VP; therefore *ne*-cliticization is excluded. In this respect, the morphologically complex passives behave in the manner of ordinary base-generated copula constructions, whereas the quite different behavior of syntactic passives follows from the fact that the direct object is base-generated in place in the post-verbal direct object position, optionally becoming the subject of S-structure by application of Move-α, or remaining in place as in (7).

Examples such as these illustrate clearly the distinction between syntactic and lexical passives, the former involving a base-generated direct object, the latter not.

The category that is commonly called "passive" may not constitute a natural class, either within or across languages. Syntactic passives are unlike lexical passives, and in languages as closely related to English as German, syntactic passives seem to behave differently and may involve a rather different rule structure.[117] In other languages, what might be translated as passive in English has still different properties; the Romance impersonal passives, discussed briefly in § 2.4.1, are a case in point. To cite another example, John McCarthy has pointed out that Classical Arabic has a lexical passive combined with a Case-assignment rule that assigns nominative Case to the first NP following the verb and objective Case to the NP following it, leading to such sentences as (9):

(9)   (i) qatala zaydun al-waladan
             ("killed-active Zeyd-nominative the-boy-objective" – "Zeyd killed the boy")
         (ii) qutila zaydun
             ("killed-passive Zeyd-nominative" – "Zeyd was killed")
         (iii) sirtu yawma ljum?ati
             ("travelled-active-I Friday-objective" – "I travelled on Friday")
         (iv) sira yawmu ljum?ati
             ("travelled-passive Friday-nominative" – "Friday was travelled)

The last example, meaning something like "one travelled on Friday," is not directly translatable into English, but follows directly from the rules of Case-assignment and morphology, which give quite a different arrangement of data from English syntactic or lexical passives.[118]

As a final case, consider the passive-like construction in Navajo, with such examples as (10):[119]

(10)   (i) horse mule *yi*-kicked   ("the horse kicked the mule")
         (ii) horse mule *bi*-kicked   ("the horse was kicked by the mule")

    (iii) man horse *yi*-kicked   ("the man kicked the horse")
    (iv) man horse *bi*-kicked   ("the man was kicked by the horse")

The *bi*-forms look like lexical passives, but a curious pattern of unacceptability and ungrammaticality appears in other cases. Thus the sentences of (11) are unacceptable and while (12) is grammatical, (13) is completely ungrammatical:

(11)   (i) horse man *yi*-kicked ("the horse kicked the man")
          (ii) horse man *bi*-kicked ("the horse was kicked by the man")
(12)   girl water *yi*-drank   ("the girl drank the water")
(13)   water girl *bi*-drank   ("the water was drunk by the girl")

Hale offered an explanation of these properties in terms of a hierarchy of nouns based on such features as human and animate, which determines word order. Witherspoon (1977) suggests a rather different interpretation. He argues that a more correct translation of (10i) would be something like "the horse exercised its power over mules by kicking the mule," and that (10ii) means approximately: "the horse let the mule kick it." Similarly, (10iii), (10iv). But horses are not supposed to have greater intelligence than men, accounting for the unacceptability of (11), and since the water cannot let the girl drink it, (13) is ruled out completely. Assuming something like this to be the case, shall we understand the *bi*-forms as passive? The question makes sense if "passive" is a natural class, though it is unclear what the answer should be. The question does not arise if we simply assume that languages have various ways to avoid focusing the "logical subject" or to avoid expressing one at all, while still observing the syntactic requirement that a subject NP be present. Similar considerations hold of the Arabic example, or of the impersonal passive in Romance, or the "passives of nominals" such as "Rome's destruction" (cf. 2.6.(7)), or the passives without movement in Romance causatives (cf. 2.6.(6) and (5i), (7), above). In short, it is not obvious that the notion "passive" refers to a unitary phenomenon, still less one that can serve as a foundation stone or even guiding intuition for a theory of syntax. It may be a useful descriptive category, and one can imagine functional explanations for the prevalence of some such device. But the range of phenomena that fall within this category in some sense appear to be rather heterogeneous in character.[120]

    In chapter 1, I pointed out that a central element in the work discussed here, as in recent work from which it evolves, is the effort to decompose such processes as "passive," "relativization," etc., into more fundamental "abstract features": the Case Filter, the binding principles, Move-α and the principles of bounding, etc.; and I also mentioned that there will in general be only a weak relation between the functional role of such general processes and their formal properties. In the case of passive, languages tend to have devices for suppressing the subject, but these can work out in many ways, depending on how options are selected from the components of UG.

Thus the Italian syntactic passive with passive morphology and the impersonal passive with the clitic *si* are both "passive" in some general sense, but the formal devices are quite different, though each may (though it need not) make use of the rule Move-α, which also figures in many other constructions. The same is true in the other cases discussed, and many others.

Even within a single language that has syntactic passives with movement and passive morphology, we may find passive morphology without movement (e.g., (14)), movement with the sense of passive but without passive morphology (e.g., (15)), and the passive sense with neither passive morphology nor movement (e.g., (16):

(14)   (i) it was believed (held, reasoned, . . .) that the conclusion was false[121]
        (ii) fu arrestato Giovanni[122]
            ("Giovanni was arrested")
(15)   Rome's destruction
(16)   (i) faire manger la pomme par Pierre
            ("to have the apple be eaten by Pierre")
        (ii) si mangia le mele
            ("the apples are eaten")

While these are more or less "passive" in sense, and have the characteristic property of suppression of subject, the selection of formal devices is quite different.

We have an explanation for the general properties of these various constructions in terms of Case theory, along the lines already discussed. In the normal syntactic passive, movement is obligatory because the passive participle is not a Case-assigner. No movement is necessary in (14i), because the clausal complement is exempt from the Case Filter; in (14ii) and (18), because Italian assigns nominative Case in the post-verbal position for reasons to which we return in chapter 4; in (16), because the verb assigns Case. Movement is necessary without passive morphology in (15) if the *of*-insertion option yielding *destruction of Rome* is not taken, because nouns are not Case-assigners. The resulting form is in effect the nominal of the passive *Rome is destroyed*. In the Italian case, movement is optional giving (17i,ii) corresponding to (14ii), (16ii), respectively, a matter to which we return in § 4.5:

(17)   (i) Giovanni fu arrestato
        (ii) le mele si mangiano

In (ii), there is verbal agreement with the derived subject; in (16ii), the verb remains in its unmarked form, perhaps because the clitic *si* serves as the AGR element in INFL, as suggested in Belletti (1980b).[123] A third form, (18), derives by the normal inversion option of Italian:

(18)   si mangiano le mele

In the French counterparts, (17ii) is the only option for reasons discussed in § 4.5, relating to the pro-drop parameter distinguishing Italian-Spanish from French-English. The relevant point, in the present context, is that the structures are passive-like and follow essentially the same principles as those discussed here.

In the normal syntactic passive, as also in (15) and (17ii), the direct object becomes the subject, but this is not a necessary property of passive, as shown by the examples (14), (16i), or by such examples as (19):

(19)   (i)   John was believed t to be stupid
         (ii) John was considered t stupid
         (iii) he was pronounced t dead on arrival
         (iv) the bed was slept in t

In (i)–(iii), the trace is the subject of an embedded clause, as in raising with the predicates *seem*, *certain*, etc. There is no grammatical relation between the passivized verb and the position occupied by the trace, and no θ-role is assigned to this position by the passivized verb. In such structures as (iv), the position of the trace is assigned its θ-role exactly as in the corresponding active, including actives that do not permit passivization. There seems to be no difference in θ-role assignment in the examples of (20), though (i) (like (19iv)) can be passivized as (iii), while (ii) cannot be passivized as (iv):

(20)   (i)   they spoke to John
         (ii) they spoke angrily to John
         (iii) John was spoken to
         (iv) *John was spoken angrily to

It may be, as has frequently been proposed, that in such cases as (19iv), (20iii), the verb-preposition construction has been reanalyzed as a verb,[124] and as is well-known, this device is more readily available when the combination is somehow "verb-like" in its semantic properties.[125] This reanalysis rule, then, assigns to the position of the trace the GF[NP, VP], but such derivative GFs, assigned through reanalysis, do not seem to affect θ-role assignment, as one can see clearly in more complex examples such as (21):

(21)   the Cadillac was driven away in t

There is no independent sense of "object" in which such examples as (19iv), (20iii) or (21) – or, for that matter, (19i–iii) – are instances of change of grammatical relation from object to subject. As these examples further illustrate, the θ-role of the phrase that becomes the subject of the passive need not be assigned by the verb that has passive morphology; in fact, there need be no such θ-role at all, as in the case of passivized non-arguments.

The traditional characterization of passive as involving a change of object to subject is correct in one important sense: this is the core case of passive. But it is otherwise unacceptable on grounds of factual inaccuracy (e.g., (14), (16i)), incompleteness (e.g., (15), (17ii)), circularity (e.g., (19)–(21)) and redundancy (in that independent principles of much broader scope determine both when movement is necessary and that the new grammatical function assigned is that of subject).

We may approach the syntactic passives with passive morphology from a somewhat more abstract point of view, along the lines of the earlier discussion of GFs and function chains in §2.2, as a preliminary to a more general and abstract treatment (in §2.8) of the entire complex of questions that I have been considering. What is usually called "passive" seems to have two crucial properties:

(22)   (I) [NP,S] does not receive a θ-role
       (II) [NP,VP] does not receive Case within VP, for some choice of NP in VP

In the D-structure (23), underlying "John was killed," the subject position is assigned no θ-role (and so may be filled by non-arguments, as in (14)) and the object is assigned no Case:

(23)   [$_{NP}$ e] was killed John

Assuming that the participle *killed* is not a Case-assigner (property (22II)), *John* must be moved or the Case Filter will be violated; the *of*-insertion option is excluded here (cf. note 49). *John* can only be moved to subject position as a consequence of the projection principle and the θ-criterion; cf. §2.2. In the subject position, it receives Case and is assigned a θ-role through the medium of its trace, which is in a θ-position. Thus movement in passive, yielding a "displaced subject," is a consequence of more fundamental considerations, and where these do not hold for one or another reason, there is no movement in passive (as in (14) or (16), for example). A similar configuration of phenomena is found in languages with no movement rules in the syntax; cf. §2.8.

It seems doubtful that properties (I) and (II) of (22) are independent. Therefore, it is reasonable to inquire into the assumptions necessary to derive one from the other. There seems no way to derive (II) directly from (I), though as we have seen, (II) virtually follows from (I) on rather reasonable further assumptions (cf. 2.6.(39)). The example just reviewed involving Move-α suggests how we might derive (I) in general from (II), quite apart from movement. Suppose that the unique property of the passive morphology is that it in effect "absorbs" Case: one NP in the VP with the passive verb as head is not assigned Case under government by this verb.

Call this NP "NP*." By the Case Filter, NP* must receive Case. By assumption (II), now taken as the defining property of passive morphology, NP* must receive Case on the basis of some GF it assumes outside of the VP. This new GF can only be [NP,S], by the projection principle and the θ-criterion. Therefore, NP* must assume the GF [NP,S] in addition to its D-structure GF, which may be [NP,VP] (as in (23)) or something else (as in (19)). The function chain of NP* in S-structure must be $(GF_1, \ldots, GF_n)$, where GF_n is its D-structure GF (a GF-θ if NP* is an argument) and $GF_i (i \neq n)$ is [NP,S]. But if a new GF [NP,S] assumed by NP* is one to which a θ-role is assigned, then the θ-criterion will be violated, as we have seen. Therefore, passive morphology must satisfy property (I) of (22).

More generally, we have the following conclusion:

(24)   If some NP governed by V is assigned no Case, then the VP of which V is the head assigns no θ-role

The conclusion extends directly from clause to NP, in which case we have N and $\bar{N}$ instead of V and VP. Plainly, (24) is closely related to 2.6.(40), and a more general formulation is possible including as well ergative verbs that assign no Case to their object and no θ-role to their subject, though the post-verbal thematic subject receives Case in place (cf. §4.5 and Burzio (1981)). I will return directly to some tacit assumptions that are required for this argument to go through in full generality. Let us assume now that these gaps can be filled.

Suppose that passive morphology is assigned to a verb V that has no NP governed by V in its complement, as in the case of (25):

(25)   it was believed (held, reasoned, . . .) that the conclusion was false
        (= (14i))

Since the verbs *believe*, etc., take clausal complements, the D-structure, projected in the usual way from lexical structure, is as in (25), with [$_{NP} e$] in place of the pleonastic non-argument *it*. Since there is no NP in VP lacking Case, no movement rule has to apply; no NP in VP must assume the secondary GF [NP,S] to satisfy the Case Filter. In fact, the S-structure is formed simply by the rule that inserts *it* in the non-θ-position of the subject. Thus, passive morphology, once again, is not necessarily associated with movement and assumption of a new GF.

Much the same will be true in languages in which intransitives can be passivized, as in Arabic, German, or Hebrew:[126]

(26)   (i) sira yawmu ljum?ati   (= (9iv))
        (ii) es wurde getanzt
             ("it was danced" – "dancing took place")
        (iii) dubar ba
              ("was-spoken about her" – "she was spoken about")

Languages differ as to how extensively passive morphology may be used. In English, it is restricted to verbs that take NP or clausal complements, but not in German or Dutch. In Hebrew, verbs with PP complements seem to take passive morphology freely. Presumably passive morphology can only appear with verbs that assign (or participate in assigning) a θ-role to the subject in the active form (i.e., not raising verbs such as *seem*), or so one would expect, if the "functional role" of passive is, in essence, to permit suppression of subject, but there are further constraints to be explored.

Thus passive morphology need not involve assumption of a new GF by movement (even in languages that use the Move-α option to overcome the Case Filter in passive) or some other device. As illustrated above, passive movement is not restricted to arguments, and where the NP that assumes a new GF has a θ-role, this θ-role may be one that is not assigned by the verb with passive morphology; and the sense and other properties of passive need not be associated with movement or passive morphology, or may be associated with movement without passive morphology or conversely. This dissociation of properties is what we would expect on our modular assumptions – that is, on the assumption that such processes as "passive" are composed of more fundamental abstract features, such as the elements of Case theory, θ-theory, etc. It does remain true, however, that the "core case" of passive involves passive morphology and assumption of a secondary GF [NP,S] by the direct object; presumably, a language will have passive morphology only if this case exists.

Examination of examples (14) with passive morphology but no movement reveals a gap in the argument just outlined.[127] We might ask why the verb with passive morphology may not still assign a θ-role to subject where there is no movement. For the argument to go through we must assume a certain "uniformity principle" for passive morphology, which may be more general, applying to other morphological processes as well. Let us consider the principle that morphological processes are uniform with respect to θ-role in given constructions:

(27)   Each morphological process either (i) transmits θ-role uniformly
                                          (ii) blocks θ-role uniformly
                                   or (iii) assigns a new θ-role uniformly

Passive inflection meets (27i) internally to VP; that is, every θ-role assigned by a verb within its VP is assigned by the corresponding passive participle. Passive inflection meets (27ii) externally in the S of which the passivized verb is the main verb; that is, a θ-role is never assigned to the subject. Other morphological processes (e.g., morphological causative) may assign new θ-roles in a uniform manner. Assuming the principle (27), and assuming further that where there is passive morphology in a language, it must at least apply to the "core case" of transitive verbs with objects, then (27ii) implies that the verb with passive inflection must always meet condition

(22I): $[NP,S]$ must not receive a θ-role. The reason is that this conclusion follows for transitive verbs with objects, as we have seen, so by the uniformity principle it must always hold. Hence no θ-role can be assigned to the subject even when there is no movement.

The uniformity principle for morphological processes has been left a bit vague. I think that something of the sort may well be correct. Suppose that it can be grounded in a theory of morphology and word-formation. Then the argument presented earlier deriving (22I) from (22II) goes through in full generality.[128] But notice that there are two respects in which we are still appealing to something like (22I) as an independent principle: in holding (i) that verbs that never assign θ-role to subject do not receive passive morphology, and (ii) that passive morphology meets condition (27ii) while the "core case" of passive is that of transitive verbs with direct objects. Both (i) and (ii) relate to the functional role of passive in suppressing subject.

We noted earlier that analogues of both (I) and (II) of (22) also hold for raising verbs (cf. 2.6). Consider (28):

(28)   John seems $[$t to be intelligent$]$

The subject of *seem* is not a θ-position (satisfying (22I)) and the position of the trace lacks Case (satisfying the obvious generalization of (22II) from $[NP,VP]$ to NP governed by the verb). In this case, we cannot deduce (I) from the generalization of (II) on the basis of the Case-absorbing property of passive morphology, but the same argument goes through, as an instance of (24).

The question of the accuracy of (24) is also raised by such impersonal passives as (17ii). We will suggest in § 4.5 that the principle holds in this case as well.

In English and similar languages, the passive construction is copular, and the verb with passive morphology is, we have assumed, of the category $[+V]$. On these assumptions, (22II) follows, and we can deduce (22I) for transitive verbs directly and for all verbs given the uniformity principle and the assumptions of note 128. In other languages (e.g., Hebrew), passive involves movement as in English but the passive construction is not copular; rather, the verb simply has passive morphology, which by stipulation absorbs Case, giving (22II), hence (22I). In other languages, the passive construction is not copular and passive involves no movement (e.g., Classical Arabic). Again, (22II) is stipulated as a property of the passive morphology and (22I) follows. Let us turn now to this case, but in a somewhat more general setting.

2.8. Configurational and non-configurational languages

I have been assuming so far that GFs are determined directly by the structural configurations of D-structures and transformationally-derived S-structures. A crucial assumption throughout has been that there is a category VP in the X-bar system of the base, thus permitting GFs to be defined in terms of structural configurations. But there are languages in which this does not seem to be true. Classical Arabic, with VSO structure, is a case in point. Aoun (1979b) suggests that in this case there is in fact a kind of "discontinuous VP." [129] Suppose we express verbal government with indices, say superscripts, in the style of Rouveret and Vergnaud (1980). The verb and its complements will be coindexed, forming an abstract VP; configurational languages are then a special case, with no discontinuities in superscripting. The analysis goes through pretty much as above.

Let us look at the matter in a somewhat different way. As mentioned earlier, Hale (1978) has suggested that languages fall into two major typological categories: configurational and non-configurational. The former are of the type we have been considering. In the latter (his W^*-languages) the full range of syntactic configurations is lacking in various degrees, [130] and order of constituents is typically fairly free, though there may be preference rules, which we will disregard. He has also suggested that in non-configurational languages there are no empty categories, hence no transformational rules in the syntax, assuming trace theory. Hale suggests that Japanese is essentially of the non-configurational type; in fact, as has often been noted, there is little if any reason to suppose that rules of the type Move-α apply in Japanese. Let us assume that these suggestions are correct and ask how the framework I have been outlining here can be generalized to accommodate a language of this type. [131]

Suppose that the central base rule of Japanese is (1), where W^* stands for a sequence of zero or more categories that are maximal projections (let us say, NP or $\bar{S}$), and X is the head of the maximal projection $\bar{X}$:

(1) $\bar{X} \rightarrow W^* X$

In particular, the base rules will generate such structures as (2), where we take $\bar{S} = S = \bar{V}$:

(2) $[_S NP_1 NP_2 \ldots NP_n V]$

Let us assume further that the lexicon of Japanese is essentially the same as that of English in respects that concern us here; for example, the verb *tabe* (*eat*) takes an NP-complement, assigning to it the θ-role patient and forming with it a VP that assigns the θ-role agent to the subject; *atae* (*award*) takes double NP-complement assigning θ-roles accordingly; etc. Japanese also has a word-forming element *sase* (causative) which takes a clausal complement as a lexical property, assigning to it the appropriate θ-role and assigning the θ-role agent to the subject of the verb V-*sase*. [132] It also has a word-forming element *rare* which serves as passive morphology. Assume further that GFs are represented exactly as in English: $[NP,S]$ for subject, $[NP,VP]$ for object, $[S,VP]$ for clausal complement in VP, and $[NP^1,VP]$, $[NP^2,VP]$ for primary and secondary object in the case of double-object constructions. The basic difference between Japanese and English, then, is that the configurations that determine GFs (whether GF-θ or GF-$\bar{\theta}$) are not represented in the syntax in the X-bar system in D- or S-structures in Japanese.

Let us now compare D- and S-structures and the rules that relate them in the two languages. For the verbs *eat-tabe*, English will have the D-structure (3i) and Japanese the D-structure (3ii):

(3)   (i) $\left[_S NP_1 \left[_{VP} \text{eat } NP_2 \right] \right]$
       (ii) $\left[_S NP_i\, NP_j\, \text{tabe} \right]$ ($i = 1$ and $j = 2$, or $i = 2$ and $j = 1$)

The D-structure assigns GF-θ. For English, the assignment is direct, given the configurations, along the lines sketched above. For Japanese, we may take the assignment to be random, which is to say that order is irrelevant. In each case, take $NP_1 = [NP,S]$ and $NP_2 = [NP,VP]$. Assuming essentially the same Case-assigning rules in the two languages, NP_1 receives nominative Case and NP_2 objective Case (GA and O, respectively, in Japanese).[133] In both languages, θ-roles are assigned on the basis of GF-θ, in the obvious way. Note that if random GF assignment had proceeded differently in the Japanese example, the θ-criterion would have been violated.

Consider next the passive D-structures (4), generated by the base rules:

(4)   (i) $\left[_S \left[_{NP} e \right] \left[_{VP} \text{was} \left[_{\overline{[+V]}} \text{eaten } NP \right] \right] \right]$
       (ii) $\left[_S NP\, \text{tabe-rare} \right]$

Example (4ii) is an instance of NP* V, with NP* = NP and V = *tabe-rare*. The general property of passive is that the passive element absorbs Case (namely, 2.7.(22II)). Therefore, as we have seen, no θ-role is assigned to $[NP,S]$ (property 2.7.(22I)). In English, Move-α applies, giving the S-structure (5):

(5) $\left[_S NP \left[_{VP} \text{was} \left[_{\overline{[+V]}} \text{eaten } t \right] \right] \right]$

Along the lines discussed earlier, NP is assigned the function chain ([NP,S], [NP,VP]). The second element determines the θ-role in LF and the first might play a role elsewhere in LF, as we have seen. Nominative Case is assigned to NP with the S-structure GF [NP,S], the initial element of the function chain.

In Japanese, the D-structure (4ii) must be converted to an appropriate S-structure in which NP can receive Case, since the passive element *rare* absorbs Case, by assumption. This cannot be done by an application of Move-α, as in English, since GF is not configurationally defined. The obvious analogue of the rule Move-α for Japanese is the rule (6):

(6)   Assume a GF

We understand (6) as assigning to an NP the function chain $(GF^*, GF_1, \ldots, GF_n)$, where $(GF_1, \ldots, GF_n)$ is the function chain it already has and GF^* is an arbitrary GF. If (4ii) is to satisfy the θ-criterion, the GF [NP,VP] must have been assigned by random GF-assignment at D-structure. Applying rule (6), we form an S-structure identical in form with the D-structure (4ii) but with NP assigned the function chain (7):

(7) $(GF^*, [NP,VP])$

What is GF^*? It must be a GF that lacks a θ-role and that will permit Case to be assigned to NP, so as to satisfy the Case Filter. By assumption, NP cannot be assigned Case within VP since *rare* absorbs Case, so GF^* must be [NP,S], just as the rule Move-α must always move α to the subject position. Therefore, NP is assigned the function chain ([NP,S], [NP,VP]) in S-structure, exactly as in English, and θ-role as well as Case are assigned exactly as in English, with the nominative GA and the θ-role patient assigned to NP. Recall that *tabe-rare* cannot assign a θ-role to [NP,S] by virtue of 2.7.(22I). Therefore the θ-criterion leads to the same choice for GF^* as in English.

Consider next *atae-award*. In English, we have (8i); in Japanese, (8ii), the only choice of D-structure that will not lead to a violation of the θ-criterion:

(8)   (i) $[_S NP_1 [_{VP} \text{award } NP_2 NP_3]]$
       (ii) $[_S NP_i NP_j NP_k \text{ atae}]$ (where (i,j,k) is some permutation of (1,2,3))

In each case, take $NP_1 = [NP, S]$, $NP_2 = [NP^1, VP]$, $NP_3 = [NP^2, VP]$. S-structure is identical in form to D-structure, and assignment of θ-role and Case (in Japanese: $NP_1 = GA$, $NP_2 = NI$, $NP_3 = 0$) is straightforward.

Consider next the corresponding passives. In English, the passive morphology absorbs the Case assigned to NP_2, so that NP_2 must move to subject position, with θ-role and Case assigned in the familiar way. In Japanese, passive absorbs either the Case of NP_2 or NP_3 (as in English dialects that permit both "a book was given Bill" and "Bill was given a book"). The rule (6) assigns the GF [NP,S] to whichever NP does not receive Case, giving either a GA-O or GA-NI form for passive. Choice of the GF [NP,S] as the new element of the function chain for whichever of NP_2, NP_3 loses Case is, again, dictated independently by the Case Filter and the θ-criterion.

Consider finally the causative forms in Japanese, namely, (9), (10):

(9) $NP_1 NP_2 NP_3 [_V \text{tabe-sase}]$
       ("NP_1 causes NP_2 to eat NP_3")
(10) $NP_2 NP_3 [_V \text{tabe-sase-rare}]$
       ("NP_2 is caused to eat NP_3")

For convenience, I pick a particular ordering.

The lexical properties of *tabe* require that it bear the GF $[V,VP_1]$, where VP_1 has an object $[NP,VP_1]$ and VP_1 assigns a θ-role to $[NP,S_1]$. By random GF assignment at D-structure, following the (arbitrary) numerical conventions adopted in (9), we take $NP_3 = [NP,VP_1]$ and $NP_2 = [NP,S_1]$. Thus the lexical structure of (9) will include (11), which is simply a convenient shorthand for a list of GFs associated with elements of (9):

(11) $[_{S_1} NP_2, [_{VP_1} NP_3, [_{V_1} tabe]]]$

Lexical properties of *sase* require that it bear the GF $[V,VP_2]$ to a verb phrase VP_2 with a clausal complement $[S, VP_2]$, where VP_2 assigns a θ-role to the $[NP, S_2]$ of a sentence S_2 containing VP_2 as its VP. Thus the lexical structure of (9) must contain the GFs represented in (12), including (11), if the θ-criterion is to be satisfied at LF:

(12) $[_{S_2} NP_1, [_{VP_2} (11), [_{V_2} sase]]]$

Once again, S-structure is identical in form to D-structure. θ-role assignment is straightforward given (12), which was derived by random assignment of GFs to the D-structure (9). Case assignment is also straightforward. On the assumptions so far discussed, we expect $NP_1 = GA$, $NP_3 = 0$, $NP_2 = GA$. For reasons that we may put to the side, the form of NP_2, the subject of *tabe*, is actually NI.

Consider next the passive (10). As noted, passive morphology precludes assignment of θ-role to the subject; therefore the D-structure (10) necessarily lacks an NP that takes on the GF $[NP,S]$ in the full sentence, i.e., $[NP, S_2]$, keeping to the notations used in (12). Random assignment of GF to (10) in such a way as to satisfy the θ-criterion therefore gives a structure that we may represent as (13), keeping to the notations used above:

(13) $[_{S_2} [_{VP_2} [_{S_1} NP_2, [_{VP_1} NP_3, [_{V_1} tabe]]] [_{V_2} sase-rare]]]$

Since *sase* is passivized as *sase-rare*, one NP in its complement will not receive Case. But there is no NP in its complement; rather only an S. Therefore this requirement is vacuous. Thus there is no reason to apply the rule (6); S-structure is identical in form to D-structure, and the function chains are unchanged. NP_2, with the GF $[NP,S_1]$, receives the nominative Case GA; NP_3, with the GF $[NP,VP_1]$, receives the objective Case 0. θ-roles are assigned exactly as in the active counterpart.

Note that (13) violates the requirement 2.1.(25) that clausal structures must have subjects. We might assume this requirement to be relaxed for non-configurational languages, or we might assume that there is an empty subject of one or another sort. At issue are questions concerning the status of PRO, pro-drop, the nature of nominative Case-assignment, and other questions concerning the structure of languages of the type under consideration. I will simply leave all of these questions open.

We might have approached the causative structures in a slightly different manner. Suppose that a general property of causative is to assign the GF indirect object (which we might identify by convention with the primary object of the double-object construction) to the subject of the clausal complement. This would account for the fact that we have GA-NI-O rather than GA-GA-O in (9), and the principle might be extended to languages that appear to have a rather different way of forming causatives, e.g., the Romance languages.[134] If so, then what we would say at this point, in connection with (10), is that this property of assigning NI (dative) to the primary object is absorbed by the passive morphology under principle 2.7.(22II), giving the same results as in the foregoing account.

Compare now the passive of a double-object verb (namely, (14)) with the passive of the causative of a single-object verb (namely, (15)):

(14)   NP NP atae-rare
(15)   NP NP tabe-sase-rare

In (14), we have the Case structure GA-O or GA-NI, depending on whether the primary or secondary object of the verb is passivized. In (15), we have only the Case structure GA-O, where the GA form is the subject of the embedded verb in the corresponding active. But no special rules are required to achieve these results, which simply fall out as the only ones possible. Since Japanese allows either object to lose Case under passive, we derive either GA-O or GA-NI for (14). Since *sase* has no NP-complement, no Case is absorbed by the passive form *sase-rare* (apart from the consideration of the preceding paragraph, not relevant here), so that the Case structure of the corresponding active is preserved.

The passive of the causative is thus analogous to the English examples such as (16) in which the rule Move-α did not have to apply to yield the S-structure of a grammatical sentence:

(16)   it was believed (held, reasoned, ...) that the conclusion was false (= 2.7.(14i))

Similarly, in the case of the passive of the causative in Japanese, the corresponding rule (6) did not have to apply. The reason, in each case, is that there was no NP in the complement of the passivized verb to lose Case under passive morphology.[135]

Summarizing, Japanese is non-configurational, English configurational. Thus, GFs are not represented in D- and S-structures in Japanese in terms of the formal structures, but are assigned randomly to D-structures and by (6) to S-structures. We may think of D- and S-structures as being pairs (α, β), where α is a formal syntactic structure and β is a representation of associated GFs such as (11)–(13): For English, β is derived from α by abstraction from order, etc. For Japanese, α is a "flat" structure formed by (1) and β is essentially the same as the corresponding element in English.

Case and binding theory crucially consider the element β of the pair (α,β) in both types of language, but we need not make the distinction in English since β is a simple abstraction from α Function chains are similar in the two cases.

Given that GFs are represented configurationally in formal structures in English, English uses the rule Move-α to permit an NP to assume a new GF, extending its function chain. Lacking this formal representation of GFs in syntactic structures, Japanese uses the analogous rule: Assume-GF – i.e., (6). The lexicons are essentially identical, as are the systems of grammatical relations and functions. The common property of passive, its only stipulated property, is that it absorbs Case. In both languages, the base rules are minimal, stipulating only the values for such parameters as order. In other respects, D-structures are projected from lexical structure, as are S-structures, given the paired rules Move-α and Assume-GF. While nothing quite as simple as this can be expected to work out without further problems, this seems a reasonable start towards generalizing the theoretical framework we have been discussing to what appear to be radically different language types. If this reasoning is correct, the differences lie essentially along the parameter that Hale identifies as configurational vs. W^*-language. Evidently, there are subtypes of each category, not dealt with here, and it may turn out that these are not two language types but rather more abstract properties that subsystems of a language may instantiate in one or another manner.

If this approach to non-configurational languages is correct in essence, two questions arise concerning our earlier discussion:

(17)   What is the import of the projection principle for a non-configurational language?
(18)   What would be the result of allowing application of random assignment of GF at D-structure and the rule (6) in a configurational language?

As for (17), the projection principle is trivially satisfied for a non-configurational language under a very slight reinterpretation, where we now understand the notions D-structure and S-structure that appear in the formulation of this principle along the lines just indicated, i.e., as pairs (α, β), with the principle referring to the element β of the pair. In case (4ii), for example, the GF $[\text{NP,VP}]$ is assigned to NP at D-structure and the function chain $([\text{NP,S}], [\text{NP,VP}])$ is assigned to it at S-structure, if the LF-representation is well-formed. Since NP is subcategorized and θ-marked by *tabe* at LF in the configuration $[\,_{VP}\text{NP } \textit{tabe-rare}]$, the same must be true at D- and S-structure according to the projection principle. But this is trivially true since exactly these configurations are assigned at the D- and S-structure levels, though they do not appear in the formal syntactic representations themselves, we have assumed. It is fairly obvious how the projection principle (and also the θ-criterion) can be formulated to ensure that they are satisfied in these cases, but there is little point in pursuing the question, since the projection principle is essentially vacuous, as is rather natural considering the role of D- and S-structure in these languages.

Turning to question (18), suppose that random GF-assignment and rule (6) were to apply in English. To make the discussion concrete, suppose that contrary to our earlier assumptions, the only structure underlying (19) is the surface structure (20):

(19)   John is considered stupid

(20) $[_S[_{NP} \text{John}][_{VP} \text{is} [_{\overline{[+V]}} \text{considered} [_{AP} \text{stupid}]]]]$

At the LF-level, we want *John* to appear as subject of a proposition with *stupid* as its predicate. For present purposes, it does not matter which of the options discussed earlier we adopt for small clauses; let us say that the proposition in question at LF is a clause S_1. Then at LF, *John* must be assigned the θ-role determined for the subject of S_1, a clause with an NP subject and the predicate $[_{AP} stupid]$.

Suppose we proceed as follows, mimicking the procedure for a non-configurational language. Take (20) to be the formal part of the D-structure, exactly as in Japanese, though with certain configurations already defined in this case. Then assign to *John* the GF $[NP,S_1]$ and to *stupid* the GF $[AP,S_1]$ (predicate of S_1) by random GF-assignment, giving the full D-structure. Suppose further that we construct the S-structure by rule (6), assigning to *John* the function chain $([NP,S], [NP,S_1])$, exactly as in a non-configurational language. The resulting S-structure is then mapped to the surface structure (20) and the LF-representation.

This procedure, however, is inconsistent with our leading assumptions and thus is ruled out within the present framework. We have assigned conflicting GFs to *John* at D-structure: $[NP,S]$ by virtue of its position in the formal configuration (20) and $[NP,S_1]$ by random GF-assignment. The projection principle is violated, since the assignment $[NP,S]$ does not correspond to selection (subcategorization and θ-marking) at LF; such inconsistent GF-assignment would be ruled out explicitly as soon as the notions outlined above are made more precise. The S-structure also violates the projection principle, since it contains no category filling the subject position of S_1, a θ-position – i.e., no category with the GF $[NP,S_1]$ in S-structure. Thus the answer to question (18) is that it is impossible to apply the "non-configurational rules" in a configurational language.

But these inconsistencies are readily overcome if we look at what we are doing in a slightly different way. Suppose we take (20) to be not the formal part of the D-structure, as in a non-configurational language, but rather just the surface structure of (19). We then proceed to construct D- and S-structures exactly as in the preceding account, with only one modification: we assign an empty category coindexed with *John* bearing the GF $[NP,S_1]$ at S-structure, so as to satisfy the projection principle. What we have now done, in effect, is to construct the D- and S-structures previously assumed. That is, this account simply spells out one way to construct an appropriate D- and S-structure that will map in the required way to LF, given a surface structure. One can narrow the procedure outlined in various ways to ensure more rapid convergence on the appropriate D- and S-structures, eliminating the random elements and providing an algorithm of some sort for making the right choices, given surface structure. We now have a parsing model, in effect. Nothing of any significance is at stake. Under this interpretation, there is no reason at all to rule out application of the non-configurational principles to a configurational language. The answer to question (18), under this interpretation, is that application of these principles is a first step towards construction of a parser.

2.9. Modules of grammar

In chapter 1, I distinguished two classes of subsystems of the theory of grammar: subcomponents of the rule system (1) and subsystems of principles (2):

(1)   (i) lexicon
         (ii) syntax
              (a) categorial component
              (b) transformational component
         (iii) PF-component
         (iv) LF-component
(2)   (i) bounding theory
         (ii) government theory
         (iii) θ-theory
         (iv) binding theory
         (v) Case theory
         (vi) control theory

Some of the properties of these systems have been discussed in the foregoing remarks, and (liib) has been generalized in terms of the parameter [±configurational]. Further properties of these systems will be elaborated as we proceed. Perhaps this a good point for a preliminary summary.

The system that is emerging is highly modular, in the sense that the full complexity of observed phenomena is traced to the interaction of partially independent subtheories, each with its own abstract structure. I have discussed two basic principles: the θ-criterion and the projection principle. As a property of LF, the θ-criterion might almost be regarded as part of a definition of well-formedness, and in this sense, is relatively uncontroversial. Combined with the projection principle, however, it is far from innocuous, with consequences extending well beyond the internal structure of grammar. Within the theory of grammar, one consequence of these principles is that the categorial component of the syntax is highly restricted, to a substantial extent a projection of properties of the lexicon.

Base rules are virtually eliminated. There are also a variety of consequences with regard to principles of grammar (e.g., movement is always to a non-θ-position, hence to subject, if not adjunction) and to specific properties of grammars (e.g., the structure of verbal complements).

Given these principles and others to which we return, the transformational component of core grammar – now reduced to the rule Move-α with perhaps some parameters as to choice of α and landing sites – can in effect be defined by the conditions 2.4.1.(2), repeated here as (3), which belong, respectively, to the theory of government, θ-theory and bounding theory:

(3)   (i) trace is governed
       (ii) the antecedent of trace is not in a θ-position
       (iii) the antecedent-trace relation observes subjacency

Recall that (3ii) derives from the θ-criterion and the projection principle.

PRO differs from trace in all three respects. It is ungoverned, its antecedent (if any) has an independent θ-role, and the antecedent-PRO relation (if it exists) does not observe the subjacency requirement. Given the first of these properties, we have the following general principle holding of empty categories, that is, categories lacking phonetic content:

(4)   If α is an empty category, then
       (i) α is PRO if and only if it is ungoverned
       (ii) α is trace if and only if it is governed

Principle (3), which restates 2.4.1. (13), is a bit too strong as we shall see. It will be refined as we proceed, and in part (namely, part (i)) will be reduced to the theory of binding. PRO is a pronominal anaphor, sharing properties of pronouns and of anaphors. The positions in which PRO appears are determined by these shared properties and by the theory of Case.

Traces are of several types. NP-trace is an anaphor, like *each other*. It is not Case-marked. A variable is a trace bound by an operator; it is an R-expression, functions in the manner of a name (with interesting exceptions), is Case-marked and assigned a θ-role. I have also briefly discussed traces left by extraposition and have noted that there may be other cases as well.[136] The distribution of trace too is determined by the theories of government, binding and Case. Given that these theories determine the positions in which empty categories and non-empty categories appear, we can maintain the projection principle without qualification, assuming all clauses to be of the form NP-INFL-VP at D- and S-structure, apart from small clauses, which are of the form NP-predicate and may or may not be of the category S.

If the analysis developed so far is basically correct, two related questions arise. First, why do we have a partitioning of empty categories into the three types: ungoverned (PRO), governed and Case-marked (variable), governed and non-Case-marked (NP-trace)?[137] Second, given the partitioning, why is it that properties are associated in just this manner? The theory of binding, to which we turn next, is particularly relevant to these questions.

Each of the systems outlined admits of some possibilities of parametric variation while certain principles are fixed. We assume that the lexicon is basically the same in character across languages, though different items may be selected within a narrow range of possibilities. By the projection principle, S-structures are also comparable across languages, differing according to the ways in which parameters for configurationality and order are fixed. At LF, there is always a category VP; languages are of the subject-predicate form at LF. In configurational languages, VP appears as a category in syntactic structures as well.[138]

S-structure is the fundamental level of syntactic representation, receiving its interpretation at the levels of PF and LF by rules of the PF- and LF-components, respectively. At S-structure, each NP apart from trace is assigned a function chain $(GF_1, \ldots, GF_n)$, whether it is an argument (including PRO) or a non-argument (idiom chunks, pleonastic *it* and *there*, etc.). GF_n determines the θ-role for arguments; the GF_i's $(i \neq n)$ may play other roles in determining LF-representations, as may other properties of S-structure.

We have decomposed S-structure into two factors: D-structure, which is a representation of GF-θ, and a rule adding GFs to a function chain: either Move-α or Assume-GF. For configurational languages, the rule Move-α has the properties (3). Property (3ii) is more general, holding as well in the case of the rule Assume-GF, since it follows from more fundamental principles. The rule Move-α plays other roles in the grammar, e.g., relating *wh*-phrases and other elements in COMP to abstract variables, extraposition, idiom interpretation. The Case Filter determines the applicability of the paired rules Move-α and Assume-GF for construction function chains. Since Move-α plays other roles as well, there might be (and apparently are) languages that use Move-α for, say, *wh*-movement in the syntax, while using its counterpart Assume-GF for the construction of function chains.

Given the projection principle and the θ-criterion and the restricted ways in which S-structure is formed from D-structure, it follows that S-structures are sharply limited in variety. X-bar theory imposes other constraints on D-structures, hence S-structures. Making no reference to the conditions derived from the lexicon via the projection principle and the θ-criterion and from X-bar theory, the base rules will stipulate idiosyncratic properties of D-structure, hence S-structure.

When the parameters of UG are fixed, a core grammar is determined, one among finitely many possibilities, lexicon apart. Marked structures are added on the basis of direct or indirect evidence (cf. chapter 1), while certain options are selected as unmarked in the absence of evidence to the contrary by the person acquiring knowledge of the language. It is possible that so-called "functional considerations" e.g., compatibility of the grammar with parsing principles, assumed given—might play a role in determining choice of grammar.[139] These and many other questions must be considered in the development of a comprehensive theory of UG, as a characterization of the initial state of the language faculty.

We will turn next to a closer examination of government and binding theory and to consideration of some parameters of language variation. Further questions, of a different sort, arise when we ask how the language faculty in its initial or steady state interacts with other cognitive systems such as systems of conceptual structure and organization, which have their own properties.[140] The lexicon is one point of contact, but not necessarily the only one. It also goes without saying that the approach I have outlined is not the only one that deserves serious consideration, either in its specific details or in its general organization and principles.

Notes

1.   Cf. Chomsky (1980b,c).
2.   For further discussion of what is at stake, see Chomsky (1975, 1980b).
3.   See May (1977) for an approach that I will follow in general. See chapter 4 for further discussion of movement rules in the LF-component.
4.   One might argue that at surface structure, *to-visit* becomes a single word. For expository purposes, I ignore this possibility here.
5.   It has occasionally been proposed that *wanna* is a lexical verb, perhaps quasi-modal, in which case the S-structure of (6ii) would be the same as its surface structure. This verb would have a highly defective morphology and unique syntactic distribution (e.g., "I wanna visit Paris," "I will wanna visit Paris," etc.; but not *"he wanna(s) visit Paris," *"I wanna(d) visit Paris (yesterday, if I could)," etc.) and semantics. Since exactly the properties that would have to be stipulated for this verb follow from the assumption that *want-to* is optionally contracted to *wanna* in the PF-component, I assume that the analysis in the text is correct. For further discussion, see § 3.2.2 and references cited there.
6.   Cf. Fillmore (1975) for discussion of a somewhat similar idea.
7.   That *he* may be associated at LF-representation with the object of *persuade* as one option is particularly clear if this matrix object is a quantified NP such as *everyone*. Then one option of interpretation of, say, the analogue to (39ii), is: "for every person x, x was persuaded that x should finish college." The option of interpreting a pronoun as identical to a variable bound by some quantifier is available only under specific structural conditions to which we return, conditions that are satisfied in this case.
8.   Confusion is not uncommon even in the technical literature. See Chomsky (1980b, chapter 4) for some discussion; and for a clear analysis of the issues, see Koster (1978b, chapter 1).
9.   For recent argument that they should be identified, see Koster (1980).
10.   See Chomsky (1975, chapter 3), (1977a, chapter 4), (1980b, chapter 4); and for a considerable improvement, Higginbotham (1979a, c). See also Milner (1979).
11.   For evidence in support of this view, see Sag (1976), Williams (1978).
12.   Note that the term "argument" is often used differently in linguistic work, referring to elements occupying "argument positions," the latter being base-generated NP positions—i.e., positions in S other than adjuncts formed by extraposition, excluding NP in COMP.
13.   The bracketed expressions in (3) are of the categories NP, $\bar{S}$, AP, PP, i.e., maximal projections in the X-bar theory. It remains an open question whether VP is a maximal projection (as I will assume below) or whether the S-system is a further projection of V. If the former, then the maximal projections are exactly the expressions filling θ-roles on the

assumption that VP is in a θ-position, namely, the position predicate, on a par with subject, perhaps both adjuncts of the head INFL of S.

14.   This is a generalization of the conditions of functional uniqueness and functional relatedness of Freidin (1978). The latter conditions stipulate only that each argument (in our sense) bears one and only one θ-role. The second clause of (4) is well-motivated. To say that each θ-role must be filled implies, for example, that a pure transitive verb such as *hit* must have an object, that a verb such as *put* or *keep* (with the sense they have in *put it in the corner, keep it in the garage*) must have the associated PP slot filled, etc. The additional requirement that each θ-role must be filled by only one argument will, for example, exclude the possibility that a single trace is associated with several argument antecedents, a possibility ruled out in principle under the Move-α theory.

Note that the θ-criterion, while not unnatural, is not obviously correct. It is rejected in Jackendoff's pioneering work on this topic (Jackendoff (1972)). He argues that, e.g., in "John deliberately rolled down the hill," *John* has a dual θ-role, as agent and as theme. I will assume that such cases should be dealt with by modification of θ-role assignment rather than by modification of the θ-criterion, though it is not obvious that this decision is the right one.

Suppose that Jackendoff is correct, and that an argument may have a multiple θ-role in the example cited and others like it. While this requires a modification of the formulation of the θ-criterion, this modification is quite irrelevant to the uses to which we will put this principle. We are concerned here with the assignment of θ-role within the basic system of grammatical relations: verb-object, verb-subject (or VP-subject), etc. If θ-roles are assigned in some different way outside this system, the principles we are considering can easily be modified to accommodate such cases while continuing to hold them as formulated here within the central subdomain that is our primary concern. Since the issue is irrelevant to the uses to which the θ-criterion will be put in the subsequent discussion, I will put it aside here, adopting the simpler formulation.

Apart from the reasons given in the text, the behavior of arbitrary PRO supports the θ-criterion. In "they think that to help Bill would be difficult," one might say that the infinitival has an unspecified subject or that *they* is its subject (violating the θ-criterion). The former interpretation is forced if we replace *Bill* by *them*, a fact that reduces to disjoint reference if we assume a PRO subject, in which case this same PRO subject will be subject of *help* in the former sentence, satisfying the θ-criterion.

15.   Note that we are interpreting the θ-criterion as stating that a single θ-role cannot be assigned in two different ways to the same argument. Thus if α is θ-marked by β and by γ ($\beta \neq \gamma$) with a single θ-role (say, agent-of-action), the θ-criterion is nevertheless violated by this dual assignment of a single θ-role. I am indebted to S.J. Keyser for pointing out this tacit assumption. See chapter 6 for a more careful account of this and other matters, based on a somewhat different notion of θ-role assignment that will be developed in chapter 3.

16.   All of this can be stated more precisely and more abstractly in terms of the theory of grammatical functions, in the sense of Chomsky (1955), rudiments of which will be discussed shortly. But this will suffice for present purposes.

17.   See chapter 1 on the problem of defining "grammatical relation." See also Hale, Jeanne and Platero (1977) for some remarks on this matter. Also Hale (1978) for a generalization to which I will return in §2.8. For more extensive discussion, cf. Marantz (1981), surveying several current approaches and developing somewhat different ideas.

18.   Cf. Chomsky (1965), or in a more general setting, Chomsky (1955).

19.   To be precise, this statement holds only for argument positions within VP. But we are assuming that apart from idioms, each NP complement of a verb is an argument; and furthermore, once an expression is restructured as an idiom by an idiom rule, movement into this expression is surely to be excluded by general convention, so that the statement in the text holds in full generality. In effect, restructured idioms are lexical items, thus immune to insertion of α under the rule Move-α. Under the assumption that idiom chunks have the θ-role $\#$, as suggested earlier, the position of an idiom-complement is a kind of θ-position, thus in any event not a target for movement.

20.   Or just heads, complements and adjuncts, if we take INFL to be head of S, and its subject and VP to be complements of the head.

21.   Note that this is in part a matter of execution. One might suppose that the *of*-phrases in (2)–(4) are base-generated, restating contextual features accordingly. Cf. Jackendoff (1977). On *X*-bar theory, see also van Riemsdijk (1978) and many papers in the current literature. Cf. George (1980), for argument that prepositions do not constitute a category.

22.   See chapter 1, note 1.

23.   On the status of clauses, see Koster (1978a) and references cited there. Also Piera (1979).

24.   Note that these cases can be unified if INFL is taken as head of S.

25.   For example, in Russian, dative Case may be assigned to the subject of an infinitival indirect question in certain cases. Or in Hebrew, where the preposition *al* (*on*) is sometimes used in roughly the sense of the English complementizer *for*, infinitival indirect questions can appear with overt lexical pronouns cliticized to *al* as subject (*ani lo yodea – ma alay la' asot* – "I don't know – what for-me to do," meaning that I don't know what I am supposed to do). The case of accusative subjects of infinitives in Greek or Latin remains more problematic, however, among a host of other questions that arise when we turn to a wider variety of languages.

26.   In case (4), Move-α will not permit the construction to escape the Case Filter, since genitive Case is not assigned in pre-adjectival position. Therefore the *of*-insertion option is obligatory. One might ask why this is so.

27.   On the assumptions of Chomsky (1977b), there is a further projection of the S-system to $\bar{\bar{S}}$ = TOP $\bar{S}$. Nevertheless, it is natural to take $\bar{S}$ to be the maximal projection in that $\bar{S}$, as distinct from NP (etc.), is an optional projection of $\bar{S}$; thus $\bar{S}$, like NP (etc.), is the maximal obligatory projection. Alternatively, we might identify $\bar{S}$ and $\bar{\bar{S}}$, appealing to other properties of the system to determine whether the expansion may be recursive, as may be possible in some languages (perhaps Japanese, if *wa*-constructions are incorporated into the $\bar{\bar{S}}$-system). It may be that properties of elements at the periphery of the clause can be determined by general principles. See Marantz (1979a) for some interesting ideas on the subject. Also Baltin (1979). I will not pursue the issue here.

28.   Perhaps the Modals also appear within INFL. I will omit any discussion of their status, as well as other questions relating to the auxiliary system which have been the topic of much study and debate. See, among others, Pullum and Wilson (1977), Akmajian, Steele and Wasow (1979), Fiengo (1979), Lasnik (1979), Milsark (1980). Perhaps other elements too (e.g., *ing* as in "I found him running on the beach") should also be associated with INFL. See Chomsky (1955) for discussion of parallels between *ing*- and *to*-clauses. For discussion of various types of *ing*-clauses within the GB-framework, see Reuland (1980).

We might regard Aux-V as a verbal complex, assigning Case and assuming clitics as a unit, analogously to causatives and restructuring constructions in the Romance languages. Cf. Rouveret and Vergnaud (1980); cf. also Rizzi (1978a), Burzio (1978, 1981), and much other work. Again, I will skirt these important questions here.

29.   On similar complementizers in French and Italian, see § 5.2. It might be, as suggested in Chomsky and Lasnik (1977) that *if* is in COMP in such structures as "I wonder if John will leave," and that *than* and *as* are not complementizers (elements of COMP) but rather, perhaps, prepositions. On this matter, see also Chomsky (1979b).

30.   Note that these assumptions raise problems if we assume that PRO moves to COMP, as in the analysis of purposive infinitivals in OB, a suggestion with considerably broader potential scope. See §§ 2.4.2, 2.6, 3.2.3; note 52, chapter 3; and chapter 6.

31.   This approach does not account for *"a man whose brother to give the book to" and other similar examples, blocked by the *[NP-*to*-VP] filter but not by the deletion-to-recoverability approach, since the *wh*-phrase is undeletable (C.L. Baker and E. Williams, personal communication). But it may be that independent considerations block this case. Thus, it is not obvious that such phrases as "a man to whose brother to give the book" are crucially different from the cited example, as predicted by the *[NP-*to*-VP] filter. The more general point may be that there is a tendency to avoid complex *wh*-phrases in infinitivals,

with deletion up to recoverability as an obligatory extreme case. There appears to be a hierarchy of acceptability; in appositive relatives, complex *wh*-phrases are fairly free; in restrictive finite relatives, they are less acceptable; in restrictive infinitival relatives, they are unacceptable. Correspondingly, *wh*-phrase deletion is excluded in appositives, optional in restrictive finite relatives, and obligatory up to recoverability in restrictive infinitivals.

For a different and quite promising approach to these questions, see Cinque (1978, 1980).

32.   Cf. Jaeggli (1980b), where it is argued that there is no *wh*-phrase deletion in COMP at all, apparent cases of this sort being in reality instances of PRO-movement. Cf. §§2.4.2, 2.6, §3.2.3, and chapter 6. See also Fiengo (1979) for arguments against deletion from a different point of view.

33.   Cf. Marantz (1979a), Baltin (1979) for further development of the assumption that *wh*-movement is a rule of adjunction to the clause itself, not involving COMP.

34.   On this matter, see Grimshaw (1979).

35.   There is a large and growing literature on these questions. For varying points of view, see Bach (1980), Bresnan (1980), Hendrick (1980), Keenan (1980), Lightfoot (1980), and references cited in these publications. See also Kayne (1980b).

36.   One might argue that in the structure of (18) there is a clausal remnant lacking INFL entirely, or with a $\emptyset$-variant of INFL, so that we have a true VP instead of a *to*-phrase. For discussion of such constructions, see Kayne (1980a).

37.   For some relevant discussion, see Lapointe (1979, 1980), Fiengo (1979), Lasnik (1979), Milsark (1980), among many others.

38.   Cf. Hale, Jeanne and Platero (1977).

39.   I assume that there is only one kind of adjunction, namely, preserving the categorial structure of the phrase to which the element is adjoined, so that no structural information is "lost" by the adjunction rule, and the S-structure of (iii) contains [$_{VP}$[$_{VP}$be here] [$_{\bar{S}}$ who John knows]]. Another possibility is that extraposition in (iii) adjoins the relative clause to S, as suggested by Baltin (1978, 1979), with supporting argument. This possibility would be excluded if we were to adopt the Principle of External Adjunction suggested in van Riemsdijk (1978b, p. 284). I will ignore these questions here.

40.   Certain examples similar to (10ii) would be acceptable, in contrast to those cited, but only in a deviant metaphoric use: e.g., "it certainly knows how to rain," in the sense of such examples as "it's been trying to rain all day, but it just can't make it." Cf. chapter 6, for further discussion of the status of "weather-*it*."

41.   Technically, the subjacency condition is not satisfied if S as well as $\bar{S}$ is a bounding node. But this cannot be what is involved here, since the sentence is also ungrammatical in dialects that do not take S to be a bounding node, and furthermore, the violation in (10iii) is far more severe than in corresponding *wh*-island violations that rely on the status of S as a (weak) bounding node. Similarly, in languages such as French or Italian for which S is not a bounding node, analogues to (10iii) are still ungrammatical.

42.   These facts were brought to my attention by Luigi Rizzi. Cf. §4.5 for some possibly related facts concerning impersonal *si* in Italian.

43.   That this alternative approach may be the correct one is suggested by some observations by Luigi Burzio, who cites the examples (i) and (ii):

(i)   i prigionieri sognavano di stare per essere liberati
(ii)   *i prigionieri sognavano di stare per liberarsi
        ("the prisoners dreamt to be about to be freed")

In both cases, the embedded *di*-clause has controlled PRO as subject, and the doubly-embedded *per*-clause has trace as subject, namely, the trace of the raised PRO. Thus in both cases the doubly-embedded clause is (iii), though (i) is grammatical and (ii) is not:

(iii)   per t_i VERB t_i

In (ii), the VERB is *liberarsi*, analogous to (18v); and in (i), the VERB is *essere liberati*, analogous to (18iv). The distinction between (i) and (ii) follows if we assume that the PRO subject of *liberarsi* is not accessible to control, but it does not follow if we take the crucial distinction to be government by *si*. See § 4.5 for further discussion.

44.   Note that there is another position in which PRO may appear, namely, in INFL, a possibility that is realized if we identify PRO and AGR, as seems plausible, given that they have the same features. We return to this question in chapter 3.

45.   Cf. Jaeggli (1980b). We return to the question in chapter 4. The tendency to take *he* to be distinct in reference from *John* is somewhat reduced when emphatic reflexives are added, as in "John would prefer his going to the movie himself." Jacqueline Guéron raises the question whether one might relate the Avoid Pronoun principle to the impossibility of such sentences as (i), given the alternative option (ii):

(i)   il$_i$ veut qu'il$_i$ vienne
(ii)   il veut venir
        ("he wants to come")

46.   We return to such examples in chapter 4. On abstract movement in the LF-component in Chinese, see Huang (1980).

47.   Whether "may govern" should be strengthened to "must govern" depends on how we treat the alternation between (7iv) and EQUI examples such as "I want to take part": as presence or absence of *for*, or as variation in properties of *for* related to deletability. We return to the question directly.

48.   We return to a more general consideration of passive and Case-assignment in § 2.7.

49.   One might ask why *of*-insertion is not possible in case (10). A narrow answer is that the *of*-insertion rule would have to be more complex to permit this option, extending the context from $[+N]$ to participles – i.e., to: $[+V]$ but not $[+V, -N]$. A more "functional" explanation might also be pursued. Intuitively, the role of the *of*-insertion rule is to permit certain D-structures that violate the Case Filter but conform to X-bar theory and the projection principle to surface, as would otherwise be impossible. Thus, such structures as "their destruction of the city" or "proud of John" can surface in no other way. But in the case of such structures as (10), Move-α is always an available option so that a complication of the *of*-insertion rule is unnecessary.

50.   The tacit assumption here, with regard to (i), is that strict adjacency is required for Case-assignment in English, excluding both (a) and (b):

(a)   John wants very much Bill to win
(b)   John believes sincerely Bill to be a fool

But the apparent similarity is illusory if the comments that follow in the text are accurate.

51.   Some of these verbs do not freely take passive morphology, but others do; e.g., "it was preferred that John leave," "what was wanted was for John to leave" (somewhat marginal, but much better than the ungrammatical (19)).

52.   As noted earlier, languages use other marked options to permit phonetically-realized subjects of infinitives to surface; e.g., nominative subjects in Portuguese with infinitives with AGR, dative subjects of indirect questions in Russian, prepositional phrase subjects in Hebrew. See note 25.

53.   For discussion, see Bresnan (1976), Postal (1977a).

54.   And if finite, indicative or subjunctive, a somewhat marginal question in English that I will ignore.

55.   In cases (iv) and (v), t is the trace of the *wh*-phrase.

56.   I am indebted to Maria-Rita Manzini for bringing these examples to my attention, in this connection.

57.   We return to questions concerning the analysis of EQUI and the status of *for*.

58.   It has been pointed out by a number of linguists (Gilles Fauconnier, Nathalie van Bockstaele, and others) that these requirements seem less strict in the Romance languages

than in English. Rochette (1980), developing ideas of Bordelois (1974) and Joan Bresnan, suggests that the difference may be traced to the fact that infinitival complements are NPs in these languages, control being freer in the case of PRO that is structurally more remote from the verb. See Manzini (1980) for further discussion from a different point of view and Lightfoot (1979, 1980) for discussion, of the status of infinitives in the history of English.
59.   Cf. Chomsky (1977a, introduction; and OB). Note that "John was promised [t to win]" is excluded by the government requirement 2.4.1.(2i) for trace.
60.   As Manzini (1980) points out, this is possible for passives but not for intransitives, as illustrated in (i)–(iii):

(i)   they decreased the price [to help the poor]
(ii)   the price was decreased [to help the poor]
(iii)   *the price decreased [to help the poor]

Thus there is some reason to suppose that passives are "agentive" in a sense in which other related constructions are not, whether or not they have an agent phrase.
61.   Cf. Jackendoff (1972).
62.   These (rather elusive) facts are noted by Mohanan (1980), who relates them to apparently much firmer facts in Malayalam and other languages.
63.   Outside its own VP, that is; compare (2).
64.   See, e.g., Hale, Jeanne and Platero (1977); Nash (1980).
65.   There has been much insightful study of similar questions in work that I will not attempt to survey, particularly, in work by Dwight Bolinger, J.R. Ross, and others.
66.   This is obvious in cases (i) and (ii), where the trace is the direct object of the verb of the embedded clause, but not in case (iii), if the analysis of relative clauses is [$_{NP}$ NP $\overline{S}$], as is sometimes assumed. In this case too, the trace is governed by the head noun of the full NP under a modification of the notion of "government" to which we return in §3.2.2. I will leave the matter open, since it is not clear that anything turns on the question of whether the trace of extraposition is indeed governed. See chapters 4 and 5 for further discussion of trace government.
67.   There are many open and much-debated questions concerning the subjacency condition that I will not discuss here, though I will return to some of them later on. It has been proposed that there is a much more intimate link between bounding and binding theories than I am assuming here (cf. Wilkins (1977, 1979), Koster (1978b,c), (1980)); I will not discuss these possibilities here, but am skeptical, for reasons implicit in the analysis that I am presenting. It has also been proposed that substantial parts of bounding theory can be derived from government theory (cf. Kayne (1980b)); problems concerning this proposal are discussed in Aoun (1980a) with reference to Arabic. I will put aside this question, and also the question of whether subjacency is a requirement on movement or on its output, as proposed by Freidin (1978), and other questions on the nature and scope of the subjacency principle; cf., among others, Marantz (1979b), Engdahl (1980), and the references of §5.3 below.
68.   In some cases of the sort reviewed, judgments are uncertain and other factors intervene. Cf. Guéron (1978) for an important discussion. But the general pattern seems clear enough.
69.   I assume here that relative clause structures are of the form [$_{NP}$ NP $\overline{S}$]. The assumption is not essential to the argument, which goes through under other possible analyses.
70.   On such constructions, see Rouveret (1978) and references cited there.
71.   The interpretation with the extraposed phrase associated with *several men* is also excluded, as has frequently been observed; perhaps because of the ambiguity that would otherwise result. Cf. Guéron, *op. cit.*, among other discussions relevant to this question.
72.   I am assuming that "across-the-board" phenomena (cf. Williams (1978)) do not involve a single movement rule applying to paired positions; cf. Taraldsen (1979), George (1980), Sjoblom (1980).

73.   In pairs of the form (8), the distinction between case (i) and case (ii) is often unclear, as noted by Ross (1967). But where there is a clear distinction in judgment, it is in the direction indicated in (8). It seems to me reasonable to assume that these configurations too illustrate (though weakly) the distinction between movement and construal, and that other facts, as yet poorly understood, interfere to cloud the issue. For an argument to the contrary, see Koster (1978b,c).

74.   An actual advertising slogan, in this case.

75.   The relevance of these examples was pointed out by Marie-Thérèse Vinet.

76.   The earliest version of trace theory in the current sense is in Chomsky (1977a, chapter 3), which appeared in Anderson and Kiparsky (1973) and was circulated in 1970. The theory is developed in various ways in MIT dissertations of the early 1970s: Wasow (1972, 1979), Selkirk (1972), and particularly Fiengo (1974, 1977, 1979); and much other work of the past several years.

77.   Cf. Burzio (1981) for discussion of *there* in a related framework; see also the the references cited there, particularly Milsark (1974, 1977), Stowell (1978). Also Couquaux (1980), (forthcoming).

78.   Pointed out to me by Guiseppe Longobardi. We return to consideration of such structures in § 4.5.

79.   Thus, depth of embedding appears to be a factor in determining permissible coindexing between a pronoun in S and a noun that appears in the specification of the category of a variable in the pre-S position in LF. Compare, for example, the sentences (i)–(iii):

(i)   which pictures of John did he like?
(ii)   which picture of the woman John married did he like?
(iii)   which people who John liked did he meet?

It is much more natural to take *John* and *he* to be coreferential in (ii) and (iii) than in (i). Further questions arise in the case of (iv) and (v):

(iv)   he attacked someone who John likes
(v)   someone who John likes, he attacked

In (iv), *he* and *John* are disjoint in reference, presumably because *he* c-commands *John*, as in (vi):

(vi)   he attacked a friend of John's

Assuming the rule QR that forms the LF-representation (vii) for (iv), and assuming further that disjoint reference is determined after the application of this rule, if (iv) is to be distinguished from (v) and considered parallel to (vi) in terms of c-command at the LF-level, we are apparently led to assume that QR places the quantifier phrase within rather than outside of S:

(vii)   for some x, x a person who John likes, he attacked x

This assumption, however, raises further problems in the case of wide scope (e.g., "everyone thinks he attacked someone who John likes," if *someone* can have wider scope than *everyone*; and many other more complex cases of this type involving multiple *wh*-constructions and other structures).

The examples above are due to Craig Thiersch. For recent discussion of a range of similar problems, see Reinhart (1976, 1979b), Higginbotham (1979a,c), Brody (1979), van Riemsdijk and Williams (1980), Aoun, Sportiche, Vergnaud and Zubizarreta (1980).

Other examples raise questions about the adequacy of a copying account in place of reconstruction of some sort. Consider, for example, cases of the type illustrated in 2.4.1.(17), such as (viii):

(viii) · it is [PRO to be 18 years old] that everyone wants most

The proper interpretation of PRO would have to involve reconstruction rather than copying if the focus element in clefts is base-generated in place. The point is even clearer in (ix), where a copying analysis is out of the question:

(ix) [PRO to be 18 years old] is what everyone wants most

For discussion of this issue, see Burzio (1981).

80.   For some discussion, suggesting that Theory Ia is preferable in this regard, see Chomsky (1980b, chapter 4). See note 94.

81.   I will not consider the internal structure of the lexicon here. While failure to consider this matter does not seem too serious with regard to the topics with which I am concerned in the case of the small selection of languages that have motivated most of this work, this is not true in general.

82.   For argument that lexical insertion should rather be at S-structure, see Otero (1976), den Besten (1976), Fiengo (1979).

83.   On this matter, see the discussion of "minor predicates" in Rouveret and Vergnaud (1980). George (1980) argues that "preposition" is not a natural class, and that those prepositional particles that are transparent to selectional features of verbs (i.e., the verb selects the object of the particle) are Case-markers, not prepositions in the X-bar system. Distinctions in status in this connection between prepositions assigning dative in French and Spanish are discussed in Jaeggli (1980b), following Vergnaud (1974). I am assuming that PP-complements receive a θ-role. Little turns on this decision in the present context.

84.   It might be that the complement for *eager* is *for*-NP or *for*-$\bar{\text{S}}$, as in "I was eager for the opportunity," "what I was eager for was for you to win," with a rule of *for*-deletion accounting for "I was eager for you to win." On such rules, see Brame (1980).

85.   If we accept the approach to "subject sentences" outlined in Koster (1978a), then there will be no movement rule applying to the disjunction: NP or clause.

86.   Cf. Aoun (1979b) for a more general approach to Case-assignment incorporating some ideas of Rouveret and Vergnaud (1980), with applications to Classical and Lebanese Arabic. Aoun shows that on his assumptions, VSO languages represent a marked (and presumably unstable) option and draws a number of other consequences. Cf. also Emonds (1980) on the status of VSO languages. Aoun extends similar notions to phonology in (1979c). Cf. also van Riemsdijk (1980). On the adjacency condition, see also Fiengo (1979).

    The adjacency principle as stated is too strong to hold in general. Thus, in SOV languages it is common for PP and other elements to intervene between the V and its NP-complement. I will not pursue the problem of developing a more adequate general version of the idea here.

87.   Another possibility is that the verb and the primary object form an internal VP (cf. Williams (1974)) which assigns Case to the secondary object. Cf. OB; also §3.2.2, below.

88.   It follows then that in languages that allow free omission of pronouns, the missing element is not PRO. It might be that such languages are W^*-languages in the sense of Hale (1978) and that, as he suggests, such languages do not have empty categories at all, hence do not have the rule Move-α. Cf. §2.8.

89.   We have given only an informal account of this property of Case-assignment, to which we return in §3.2.2. What must be assumed, clearly, is that there is no Exceptional Case-marking across clause boundary for secondary Case, as a matter of principle. This is quite natural, given the semantics of double-object verbs. We return to a gap in this argument in §2.6 (cf. 2.6.(20)–(22)).

90.   Alternatively, the embedded phrase might be taken to be [$_{\overline{VP}}$ to VP], with a rule similar to control to assign the subject of $\overline{VP}$ at LF. As noted earlier (§2.1), this approach

introduces a superfluous category $\overline{VP}$ with complex properties, and in addition suffers from the defects of (8ii).

91.   Nor is it a GF-$\bar{\theta}$ in the sense of the preceding discussion, though it would be if we adopt a variant of GR' involving raising to object in essentially the sense of Postal (1974), with base-generated $[_{NP}\ e]$ as object of the verb. This variant is ruled out by the requirement that trace be governed (cf. 2.4.1.(2i)), unless we require $\overline{S}$-deletion in addition to raising, in which case raising is superfluous. Such $\overline{S}$-deletion would have to be restricted to the case in which the base-generated object is a non-argument or the θ-criterion will be violated. There is surely no point in complicating the grammar by extending the class of $\overline{S}$-deletion cases to include the context: $V[_{NP}\ e]-$; i.e., exactly the context that violates the projection principle and θ-criterion. Cf. also note 108.

92.   Note, however, that the interpolated adverbial cannot relate to the matrix clause in such sentences as "John promised Bill that Tom sincerely would win," "John preferred for Bill sincerely to win." These are much lower in acceptability than (21). The reason may be that $\overline{S}$ is an absolute barrier to such interpretation while S is a weaker barrier, and that $\overline{S}$ is in fact deleted or non-functional in such sentences as (21), in accordance with the theory of Exceptional Case-marking that we have been assuming.

93.   Baltin notes such pairs as "persuade him though I may to be polite," versus *"expect him though I may to be polite." Again, while the distinction is not sharp, the tendency is in the predicted direction. See Williams (1979) for additional evidence.

94.   Following Lasnik and Kupin (1977), we may think of an idiom rule for an idiom with a verbal head as a rule adding the string $\alpha V \gamma$ to the phrase marker of each terminal string $\alpha \beta \gamma$, where β is the idiom, now understanding a phrase marker to be set of strings. As a matter of execution, we might assume that the idiom rule assigns special features to the verb which, at the LF level, will determine the meaning of the idiom. Some idioms require the verb to have a lexical complement at LF (e.g., *kick the bucket = die ≠ the bucket was kicked t*); others permit the idiomatic interpretation to be assigned indirectly through trace, as in *good care was taken of the orphans, how much care was taken t of the orphans* (at LF: "how much x, x care, x was taken t of the orphans," where x is coindexed with t). See Fiengo (1974) for some discussion of the distinction. Thus idioms in general have the formal properties of non-idiomatic structures, and appear either in D-structure or S-structure form, but not only in S-structure or LF-form. D-structure, not S-structure or LF, appears to be the natural place for the operation of idiom rules, since it is only at D-structure that idioms are uniformly not "scattered" and it is only the D-structure forms that always exist for the idiom (with marked exceptions), S-structure sometimes being inaccessible to idiomatic interpretation. Thus at D-structure, idioms can be distinguished as subject or not subject to Move-α, determining the asymmetry just noted.

It may be that the fundamental distinction is between idioms that require a subject (such as *kick the bucket*) and those that are strictly internal to VP (such as *take care of*) and can therefore freely undergo Move-α. On this assumption, one can perhaps explain some important observations of Kayne (1975) on the two types of idioms in French, particularly, in causative constructions where there is no overt movement but where only the non-passivizable idioms may appear. See Jaeggli (1980c) where this suggestion is proposed and developed.

It is not at all clear that there is a sharp distinction between idioms and figurative interpretations of a variety of types. These are questions that deserve much more study, as do properties of idioms in general. Cf. Higgins (undated) and Vergnaud (forthcoming).

See chapter 6 for a slightly different interpretation of θ-role assignment in idioms.

95.   Cf. Higginbotham (1979b) for a much more far-reaching analysis of the semantics of reciprocals.

96.   Perhaps these operators are also quantifiers. Cf. Chomsky (1977a, chapter 1), Cushing (1979) on definite determiners, and a considerable literature on indefinites.

97.   In the terminology of Williams (1980b), subject is an "external argument" of the verb, while complements are internal arguments.

98.   There are issues at stake here, but we can put them aside now. The statement is accurate if VP appears only in the expansion of S. This would follow, for example, if the S-bar system is regarded as a projection of verb and if the expansion of $\bar{X}$ as ... X ... is restricted to

maximal projections in ... If the assumption is wrong, as we have been assuming, then it still may be that VP appears only in the expansion of S. If, contrary to our assumptions here, VP also appears as a complement, then the statement in the text must be modified in obvious ways that are not relevant here.

99.   More strictly, of the copular VP construction. This assumption is not only natural, but enters into an explanation for the fact, noted in Chomsky (1965), that verbs of subject control lack passives under certain conditions. See Chomsky (1977a, introduction), OB, and § 2.4.3 above for some discussion.

100.   The agent phrase need not be a *by*-phrase. Thus, in "it is known to everyone that S," the phrase *to everyone* has the same function as the *by*-phrase in "it is believed by everyone that S." Note that a generalization of θ-theory beyond the framework assumed here is necessary to accommodate the role of the optional adverbial in (5i). On the θ-role of agent phrases, see Fiengo (1979).

101.   Nevertheless, there is some reason to believe that passives are "agentive" in a sense in which other related constructions are not, even where there is no expressed agent. Cf. note 60 above.

102.   We consider here the derived nominal, not the mass noun *destruction* as in "all that destruction was awful" (compare *"all that destruction of the city was awful"). Note that (iv) does not correspond to the generic "barbarians destroy," a construction that lacks an associated derived nominal. We also disregard possible elliptical interpretations of (iv) and the associated clause.

103.   The dissociation of movement and passive interpretation is also illustrated in the Romance impersonal constructions noted in § 2.4.1 (cf. (18)), to which we return in § 4.5. For discussion of constraints on NP-movement in NP, see M. Anderson (1977), Kayne (1980b).

104.   Fiengo (1974, 1979) and Burzio (1981) assume that (ii) derives by Move-α from a construction analogous to (i), considerably improving earlier proposals to this effect. If this is correct, then θ-role assignment and grammatical relations are still more closely related.

105.   Assuming $\bar{\text{S}}$-deletion in (16iii–v), we expect to find that heavy NP-shift is applicable, as in "they'd consider foolish any candidate who would take the trouble to run in every primary," corresponding to (iv). Cf. 2.4.2.(22i).

106.   Cf. Schein (1980) for discussion of this pattern in Russian, though he suggests somewhat different conclusions.

107.   This is the gap referred to in note 89.

108.   Similar and perhaps related questions arise in connection with such verbs as *force* that take NP-clause complements, as in (i):

(i)   they forced – John –[$_S$ PRO to wait]

One would expect, then, that such examples as (ii) would be ungrammatical:

(ii)   (a) they forced it to rain (by seeding the clouds)
        (b) they forced better care to be taken of the orphans (by passing new laws)

But the examples (ii) seem moderately acceptable. It may be that these examples are only derivatively generated (in the sense of Chomsky (1965, p. 227; 1972, pp. 27f.)). Evidence supporting this conclusion is that these examples are resistant to further grammatical operations; cf. (iii):

(iii)   (a) *it was forced to rain
        (b) *better care was forced to be taken of the orphans

The same may be true of examples such as (iv) (discussed in Postal (1974, 1977a), Bresnan (1976)), which should also be ungrammatical if *prevent* assigns a θ-role to its object:

(iv)   they prevented it from raining

In this case too, further grammatical operations are blocked:

(v)   *it was prevented from raining

The example (iv) has been proposed as an argument for raising-to-object, but quite apart from its dubious status, it is difficult to see how any argument can be based on it, since the rules for generating it would appear to be idiosyncratic, even if it is accepted as grammatical.

On derivative generation, see George (1980), particularly, his "law of aggravation."
109.   Other examples might be treated in a similar way, but without obvious motivation. Thus consider (i), (ii), where *him = John*:

(i)   John turned the child against him (*himself)
(ii)   John turned the argument against himself (*him)

Considerations of binding theory would lead us to assign a clausal structure to the complement of *turn* in (i) but not in (ii). But there is no independent LF-form *John-turned-clause*. The problem is not one of finding a descriptive device within the present framework, but of motivating it – that is, the problem is to gain some understanding of the nature of these constructions.

In some cases, a clausal structure, involving some kind of predication in the sense of Williams (1980a), seems quite plausible for examples of type (i); e.g., (iii), (iv):

(iii)   he kept the car in the garage (the car is in the garage)
(iv)   he left the table near the armchair (the table is near the armchair)

In others, the device seems quite artificial, e.g., (i), or (v) and (vi), where choice of *himself* or *him* in the case of coreference seems somewhat indeterminate:

(v)   he pulled the table towards him
(vi)   he pushed the book away from him

Cf. § 5.2. for further discussion.
110.   To say that *easy* or *certain* is "dyadic" is a bit misleading, in the present framework. Rather, *easy* and *certain* assign a θ-role to their clausal complement and take part on the compositional assignment of a θ-role to the matrix subject. On (29iv), see § 5.4.
111.   We might then expect coordinate structures as counterparts to (31) in some languages. This is the case in Arabic, Aoun observes. Manzini (1980) suggests treating PRO in (32) as the AGR element for adjectives, and generalizes this idea in an interesting way to the entire class of control structures. See also Stowell (1980a).
112.   The following remarks on *SEEM* and *SEEM'* are prompted by problems noted by Luigi Burzio. See Burzio (1981) for discussion of the biconditional (40), to which we return in the next section. On these topics, see also Borer (1979, 1980). We return to these examples from a different point of view in chapter 6.
113.   There are, of course, exceptions; e.g., "John received a book from Bill." But there seem to be few transitive verbs – that is, verbs that assign Case to their grammatical objects – that assign no θ-role to their subject, e.g., *KILL*, like *kill* except that it permits "it KILLed John" with impersonal *it*, meaning that John was killed. There are some exceptions among idioms (e.g., "it rained cats and dogs"), but the observation seems to hold quite generally. Cf. Hall (1965). Note that this observation does not exclude "ergative verbs" in the sense of Burzio (1981), which assign to their grammatical object the θ-role of subject. These verbs are not Case-assigners, hence not transitive in the relevant sense. We return to such constructions in § 4.5.
114.   More precisely, in our terms, participates in assigning a θ-role to the subject of the VP of which it is the head.
115.   The fact is quite general, holding of the empty category in COMP not only in

purposives, but in all the constructions of the type studied in Chomsky (1977b), and of course normal relative clauses. On the other hand, PRO in S in these constructions can be arbitrary in reference. In chapter 4, we suggest that in pro-drop languages PRO can appear as the subject of tensed clauses, but here too the arbitrary interpretation is excluded. The latter, then, is restricted to subject of infinitival or gerund. See the discussion of 4.5.(25). See chapter 6 for an approach that may provide an explanation for the fact.

In the case of purposives, there is significant evidence to support the analysis involving movement-to-COMP that we are assuming here (cf. OB, appendix; Chomsky (1980b)). Further evidence based on binding properties will appear in § 3.2.3 (cf. note 54 of chapter 3). In a review of Chomsky (1980b), P.H. Matthews (1980) argues that this analysis of purposives is undermined by the fact that PRO in COMP cannot be arbitrary in reference, as noted in OB. His argument deserves some attention, since it is far from unique. The work to which he refers noted some curious properties of purposive constructions that had not previously been investigated or even observed, to my knowledge. Extension to these constructions of an approach that was independently motivated in Chomsky (1977b) explained some of these properties, but left one unresolved, namely, the failure of arbitrary reference for the non-subject "gap" in purposives. Matthews' conclusion that this inadequacy undermines the approach entirely follows only if we adopt the principle that if something is unexplained, then nothing is explained. His argument might have some merit if the problem left unresolved were specific to the movement-to-COMP analysis that resolves the other problems, but of course it is not. The same problem arises, so far as is known, on any other analysis of these constructions. One might even argue to the contrary that the movement-to-COMP analysis is actually supported by the fact that the non-subject gap in purposive constructions may not be arbitrary in interpretation, since the problem is now localized to the COMP position, where it arises quite generally: in relatives, clefts, complex adjectival constructions, topicalization, etc.

Arguments of the sort that Matthews presents are unfortunately all too common in the linguistic literature. They are based on assumptions that can only be regarded as pathological. Any non-trivial proposal is likely to unearth new problems, while solving others. The present example is a case in point: new problems were discovered, and some were resolved by the principle proposed, which, as noted, was independently motivated elsewhere. If the fact that some problems (in this case, newly-discovered problems) remain open undermines the proposal, then all rational inquiry must cease. Surely this is obvious.

116. On these matters, see Wasow (1977), S. Anderson (1977), and the references of note 35, above.

117. See Thiersch (1978).

118. McCarthy (1976).

119. Cf. Hale (1973). I omit the Navajo forms and the required morphological changes.

120. See Keenan (1979) for an illuminating survey of so-called passive constructions, which he characterizes in terms of identity of semantic relations in the active-passive pair when names are in argument position (thus, *John saw Bill* is synonymous with *Bill was seen* (*by John*) but *many arrows didn't hit the target* has a different range of meaning from *the target wasn't hit by many arrows*). Keenan's own proposal for the analysis of passives in effect treats *believe . . . to be incompetent* as a transitive verb with the object *Bill* in *I believe Bill to be incompetent*; similarly, in related constructions. Clearly, recursion must be introduced into the system, since there are infinitely many propositions of the form NP-*to*-VP that yield such "transitive verbs" as V-NP-*to*-VP, where V-*to*-VP is, in effect, the transitive verb, and NP is its object. See Chomsky (1955) for development of an approach based on generalized transformations incorporating the recursive property and adopting this "complex verb" analysis.

121. Williams (1980b) observes that some of these verbs do not allow the "extraposed" S to appear in the pre-verbal position (e.g., *"that S was held (reasoned)," as compared with "that S was believed"). Thus we cannot assume that in general there is passive-fronting followed by extraposition in such cases.

122. Cf. Burzio (1981) for discussion of such examples, which he argues are base-

generated in this form, with *Giovanni* optionally moved to subject position leaving a trace that can then be "spelled out" by an emphatic pronoun, as in (i), where *lui* fills the position of the trace left by *Giovanni*:

(i)   Giovanni fu mandato lui ad occuparsi di quella faccenda
          ("Giovanni was sent himself to deal with that matter")

The behavior of the Italian emphatic pronouns is rather different from that of their English counterparts. Burzio argues that quite generally, they fill the position of trace, and that passive structures such as (i) therefore differ crucially from such copula-adjective constructions as (ii), which he takes to be much less acceptable than (i):

(ii)   Giovanni era orgoglioso lui di aver terminato la tesi
          ("Giovanni was proud himself to have completed the thesis")

The difference of acceptability seems to me fairly clear in the English counterparts, where perhaps it may be attributed to derivation of (i) from (iii), with Move-α applying to *Giovanni* instead of *Giovanni himself*, an option that is impossible in (ii):

(iii) $[_{NP} e]$ was sent Giovanni himself to deal with that matter

123.   Cf. § 4.5 for further discussion of these structures. See also Burzio (1981), and for a lexicalist analysis, Grimshaw (1980). Some problems in the latter, or in any analysis that does not involve movement or some equivalent and that does not include his tripartite classification of verbs as transitive, intransitive and ergative, are discussed by Burzio (1981).
124.   The device may be assignment of a new string to the phrase-marker, the latter taken to be a class of strings as in Lasnik and Kupin (1977). See note 94.
125.   Cf. Davison (1980) for an illuminating discussion.
126.   I owe example (iii) to Hagit Borer. See Borer (1979) for discussion of Hebrew passive. Note that Hebrew does not require that the subject position be filled, as by English *it* or German *es*. Cf. §§2.1-2, 4.5.
127.   This was pointed out to me by Alec Marantz.
128.   There are auxiliary assumptions, discussed earlier: that the θ-criterion holds at D-structure, that a θ-role is assigned to every position governed by the head verb apart from idioms, and that movement into idioms is impossible, either by virtue of their lexical status or because the idiom chunk has the θ-role the symbol " $\#$ ".
129.   See note 86.
130.   As noted earlier, we might look at the matter a bit differently, taking these categories to be not properties of languages but of subsystems of languages. I will disregard this possibility here.
131.   The following discussion, largely excerpted from Chomsky (1980c), adapts some recent work of Farmer (1980). See also Otsu and Farmer (1980) and Kayne (1980d,e) for further discussion of some of the issues that arise, often reaching quite different conclusions from those I am assuming here.
132.   This is an example of 2.7.(27iii).
133.   Note that we are by-passing a problem concerning assignment of nominative Case in Japanese.
134.   This proposal has been developed by relational grammarians; cf. Aissen and Perlmutter (1976), Postal (1977b). I am indebted to Paul Postal for these references. See Marantz (1981) for extensive discussion.
135.   Whether the rule Move-α may apply when it need not apply depends on how we treat such sentences as "that the conclusion was false was believed." See the references of note 23. The question does not arise in the case of (6) in any meaningful way.
136.   I have said little or nothing about many other important questions, among them, the status of PP-movement, minor movement rules and root transformations in the sense of

Emonds (1976), movement rules in the PF-component (on movement rules in the LF-component, see chapter 4). There is no obvious reason why application of Move-α in the PF-component should leave trace. Fiengo (1979) argues that minor movement rules (or more accurately, a similar category) are restricted to the PF-component and that other applications of Move-α are excluded from this component. There is a great deal more to say about these topics, but I will not pursue them here.

137.   Again, we ignore other kinds of trace. The fact that these types of empty category are in exhaustive complementary distribution suggests the possibility of a more abstract inquiry into the concept "empty category" and its subvarieties. We return to this topic in chapter 6.

138.   See Vergnaud and Zubizarreta (1980) for a formalization of similar ideas that assumes an abstract VP constituent at S- and D-structure in languages of both configurational and non-configurational types, with realization in surface structure only in the former type; and Kayne (1980c, d) for a quite different approach to this range of problems. Recall also the suggestion of Aoun (1979b) that VP appears as a continuous constituent in SVO languages but as a discontinuous constituent in VSO languages. On the latter type, see Emonds (1980).

139.   It is often regarded as obvious that this is so, but the point is much harder to establish than is commonly assumed. See Chomsky (1975, chapter 2), (1978), and (1980b, chapter 3), for discussion of some fallacious arguments. See also Miller and Chomsky (1963), Chomsky and Lasnik (1977) on ways in which functional considerations might be expected to enter into the theory of grammar, with some examples. Cf. Weinberg and Berwick (forthcoming) for discussion of many fallacies in interpretation of both experimental and mathematical results relating to parsing theories, in particular, results concerning parsability of context-free languages. As they observe, the experimental results are compatible with just about any grammatical theory, depending on what processing systems are assumed, and the mathematical results, if they have empirical relevance at all, suggest that functional considerations should favor extremely rich theories that provide short grammars for given languages. See chapter 4, note 39.

140.   Cf. Chomsky (1975, 1980b). Also the discussion by several authors of excerpts from Chomsky (1980b) in *The Behavioral and Brain Sciences*, vol. 3, number 1, March 1980, and articles and discussion in Piattelli-Palmarini (1980).

Chapter 3

On government and binding

3.1. The OB-framework

So far, I have been assuming the theory of government and binding outlined in OB. The binding theory characterizes two domains as opaque in
the sense that an anaphor cannot be free in these domains and a pronoun
is disjoint in reference from an "antecedent" within them. These two
notions of "freedom" are generalized in the OB-framework in terms of the
notion "free(i)" (cf. OB, appendix). Thus, anaphors and pronouns cannot
be free(i) in an opaque domain, in the sense made precise there. The two
opaque domains are: (1) the subject of a tensed sentence (the Nominative
Island Condition: NIC); (2) the c-command domain of the subject of an
NP or S (the (Specified) Subject Condition: SSC). These two binding
principles have a wide range of application, and relate in an interesting way
to the theory of movement in that the transparent (non-opaque) positions
within clauses are those from which movement is free out of the clause
(namely, COMP and subject of infinitive).

Let us briefly review the major examples of opacity. Consider the
structures (1) and (2), clauses and NPs, respectively, with only the basic
structure exhibited:

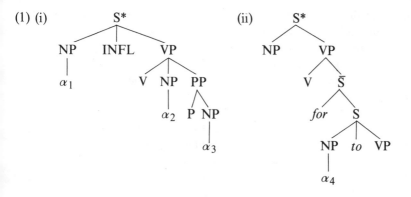

(1) (i), (ii)

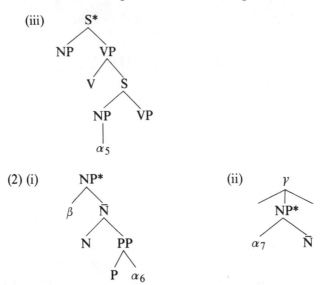

Where the α_i's are anaphors (say, *each other*), α_1 cannot be free in S* if INFL = [[+Tense], AGR] (NIC: *"we thought [$_{S*}$ each other gave the books to Bill]"); α_2 must be bound by α_1 (SSC: "they introduced each other to Bill," *"they expected [$_{S*}$ me to introduce each other to Bill]"); α_3 must be bound by either α_1 or α_2 (SSC: "they pointed the guns at each other," with ambiguous antecedent; *"they expected [$_{S*}$ me to point the gun at each other]"); α_4 cannot be free in S* (SSC: "they'd prefer [for each other to win]", *"we expected [$_{S*}$ Bill to prefer [for each other to win]]"); α_5 cannot be free in S*(SSC: "we believed [each other to be incompetent]", *"we expected [$_{S*}$ him to believe [each other to be incompetent]]").

In (2), α_6 cannot be free in NP* if β is a subject NP (SSC: "their stories about each other," *"we heard [$_{NP*}$ his stories about each other]," "we heard [$_{NP*}$ some stories about each other]"); α_7 cannot be free in the domain of the subject of γ, whether γ = S or NP (SSC: "we read [$_{NP*}$ each other's books]," *"they expected [$_{\gamma}$ me to read [$_{NP*}$ each other's books]]," *"they read [$_{\gamma}$ my reviews of [$_{NP*}$ each other's books]]," "they read [$_{\gamma}$ reviews of [$_{NP*}$ each other's books]]").

The instances of (2) illustrate the fact that it is a configurational property – presumably, c-command – that determines the operation of the binding theory, not a requirement that anaphors (or pronominals, see below) search for subjects or objects as antecedents, in some sense of this notion that has any independent sense apart from the configurational properties. Thus, in nominals corresponding to verbal constructions the antecedent-anaphor relation holds when the anaphor is within the head $\bar{N}$ (as in "their [$_{\bar{N}}$ hatred of each other]," "their [$_{\bar{N}}$ admiration for each other's work]," etc.), but not when it is outside this $\bar{N}$, in which case c-command would be violated (e.g., *"their departure after each other's parties," etc.). Similarly, when the configurational properties hold, the relation of the possessive NP to the nominal head may be quite arbitrary (e.g., "their attitudes towards each other" ("... towards each other's friends"), "their pleasure in each other's company," "their stories about each other," etc.). While other factors intervene leading to a range of uncertainty of judgment, nevertheless the basic operative principle appears to be as just indicated.

If we have $[_{VP}$ V-*ing* $\alpha_6]$ instead of $\bar{N}$ in (2i), the situation is essentially the same. Suppose that we have $[_{VP}$ V-*ing* ... $]$ in place of $\bar{N}$ in (2ii), as in (3):

(3)   *we preferred $[_{NP*}$ each other's reading the book$]$

This is ungrammatical, contrary to what is predicted in the OB-framework.

Where α_i is a pronoun, the situation is reversed; it must be free where the corresponding anaphor cannot be. The one exception is α_7 in (2ii), which may be bound in γ ("they read $[_{NP*}$ their books$]$"). Thus, *she* (*her*) may refer to Mary in S*, NP* and *he* (*him*) is disjoint in reference from *John* and not in the scope of *everyone* in (4):

(4)   (i) Mary thought $[_{S*}$ she gave the books to Bill$]$ ((li), *she* = α_1)
       (ii) John (everyone) introduced him to Bill   ((li), *he* = α_2)
       (iii) Mary expected $[_{S*}$ me to introduce her to Bill$]$ ((1i), *her* = α_2)
       (iv) everyone introduced John to him   ((li), *him* = α_3)
       (v) Mary expected $[_{S*}$ me to point the gun at her$]$ ((li), *her* = α_3)
       (vi) John (everyone) would prefer $[$for him to win$]$ ((lii), *him* = α_4)[1]
       (vii) Mary expected $[_{S*}$ Bill to prefer $[$for her to win$]]$ ((lii), *her* = α_4)
       (viii) John (everyone) believed $[$him to be incompetent$]$ ((liii), *him* = α_5)
       (ix) Mary expected $[$Bill to believe $[$her to be incompetent$]]$ ((liii), *her* = α_5)
       (x) John's (everyone's) stories about him   ((2i), *him* = α_6)
       (xi) Mary heard $[_{NP*}$ Bill's stories about her$]$ ((2i), *her* = α_6)
       (xii) John (everyone) heard $[_{NP*}$ some stories about him$]$ ((2i), *him* = α_6)[2]

These examples are counterparts, respectively, to those involving *each other*.

R-expressions (e.g., names and variables) must be free everywhere. NP-trace behaves exactly like the anaphor *each other* in (1), but meets additional constraints, as we have seen in chapter 2. Thus, as α_3 NP-trace cannot have α_2 as antecedent, a consequence of the θ-criterion and the projection principle, which prevent movement to the subcategorized position. Apart from this, NP-trace can appear as α_3 – including parallel cases where α_2 is not present – only under conditions that permit pre-position stranding (cf. §5.2). NP-trace cannot appear as α_4 because of the government requirement for trace; we return to this class of cases below. Conditions on preposition stranding exclude NP-trace from the position of α_6 in (2), and other conditions exclude it from the α_7 position in (2); cf. 3.2.1. (18). Thus the only positions open to NP-trace are α_1, α_2 and α_5 (and the parallel structures with a raising predicate in the matrix sentence S*), and α_3 subject to conditions on preposition stranding. In these positions, NP-trace exhibits the same behavior as overt anaphors.

PRO is like other anaphors in its behavior with regard to opacity, but it must meet the additional condition that it be ungoverned (cf. §§2.4.1–2). Its properties are only partially captured in the OB-framework, as we have seen. Note incidentally that PRO may also appear in INFL as AGR, and possibly in COMP, depending on the resolution of the questions discussed in §2.6.

These are the basic examples to be dealt with in the theory of binding, though there are other cases to be considered as well, raising further questions to which we return. In chapter 4, we will turn to some additional constraints on variables in the position of α_1 of (1).

While the OB-framework of assumptions has many desirable properties and considerable empirical support, nevertheless there are a number of technical and conceptual problems, some of which have arisen in the preceding discussion. The technical problems have to do primarily with some unexplained differences between PRO, on the one hand, and NP-trace and overt anaphors, on the other (the distinction between the latter two categories being reduced now to Case theory). The positions of PRO are determined in large measure by the binding principles for anaphors. PRO, like other anaphors, may appear as subject of infinitive or NP, a fact that figured crucially in support of the projection principle. But the antecedent-anaphor relation of PRO is not subject to these principles in the case of "long distance" control, as in (5):[3]

(5)
$$\text{they thought I said that } \left[\text{PRO} \left\{ \begin{array}{l} \text{to feed} \\ \text{feeding} \end{array} \right\} \text{each other} \right] \text{would be difficult}$$

In (5), *they* is antecedent of PRO, violating SSC in the OB-framework. Furthermore, the binding principles of OB do not explain why PRO may appear in certain positions from which trace is excluded, as in (6), where *t* is the trace of *John*; and why PRO is excluded from certain positions that accept overt anaphors, as in (7):

(6)   (i) (a) John tried [PRO to win]
       (b) *John tried [t to win]
       (c) it is difficult [PRO to win]
       (d) *John is difficult [t to win]
      (ii) (a) John wanted [PRO to win]
       (b) *John wanted [t to win]

       (c) *John was wanted [t to win]
   (iii) (a) it is unclear [how PRO to solve the problem]
       (b) *John is unclear [how t to solve the problem]
(7)   (i) *they expected that pictures of PRO would be on sale
     (ii) they expected that pictures of each other would be on sale

In the examples (6ib, iib) we know that trace is impossible from the fact that non-arguments cannot appear in the matrix subject position. In OB, it was suggested that (7i) is excluded by a subjacency requirement for empty categories, but this is falsified by long distance control, as in (5).

A principle was suggested in §2.4 to account for the examples of (7), namely, the principle that PRO must be ungoverned. This constituted one part of a more general principle concerning government of empty categories, the principle 2.4.1.(13) (= 2.9.(4)) which states that an empty category is PRO if and only if it is ungoverned and trace if and only if it is governed. The principle is sufficiently general so that it would not be unreasonable to adopt it as an irreducible principle of the theory of government. Nevertheless, it would be interesting to see to what extent it can be related to other principles of the GB-framework. As we will see, the part referring to PRO is reducible to the principles of binding theory when these are formulated in a way that will overcome the other problems as well.

There are other problems in the OB-framework that are more conceptual in nature. In the first place, there are various redundancies in this system and earlier versions of similar ideas, a fact that provided part of the motivation for the development of very suggestive alternative models by Jan Koster and Richard Kayne.[4] For example, the theory of Case and the theory of binding have rather similar properties. Consider the three basic positions for NP in S: nominative subject of Tense, subject of an infinitive, complement of a verb. The theory of Case singles out the subject of an infinitive as the one position that is not marked for Case. The theory of binding independently selects this position as the single transparent domain.

In a footnote in OB (note 30), I mentioned that one might characterize the properties of PRO in indirect questions and other control structures in terms of a theory of Case rather than a theory of binding by stipulating that PRO cannot have Case. That will permit PRO to appear exactly in the one transparent position, namely, subject of an infinitive. I rejected this approach because it did not generalize to other cases of binding and because the stipulation seemed rather *ad hoc*. Still, the similarity between the structural properties of Case and binding seems more than fortuitous, and raises the question whether opacity cannot somehow be reduced to Case theory just as the Tensed-S (Propositional Island) Condition was reformulated in terms of considerations of Case within the OB-framework, as the NIC.

A related question about the OB-framework is whether there is some explanation for the fact that the two opaque domains should be the subject of a tensed sentence and the c-command domain of the subject of any category. As formulated in OB and earlier work along the same lines, the two opaque domains are in no way related, and neither is particularly motivated except in terms of rather vague functional considerations. Of course, some of the principles of UG must simply be stipulated, at least if the language faculty is an independent cognitive system, and the two binding principles do serve to unify a fairly impressive range of observations and also interact as one would hope with other principles, as noted above. But nevertheless it is reasonable to ask whether there are some more fundamental considerations from which the distribution of transparency and opacity derives.

A third problem arises from a consideration of some asymmetries between the NIC and SSC, and what appears to be a near internal contradiction concerning NIC. Rizzi (1978b) observed that in languages such as Italian that tolerate certain violations of the *wh*-island constraint (namely, violations that follow from taking only $\bar{S}$, not S, to be a bounding node for subjacency in his theory), the SSC does not hold for *wh*-movement, as illustrated in (8):

(8)   tuo fratello, a cui mi domando [che storie abbiano raccontato t], era molto preoccupato
("your brother, to whom I wonder [which stories they told t], was very troubled")

Here the *wh*-phrase *a cui* moves in a single step to its S-structure position from the position marked by the trace *t*, violating the SSC. This violation appears very natural in the light of the similarity between variables and names, as illustrated for example under the conditions of strong crossover in the sense of Wasow (1972, 1979), modifying ideas of Postal (1971). What is more, as Freidin and Lasnik (1979a) point out, the similarity between variables and names revealed by the strong crossover phenomenon extends to the domain of Tense, i.e., to the NIC. In (9), the variable *t* cannot be coindexed with the pronoun *he*:

(9)   (i) who did he say [Mary kissed t]
(ii) who did he say [t kissed Mary]

In this respect, the NIC and SSC are alike: neither applies to variables, which behave in the manner of names in these constructions.

Nevertheless, *wh*-movement does appear to observe the NIC – or, as I will suggest later, a condition rather like it. That is, *wh*-movement out of a clause is impossible from the nominative subject position in constructions in which *wh*-movement is possible from the domain of a subject. Compare, for example, the English translation of (8) with (10):

(10)   the men, who I wonder [which stories t told to your brother], were
        very troubled

In (10), the *wh*-phrase *who* moves from the position marked by *t*, just as
to whom moves from the position marked by *t* in the translation of (8).
Clearly, the status of these sentences is quite different, even for dialects
that mark (8) unacceptable because of a *wh*-island violation. In (10), it
appears that the NIC applies over and above the conditions (subjacency
with S a bounding node, I assume) that lead to *wh*-island violations. Thus
we have an asymmetry between the NIC and the SSC; the former appears
to hold in some manner of *wh*-movement while the latter does not. Furthermore, while examples such as (10) appear to indicate that the NIC holds
of the variable left by *wh*-movement, example (9ii) shows that it does not
hold.

The effect of the NIC (or something like it) on *wh*-movement, as in
(10), cannot be directly observed in Italian because of an interaction with
the pro-drop parameter and its consequences. But it is clear in French
(cf. Sportiche (1979), who extends Rizzi's theory to French), and can be
observed in English as well, as examples (8) and (10) indicate. To detect
the phenomenon is a bit difficult in English because of the effect of the
wh-island condition, which renders the relevant sentences unacceptable
to a greater or lesser degree, but it can nevertheless be observed as in the
examples (8), (10), or in structures in which, for some reason, the *wh*-island
condition is relaxed. In these we find a sharp difference between extraction
from nominative subject and from other positions. Consider the examples
(11):

(11)   (i) this book, I wonder how well John understands
        (ii) these men, I wonder how well John knows
        (iii) what did John wonder how well Bill did
        (iv) what does John know how well Bill did

In each of these cases, the embedded clause is of the form (12), where *t* is
the trace of the element extracted from the clause and we omit the trace of
how (*well*):

(12) $[_{\bar{S}} [\text{how (well)}] [_{S} \text{NP V t}]]$

Consider in contrast the examples (13), with the embedded clause of the
form (14):

(13)   (i) John, I wonder how well understands this book
        (ii) John, I wonder how well knows these men
        (iii) who did John wonder how well did his work
        (iv) who does John know how did his work
(14) $[_{\bar{S}} [\text{how (well)}] [_{S} \text{t V NP}]]$

While the sentences of (11) are perhaps somewhat marginal, such examples as (13) are completely unacceptable, on a par with (10). In short, even in constructions in which the *wh*-island effect is somewhat relaxed, extraction from the *wh*-island is still impossible from the nominative subject position.

These observations indicate that the *wh*-island condition has two quite separate components.[5] One of these relates to the choice of bounding nodes in Rizzi's theory. The second, illustrated by (10) and (13), relates to something else – the NIC, one might suppose, comparing (12) and (14), the latter apparently a violation of the NIC. While *wh*-movement is not constrained by the SSC, it is apparently constrained by the NIC. It is not at all clear, within the OB-framework, why there should be this asymmetry. The fact that the *wh*-trace does not appear to be subject to either the NIC or the SSC in the strong crossover contexts simply extends the problem.

We are, therefore, led to the conclusion that the NIC, in the OB-framework and earlier work along the same lines, expresses a spurious generalization, and that in fact two distinct principles are involved in the category of phenomena that had been classified under the NIC. Pursuing this possibility, let us restrict the NIC proper to the category of phenomena in which we find complete symmetry between the NIC and the SSC. Thus variables are exempt from both conditions, while NP-trace is subject to both. Some distinct principle, then, will account for the fact that *wh*-movement appears to be subject to something like the NIC, as in (10), (13). I will return to this distinct principle – call it "the residue of the NIC" (RES(NIC)) – in chapter 4, where it will be related to the question of government of trace. Where there is symmetry between the NIC and SSC, it is reasonable to assume that the phenomena fall under binding theory.

Such examples as (10), (13) are reminiscent of the *[that-t] filter of Chomsky and Lasnik (1977) and the set of phenomena related to it: deletability of subject, free inversion of subject, etc. In fact, these examples suggest that the NIC and the *[that-t] filter are related phenomena, a possibility investigated by Taraldsen (1978b) and Pesetsky (1978b), who developed Taraldsen's idea that the *[that-t] filter can be reduced to the NIC in a different way. Kayne (1980a) simultaneously developed a different and independent approach to explaining the phenomena related to the *[that-t] filter in terms of the NIC – actually, a modification of the NIC that he proposes. These various studies are motivated by another problematic feature of the OB-framework, namely, the curious character of the *[that-t] filter. Again, some properties of UG just have to be stipulated, and this particular stipulation does serve to unify many phenomena related to "long movement" of nominative subjects in an enlightening way. But nevertheless the filter is so strange-looking that one would certainly want to derive it, if possible, from more natural principles. I will pursue the possibility of deriving the filter from RES(NIC), properly formulated, in chapter 4.

Recall that the *[*that-t*] filter does not apply in languages that allow missing subjects ("Perlmutter's generalization"; cf. Chomsky and Lasnik (1977)). Let us continue to refer to the latter option of UG as the "pro-drop parameter." Several properties of languages cluster in this connection, including applicability of the *[*that-t*] filter. We want to explain this clustering, if possible, in terms of a single parameter, which should be related to RES(NIC). I will return to these topics in chapter 4.

The indexing conventions of the OB-framework are another aspect of the theory where improvement is desirable, if possible. While they work quite neatly, they are fairly complicated and it is worth asking whether it is not possible to eliminate the concept of "anaphoric index" entirely in terms of some more basic and simple notion, while retaining the desirable properties of the OB-system.

A related question arises in connection with the phenomenon of disjoint reference. As is well-known, pronouns enter into disjoint reference under essentially the conditions under which other anaphors enter into coreference, as illustrated above. This seems an odd state of affairs. Why should languages have this peculiar design, which in fact gives rise to the complexity of the indexing conventions and of the notion "free(i)" defined in OB? Why shouldn't pronouns have coreference, rather than disjoint reference, where, for example, reciprocals do? Again, it is worth asking whether there is some different approach that would give a somewhat more natural account of these phenomena.

Summarizing, I have mentioned six conceptual problems that arise in the OB-framework and earlier work along similar lines: (1) redundancies, specifically, between Case theory and binding theory; (2) the problem of explaining why the subject of Tense and the domain of a subject should be the two opaque domains; (3) the failure of correspondence between the theory of movement and of binding as reflected in the phenomena that I have assigned to RES(NIC); (4) the problem of deriving the *[*that-t*] filter from more fundamental considerations and relating it to RES(NIC) while determining the exact nature of the pro-drop parameter; (5) the problem of simplifying the indexing conventions; (6) the problem of finding some more natural account of the relation between coreference and disjoint reference. In addition, there are certain technical problems.

3.2. The GB-framework

I would now like to develop and explore an approach to the problems just reviewed that seems to me more principled than the OB approach, to show how it deals with these problems, and to examine its further empirical consequences. As in chapter 2, I will proceed in stages, first giving a preliminary version in which the basic ideas are sketched and then turning to refinements, problems and ramifications. In the course of this discussion, I will return to notions introduced in chapter 2 and will suggest some possibilities for developing them further as well. At this point, matters become rather delicate, and decisions about execution have complicated consequences.

3.2.1. The concept of government

A preliminary discussion of the theories of Case and government and their connections was presented in §2.3. Let us now consider these matters more carefully. The basic concept we have to develop is the concept of government. We have such examples as the following:

(1) (i) $[_{VP} V NP (NP')]$
     (ii) $[_{PP} P NP]$
     (iii) $[_{\bar{S}} for [_S NP_1 to [_{VP} V NP_2]]]$
     (iv) $[_{XP} X [_S NP to VP]]$
     (v) $[_{VP} V [_{\bar{S}} COMP [_S NP INFL VP]]]$
     (vi) $[_{VP} V [_{NP_1} NP_2\text{'s } N]]$
     (vii) $[_{VP} V [_{AP} A (of) NP]]$
     (viii)$[_{VP} V [_{PP} P NP]]$

In (i), V governs NP (and NP'). In (ii), P governs NP. In (iii), the prepositional complementizer *for* governs NP_1 but not NP_2; the latter is governed by V. In (iv), X governs NP, where X may be a verb such as *believe* that induces $\bar{S}$-deletion (a marked case in English), a normal raising verb such as *seem*, or a raising predicate such as *certain, likely*; then XP is VP or AP as X is V or A. There are also some cases of raising predicate nominals, generally more idiom-like (e.g., "John is a cinch to win"). Note that (iii) is similar to (iv), and is a special case of (iv) if we regard COMP as the head of $\bar{S}$. Structures (iii) and (iv), where the V of (iv) is a marked verb such as English *believe*, are the instances of Exceptional Case-marking. In (v), V does not govern NP but INFL does if it is tensed, i.e., if INFL = $[+\text{Tense, AGR}]$. More generally, INFL governs the subject NP if it contains AGR, which we have assumed to be indistinguishable from PRO, hence an N. COMP in (v) may be null ("John tried $[$PRO to win$]$") or lexically filled ("John wondered $[$what PRO to do$]$"), or it may be the complementizer *that* or *for*, INFL varying accordingly. In (vi), V governs NP_1 but not NP_2. In case (vii), V does not govern NP; the latter is governed by *of* and the phrase *of*-NP (which may be a PP, or perhaps an NP if *of*-insertion is regarded as adjunction)[6] is governed by A. In (viii), NP is governed by P but not by V; PP is governed by V.

These are the basic cases; we return to some extensions and possible modifications.

In a general way, then, we are assuming that a lexical head governs its complements in the phrase of which it is the head, and that INFL governs its subject when it contains AGR (and in the unmarked case, is tensed). The two cases fall together if we regard INFL as head of S. Furthermore, we have government across S but not across $\bar{S}$ in structural configurations that are formally similar to those of a head and its complements, as in (iii), (iv).

As is often true, the "core notion" of government has clear thematic content, but the operative notion involves structural configurations generalizing the core notion.

The notion of government must meet several kinds of conditions:

(2)   (i) conditions on choice of governor
            (ii) conditions on governed terms
            (iii) structural conditions on the relation of government

Thus under (i), V is a governor but not VP or $\bar{N}$; under (ii), the NP in PP but not the P is the governed term. As for (iii), in a language such as English we would expect the conditions in question to be configurational; perhaps this is true generally.[7]

There are a number of specific proposals concerning the condition (2) in the literature. One approach is in terms of the notion "minimal c-command," construed as in (3):

(3) α governs β if and only if
            (i) $\alpha = X^0$
            (ii) α c-commands β and if γ c-commands β then γ either
                 c-commands α or is c-commanded by β

Thus α is $[\pm N, \pm V]$; i.e., it is one of N, V, A or P. For this approach to work properly the notion "c-command" must be revised so that there is no distinction between branching and non-branching in such categories as VP, since neither transitive nor intransitive verbs govern their subjects (similarly in other cases); and stipulations must be added to ensure that NP and $\bar{S}$ are absolute boundaries to government.

I will pursue a slightly different approach. Consider the structure (4):

(4) $[_\beta \ldots \gamma \ldots \alpha \ldots \gamma \ldots]$, where
            (i) $\alpha = X^0$
            (ii) where φ is a maximal projection, if φ dominates γ then φ domi-
                 nates α
            (iii) α is an immediate constituent of β

Again, α is one of N, V, A, P. In the usual case, $\beta = \bar{\alpha}$ (but not in (1iii), where $\alpha = for$ and $\beta = \bar{S}$, unless we take $\bar{S}$ to have COMP as its head with either $\bar{S} = \bar{P}$ and *for* a P, or $\bar{S} = \overline{COMP}$ with *for* of the category $[P,COMP]$ properly specified in feature terms). Here and below, we mean (4) and later modifications to be interpreted with γ either to the right or left of α.

Let us assume further that VP is a maximal projection and that the S-system is not a projection of V but rather of INFL; and that INFL may contain the element AGR and must contain it when INFL contains [+Tense], where AGR is identified with PRO and hence is a lexical category (N) and thus a proper choice for α in (4). We may think of INFL itself as a proper choice for α in (4) where INFL contains AGR, regarding INFL as a feature complex including [+N,−V] in this case. Then we define "government" as in (5):

(5) α *governs* γ in (4)

Thus the maximal projections ($\overline{S}$, NP, AP, PP, VP) are absolute barriers to government; by (4ii), none of these maximal projections may dominate γ unless it also dominates α, if α governs γ.

Note that government is closely related to subcategorization. We might (almost) say that the subcategorization features of V are actually the governors, and that the category V inherits government from these features; similarly, for other categories. But as we have defined "government," this would not be quite accurate; in cases (iii)–(v) of (1) (namely, the cases of Exceptional Case-marking and raising), the head governs the NP that follows it but is not subcategorized for this element.[8] We may, however, take the subcategorization features to be the Case-assigners, without exception. Thus *for* in (1iii) or *believe* as X in (1iv) has the subcategorization feature −NP (and in addition, *believe* has the feature −$\overline{S}$) and can therefore assign Case to the subject of the embedded infinitive, while the elements *seem, certain*, etc., taken as X in (1iv), govern but do not assign Case to the subject of the embedded infinitive. Similarly, if X in (1iv) is the passive participle *believed*, it will govern but not assign Case, for reasons discussed in §2.7. Only transitive verbs can be Exceptional Case-marking verbs; and if we take variables to be Case-marked traces, as suggested in chapter 2 (cf. 2.4.2.(17)), then raising verbs must be intransitive, since the NPs they govern in raising constructions are not variables.[9] We now take INFL to subcategorize for NP (and VP), which is a way of expressing 2.1.(25) (obligatoriness of subject in clausal structures).

A variant of definition (4)–(5), proposed by Dominique Sportiche and Youssef Aoun, strengthens the *if-then* in (4ii) to *if-and-only-if* and deletes (iii). Thus we have (6) instead of (4) and a corresponding change in the notion of "government":

(6) $[_\beta \ldots \gamma \ldots \alpha \ldots \gamma \ldots]$, where
        (i) $\alpha = X^0$
        (ii) where ϕ is a maximal projection, ϕ dominates α if and only if ϕ dominates γ

Then α and γ are contained in all the same maximal projections. Sportiche and Aoun point out that this modification has empirical consequences in connection with the distinction between gerunds and NPs noted but left unexplained in § 2.4.2. We have such examples as (7), (8):[10]

(7)   (i) I like $[_{NP}$ PRO reading books $]$
       (ii) I like $[_{NP}$ his reading books $]$
(8)   (i) *I like $[_{NP}$ PRO book $]$
       (ii) I like $[_{NP}$ his book $]$

The NP objects of (7), (8) are (9i), (9ii), respectively:

(9)   (i) $[_{NP}$ NP* VP $]$
       (ii) $[_{NP}$ NP* $\bar{N}]$

Under the definition of "government" based on (6), the head of VP in (9i) does not govern NP* since it is dominated by a maximal projection (namely, VP) that does not dominate NP*. But the head of $\bar{N}$ in (9ii) does govern NP*, since NP is the least maximal projection dominating NP* or the head of $\bar{N}$, and it dominates both of them, so they are contained in all the same maximal projections. Thus PRO is a possible choice for the ungoverned NP* in (9i) (as in (7i)), but not for the governed NP* in (9ii) (as in (8i)). A phonetically-realized NP (e.g., *his*) is a possible choice for NP* in either (9i) or (9ii), since genitive Case is assigned in this structure.

On the same assumptions, if the structures of (10) are as indicated, then *proud* will govern its complement and *certain* will govern the embedded trace subject despite the failure of c-command, as required:

(10)   (i) John was $[_{AP} [_{\bar{A}}$ very $[_A$ proud $]] [$ of Bill $]]$
       (ii) John is $[_{AP} [_{\bar{A}}$ quite $[_A$ certain $]] [_S$ t to win $]]$

Note that *proud* and *certain* do c-command their complements, just as the head of $\bar{N}$ c-commands NP* in (9ii), in the extended sense of c-command discussed by Reinhart (1976). Pursuing this observation further, we might restate (6) as (11), redefining "government" accordingly:

(11) $[_\beta \dots \gamma \dots \alpha \dots \gamma \dots]$, where
       (i) $\alpha = X^0$
       (ii) where ϕ is a maximal projection, if ϕ dominates γ then ϕ dominates α
       (iii) α c-commands γ

The structure (11) differs from (4) only in that (4iii) is replaced by (11iii) – i.e., the requirement that α be an immediate constituent of β is changed to the requirement that α c-command γ. We now understand "c-command" as in (12):[11]

(12) α c-commands β if and only if
    (i) α does not contain β
    (ii) Suppose that $\gamma_1, \ldots, \gamma_n$ is the maximal sequence such that
       (a) $\gamma_n = \alpha$
       (b) $\gamma_i = \alpha^j$
       (c) γ_i immediately dominates γ_{i+1}
       Then if δ dominates α, then either (I) δ dominates β, or (II)
       $\delta = \gamma_i$ and γ_1 dominates β

To illustrate the sense of (12), consider the examples (13):

(13)   (i) $[_S \text{NP} [_{VP} \text{V} \ldots]]$
    (ii) $[_{AP} [_{\bar{A}} \text{quite} [_A \text{certain}]] [_S \text{t to VP}]]$
    (iii) $[_{VP} [_{VP} \text{V NP}] \text{NP*}]$
    (iv) $[_{NP} [_{NP} \text{Det N}] [_S \text{NP*} \ldots]]$

In (i), V does not c-command NP since VP ($= \gamma_1$ of (12ii)) dominates V but not NP. In (ii), however, *certain* c-commands the trace subject of S, since AP ($= \gamma_1$ of (12ii)) does dominate the trace. Similarly in (iii), a structure to which we will return in chapter 4, V c-commands NP*, just as N c-commands NP* in (iv).

Suppose that we now construe "government" so that α governs γ in (11), with "c-command" defined as in (12). Earlier results stand, but there are some new possibilities. The structures (13iii) and (13iv) illustrate some of these. In (13iii), V c-commands NP* in the sense of (12), and therefore governs NP* if "government" is defined in accordance with (11), though not (6), since there is a maximal projection (namely, the internal VP) that dominates V but not NP*. We will see subsequently that there is evidence that V governs NP* in (13iii); namely, *wh*-movement can take place from the NP* position in Italian, and the trace left by this movement is governed by V, as required by 2.4.1.(2i). On the other hand, there is also conflicting evidence. In (13iii), V does not "c-command" NP* in whatever sense of "c-command" is relevant to permitting *ne*-cliticization in Italian, which is impossible from the position of NP* to V. It appears, then, that c-command must be understood in both a stronger and a weaker sense, the stronger sense being the one relevant to government of trace and the weaker sense being the one relevant to trace-binding. But the basis for the distinction remains unclear for the time being.

The structure (13iv) also may serve to illustrate some of the empirical possibilities allowed by the characterization of "government" in terms of c-command as defined in (12). Consider the examples (14):

(14)   (i) they gave me [something broken]
    (ii) they gave me [something broken into small pieces]
    (iii) *they gave me [a vase broken]
    (iv) they gave me [a vase broken into small pieces]
    (v) they gave me [a vase that was broken into small pieces]

Throughout, the bracketed expression is an NP. Comparison of (iv) and (v) suggests that in (iv) the relative is a small clause in the sense of Williams (1974, 1975), with the structure of (15):

(15) $[_{NP}[_{NP}$ a vase $] [_{\bar{S}}[_S$ NP* $[_{AP}[_A$ broken $]$ into small pieces $]]]]$

In (15), NP* is ungoverned and lacks Case. Therefore it may be PRO, and must be PRO. We noted in §2.6 that $\bar{S}$-deletion appears to be the unmarked case for small clauses. Suppose we now modify the requirement 2.6.(18) that $\bar{S}$-deletion is obligatory for small clauses, restricting the application of this rule to "short adjective phrases" such as *broken* but not *broken into small pieces*. Then (14iv) is grammatical with the relativized NP of the form (15), NP* being PRO. Turning to (14i–iii), the NP is of the form (16i–iii), respectively:

(16)   (i) $[_{NP}$ something $[_S$ NP* broken $]]$
        (ii) $[_{NP}$ something $[_{\bar{S}}[_S$ NP* broken into small pieces $]]]$
        (iii) $[_{NP}[_{NP}$ a vase $] [_S$ NP* broken $]]$

NP* lacks Case throughout and therefore can only be trace or PRO. In (ii), it may be PRO but not trace since it is ungoverned; therefore (ii) is grammatical with NP* = PRO. In (i) and (iii) the question reduces to one of interpretation of the θ-criterion in an area where we have so far left the question ambiguous. Suppose we were to understand the θ-criterion in such a way that a θ-role is assigned to the NP head of the relative construction. This is not obviously correct – for example, it excludes the possibility of a "raising" analysis of relatives as in Vergnaud (1974) – but let us assume that it is correct. Then trace is excluded as a choice for NP* in (i) and (iii). Therefore, NP* can only be PRO. In case (iii), NP* is governed by *vase*; this is an instance of (13iv). Therefore, (14iii) is ungrammatical, as required.[12] In case (i), while NP* is not protected from government by a maximal projection as it is in (ii), nevertheless it is plausible to argue that there is no lexical category to serve as a governor for NP* in the full NP. Therefore NP* may be PRO, giving (14i). Whether or not this analysis is correct, it illustrates the empirical differences between (11) and (6).

The argument could be presented a bit more narrowly so as to be independent of the question of a raising analysis for relatives. It would suffice for small clause relatives to lack COMP, so that internal *wh*-movement is impossible and the question of raising to the matrix NP does not arise. We would then be treating the relative clauses in (14) analogously to such infinitival relatives as "I found a man [to fix the sink]." In Chomsky and Lasnik (1977), these were analyzed in terms of *wh*-movement, but that analysis is excluded in the present framework since the embedded subject is ungoverned and not case-marked, and must therefore be PRO (cf. Williams (1980a)). There are, however, further consequences with regard to the motivation for a raising analysis in terms of idiom chunk heads, which I will not pursue.

Luigi Burzio points out that evidence from Italian supports the conclusion that the subject of a small clause relative is indeed PRO. Examples of the sort cited in note 43 of chapter 2 illustrate the fact that impersonal *si* is impossible in a control structure, though it is possible in a raising structure as noted in the text at that point. Other types of *si* (e.g., reflexive) permit both raising and control. But small clause relatives allow only other types of *si*, not impersonal *si*. Thus consider (17):

(17)   (i) il vaso rottosi ieri è quello cinese
        ("the vase broken yesterday is the Chinese one")
        (ii) il vaso che si è rotto ieri è quello cinese

In (17i), with the small clause "rottosi ieri," the impersonal-*si* interpretation is barred, but (17ii) with a full clausal relative is ambiguous, with a possible impersonal-*si* interpretation (roughly, "the vase that broke (itself) yesterday is the Chinese one"). It follows that the subject of the small clause in (i) is PRO, barring impersonal *si*. The argument is not entirely persuasive, as Burzio notes, because there may be other reasons why impersonal *si* is barred. Cf. Burzio (1981).

Let us now return to the examples (7)–(9). As we have seen, NP* must be governed in (9ii) to bar PRO from this position, and if "government" is interpreted in accordance with (6) or (11) the position is indeed governed, as required. However, trace is also barred from this position, as in (18i) derived from (18ii):

(18)   (i) *who(se) did you see $[_{NP}$ t book$]$
        (ii) you saw $[_{NP}$ who(se) book$]$

We cannot appeal to subjacency to account for (18), since the same situation obtains in languages (e.g., Italian) in which S is not a bounding node, so that subjacency fails to block the equivalent of (18i), assuming the theory of Rizzi (1978b). The natural conclusion is that while NP* is governed in (9ii), this kind of government is somehow "not strong enough" to permit trace. We will see in chapter 4 that there is good reason to suppose that trace must not only be governed, as we have been assuming since § 2.4.1, but also *properly governed*, where "proper government" is a narrower notion than "government": i.e., α properly governs β only if α governs β and some additional condition is satisfied. There is, then, a gap between "government" and "proper government." What we want to say, then, is that in (9ii), NP* is governed but not properly governed by the head of N̄. The extra conditions on "proper government" will be formulated in § 4.5 so as to establish this conclusion. Where an NP position is governed but not properly governed, neither PRO nor trace can appear. The position of NP* in (9ii) is such a case.

Suppose that an NP position is governed but not properly governed, and furthermore is not a position to which Case is assigned. In this case,

NP cannot be PRO or trace, but it also cannot be phonetically realized, by virtue of the Case Filter. Therefore such constructions cannot exist; any such construction would necessarily be ungrammatical, for any choice of NP. The configuration (9ii) escapes this consequence because, even though the governing element for NP* (namely, the head of N̄) is not a Case-assigner, nevertheless genitive Case is assigned in this configuration.

Bearing in mind these characteristics of government, proper government and Case-assignment, we may return to a problem left unresolved in § 2.6. We noted there that S̄-deletion is obligatory in such small clauses as (19)(= 2.6.(17)):

(19) (i) *John considers $\left[_{\alpha} \text{PRO foolish}\right]$
      (ii) John is considered $\left[_{\alpha} \text{t foolish}\right]$
      (iii) they consider $\left[_{\alpha} \text{each other foolish}\right]$

In (19), α is not S̄, for reasons that are now familiar. But we offered no explanation for the fact, that is, no reason why there could not be a verb like *consider* but with the analogue of (19i) grammatical and the analogue of (19ii,iii) ungrammatical. We are now in a position to explain the fact that α in (19) cannot be a maximal projection, if we combine the concept of "government" expressed in (6) or (11) with the analysis of small clauses proposed by Stowell (cf. 2.6.(34)). Suppose, then, that α in (iii) is taken to be some projection of adjective (i.e., $[+N, +V]$); thus $\alpha = A^i$, for some choice of i. Call it A*. Then the small clause of (19) is a configuration exactly like (9ii) in relevant respects, namely, (20):

(20) $\left[_{A*} \text{NP*} \left[_{A} \text{foolish}\right]\right]$

In (20), NP* is governed by the adjective *foolish*, but – exactly as in (9ii) – it is not properly governed by *foolish*. Therefore NP* cannot be PRO, because it is governed; and NP* cannot be trace if α is a maximal projection. The only remaining possibility is that NP* is a phonetically-realized NP. But (20) differs from (9ii) in that there is no rule that assigns Case to NP* internal to the category α; there is no analogue to the genitive Case-assignment rule for adjective phrases. Therefore, if α is a maximal projection in (20), NP* cannot be a phonetically-realized NP either. Therefore, there is no possible choice for NP* if α is a maximal projection, assuming that it is a projection of its predicate.

We thus establish principle 2.6.(18) in the relevant cases: if the small clause α is of the same category as its predicate – i.e., if what is selected by the matrix verb is the predicate of the small clause as in (19) – then α is not a maximal projection. Therefore NP* of (20) can be properly governed by the matrix verb, and can be trace or a phonetically-realized NP, but not PRO, as in (19). Note that this conclusion does not affect the analysis of (14) discussed earlier, or other proposed analyses in which the small clause is of the category S, since there is no selection of its predicate; e.g., 2.6.(31).

It follows, then, that there can be no verb like *consider* except that it inverts the distribution of * in (19). Analogous moves can be made in the case of other types of small clauses, as, e.g., in (21):

(21)   John considers Bill a fool

The pattern of argument here is similar to the one followed in §2.6 to show that in (22), the complement clause must be a maximal projection:

(22)   John persuaded Bill – Clause   (= 2.6.(19))

Thus, the complement clause in (22) cannot be a small clause, nor can it be an infinitive with $\bar{S}$-deletion. We established the fact in §2.6 by showing that if the complement clause in (22) were not a maximal projection, then there would be no possible choice for its subject. In the case of (19), following similar reasoning, we showed that α *cannot* be a maximal projection, because if it were, there would be no possible choice for its subject. In the case of (9ii), the same reasoning shows that PRO and trace are excluded as possible subjects, but not a phonetically-realized NP; thus in this case the category analogous to α of (20) *is* a maximal projection, namely, NP. The principles of government and Case theory thus interweave to explain a variety of phenomena that seem to hold quite generally.

Later on, in §5.3, I will discuss some other possible modifications of the notion "government." These and other suggestions have various ramifications, which become rather complex as the notion "government" is embedded in a richer theory, given the central role of this notion in the GB-framework. For the moment, we may assume some notion of "government" with the general character of those just discussed, examining consequences of various decisions as we proceed.

3.2.2. *Case theory and θ-roles*
Turning now to Case theory, let us suppose (following OB) that the fundamental properties of Case-assignment are as in (1):

(1)   (i) NP is nominative if governed by AGR
        (ii) NP is objective if governed by V with the subcategorization feature: – NP (i.e., transitive)
        (iii) NP is oblique if governed by P
        (iv) NP is genitive in $[_{NP} – \bar{X}]$
        (v) NP is inherently Case-marked as determined by properties of its $[-N]$ governor

Let us refer to the Case assigned under (i)–(iv) as "structural Case," and the Case assigned under (v) as "inherent Case." The only example of the latter we need consider here is the "double NP" construction, as in (2):

(2)   John gave Bill a book

Let us say that *Bill* in this construction receives its structural Case under (ii) and that *a book* receives inherent Case under (v). Structural Case in general is dissociated from θ-role; it is a structural property of a formal configuration. Inherent Case is presumably closely linked to θ-role.[13] If this is correct, then in (2) we have a structure with a verb head followed by structural Case (*Bill*) and inherent Case (*a book*), whereas in (3) we have just structural Case:

(3)   John gave a book to Bill

But the θ-role of *a book* is the same in (2) and in (3), so that θ-role and Case are not associated. Exceptional Case-marking is another example of this dissociation. In general, various θ-roles may be assigned to an element with a given structural Case.

An alternative to the analysis of (2), suggested in OB, would be to assume that the VP contains an internal VP in the sense of Williams (1975), so that its structure is (4):

(4)   John $[_{VP}[_{\bar{V}}$ gave Bill$]$ a book$]$

We might then assume that *Bill* receives structural Case by (1ii) in the normal way and *a book* receives structural Case from $\bar{V}$ (now admitted as a governor) by (1ii) as well. Then each governor assigns only a single Case.

Jaeggli (1980b) points out that this last assumption has interesting consequences in the Romance languages. There is evidence that in French the structure analogous to (3) is (5i), while in Spanish it is (5ii):

(5)   (i) NP $[_{VP}[_{\bar{V}}$ V NP$]$ Dative$]$
        (ii) NP $[_{VP}$ V NP Dative$]$

The evidence derives from causative constructions. In French, the structure $\bar{V}$ is preposed, as in (6); while in Spanish, the structure VP (= $\bar{V}$) is preposed, as in (7):

(6)   (i) je ferais $[_{\bar{V}}$ téléphoner$]$ Jean à ses parents
             ("I'll make Jean telephone to his parents")
        (ii) je ferais $[_{\bar{V}}$ manger cette pomme$]$ à Jean
             ("I'll make Jean eat this apple")
(7)   le hicimos $[_{VP}$ llamar a sus padres$]$ a Pedro
        ("we made Pedro call his parents")

Thus the dative phrase is preposed in Spanish causatives along with the verb, but not in French. There is a second difference between French and Spanish in these constructions. The dative in Spanish behaves in the manner of a true prepositional phrase, while the corresponding à-phrase in French is an NP, Jaeggli argues following Vergnaud (1974); cf. note 6. These two differences can be correlated, Jaeggli observes, on the assumption that a verb can in principle assign only one Case, so that Case-assignment in (5i) to the second NP must be by $\bar{V}$. Then the dative in French is a structural Case assigned by $\bar{V}$ to an NP, whereas the dative in Spanish is a structural Case assigned in a PP by the governing P, there being no "small $\bar{V}$", as the causative constructions show. Jaeggli goes on to show that the properties of clitic-doubling in several varieties of Spanish and in French follow from these and related assumptions. If we take the assumption that verbs assign only a single Case to be general, then it follows that (4) is the correct analysis for the double object constructions.

Returning to the rules (1) for Case-assignment, a few further comments are in order. While assignment of nominative Case under government by AGR is natural for English on the assumption that the base structure is NP-INFL-VP, it may be that this should be regarded as a special case, and that the general property is that nominative is assigned as a concomitant of agreement (i.e., the NP-AGR relation), which may or may not involve government. We return to the question in §4.5. Case (ii) will be modified slightly in the next chapter to accommodate verbs that are "ergative" in the sense of Burzio (1981); i.e., verbs that subcategorize for a formal NP object but do not assign Case to it. As for (iii), I have tentatively been adopting Kayne's proposal that the Case system has in part been lost in English even at the level of abstract Case, so that prepositions assign objective rather than oblique Case. Cf. §5.2. In languages with richer Case systems, assignment of Case by inherent properties of the governor would require a much more extensive analysis, and examples of many other types would have to be considered. Furthermore, languages may have other Case-assignment rules not involving government in addition to (iv). These comments are only the bare outline of a possible approach to the development of a proper theory of abstract Case and its morphological realization.[14]

Reviewing some related topics, I have been assuming that Exceptional Case-marking in the case of verbs such as *believe* involves $\bar{S}$-deletion, an idiosyncratic marked property of these verbs. Rizzi points out that we could not assume that the structures in question are base-generated with S rather than $\bar{S}$ complements, or it would follow that such sentences as (8) would be on a par with *wh*-island violations such as (9), with "long movement" of the *wh*-phrase directly to the COMP of the matrix sentence:

(8)   who did you believe [John to have seen t]
(9)   (i) what did you wonder [who saw t]
        (ii) to whom did you wonder [what to give t]

Recall that Exceptional Case-marking is impossible in such structures as (i) of note 13 or (10):

(10)   it is unclear [what NP to do t]

In place of S̄-deletion, we might assume S̄-transparency to Case-assignment (as in OB), or a rule changing S̄ to S. In the framework of Lasnik and Kupin (1977), the latter option coincides with S̄-deletion in the case of missing COMP. I will return to this and related questions in §§5.2, 5.3.

Consider next the problem of assigning Case in *wh*-movement constructions, as in (11):

(11)   (i) who(m) did you see
          (ii) who did you think [t saw Bill]
          (iii) *whom did you think [t saw Bill]

The phenomenon is rather marginal in English, and is perhaps an artificial one. Suppose we assume it to reflect a property of core grammar. Then some device is needed to assign Case appropriately to the *wh*-phrase. In OB, it was assumed that Case is assigned by the rule Move-α itself, so that the *wh*-phrase receives the Case of the position from which it is moved to COMP. Freidin and Lasnik (1979b) argue that this suggestion is dubious on the grounds that it undermines the homogeneity of the principles of Case-assignment. There might also be problems with resumptive pronouns. Consider the examples (12):

(12)   (i) the man who(m) I don't believe the claim that anyone saw him
          (ii) the man who (*whom) I don't believe the claim that he saw anyone

The examples are very dubious. The resumptive pronoun strategy is marginal in English, and probably involves a dialect clash with the *who-whom* distinction where it exists, so it is not at all clear that a real phenomenon is illustrated in (12). If it is, then the OB approach cannot be sustained, since there is no movement in (12). One might search for relevant examples in a language with a live resumptive pronoun strategy combined with manifestation of Case in the *wh*-phrase position.

The question relates to the proper treatment of free relatives, in the situation in which the Case of the *wh*-phrase head of the construction is determined by its structural position; e.g., accusative, if the free relative is the object of a verb.[15] Aoun observes that on the OB assumptions, if there is a resumptive pronoun in such cases then it should receive its Case on the basis of its position in the free relative while the *wh*-phrase head should receive its Case on the basis of the structural position of the free relative.[16]

Another possibility would be to assume that the *wh*-phrase in COMP, whether moved or base-generated, "inherits" the case of the variable that it binds (apart from free relatives of the sort just mentioned), which may be a trace or a resumptive pronoun. Suppose that the *wh*-phrase is coindexed with more than one trace in an A-position. Then it will follow from other considerations that only one of these is Case-marked, so that no ambiguity arises. Note that there is no motivation for assigning to a trace in COMP the Case of the variable it binds, so we will add no convention to provide for such assignment. It remains possible, however, that a trace in COMP receives Case from a verb governing the COMP position, as suggested by Kayne in work to which we return.

An interesting confirmation of the latter possibility is reported by Julia Horvath, in Hungarian. Consider examples of the following abstract form (the actual form is somewhat different, for reasons that we may put aside):

(13)   *wh*-phrase $[_S$ NP V $[_{\bar{S}}$ t $[_S \ldots [_S$ t VP$] \ldots]]]$

This is an example of successive-cyclic *wh*-movement from the position of the most deeply embedded trace, as in the English analogue (14):

(14)   who do $[_S$ you think $[_{\bar{S}}$ t $[_S$ Bill said $[_{\bar{S}}$ t $[_S$ t saw John$]]]]]$

In Hungarian, in case (13) the *wh*-phrase is not nominative, as in the English example (14), but rather takes the case assigned by the matrix verb. A natural explanation is that this verb assigns Case in the COMP position of the embedded $\bar{S}$, this Case being inherited by the *wh*-phrase (or, on the OB assumptions, that this verb assigns Case to the *wh*-phrase in the last stage of movement replacing its Case, a clumsier mechanism). The example is interesting for three reasons. First, it illustrates that Case may be assigned in the embedded COMP position, as Kayne suggests. Second, it provides an argument for successive cyclic movement.[17] Third, it overcomes an apparent problem relating to "Perlmutter's generalization" concerning the *[that-t] phenomenon (e.g., *"who do you think that t saw Bill"). The generalization states, in effect, that the *that*-trace phenomenon holds if and only if the language in question is not a "pro-drop" language such as Italian or Spanish, a fact that is a consequence of the analysis in terms of a *[that-t] filter (cf. Chomsky and Lasnik (1977) for discussion). Hungarian appears to be an exception to the generalization, in that it is a pro-drop language but excludes such structures as (13) where the *wh*-phrase is nominative and the trace in the D-structure position of the *wh*-phrase – the variable that it binds in (13) – follows the overt complementizer; i.e., it appears that Hungarian observes that *[that-t] filter though it is a pro-drop language. But as Horvath points out, the exception is only apparent. While it is true that a nominative *wh*-phrase does not appear, the reason lies in the factors just reviewed. Thus the *[that-t] filter does not apply, as expected.

Another possibility that might be considered is that Case is assigned not to the NP itself but rather to its index. Then any NP with this index may (optionally) be assigned Case. This mechanism provides a sense for the notion of "Case-inheritance" just discussed, though it must be sharpened to deal with a wider range of structures. The same might be true of θ-role assignment in the case of antecedent-trace relations. In the case of *wh*-movement, then, the index of the variable bound by the *wh*-phrase is assigned Case, and any phrase bearing this index may (optionally) realize the Case: the variable, the *wh*-phrase, or both. Interaction of other principles will then require that Case be assigned to the variable and the *wh*-phrase. Principles of θ-theory will require assignment of θ-role as appropriate. The suggestion is developed by Aoun (1980b), who notes further consequences. We return to some relevant considerations directly and to a more precise formulation in chapter 6.

Consider again the Case Filter, a fundamental principle of the theory of abstract Case as we are developing it, following Vergnaud. We gave this filter in §2.3 as (15):

(15)   *NP, where NP has a phonetic matrix but no Case (= 2.3.(6))

We have also been toying with the principle (16):

(16) $[_{NP}$ e$]$ is a variable if and only if it has Case (= 2.4.2.(17))

Suppose that (16) is indeed a principle of GB theory. Then the Case Filter can be extended to the Extended Case Filter (17):

(17)   *$[_{NP}$ α$]$ if α has no Case and α contains a phonetic matrix or is a variable

Again, variables behave like names, in this respect.

What about the status of (16)? Note that from left to right it almost follows from the Case Filter (cf. OB). By the Case Filter, the *wh*-phrase must have Case, but if the variable it binds lacks Case, then it will not be able to inherit Case. Hence this variable must have Case, establishing (16) from left to right. Consider, for example, (18):

(18)   *who does it seem $[$t to see Mary$]$

Here, *who* cannot inherit Case from its trace, which, while governed by *seem*, is not assigned Case. So the sentence is blocked by the Case Filter; i.e., by the violation of (16) from left to right.

There are, however, some problems in this approach. One is that in cases of PRO-movement to COMP the variable must still be Case-marked, although PRO requires no Case. A second problem is that in examples of the Hungarian type just discussed, the Case Filter is not violated by the *wh*-phrase whether or not the D-structure trace of the *wh*-phrase has Case, but here too the variable must be in a Case-marked position. The same is true of free relatives in which the *wh*-phrase is assigned Case by virtue of the structural position of the entire construction. A third problem, noted by Freidin and Lasnik (1979b), is illustrated by such examples as (19), where *t* is the trace left by relativization:

(19)   (i) *the man $[_\bar{S}$ that $[_S$ you tried $[_\bar{S}[_S$ t to win $]]]]$
        (ii) *the man $[_\bar{S}$ that $[_S$ I wonder $[_\bar{S}$ what $[_S$ t to see $]]]]$

In (19), if we assume that the *wh*-phrase is deleted and therefore not submitted to the Case Filter,[18] the latter provides no basis for excluding these examples and thus guaranteeing that the variable has Case.

Such examples as these illustrate gaps in the attempt to derive (16), left-to-right, from the Case Filter.

One possible approach to such examples as (19) is to assume (contrary to OB) that the Case Filter is in the LF- rather than the PF-component, or that it applies at S-structure, prior to deletion in the PF-component. In either case, the *wh*-phrase of (19) would suffice, by means of the Case Filter, to exclude examples (19). As between these alternatives, it seems preferable to assume the Case Filter to be at S-structure, because of such examples as (20):

(20)   *John tried $[$everyone to leave$]$

The example is blocked by the Case Filter applying at S-structure (or in the PF-component), but if the rule of quantifier-movement[19] assigns to (20) the LF-representation (21), the Case Filter applying at LF would not assign * unless we were to assume that the quantifier itself requires Case, which seems artificial:

(21)   John tried, for all *x*, *x* to leave

Assume then that the Case Filter applies at S-structure. One consequence of this assumption, pointed out by Freidin and Lasnik, is that there can be no *self*-deletion analysis of EQUI, at least on the assumptions of Chomsky and Lasnik (1977) and OB. This is not an unacceptable result, however; we have already found good reason to suppose that EQUI involves PRO, not *self*-deletion. The motivation for the contrary assumption in earlier work is not operative in the current framework, for the most part.

Nevertheless, it seems reasonable to expect that the Case Filter will be in the PF-component. Some direct evidence in Arabic is offered by Aoun (1979b). If this is correct, then a different analysis is required for (19), as it is for the other two problems cited.

The approach to this complex of problems that seems to me most promising is one that integrates Case theory with θ-theory. Let us assume that elements of the form $[_\alpha \beta]$ are "invisible" to rules of the LF-component unless β contains some feature. Thus PRO is visible as is Case-marked trace, but $[_{NP} e]$ is invisible when it contains no Case. If so, then no θ-role will be assigned to the invisible trace in (18), (19), and in fact in all of the problematic cases noted. It follows that the D-structure position of the *wh*-phrase – and in general, any D-structure position that is ultimately the position of a variable – must be one to which Case is assigned, as a consequence of the θ-criterion.[20]

The exact formulation of this principle requires some care, since there is a sense in which a θ-role is assigned to an NP-trace in a θ-position even though it lacks Case; namely, this trace transmits a θ-role to its antecedent. In the light of this fact, we might formulate the principle in question as (22):

(22) $[_\alpha \beta]$ cannot retain (though it may transfer) a θ-role if β lacks features

Now (16) follows from left to right; variables must have Case. For if a variable lacks Case, it will not retain a θ-role, thus violating the θ-criterion.

It might be argued that the requirement that variables have Case is too strong. One possible counterexample to this requirement is discussed in May (1977). He observes that (23) is three-ways ambiguous as in (24), while (25) is unambiguously interpreted as (26), corresponding to (24i):

(23)   some senator is likely to speak at every rally
(24)   (i) there is a senator S, such that it is likely that for every rally R, S speaks at R
            (ii) it is likely that there is a senator S, such that for every rally R, S speaks at R
            (iii) it is likely that for every rally R, there is a senator S such that S speaks at R
(25)   some senator wants to speak at every rally
(26)   there is a senator S, such that S wants that for every rally R, S speaks at R

If these judgments are correct, then (24ii,iii) violate the requirement that variables be Case-marked. May offers an explanation in terms of his rule of quantifier-movement, which, he suggests, can "lower" the quantifier from a non-θ-position. For a possible alternative explanation, which preserves the essential idea that variables have Case, see chapter 6, note 4.

Note that if May is correct, we have another distinction between trace and PRO illustrated in the different ranges of interpretation of (23) and (25). In the same connection, May notes the examples (27):

(27)   (i) someone expected $[_\alpha$ everyone to bring the wine$]$
            (ii) some senator promised $[_\alpha$ to address every rally in John's district$]$
            (iii) we persuaded some senator $[_\alpha$ to address every rally in John's district$]$

      (iv) it is difficult for some member of the band $[_\alpha$ to play every piece by Ellington$]$

      (v) every piece by Ellington is difficult for some member of the band $[_\alpha$ to play$]$

While judgments are insecure, it seems that (i)–(iv) are unambiguous while (v) is ambiguous, with either order of quantifiers. These judgments could be explained on the assumption that the bracketing is as indicated with α = clause throughout, with PRO subject in (ii)–(v), where clauses tend (in the unmarked case) to bound quantifier raising, while the *for*-phrase is in the matrix clause in (v).

    Another possible counterexample to the requirement that variables must be Case-marked is raised by the analysis of *there*-constructions in Stowell (1978).[21] He takes the base form to be (28), with NP-movement yielding (29):

(28) $[_{NP}$ e$]$ is NP . . . (e.g., "there is a man in the room," after *there*-insertion)

(29) NP_i is t_i . . . ("a man is in the room")

But *wh*-movement may also apply from (28), yielding (30):

(30) *wh*-phrase$_i$ is $[_{NP}$ e$]$ t_i. . . ("who is there in the room," after *there*-insertion)

Thus both NP-movement and *wh*-movement apply from the same position; if it is Case-marked, then NP-movement should not apply, and if it is not Case-marked, then *wh*-movement should not apply, on the assumptions we are now considering. From these and other examples, Borer (1979, 1980) concludes that the requirement that variables must be Case-marked is too strong. Aoun (1980b) points out that many of the problems do not arise if we assume that Case is assigned to indices, then optionally to elements bearing these indices; cf. his paper for further development of this idea.

    Assuming that variables must indeed be Case-marked, we might approach the questions we have been considering from a slightly different point of view. Recall the discussion of grammatical functions (GFs) in §2.2. We distinguished there between A-positions in which A-GFs are defined, corresponding to what are often called "argument positions," and Ā-positions with Ā-GFs. The A-GFs are subject, and complements to heads of constructions:[22] object, clausal complement, etc. Ā-GFs are adjuncts in constructions formed by Move-α: for example, the GF of the *wh*-phrase in COMP, or of an extraposed item, or of an NP adjoined to a VP by inversion in pro-drop languages (cf. 3.2.1.(13iii) and chapter 4). Recall that each NP has a grammatical function GF_1 given by its S-structure position, and a function chain $(GF_1, \ldots, GF_n)$ which represents its derivational history, GF_n being the GF of its D-structure position, an

A-GF, a θ-position in the case of an argument. Suppose that we now restrict attention to function chains in which each GF_i is an A-GF – call these "A-function chains." An element in COMP will not have an A-function chain, but an NP in an A-position will have one (we return in chapters 4, 6 to the case of inverted NP in Italian or Spanish). In the S-structure (31), for example, where t and t' are the traces of *who, t* has an A-function chain (namely, ([NP,S], [NP,VP])), but *who* does not:[23]

(31)   who $[_S$ t was $[_{VP}$ killed t$']]$

The items that fill the positions associated with the A-function chain all have the same index. We may now bring together the principle (22) and the suggestion made informally above that θ-role (like Case) is assigned to an index, then optionally assumed by elements with that index, reformulating (22) as (32):

(32)   Suppose that α has the A-function chain $(GF_1, \ldots, GF_n)$ and that β^i is the element bearing GF_i. Then the chain is assigned a θ-role only if for some i, β^i has features

Specifically, β^i may have the features of PRO, or it may have Case (and must have Case by the Case Filter if it is phonetically realized). But if for each i, β^i is $[_{NP}\ e]$ lacking Case, then the A-function chain is assigned no θ-role; and derivatively, the elements β^i including $\alpha = \beta^1$, have no θ-role.

Suppose that other properties of the system require that the element β^i with features be α itself. Then we can reduce (32) to (33):

(33)   Suppose that α has the A-function chain $(GF_1, \ldots, GF_n)$. Then the chain is assigned a θ-role only if α has features

By definition, each β^i is a trace for $i \neq 1$. Therefore, to guarantee reducibility of (32) to (33) it suffices that β^i lack Case for $i \neq 1$. Such β^i cannot be a subject with nominative Case, or the NIC will be violated. If it is assigned genitive Case in the configuration $[_{NP}\beta^i X]$, the trace left by movement will not be properly governed, as we have seen, so this case is excluded too. Conditions on preposition stranding exclude the possibility that β^i is assigned Case by a preposition (cf. § 5.2). The only remaining possibility is that β^i is assigned Case by a transitive verb V, but this case is ruled out by 2.6.(39) and the requirement that movement be to a non-θ-position, along with the SSC which guarantees that movement cannot be past the subject of the verb to an A-position. (If 3.2.2.(4) is the correct analysis for double-object verbs, then 2.6.(39) must be extended to $\bar{V}$, which raises no problems.) This exhausts the possibilities, with the exception of post-verbal NP with nominative Case, which we will consider in the next chapter. As we shall see, however, these structures are grammatical only if α has features, so we may disregard this possibility. Therefore, we can reduce (32) to (33).

Restriction of (33) to A-function chains is natural in that it makes no sense to assign a θ-role to an operator in COMP, but only to the variable that it binds. Furthermore, the case of movement-to-COMP requires this restriction. Thus consider (34):

(34)   John $_i$ found a book [which $_j$ [he wanted [PRO $_i$ to give t $_j$ to Mary]]]]

Here, *which $_j$* has features, but it is the Case-feature of t_j, the sole element of the A-function chain with index j, which permits assignment of θ-role. Thus (35) is ungrammatical, since t_j lacks Case:

(35)   John $_i$ found a book [which $_j$ [he wanted [it to seem [t $_j$ to please Mary]]]]

The point is made still more clearly by consideration of free relative constructions in which the *wh*-phrase in COMP receives Case from outside the construction, as in the examples noted earlier. As we have seen, such a construction will be grammatical only if the variable is in a Case-marking position (but see note 16).

Principle (33) states an "only if" condition for assignment of θ-role. To strengthen it to "if and only if," we add the requirement that some element of the chain be in a position that is θ-marked. In effect, then, θ-role is assigned to the chain and derivatively to the argument that is the head of the chain, i.e., that bears GF $_1$. We develop these notions more carefully in chapter 6.

Summarizing, a θ-role is assigned to an A-function chain that has a visible category (a category with lexical features, PRO, or Case-marked trace) and a category in a θ-position. Note that we derive principle 2.6.(47); specifically, though *a book* and the trace t_j have the same index in (34), they receive θ-roles independently since they belong to different A-function chains. We return in § 3.2.3 to some problems that arise in this connection.

It now follows that a variable must have Case; i.e., (16) is true from left to right. It remains to determine whether it is also true from right to left, i.e., whether Case-marked traces are variables, and also to deal somehow with such cases as (23) and those cited in note 16, where the requirement appears to be too strong.

The principle (33) refers to the LF-component, but it is quite similar to a principle that applies in the PF-component. Recall the discussion of contraction in § 2.1. The basic examples are these, in S-structure representation:

(36)   (i) they want [PRO to visit Paris]
         (ii) they want [Bill to visit Paris]
         (iii) who do they want [[$_{NP}$ e] to visit Paris]
         (iv) who do they want [PRO to visit [$_{NP}$ e]]

The simplest form for the (optional) contraction rule is (37):

(37)   want+to ⟶ wanna

Let us assume, then, that the rule in question is (37). It applies in (36i) and (36iv), but not in (36iii) or, obviously, in (36ii). Thus we have (38) corresponding to (36):

(38)   (i) they wanna visit Paris
        (ii) they want Bill to visit Paris
        (iii) *who do they wanna visit Paris
    ·   (iv) who do they wanna visit

Evidently, the trace in (36iii) acts in the same way as the lexical NP *Bill* in (36ii), blocking contraction – another respect in which variables behave like names. But PRO does not block the rule (37). It is "invisible" to the rule.

Now consider (36iv), which does undergo contraction, more carefully. Under successive-cyclic *wh*-movement, the S-structure, which enters the PF-component, is (39):

(39)   who do they want $[\, _{\bar{S}}t[\, _S PRO$ to visit t$'$ $]]$

Here too contraction may apply. We must therefore conclude either that the trace in COMP may be optionally erased, or that it does not block contraction for some reason. Deletion of trace in COMP was a reasonable assumption in the framework of Chomsky and Lasnik (1977), as a special case of the general rule of free deletion in COMP. In the OB-framework, which I have been assuming and extending here, there is no such general rule for deletion, as we have seen. Hence there is no general rule that will subsume deletion of trace in COMP as a special case. We therefore look for some other reason why trace in COMP will not block contraction, while trace with an A-GF will, as in (36iii). The obvious answer is that trace with Case is "visible" to the contraction rule (37) while trace without Case is not; recall that we added no convention to assign Case to trace in COMP, and if we pursue the idea of assigning Case to indices, then realization of Case on trace in COMP is optional, corresponding in this case to the option of applying (37). Then we conclude that to be visible to a PF-rule, an empty category must have the feature Case.[24]

It is quite natural that the features of PRO should not be visible in the PF-component. These are features with purely semantic, morphological or syntactic content. So we may assume that such features as person, gender, number are not visible to phonological rules. We might say that these features may participate in morphological rules of the PF-component, but are eliminated by the operation of this subsystem, which precedes the phonological rules. We are then left with a principle very similar to (33);

(40) α is invisible to phonological rules if it lacks appropriate features

The "appropriate features" are the phonological features, and also Case. The common property of (33) and (40) is that Case acts as a "marker" for empty categories, marking them as "visible" to rules of both interpretive components of the grammar.

If all of this is on the right track, then it follows that *wh*-traces and NP-traces will differ in their phonetic consequences; the latter are invisible to phonological rules, while the former are not. There has been much discussion of this topic since the work of Selkirk (1972), who suggested such a distinction on the basis of properties of French liaison, in particular. Pullum and Postal (1979) argue for the same distinction on the assumption that semi-auxiliaries such as *have to, ought to* ("he has to go," with obligatory contraction of *have-to*; "he ought to go," with optional contraction of *ought-to*), etc. are raising verbs, with an NP-trace (in our terms) between the verbal part and *to*. A stronger argument is given by Longobardi (1978), who shows that a filter preventing successive infinitives in Italian is blocked by an intervening *wh*-trace but not an intervening NP-trace.[25] The idea that Case is the relevant feature distinguishing NP-trace and *wh*-trace in this connection has been suggested independently several times,[26] and follows in a very natural way in the framework we are now developing.

Returning to the principle (16) characterizing variables in terms of Case, we see that the requirement that variables be Case-marked ((16) from left to right) follows from a reasonable principle that relates closely to a similar principle operative in the PF-component and probably falls together with it, though questions remain. As for the condition that Case-marked trace is a variable ((16) from right to left), its validity and basis (if it is valid) remain open. We return to these questions in a somewhat different framework in chapter 6.

The condition that Case-marked trace is a variable has some desirable consequences but also some questionable ones –though none of these consequences follow if we assign Case to indices in the matter discussed earlier. Consider, for example, (41) and (42):

(41)   (i) *John$_i$ hit t$_i$
        (ii) *advantage took t$_i$ of John
(42)   (i) the ship sank
        (ii) the book reads easily

The sentences of (41) are marked ungrammatical by the theory of binding if the Case-marked trace is a variable. The θ-criterion rules out (41), and all such cases for which 2.6.(39) is valid, requiring that a verb that assigns objective Case assign a θ-role to its subject. If the structures of (42) are derived by NP-movement from the direct object to subject position, as has sometimes been proposed,[27] then some mechanism is required to block objective Case-assignment if Case-marked traces are variables. We return to examples of this sort in pro-drop languages in the next chapter. There are many related questions, some of which we will consider below.

I have so far left open the question of where and how Case is assigned in the grammar. In OB, it was proposed that inherent and oblique Case are assigned at D-structure, that structural Case is assigned at S-structure, and that a *wh*-phrase and its trace are assigned Case as Move-α applies. The last of these conditions might be replaced by Case-inheritance, as discussed earlier, and more carefully in chapter 6. It has been suggested that Case should be assigned as a lexical property of nouns and that instead of Case-assignment rules, a filter (not to be confused with the Case Filter) should determine whether it has been properly assigned.[28] We are now assuming that such Case-checking is in the PF-component or at S-structure. Case-assignment can be no later than S-structure since it figures in the LF-component as well as the PF-component, if the preceding discussion is correct in essence. I will leave the question in this state for the time being, returning to it in subsequent discussion.

3.2.3. The theory of binding

In its essentials, Case theory forms part of the theory of government. That is, the basic and central instances of Case-assignment are instances of government by a Case-assigner. One of the problems in the OB-framework noted earlier (§ 3.1) was that there was considerable redundancy between notions of Case and binding. This suggests that binding theory too should be developed within the framework of the theory of government, with the latter expressing their common core. Let us now proceed to investigate this possibility.

Notice that we have been using the term "binding" in several senses. In the sentence (1), the trace t is bound in one sense by the *wh*-phrase – a kind of quantifier at LF – and the trace t' is bound in another sense by t as its antecedent:

(1)   who [t was killed t']

The trace t is a variable with Case; let us say that it is *operator-bound* by *who*. The trace t' is an anaphor lacking Case; let us say that it is *antecedent-bound* by the variable t.

Consider a case of crossover, say (2):

(2)   (i) who did he say Mary kissed t
        (ii) [$_{\bar{S}}$ who [$_S$ he said [$_{\bar{S}}$ t [$_S$ Mary kissed t']]]]

Here t' is operator-bound by *who* (or perhaps by its trace t in the lower COMP), but it cannot be antecedent-bound by *he*. In fact, the relation of disjoint reference holds between this trace and *he*, so that (2) does not have the interpretation (3):

(3)   for which *x*, *x* said that Mary kissed *x*

It may be that the two notions – operator- and antecedent-binding – reduce to the same more general notion, but it is not obvious that this is the case. Antecedent-binding relates anaphors and proximate pronominals to their antecedents, controllers in the case of PRO. Variable-binding relates variables to the operators that bind them, perhaps through the medium of a trace. The notions seem conceptually distinct. One is a logical notion, the other (antecedent-binding) a syntactic notion relating to the syntax of LF.

In fact, the appropriate distinction for our purposes may not be that of antecedent- versus operator-binding but rather antecedent-binding versus peripheral-binding, where the former holds when the c-commanding element is in an A-position and the latter when it is not.[29] Thus, movement of an empty category to COMP – PRO or trace; see § 2.6 – leaves a variable, but the empty NP is not an operator in the intuitive sense.[30] Furthermore, the notion "operator" has been left too vague. Let us therefore distinguish the two notions "A-binding" and "$\bar{\text{A}}$-binding," the former holding when the binder is in an A-position and thus has an A-GF and the latter when it is in an $\bar{\text{A}}$-position with an $\bar{\text{A}}$-GF; the former notion is what I have been calling "antecedent-binding" and the latter, "operator-binding."

I will use the terms of binding theory ("bound," "free," etc.) for both types of binding adding the specification "A-" or "$\bar{\text{A}}$-" when the context does not suffice to indicate which kind of binding is under discussion. The theory of binding is a theory of A-binding.

A trace in S is an anaphor if it is A-bound, and a variable if it is $\bar{\text{A}}$-bound (cf. 2.6.(4)). Note that it is a kind of "local binding" that is involved in these characterizations. Consider (4):

(4)   who $[_S$ t seemed $[_S$ t' to have been killed t'' $]]$

Of the three traces *t*, *t'* and *t''*, only *t* is a variable; the others are anaphors, though they are coindexed with the trace *t* that is locally $\bar{\text{A}}$-bound by *who*, hence a variable. In the sense in which I will use these terms, then, *t*, in (4) is $\bar{\text{A}}$-bound and locally $\bar{\text{A}}$-bound by *who*, *t'* is $\bar{\text{A}}$-bound by *who* and is A-bound and locally A-bound by *t*, and *t''* is $\bar{\text{A}}$-bound by *who*, A-bound by *t*, and both A-bound and locally A-bound by *t'*.

The basic notions of the theory of binding may be defined as in (5) and (6):

(5)   (i) α is *X*-bound by β if and only if α and β are coindexed, β c-commands α, and β is in an *X*-position[31]

(ii) α is X-free if and only if it is not X-bound

(iii) α is locally bound by β if and only if α is X-bound by β, and if γ Y-binds α then either γ Y-binds β or $\gamma = \beta$

(iv) α is locally X-bound by β if and only if α is locally bound and X-bound by β

(6) α is a variable if and only if

(i) $\alpha = [_{NP} e]$

(ii) α is in an A-position (hence bears an A-GF)

(iii) there is a β that locally $\bar{A}$-binds α

Cases (i) and (ii) of (5) define "bound" and "free" with "X" replaced by "A" or "$\bar{A}$". Similarly, case (5iv). In (iii), "X" and "Y" may be independently replaced by "A" or "$\bar{A}$". We have excluded the possibility that an element may be locally bound by two different elements, hence that it may be both locally A-bound and locally $\bar{A}$-bound. Note further that if α is A-bound by β and $\bar{A}$-bound by γ, then β binds γ or conversely by properties of c-command.

In the case of a variable, the binder β in (6) may be an operator, a trace in COMP, an empty NP in COMP, or some other element adjoined to S or $\bar{S}$.[32] This formulation leaves open a variety of questions about the class of rules I have been calling "movement-to-COMP," as a loose designation.

These notions suffice for our purposes, with one significant exception: they do not provide an appropriate notion of variable for such cases as (7):

(7)   (i) the man [to whom I gave the book t]

(ii) the man [whose picture I saw t]

(iii) John, [a picture of whom I saw t yesterday]

The trace t is not the variable bound by the phrase in COMP in such cases as these. I will leave this problem open, pending answers to the questions raised in §2.4.6 concerning movement-to-COMP in such cases: does such movement leave a full copy as trace, or is there a reconstruction rule, or should we distinguish NP-movement from movement-to-COMP in some fundamental respect, perhaps as suggested by van Riemsdijk and Williams (1980)? And what is the proper way to handle examples of the sort mentioned in chapter 2, note 79? Let us put these problems – which are far from trivial – to the side, restricting our attention to structures in which they do not arise.

So far, I have been assuming a very simple indexing theory; see §2.6. Plainly every trace must be coindexed with the moved element, a requirement in the case of A-binding since the trace transfers θ-role, and in the case of $\bar{A}$-binding to account for the association of the variable to its binder. Our assumption has been that coindexing of moved element and trace is simply a part of the rule Move-α by convention, but we have not yet stipulated that distinct indices be assigned by different applications of Move-α, obviously a necessity. Thus consider (8):

(8)   whom$_i$ did John$_j$ seem $[_{\bar{S}} t_i [_S t_j$ to have wanted $[_{\bar{S}} t'_i [_S \text{PRO}_k$ to visit $t''_i]]]]$

Here t''_i is the variable bound by *whom*, and t_j is A-bound by *John*. The association of the traces and their binders is determined by the rule Move-α. Successive-cyclic movement preserves indices. Suppose that i had been chosen identical to j in (8). The theory of binding requires that the variable t''_i be A-free; cf. the crossover example (2). Therefore the binding conditions will be violated if $i = j$, and the sentence assigned *. The same condition requires that $k \neq i$. The theory of control requires that PRO in (8) be A-bound. Therefore, $j = k$. In short, no indexing convention is required to ensure proper indexing in (8).

Apart from trace, I have been assuming that indexing is free; in fact, we might assume that traces and moved elements are also freely indexed, say at S-structure, but for convenience of exposition I will continue to suppose that the rule Move-α coindexes in the manner already indicated. To persist with these optimal assumptions, we must show that example (8) is typical in that unwanted indexing is ruled out by independent conditions. To illustrate with another example, consider (9) in English and Italian:

(9)   (i) the man $[$ who$_i [$ I don't know $[$ who$_j [t_k$ knows $t_l]]]]$
        (ii) l'uomo $[$ *wh*-phrase$_i$ che $[$ non so $[$ chi$_j [t_k$ conosca $t_l]]]]$

The traces must be bound, and $k \neq l$ by the requirement that variables be A-free. Suppose $i = l$ and $j = k$. In English, this is a *wh*-island violation (i.e., a violation of subjacency, with S a bounding node), hence assigned the degree of unacceptability accorded such examples, depending in part on dialect. But in Italian, the sentence is grammatical; according to the theory of Rizzi (1978b), the reason is that Italian does not have S as a bounding category, so there is no *wh*-island violation in this case. Suppose alternatively that $i = k$ and $j = l$. In English, the example is ruled out by the condition that I called RES(NIC) in § 3.1, but in Italian this condition applies in such a way as to permit this assignment of indices, a distinction between the two languages contingent on the pro-drop parameter. Cf. § 3.1. Therefore the sentence (9) is ambiguous in Italian but ungrammatical in English (subject to dialect variation in the case of $j = k$, $i = l$). Again, the choice of indices is determined by independent conditions, and no stipulations are required in the indexing theory. The same is true in all such cases.

What about pronouns? I will assume that the same indexing theory applies to pronouns. Thus pronouns are "proximate" if they are coindexed with some other element and "obviative" if not coindexed with any other element. Note that this is a departure from the OB-framework, in which anaphoric and referential indices were assigned to pronouns and names to account for the proximate-obviative distinction, and more generally, for disjoint reference; I am now assuming only referential indices, in the sense of OB. This is also a departure from the spirit of Lasnik's well-known proposal (Lasnik (1976)) that pronouns are free in reference, subject to other conditions. I will tentatively adopt this approach, putting questions of disjoint reference to the side. If this simplified approach is workable, then one of the conceptual problems in the OB-framework noted in §3.1 is overcome. The proposal does not appear to be feasible, however, a matter to which I will return in §5.1; but let us assume it now anyway, for ease of exposition.

At the level of LF-representation, each NP must be indexed by a single index. Let us assume that each lexical element is inserted in D-structure with an index (including PRO), indices being copied by Move-α. Then consider such structures as (10):

(10)   (i) John$_i$ was killed α
        (ii) John$_i$ seems $[\alpha$ to have been here$]$

In these examples, $\alpha = [_{NP} e]$ with index i, after movement. Suppose (10) had been generated directly with PRO in the position of α. This is impossible by the requirement that PRO be ungoverned. What of the possibility of generating (10) with *John* in its S-structure position and $[_{NP} e]$ in the base, with the coindexing assigned by a free indexing convention? Kayne points out that this possibility should be barred on general grounds; since there is no ambiguity in (10), we do not want to have an interpretive option alongside of the movement option. In fact, the interpretive option is ruled out by the projection principle, since *John* appears in a non-θ-position in D-structure.

Therefore all interpretive options are eliminated, and we can distinguish the class of phenomena that arise in movement cases from those found in interpretive cases appropriately, along the lines discussed earlier.

Let us now turn to the binding theory itself. Recall that in the OB-framework, anaphors and pronouns were subject to the NIC and SSC. The theory had many good consequences and unified quite a wide range of facts in a principled way, but faced a variety of problems, some empirical and some conceptual, as discussed in §3.1. When we have a fairly successful theory that faces a number of problems, a reasonable strategy is to try to derive its desirable aspects from a more principled theory that avoids these problems – a never-ending quest. I will now explore two different approaches to this question, then suggesting a way of combining them to yield a principled and I think rather successful theory of binding.

Let us investigate the possibility that the theory of binding, like Case theory, is developed within the theory of government. It makes use of the fundamental notion "governing category," which we may characterize as

(11) α is the governing category for β if and only if α is the minimal category containing β and a governor of β, where $\alpha = $ NP or S

We may assume that β has at most one governing category. Note that if β is Case-marked by a governor (cases (i), (ii), (iii), (v) of 3.2.2.(1)), then it is Case-marked within its governing category. The same is true in case (iv) where $X = $ N.

We have come across several possible exceptions to Case-marking under government: nominative Case-assignment contingent on agreement, genitive Case-assignment, and idiosyncratic Case-marking as in the subject of infinitives in certain languages (e.g., Russian, Latin). In terms of the definition (11), there is no governing category for the Case-marked element in these instances (but see the discussion of 3.2.1.(8)). The first possibility was left as an open option perhaps realized in languages in which the agreement element AGR does not govern the subject as we have assumed to be the case in English. Genitive Case-assignment might be reduced to Case-assignment by government by assuming an abstract element GEN adjoined to the NP that receives the CASE, where GEN is both a governor and a Case-assigner, in the spirit of Siegel (1974). In the third case, there seems no reason to suppose that the Case-marked element has a governing category, and I will tentatively assume that this is true in the case of genitives as well, leaving the question of nominative Case-assignment by agreement for later discussion.

Let us tentatively assume that the binding conditions apply at the level of LF.[34] We have subdivided nominal expressions into three basic categories: (I) anaphors, (II) pronominals, and (III) R-expressions; cf. 2.6.(1). Intuitively, anaphors are NPs that have no capacity for "inherent reference." We return to some further comments on this category of elements. For the present, we consider two types of anaphors: lexical anaphors, such as reciprocals and reflexives; and NP-trace.

Let us now propose that the binding theory has one principle for each of these categories; namely, (12):

(12)   *Binding Theory*
        (A) An anaphor is bound in its governing category
        (B) A pronominal is free in its governing category
        (C) An R-expression is free

Throughout, the binding is A-binding.[35] Apart from inverted post-verbal NP, to which we turn in §4.5, each anaphor, pronominal and R-expression is in an A-position, within the range of constructions that I am considering here.[36]

Let us now return to the major examples of opacity reviewed in §3.1. We consider first binding within clauses with the basic structure of 3.1.(1), repeated here as (13):

(13)

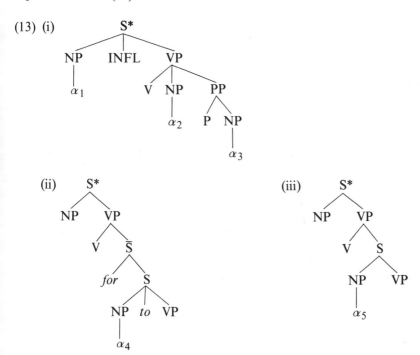

Consider first the case of overt anaphors such as *each other*. Since this element has phonetic content, it must be assigned Case and therefore must have a governing category in (13). By binding principle (A), it must be bound in this governing category.

Beginning with α_1 of (13i), suppose that *each other* in this position is the subject of a tensed clause, with INFL $= [[+\text{Tense}], \text{AGR}]$. Then it is governed by INFL and its governing category is S*. But *each other* must be bound in S*, which is impossible, so the sentence is ruled ungrammatical. This is the case of NIC.

Suppose that *each other* is the object of a verb or a preposition in VP, cases α_2, α_3 of (13). Then the governing category once again is S* and *each other* must be bound in S*. If in α_2, it must be bound by the subject in α_1; if in α_3, it must be bound by either the subject in α_1 or the object in α_2.[37] This is one case of SSC.

Suppose next that *each other* is the subject of an infinitive, as in the two marked constructions (13ii,iii); such constructions as (14), (15), respectively:

(14)   (i) $[_{S*}$ they'd prefer $[_{\bar{S}}$ for $[_{S}$ each other to win$]]]$
         (ii) $[_{S*}$ they want $[_{\bar{S}}$ for $[_{S}$ each other to win$]]]$
         (iii) $[_{S*}$ they would be happy $[_{\bar{S}}$ for $[_{S}$ each other to win$]]]$
         (iv) $[_{S*}$ they would hate it $[_{\bar{S}}$ for $[_{S}$ each other to win$]]]$

(15) $[_{S*}$ they believe $[_{S}$ each other to be intelligent$]]$

In (14), where *each other* is in the position of α_4 of (13ii), the anaphor is governed and assigned Case by *for*, so that its governing category is S* and it must be bound in S*,[38] as required by SSC. In (15), where *each other* is in the position of α_5 of (13iii), the anaphor is governed and assigned Case by *believe*; again, S* is the governing category in which *each other* must be bound.

In clauses, then, we derive NIC and SSC from the binding theory. The major conceptual problem of the OB-framework receives a natural solution. In place of the two unrelated opacity conditions NIC and SSC, we have the very simple principle (A) of the binding theory from which both NIC and SSC derive.

Consider next the case of the non-overt anaphor NP-trace. If principle 3.2.2.(16) (namely, NP-trace is a variable if and only if it is Case-marked) holds in full generality, then NP-trace lacks Case. Nevertheless, NP-trace is governed, a property of trace that was noted in § 2.4.1 (cf. 2.4.1.(2)) and that we will relate to RES(NIC) in chapter 4. Therefore, NP-trace has a governing category, and as an anaphor, must be bound in this category. As we saw in § 3.1, NP-trace is excluded from positions α_3 and α_4 of (13) by other conditions. It can appear as α_2 or α_5 with the subject of S* as antecedent, exactly as in the case of *each other*; but NP-trace differs from *each other* in that its governor must be a non-Case-assigning element, namely, a passive participle in (13i) or a raising predicate in (13iii). NP-trace is excluded from position α_1 if INFL is tensed (contains AGR), since it is free in its governing category. Thus we derive NIC and SSC just as in the case of overt anaphors.

Note that while overt anaphors differ from NP-trace with respect to Case theory, they are on a par with respect to government and thus behave alike under the principles of the government-based binding theory of GB.

Let us now turn to pronominals, considering first overt pronominals, i.e., pronouns. A pronoun is necessarily Case-marked, hence has a governing category in which it must be free by principle (B) of the binding theory (recall that we are now considering positions within S, not NP). Once again, the NIC and SSC follow, with examples of the sort given in § 3.1.(4), illustrating the fact that pronouns are free in positions in which an anaphor is bound, the basic property of disjoint reference for pronouns.[39] Thus we have such examples as (16), with disjoint reference, and (17), with free reference of the pronoun:

(16)   (i) John saw him
        (ii) John told Bill about him
        (iii) John expected him to win
        (iv) John would prefer for him to win
        (v) John would hate it for him to win
        (vi) John is too clever for him to expect us to catch him

(17)   (i)   John expected Mary to catch him
          (ii)   John expected that he would catch Mary

In (16), *him* cannot be coindexed with *John* or *Bill*. Similarly, if either *John* or *Bill* is replaced by *everyone*, *him* cannot be coindexed with *everyone*, hence ultimately interpreted as identical with the variable bound by this quantifier; cf. § 5.1 and note 2, above. Example (16iv) might be regarded as falling under the Avoid Pronoun Principle 2.4.2.(5), since there is a corresponding EQUI case with PRO instead of *him*, but this is not the case for (16v) in some dialects or for (16vi). In (17), the pronoun is free in its governing category and thus not subject to these constraints.

     We might, incidentally, ask why there is no EQUI analogue to (16vi), i.e., (18):

(18)   John is too clever [PRO to expect us to catch][40]

Note that (18) is not ungrammatical, but rather is interpretable only with the PRO subject of *expect* taken as arbitrary in reference, not controlled by *John*, though this is a position of control as illustrated in (19):

(19)   John is too clever to expect us to catch Bill

I will return to these examples in discussing principle (C) of the binding theory, from which their properties follow.

     Consider next pronominals without a phonetic matrix, i.e., PRO. Note that PRO is like overt pronouns in that it never has an antecedent within its clause or NP. PRO also resembles anaphors in that it has no intrinsic referential content but is either assigned reference by an antecedent or is indefinite in interpretation, lacking specific reference. It is reasonable, then, to regard PRO as a pronominal anaphor. If so, it is subject to both the binding conditions (A) and (B). Then PRO is bound and free in its governing category, a contradiction if PRO has a governing category. Therefore PRO has no governing category and is therefore ungoverned. We therefore derive the principle (20), which as we found in § 2.4, is the essential property of PRO:[41]

(20)   PRO is ungoverned

If PRO is ungoverned, then it satisfies principles (A) and (B) of the binding theory vacuously (cf. note 35). We therefore derive the basic properties of PRO reviewed in § 2.4. The binding theory determines that the positions of PRO are essentially those of other anaphors (among them, subject of infinitive or of NP), but the relation of PRO to its antecedent (if any) is not determined by the binding principles, so that we have long-distance control as in (21):

(21)   they thought I said that $\left[\text{PRO}\begin{Bmatrix} \text{to feed} \\ \text{feeding} \end{Bmatrix}\text{each other}\right]$ would be difficult (=3.1.(5))

Furthermore, PRO is permitted in the structures of 3.1.(6) from which trace and overt anaphors are excluded, and PRO is excluded from the structures of 3.1.(7), where overt anaphors are permitted (trace being excluded by subjacency), by virtue of principle (20), which in turn follows from the binding theory, given that PRO is a pronominal anaphor. The fact that PRO is ungoverned – namely, (20) – now follows in a principled way from the theory of binding. The fundamental principle 2.9.(4) of the theory of government must therefore be stipulated only for trace.

We thus overcome the technical problems of the OB theory noted at the outset of §3.1. One of the conceptual problems is also resolved, namely, the first: redundancies between the theory of Case and the theory of binding. These redundancies are now eliminated, reduced to the common contribution of the theory of government to these two sub-theories. The suggestion in OB cited in §3.1 (namely, note 30 of OB) was more or less on the right track, but was mistaken in that it was based on Case rather than the more fundamental concept of government.

Note that the full range of properties of PRO and trace discussed in §2.4, as well as the partially similar properties of overt anaphors, are determined by the interaction of four theories: the theory of bounding (for trace), the theory of control (for PRO),[42] the theory of Case (for elements with phonetic content, including overt anaphors), and the theory of binding (for all NPs). The latter two theories are developed within the theory of government. Again, we see the highly modular character of the theory of grammar, with the basic subsystems of principles discussed in chapter 1 serving as quite simple and fundamental abstract components that interact to yield a complex range of properties.

I have so far been assuming a very simple indexing theory: namely, indices are freely assigned, where we are considering only referential indices in the sense of OB. In OB, PRO was assigned a referential index in the cases of control and the index *arb* (distinct from all referential indices) in the case of indefinite reference, as in (22):

(22)   it is unclear [what [PRO to do]]

But the OB approach does not work,[43] as we can see in the case of PRO-movement, as in (23):

(23)   it is annoying [PRO to be cheated t]

Here, PRO and its trace are coindexed by the rule Move-α, so that PRO cannot be assigned the designated index *arb* by the control rule, as in the OB theory. Yet it must receive the arbitrary interpretation. So the OB theory would require a rather obvious, but *ad hoc* supplementation to account for these cases. We obtain the same positive results, also accommodating (23), with the simpler – essentially null – theory of free indexing. PRO$_{arb}$ is simply PRO that is free. Cf. §2.4.3.

While such examples as (23) certainly exist, still it seems to be true that PRO with arbitrary reference is rather resistant to movement in indirect questions. Examples such as (24) are awkward if possible at all, whatever the reason may be:[44]

(24)   (i) it is unclear how to be fed
         (ii) it is unclear what presents to be given

Recall that the term "pronominal" is used here as a purely descriptive term for an item containing PRO – PRO or pronouns – rather than as an explicit feature. At the level of execution, we might assume that the lexical rules insert the features person, number, gender in the context $[_{NP}[_{N}-]]$, and may or may not insert a phonetic matrix as well, preferring (or requiring) non-insertion where possible by the Avoid Pronoun principle 2.4.2.(5). If a phonetic matrix is inserted, we have a pronoun; if not, PRO. There is no feature "pronominal." A proximate pronominal bound by NP must match NP in the features gender, number and person, whether it is PRO or a pronoun. Recall as well that the inherent number of unbound PRO is a parameter of UG; cf. 2.4.1.(11).

We have briefly discussed principles (A) and (B) of the binding theory, where they are plainly closely related. Let us turn now to principle (C), which asserts that R-expressions are free. For names, this gives the familiar properties, as illustrated in (25):

(25)   (i) he said that John would win
         (ii) John said that John would win

Where there is no emphatic stress, these are understood with the embedded occurrence of *John* distinct in reference from the matrix subject. There is, in fact, a strong tendency to take names to be distinct in reference even apart from c-command, a matter that I will not pursue.[45]

The case of variables is more interesting. Principle (C) gives the basic facts of strong crossover in the sense of Wasow (1972, 1979), for example (26):

(26)   (i) who did he say Mary had kissed   (for which x, he said Mary had kissed x)
         (ii) who did he say had kissed Mary   (for which x, he said x had kissed Mary)
         (iii) who said Mary had kissed him   (for which x, x said Mary had kissed him)
         (iv) who said he had kissed Mary   (for which x, x said he had kissed Mary)

In (i) and (ii), *he* cannot be replaced by the variable x in the associated LF-representation, whereas in (iii) and (iv) it can; (27i,ii) are not possible interpretations of (26i,ii), respectively, but they are possible interpretations of (26iii,iv), respectively:

(27)   (i) for which x, x said Mary had kissed x
        (ii) for which x, x said x had kissed Mary

Whatever the exact mechanisms of interpretation may be,[46] we can express the central facts in terms of the binding theory. In the LF-representation for (26i,ii), *he* must be indexed differently from x, whereas in (26iii,iv) it may or may not be, giving the interpretations just indicated, where the option of interpreting *he* as identical to the variable bound by "for which x" is contingent on coindexing. These possibilities are consequences of principle (C) of the binding theory, with variables behaving like names in this respect.[47]

The same basic observations hold with quantifiers in place of *wh*-phrases; thus variables left by the quantifier-movement rule of the LF-component behave exactly like those left by overt *wh*-movement.[48] In (28), for example, *he* cannot be replaced by x in the LF-representation, as a consequence of principle (C):

(28)   he kissed everyone   (for every x, he kissed x)

Insofar as wide scope of *everyone* is possible in (29), the facts are exactly parallel to (26):

(29)   (i) he said Mary had kissed every-   (for every x, he said Mary
           one   had kissed x)
        (ii) he said everyone had kissed   (for every x, he said x had
            Mary   kissed Mary)
        (iii) everyone said Mary had kissed   (for every x, x said Mary
             him   had kissed him)
        (iv) everyone said he had kissed   (for every x, x said he had
            Mary   kissed Mary)

The crossover facts indicate that variables, whether bound by quantifiers or by quasi-quantifiers such as *wh*-phrases, behave alike; furthermore, they behave as names generally, though as the weak crossover facts show, the analogy to names is not total, an apparent fact of natural language as yet unexplained. The similarity of the several types of variables suggests that principle (C) of the binding theory applies at the level of LF-representation as we have so far been assuming, though other facts, to which we turn directly, run counter to this assumption.

The similarity between bound variables and names is reflected in the fact that variables are not subject to the SSC, as illustrated, for example, in (26i), where x is free in the domain of the subject *Mary* of its clause. And such examples as (26ii), as pointed out by Freidin and Lasnik (1979a),

indicate that they are also not subject to NIC (or the Tensed-S or Propositional Island Condition of earlier work). That is, they do not fall under
principles (A) and (B) of the binding theory, from which SSC and NIC
follow in their essentials, but rather from principle (C). We therefore face
the apparent paradoxes noted in §3.1, since in other respects bound
variables seem to fall under something like the NIC, as illustrated in
(30):

(30) (i) *who do you wonder $[_{\bar{S}}$ how well $[_S$ t liked Bill$]]$
     (ii) *who does John know $[_{\bar{S}}$ how well $[_S$ t explained the theory$]]$
     (iii) *who does John know $[_{\bar{S}}$ how $[_S$ t did his work$]]$

As noted earlier, such examples, involving *wh*-movement of nominative
subject, are not to be confused with other violations of the *wh*-island
condition, as in (31):

(31) (i) who do you wonder $[_{\bar{S}}$ how well $[_S$ Bill liked t$]]$
     (ii) what does John know $[_{\bar{S}}$ how $[_S$ Bill did t$]]$
     (iii) which theory does John know $[_{\bar{S}}$ how well $[_S$ Bill explained t$]]$

See the discussion of examples 3.1.(9)–(14). Contrary to earlier work of
mine and of others cited above, I will assume that the generalization of the
NIC to such examples as (30) is spurious, and that in fact RES(NIC), an
entirely different principle, applies in these cases. We return to this topic
in chapter 4.

   Principle (C) of the binding theory also eliminates cases of improper
wh-movement, as in (32):

(32) (i) *who $[_S$ t tried $[_{\bar{S}}$ t' $[_S$ t'' to win$]]]$
     (ii) *who $[_S$ t thought $[_{\bar{S}}$ t' $[_S$ John would see t''$]]]$
     (iii) *who $[_S$ t is possible $[_{\bar{S}}$ t' $[_S$ John will see t''$]]]$

The examples of (32) can be derived by successive application of the rule
Move-α, moving *who* from the D-structure position of t'' to the COMP
position of t', then to the matrix subject position of t, and finally to the
matrix COMP position of *who*. Since t'' is a variable, by definition, it is
subject to principle (C) of the binding theory, and therefore cannot be
A-bound by t, so that the structures are ungrammatical. The argument
is essentially that of May (1979), recast in the GB-framework.

   Examples (i) and (ii) might be excluded on different grounds, namely,
by a revision of the θ-criterion requiring that all occurrences of a variable
must be assigned a θ-role by a single θ-position. But this is an unmotivated
move which is, furthermore, dubious in several respects; for one thing, it
conflicts, at least in spirit, with the conclusion in 2.6.(47) that t'' does
not assign a θ-role to t in (32). Note that we would have to appeal to this
principle to bar (iii) if the binding theory were inapplicable; recall that the

variable *t*, an R-expression, must be assigned a θ-role. Given 2.6.(47), then, (iii) is barred independently of the binding theory.

We have so far been assuming that the binding theory applies at the LF-level. Another possibility is that it applies at S-structure. The choice has no effect on the foregoing discussion of principles (A) and (B), but it does affect the applicability of principle (C). There are a number of considerations that suggest that in fact the binding theory does apply at S-structure, contrary to the assumption of the OB-framework that we have so far adopted here. S-structure differs from LF-representation by the rules of the LF-component. There are three such rules that enter into our discussion, namely, (33):

(33)   (i) the rule of quantifier-movement
        (ii) the LF-rule of *wh*-movement
        (iii) the rule of focus

Rule (33i) maps the S-structure (34i) to (34ii); rule (33ii), in conjunction with the rule interpreting *who*, maps the S-structure (34iii) to (34iv)[49]; rule (33iii) maps the S-structure (34v) to (34vi):

(34)   (i) his mother loves everyone
        (ii) for every person *x*, his mother loves *x*
        (iii) I don't remember [who [t expected [his mother to love whom]]]
        (iv) I don't remember [for which persons *x*, *y* [*y* expected [his mother to love *x*]]]
        (v) his mother loves JOHN   (*JOHN* with focal stress)
        (vi) for *x* = John, his mother loves *x*

The examples illustrate the phenomenon of weak crossover (cf. the references of notes 46, 47). In each case, we have the clause "his mother INFL love *x*" at LF-representation. In this structure, *his* may of course refer to someone understood from the discourse. But it cannot be interpreted as a variable identical to *x*, as it can, say, in "everyone loves his mother" (= "for every person *x*, *x* loves *x*'s mother," under one interpretation); though, as Wasow notes, the effect is weaker than in the strong crossover cases.

To determine whether the binding theory applies at S-structure or LF, we ask what effect the rules of the LF-component have on the functioning of the binding theory. In the case of each of the rules of (33), it appears that the binding theory applies prior to the application of the rule. Therefore, we conclude that the binding theory applies at S-structure rather than at LF.

To illustrate, consider the following examples:[50]

(35)   (i) which book that John read did he like

(ii) he liked every book that John read
(iii) I don't remember who thinks that he read which book that John likes
(iv) John said that Bill had seen HIM   (*HIM* with focal stress)

In (i), *he* may be proximate to *John,* but not in (ii) or (iii); and in (iv), *HIM* may be proximate to *John.* These are the predicted results if the binding theory applies at S-structure. At this level, *he* does not c-command *John* in (i), but it does c-command *John* in (ii) and (iii); and *HIM* in (iv) is a pronominal, so that it may be bound by *John.* But at the LF-level we have the representations (36i–iv) for (35i–iv), respectively:

(36)   (i) for which book x that John read, he liked x
         (ii) for every book x that John read, he liked x
         (iii) I don't remember for which person y and which book x that John likes, y thinks that he read x
         (iv) for x = he, John said that Bill had seen x

In (36ii,iii), as in (36i), *he* does not c-command *John*; and in (36iv), *HIM* has been replaced by a variable which must be free, hence not bound by *John*, in accordance with principle (C) of the binding theory. Thus the rules (33) of the LF-component obliterate the distinction between (35i) and (35ii,iii), and they convert (35iv) to a structure that prevents binding, contrary to fact.

Such examples indicate that syntactic movement and movement in the LF-component have quite different effects with respect to the binding theory. This theory applies properly after syntactic movement, but each rule of the LF-component converts S-structures to which the binding theory applies correctly to LF-representations to which it applies incorrectly. Therefore these examples provide *prima facie* evidence that the binding theory applies at S-structure, a conclusion that I will now adopt. It should be noted, however, that the argument is only of limited weight. There are many open questions about examples of these types. Thus, examples (35i,ii,iii) are drawn from the class of largely unsolved problems briefly noted in chapter 2, note 79, and in the text at that point; and as we shall see in chapter 4, there remain open questions about the interpretation of focus at LF, in addition to well-known problems about the effect of focal stress on choice of referent in other constructions that do not seem to relate to binding theory (e.g., "John hit Bill and then HE hit HIM").

As noted, this revision – placing the binding theory at S-structure rather than at LF – leaves the preceding discussion unaffected except as regards principle (C). Previously, we treated variables created by syntactic movement-to-COMP and those created by quantifier movement in the same way, under principle (C). But with the binding theory applying at S-structure, only the former variables appear; in place of the latter, we have the quantifier phrases *everyone*, etc. Principle (C) still applies as before, since quantifiers are R-expressions (cf. §2.6). We can thus retain the binding theory in the form (12). The principles apply at S-structure; the binding in question is A-binding. The results outlined earlier follow. We might take principle (C) to be an "elsewhere condition," reading: "Other NPs are free."

The conclusion that the binding theory applies at S-structure yields considerable insight into the properties of this level, since these properties must be such as to permit the principles of the binding theory to apply. To mention a few examples, consider (37):

(37)   (i) *they persuaded Bill to visit each other
        (ii) they $_i$ regard [Bill as too critical of them $_i$ (*themselves, *each other)]
        (iii) Bill regards [them $_i$ as too critical of themselves (*them $_i$, each other)]
        (iv) I impressed them $_i$ [t as too critical of them $_i$ (*themselves, *each other)]
        (v) they $_i$ impressed me [t as too critical of themselves (*them $_i$, each other)]

Cf. also chapter 2, note 109. For the binding theory to apply properly in the case of examples (37), it is necessary to assume appropriate S-structures. In the case of (i), the correct results follow from the assumption that the *to* complement is clausal with **PRO** subject, as implied by the projection principle. In §2.6, we concluded that the projection principle implied the analysis exhibited in (ii) and (iii) (cf. the discussion of 2.6.(25)–(27)), though some questions remained. This analysis yields the binding properties illustrated in (ii), (iii). The analysis exhibited in (iv), (v) follows from the projection principle and Case theory (cf. the discussion of 2.6.(28)), and again yields the correct binding conclusions.

The general point is that if the binding theory holds at S-structure, considerations of binding provide evidence as to the nature of S-structures. We may therefore ask whether this evidence supports postulation of S-structures that are independently predicted by the projection principle and the system of principles in which it is embedded: specifically, Case theory and the principle that clauses have subjects at every level of syntactic structure (cf. 2.1.(25)). If this is the case, we have independent confirmation of this system of principles. In many interesting cases, the conclusions seem to hold.

While the binding theory applies at S-structure, there are other principles that must apply at the level of LF. One is the principle involved in weak crossover (see (34) and references of notes 46, 47), since this principle applies to variables created by LF rules as well as those resulting from the application of syntactic movement rules. Another example, to which we turn in the next chapter, is the principle that we have so far labelled "RES(NIC)." Some further LF phenomena are discussed in May (1980). The principle that $[_\alpha e]$ must be bound (cf. §2.6) is also, presumably, an

LF principle. It remains to give a principled account of the distinction between the conditions that hold at the two levels and the distinction between their formal properties, and indeed, to determine the nature of these properties more closely. We continue to consider these questions in connection with the binding theory and RES(NIC) in this and the following chapter, respectively.

Let us now return to the examples (32) illustrating improper movement. Note that there are examples exactly like those of (32) except that the c-commanding element with index i is in an A-position rather than in an $\bar{\text{A}}$-position, as it was in (32), i.e., examples which omit the final step in the derivation of (32); for example, (38):

(38)　　(i) *John tried $[_{\bar{S}} t [_S t' \text{ to win}]]$
　　　　(ii) *John seemed $[_{\bar{S}} t [_S \text{Bill would see } t']]$
　　　　(iii) *John is possible $[_{\bar{S}} t [_S \text{Bill will see } t']]$
　　　　(iv) *it seems $[_{\bar{S}} t [_S t' \text{ to rain}]]$
　　　　(v) *it seems $[_{\bar{S}} t \text{ that } [_S \text{John expected } [_{\bar{S}} t' [_S t'' \text{ to rain}]]]]$

The surface structures of (i) and (iv) are grammatical, but not with the derivation indicated, with the matrix subject moving from the D-structure position of t' to the COMP position of t and then to its matrix position. Examples (ii), (iii), (v) are excluded. These structures are, once again, barred by principle (C) of the binding theory, exactly as in the case of (32).

This conclusion, however, is problematic, as we can see by returning to certain examples rather similar in form to (38) that we discussed in § 2.6, for example, (39i) derived by Move-α from the D-structure (39ii):

(39)　　(i) John bought a book $[_{\bar{S}} [_{NP_i} \alpha] \text{ for } [_S \text{Mary to read } t_i]]$
　　　　(ii) John bought a book $[_{\bar{S}} \text{for } [_S \text{Mary to read } [_{NP_i} \alpha]]]$

We assumed in § 2.6 that the empty NP is assigned the feature $[wh\text{-}]$ permitting movement-to-COMP (cf. 2.6.(45)), though the motivation was not strong. Two other questions were discussed, namely, the options of (40):

(40)　　(i) $\alpha = e$ or $\alpha = \text{PRO}$ in (39)
　　　　(ii) Move-α applies in the syntax or in the LF-component to form (39i) from (39ii)

If syntactic movement is selected in (40ii), then (39i) is the S-structure; if LF-movement is selected, then (39ii) is the S-structure. In either case, (39i) is the LF-representation, with t_i a variable bound by $[_{NP_i} \alpha]$. As for (40i), we saw that although there might be some advantages to choice of $\alpha = e$, this choice is inconsistent with the projection principle, which requires that $\alpha = \text{PRO}$ (see chapter 6 for dissolution of the issue, from another point of view).

However we answer the questions (40), the LF-representation (39i) is quite similar to (32) and (38). Clearly, the NP *a book* in (39i) is coindexed with $[_{NP_i} \alpha]$, so that the LF-representation is in fact (41):

(41)   John bought $[_{NP_i}$ a book$]$ $[_{\bar{S}}[_{NP_i} \alpha]$ for $[_S$ Mary to read t$_i]]$

As distinct from (32), (38), however, the structure (41) is grammatical. We must therefore determine why principle (C) does not apply to (41) barring this construction on the grounds that the variable t_i is A-bound, whereas in (32) and (38) it does apply, barring these very similar constructions.[51]

The structures we are now considering are of the form (42) at LF:

(42)   (i) $[_{wh\text{-phrase}_i}[\ldots \alpha_i \ldots [_{\bar{S}} t_i \ldots [_S \ldots t'_i \ldots]]]]$
        (ii) $[\ldots \alpha_i \ldots [_{\bar{S}} t_i \ldots [_S \ldots t'_i \ldots]]]$

The examples of (32) are of the form (42i); the examples of (38) and (41) are of the form (42ii). In (42i), α_i is a trace, whereas in (42ii) it is a lexical NP. Where (42ii) represents (38), α_i is moved from the D-structure position of t'_i; where (42ii) represents (41), α_i is base-generated in place. Our problem is to explain why (42i) is always ungrammatical, whereas (42ii) is ungrammatical when it represents (38) but grammatical when it represents (41).

We can try to account for these facts in terms of differences in manner of derivation or differences in form. Let's first consider manner of derivation. There is an obvious difference in this respect between (32) and (38) on the one hand, and (41) on the other; namely, in (32) and (38) the variable t'_i of (42) is coindexed with the NP α_i that A-binds it by double application of a syntactic movement rule, whereas in (41) the coindexing of t'_i and α_i involves a rule of control associating α_i with t_i in COMP.[52] Looking at the S-structures, in the ungrammatical cases (32) and (38), α_i is coindexed with and therefore binds t'_i, whereas in the grammatical case (39) the coindexing illustrated in (41) is not yet established. But the binding theory applies at S-structure. Therefore principle (C) marks (32) and (38) ungrammatical while not applying at all to (39) (whether (i) or (ii) is assumed to be the S-structure, i.e., whatever answer we select for (40ii)); therefore (39) is grammatical. Thus we make the proper distinctions if the binding theory applies at S-structure.

The argument, while attractive, is based on a dubious and probably incorrect assumption concerning indexing. Under the simplest indexing conventions, the rule of control that relates a *book* and $[_{NP} \alpha]$ in (41) is not a rule assigning indices but rather a rule that checks indices already assigned by random index assignment at S-structure. Thus at the S-structure level, we already have coindexing as in (41), (42ii). Therefore the structures are incorrectly ruled ungrammatical by principle (C) of the binding theory, even though the control rule that determines that the coindexing of α_i and t'_i of (42) is legitimate applies later. We can therefore sustain the argument based on manner of derivation only if we adopt a theory of indexing in which the control rule of the LF-component assigns indices, a slight but undesirable complication.

Let us try, then, to appeal to a difference of form. Putting (38) aside for the moment, let us compare the ungrammatical (32), which is of the form (42i), with the grammatical (41), which is of the form (42ii). There is an obvious difference between (42i) and (42ii), namely, in (42i) the variable t'_i and the NP α_i that binds it are both within the scope of an operator, the *wh*-phrase, which $\bar{A}$-binds both α_i and t'_i; whereas in (42ii) the A-binding NP α_i is outside the scope of the unique operator t_i that $\bar{A}$-binds the variable t'_i. Suppose that we recast definition (5ii) as follows:

(43) α is X-free if and only if there is no β, γ such that
   (i) β X-binds α
   (ii) if γ $\bar{A}$-binds α, then $\gamma = \beta$ or γ binds β

This modification is vacuous for names and is reasonable for variables. Its content is, in effect, that principle (C) of the binding theory requires that a variable must be A-free in the maximal domain in which it is $\bar{A}$-bound; only elements within the scope of the maximal operator that binds a variable "count" as potential A-binders for it. We might think of the definition (43) as analogous to a notational convention in standard quantification theory that takes two occurrences of the variable x to be distinct if one lies within the scope of a quantifier Q while the other lies outside the scope of Q.

The definition of "X-free" in (43) is, in effect, a definition of "A-free" for variables; it reduces to the former notion "X-free" in other cases. The concept defined in (43) is already familiar from θ-theory. In §2.6, we saw that an argument can be assigned a θ-role by a coindexed trace only if the trace is "operator-free"; cf. 2.6.(47). The definition (43) is similar in its import.

The effect of the revision to (43) is to permit (41) while barring (32). But the examples of (38) remain a problem; they are not barred by principle (C) of the binding theory, since they are just like (41) under the revision of the notion "A-free." Is there, then, some independent consideration that blocks the examples of (38)? In fact, these examples are barred by principle 2.6.(45) which restricts movement-to-COMP to elements with the feature [*wh-*]. But the matrix subject in the examples of (38), being lexical, cannot have the feature [*wh-*]. There is, then, a distinction of form between the grammatical and ungrammatical instances of (42ii). In the grammatical instances such as (41), α_i does not have the feature [*wh-*] (since it is base-generated in place); whereas in the ungrammatical instances of (38) α_i has the feature [*wh-*], since it is moved from the COMP position t_i, and this is impossible, under obvious interpretive conventions.

On the assumption that 2.4.(45) is valid, it follows that the notion "X-free" defined in (43) suffices to establish the distinctions we require.

But this conclusion is still somewhat unsatisfactory, since 2.4.(45), while not unreasonable, was not very strongly motivated empirically. Its only function, in fact, was to ensure that non-operators will not move to COMP, a result that could easily be obtained by alternative conventions. Let us ask, then, whether there are independent considerations that bar the examples of (38).

In fact, considerations of θ-theory show, more indirectly, that the examples of (38) are ungrammatical. Repeating (38), we have the following cases:

(38)   (i)   *John tried $[_{\bar{S}} t [_S t'$ to win$]]$
        (ii) *John seemed $[_{\bar{S}} t [_S$ Bill would see $t']]$
        (iii) *John is possible $[_{\bar{S}} t [_S$ Bill will see $t']]$
        (iv) *it seems $[_{\bar{S}} t [_S t'$ to rain$]]$
        (v)   *it seems $[_{\bar{S}} t$ that $[_S$ John expected $[_{\bar{S}} t' [_S t''$ to rain$]]]]$

These examples exhaust the range of relevant cases. Investigating them, we see that each is ruled out by the θ-criterion, under the projection principle. In case (i), the D-structure violates the θ-criterion since the matrix subject position lacks an argument. Examples (iv) and (v) are ruled out by the θ-criterion applying at LF, since the variable has no θ-role, and variables, being R-expressions and hence arguments, must have a θ-role. The same consideration excludes such examples as "what $[t$ rains$]$," "what do you think $[t$ seems that John will win$]$." Now consider (ii) and (iii). In these examples, the argument *John* appears in a non-θ-position in LF, so that the examples are grammatical only if *John* is assigned a θ-role by its trace. The trace t is not in a θ-position, so cannot assign a θ-role. The trace t' is in a θ-position, but it is not "the trace of *John*" in accordance with 2.6.(47). Returning to the considerations of §3.2.2, principle 3.2.2.(32) assigns a θ-role to an A-function chain, but in (38ii,iii) there are two A-function chains, one containing just t' and one containing just *John*; the latter is assigned no θ-role, so the examples are ungrammatical by the θ-criterion applying at LF. Therefore, all the examples of (38) are barred by the θ-criterion.

Note that this argument does not exclude the grammatical example (41), which is similar in form to (38i). The reason is that the D-structure (39ii) in this case satisfies the θ-criterion, since α_i of (42ii) is base-generated in place. The projection principle thus distinguishes properly between the case of movement and the case of control, even though the resulting structures are identical at LF, and also at S-structure if we assume that it is syntactic movement that produces the form (41), that is, if we select syntactic movement as the required option in (40ii). But we must select this option, since otherwise the example will be ruled ungrammatical at S-structure by the θ-criterion. The reason is that if the S-structure is (39ii) (where *a book* is now assigned the index i by random indexing at S-structure), then *a book* and $[_{NP} \alpha]$ belong to the same A-function chain, but two distinct θ-roles are assigned, violating the θ-criterion.

This analysis provides an answer to question (40ii): Move-α must apply in the syntax to ensure that the matrix NP *a book* and the trace in the embedded clause (namely, α and t' of (42ii), respectively) are in different A-function chains. Furthermore, indexing must be at S-structure, after the appropriate A-function chains are distinguished by application of Move-α, or the θ-criterion will again be violated. As for question (40i), the projection principle requires that $\alpha = $ PRO, though as we shall see in chapter 6, nothing is really at stake in the choice between PRO and $[_{NP}e]$ for the moved element.

Note further that the same analysis rules out examples (42i) independently of the binding theory, for exactly the reasons just reviewed in connection with (38), which is of the form (42ii). James Higginbotham points out that there are other examples of improper movement that are not blocked by the binding theory though they are barred by the argument just outlined in terms of θ-theory. Consider, for example, (44):

(44)   *who did you give [pictures of t] to t'

Suppose (44) to have been derived by *wh*-movement from the position of t' to the position of t (or conversely), and then to the matrix COMP position, yielding the interpretation: "for which person x, you give pictures of x to x." There is no semantic constraint against this interpretation; nevertheless, it is not an interpretation assigned to (44), which is ungrammatical. The binding theory is not violated by the structure (44). The operator *who* binds the variables t and t', but neither variable binds the other, so that condition (C) of the binding theory is not violated. But the θ-criterion is violated if (44) is derived in the manner just described. Since the variables are arguments, they must appear in θ-positions. But at least one of these positions must be a non-θ-position since it is filled by a non-argument – in fact, $[_{NP}e]$ – at D-structure, or the derivation will violate the recoverability condition, which in this case guarantees that D-structure is an accurate characterization of GF-θ. But this is a contradiction. Examples of the type of (42ii) and (44) therefore indicate that it is θ-theory rather than binding theory that provides the fundamental reason why improper movement is barred in (42i).

Notice that it is the *derivation* of (44) just considered rather than the structure itself that must be barred. The structure itself does not violate any of the subsystems of principles 1.(2) of the GB-theory, but it is not derivable by the rule system 1.(1) of this theory. Thus, it would be possible to add rules (presumably, marked rules) of some sort that would allow us to derive structures with the general properties of (44). Cf. Taraldsen (1979) for discussion that bears on this possibility. Examples of "across-the-board deletion" in the sense of Williams (1978) are a possible case, though we have assumed that they are in fact generated in accordance with the rule system 1.(1). See the references of chapter 2, note 72.

Note also that there is again crucial reliance on properties of D-structure in connection with (44).

Summarizing this discussion, θ-theory – i.e., the θ-criterion under the projection principle – distinguishes the grammatical examples (39), (41) from the ungrammatical cases (32), (38), (44), relying crucially on the distinction between movement and base-generation, the properties of D-structure and the rule system including the syntactic rule Move-α. We have also considered two other possibilities, each worth considering but with lesser explanatory force in these cases: (1) with a complication of the indexing theory, the examples are distinguished by the binding theory at S-structure; (2) the principle 2.6.(45) requiring $[wh\text{-}]$ for movement-to-COMP combines with the definition (43) for "X-free" to make the appropriate distinctions. Neither (1) nor (2) accounts for (44). It seems clear that the argument in terms of θ-theory is the most principled approach, as well as the one with broadest empirical coverage. I will therefore assume that it is correct.

In the light of these considerations, let us return to examples (18), (19), repeated here as (45):

(45)   (i) John is too clever $[$PRO to expect us to catch$]$
        (ii) John is too clever $[$PRO to expect us to catch Bill$]$

As noted earlier, (45i) is interpretable only with the PRO subject of the embedded clause taken to be arbitrary in reference, not controlled by *John*, even though it is in a position of control as shown by (45ii), where PRO is controlled by *John*. This was left as an open problem in the earlier discussion. Let us now have another look at it.

The embedded clause of (45i) is (46) at the level of S-structure and LF:

(46) $[\,_{\bar{S}}[\,_{NP_i}\alpha][\,_S PRO_j$ to expect $[\,_S$ us to catch $t_i\,]]]$

Suppose that PRO in (45i) (i.e., PRO$_j$ in (46)) is coindexed with *John*, as in (45ii). Therefore *John* has the index j. The empty category in COMP must be coindexed with *John*; cf. § 2.6. Therefore $i = j$. But now the variable t_i in (46) is bound by PRO$_j$, which is within the scope of the operator that $\bar{A}$-binds t_i. Therefore, (46) violates principle (C) of the binding theory. The sentence (45i) has a grammatical interpretation only when PRO ($=$ PRO$_j$) is free, i.e., arbitrary in reference. The question does not arise in case (45ii). Therefore it may receive the (highly preferred) control reading. The crucial properties of (45), as of (41), are once again captured by the concept of binding defined in (43), or equivalently, by the closely related notion of θ-role assignment to A-function chains. Note that the same analysis applies to (16vi), even if *him* is permitted to be coindexed with *John*; cf. note 40.

A similar analysis is applicable to such examples as (47):

(47)   (i) they are too stubborn for each other to talk to

      (ii) they are easy for each other to talk to
      (iii) John is too stubborn to talk to

The corresponding representations at S-structure and LF are (48):[53]

(48)   (i) they are too stubborn $[_{\bar{S}} \alpha_i$ for $[_S$ each other to talk to $t_i]]$
        (ii) they are easy for each other $[_{\bar{S}} \alpha_i [_S PRO_j$ to talk to $t_i]]$
        (iii) John is too stubborn $[_{\bar{S}} \alpha_i [_S PRO_j$ to talk to $t_i]]$

Bochner (1976) notes that case (iii) is necessarily interpreted with the embedded subject arbitrary in reference, though control is possible in this position, as in (49), and would lead to no semantic anomaly:

(49)   John is too stubborn to talk to Bill

But in (48iii), as in (45i), α in COMP is necessarily controlled by the matrix subject. Therefore, if PRO_j is controlled by the matrix subject, it follows that $i = j$, so that principle (C) of the binding theory is violated in (48iii). Therefore, PRO_j must be free, accounting for the interpretation of (47iii). Example (47iii), (48iii) contrasts with such cases as "they would be happy for each other to talk to Bill"; cf. note 38.

    Turning to (47i,ii), in case (ii) PRO_j of (48ii) must be controlled by the matrix *for*-phrase in such structures, as in (50):

(50)   they are easy for Bill $[_{\bar{S}} \alpha_i [_S PRO_j$ to talk to $t_i]]$

But *each other* in (48ii) is controlled by *they*. Again, it follows that $i = j$, since α_i is also necessarily controlled by *they*, as in (50). Therefore (47ii) is also barred by principle (C) of the binding theory. A similar argument applies in case (47i).[54]

    There are many other questions about the choice of antecedents for pronouns that are not answered by the binding theory; see for example 2.4.3.(7), repeated here as (51):

(51)   (i) John asked Bill his plans
        (ii) John told Bill his plans
        (iii) John promised Bill his consent
        (iv) John promised Bill his admission to the university

Among other examples are (52):[55]

(52)   (i) John told Bill too many things for him to understand
        (ii) John told Bill things that were too difficult for him to understand
        (iii) John heard too many things for him to understand
        (iv) John considers Bill too stupid for him to pass algebra
        (v) John gave Bill a book for him to read

The determined or preferential choice of antecedent for the pronoun when taken as proximate in these cases and others like them varies in part on the basis of conditions extrinsic to this discussion, but in part raise questions – which I will not pursue here – that are relevant to it. The binding theory, however, extends to a considerable range of cases where choice of antecedent depends on structural configurations involving empty categories, as the discussion indicates.

There are a few related problems that deserve some mention.[56] Consider again the structures (53):

(53)   (i) John$_i$ V $[_{\bar{S}} t_i (for) [_S \ldots t'_i \ldots]]$
        (ii) John$_i$ is possible $[_{\bar{S}} t_i (for) [_S \ldots t'_i \ldots]]$

These might arise from successive-cyclic application of Move-α, with *John* moving from the D-structure position of t'_i to COMP and then to the matrix position, exactly as in (38). We have seen that these derivations are excluded by the θ-criterion. So far there is no problem.

But how do we ensure that structures of the form (53) are not base-generated with *John* in the matrix subject position, coindexed with the empty categories of the embedded clause by a control rule as in (41)? We might exclude this possibility on the grounds that the base rules do not permit generation of NP in COMP, but suppose that we do not adopt this constraint, thus permitting base-generation of (53). The only possible interpretation of (53) is as a purposive clause. Suppose that the embedded clause is finite, as in (38ii,iii). This possibility is excluded by the principle, whatever it may be, that requires that purposive clauses be infinitival, and more generally, that clauses of the form of the embedded clause in (53) are infinitival in many other structures as well – e.g., complex adjectival constructions of various sorts.

Suppose then that the embedded clause in (53) is infinitival, as in (54):

(54)   (i)   *John thought [for [Bill to visit]]
        (ii) *John came over last night [for [Bill to speak to]]
        (iii) the book was left [for [Mary to read]]
        (iv) the book is here [for [you to read]]

As (iii) and (iv) indicate, the structures are permissible and therefore should not be ruled out by any structural condition of the sort we are considering. Properties of thematic structure presumably rule out the interpretation as a purposive clause in (i) and (ii), this being the interpretation assigned to these constructions at the LF-level.

This takes care of examples of the form (53i). What of (53ii)? Whether the embedded clause is finite or infinitival, these are excluded by the θ-criterion, since *John* is not in a θ-position and cannot be assigned a θ-role by t'_i, since the two belong to distinct A-function chains. Redundantly, these cases are ruled out by the considerations just mentioned if the embedded clause is finite.

In §2.4.6, we discussed the very marginal, and perhaps ultimately vacuous question of whether the rule Move-α should be interpreted as a mapping of D-structure to S-structure or, alternatively, as an interpretive rule of the LF-component with exactly the special properties of Move-α, these being crucially distinct from the properties of the rules of construal of the LF-component (the latter distinction being substantive). The analysis just presented of (53) in effect corresponds to the second of these options: interpretation of Move-α as a special rule of the LF-component. Once again we see that exactly the same principles operate – crucially, the assignment of θ-role to A-function chains or equivalently, adoption of (43) – whichever option is selected, revealing again the marginal character of this question if the projection principle (hence trace theory) is adopted.

The preceding discussion has been limited to the functioning of the binding theory for arguments within clauses. The principles (12) are close to bare statements of fact and are minimal, so far as I can see. The binding theory has one problematic feature, however, at the conceptual level: it gives no answer to the question (55):

(55)   Why are NP and S the two governing categories?

I will return to this question shortly.

Before doing so, let us briefly consider the application of the binding theory to arguments within NPs, as in 3.1.(2), repeated here as (56):

(56) (i)   NP*   (ii) γ

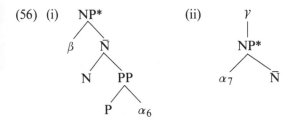

Principle (C) applies unproblematically. As for anaphors, we need only consider overt anaphors such as *each other*, since trace is excluded from positions α_6 and α_7 in general for reasons noted in §3.1, though there is more to say about the subject, which goes beyond the bounds of this discussion. See the references cited in §5.2; also Obenauer (1976), Milner (1979), Cinque (1979), Steriade (1980).

In position α_6, the anaphor is governed by P so that NP* is its governing category, in which it must be bound. This gives the right results where β is a subject, as in (57i,ii), but the wrong results where β is not a subject, as in (57iii,iv):

(57)   (i)   their stories about each other
        (ii) *we heard [their stories about each other]
        (iii) we heard [some stories about each other]

(iv) we heard [the stories about each other (that are being circulated)]

In this case, SSC gives the right results throughout; note that in this case SSC does not follow in general from the binding theory of the GB-framework, in contrast to the case of arguments within clauses. The same is true in more complex cases, e.g., (58):

(58)   we thought [that [pictures of each other] would be on sale]

Here, the OB-theory marks the sentence grammatical while the GB-theory incorrectly rejects it. While (58) is perhaps somewhat marginal and may be a marked construction, as consideration of some other languages suggests (cf. Milner (1979)), nevertheless in English it surely has a different status from such violations of the SSC as (59):

(59)   we thought [that [John's pictures of each other] would be on sale]

Turning to position α_7, the question of whether or not it is governed with the governing category NP* depends on the resolution of a question discussed in § 3.2.1. Neither decision concerning government gives exactly the right results. Suppose that α_7 is ungoverned and thus lacks a governing category (though it has Case). Then we derive the right results for (60), but long-distance binding is incorrectly admitted in (61):[57]

(60)   we read [$_{NP*}$ each other's books]
(61)   *they forced me [PRO to read [$_{NP*}$ each other's books]]

Suppose that α_7 is governed by the head of $\bar{N}$, so that NP* is the governing category. Then (60) is incorrectly barred and (61) is correctly barred, though for what seem to be the wrong reasons.

Suppose we have [$_{VP}$ V-*ing* . . .] in place of $\bar{N}$ in (56ii), as in (62):

(62)   *they preferred [$_{NP*}$ each other's reading the book]   (= 3.1.(3))

Under any of the concepts of government discussed in § 3.2.1, *each other* is ungoverned in (62). Therefore (62) is not excluded by the binding theory, since *each other* lacks a governing category in this case. Similarly, (62) is admitted in the OB-framework, incorrectly. But the example may not be crucial, since it might relate to the plurality requirement for reciprocals (see note 57). Comparative evidence should be relevant in this case.

Turning now to pronominals in (56), we need only consider pronouns, PRO being excluded from the governed positions α_6 and α_7, and unproblematic in α_7 if $\bar{N}$ is replaced by [$_{VP}$ V-*ing* . . .]. The predictions of the GB-theory are that a pronoun must be free in its governing category NP* in case (56i), giving (63) for the case of *him* proximate to *John*:

(63)   (i)   John saw [$_{NP*}$my picture of him]
         (ii) *I saw [$_{NP*}$John's picture of him]
         (iii) John saw [$_{NP*}$a picture of him]
         (iv) John thought I saw [$_{IV*}$a picture of him]

The OB-framework gives the same results for (i) and (ii) but marks (iii) ungrammatical, which appears to be the correct result for such cases. Cf. note 2.

With regard to case (56ii), consider the examples (64); and example (65), where we have VP in place of $\bar{N}$ in (56ii):

(64)   (i)   John read [$_{NP*}$ his book]
         (ii) John thought I saw [$_{NP*}$ his book]
(65)   John preferred [$_{NP*}$ his reading the book]

Suppose *his* to be proximate to *John*. If *his* is governed in (56ii), then (64i) is predicted to be grammatical by the GB-theory, as is (64ii). If *his* is not governed and thus lacks a governing category, the predictions are the same. The OB-framework predicts that (64i) is ungrammatical and (64ii) grammatical. As for (65), it is marked unacceptable by the Avoid Pronoun principle 2.4.2.(5), which may account for its status.[58]

Summarizing, the GB-framework is a considerable improvement over OB on empirical and conceptual grounds, but there are still problems in the case of arguments within NPs, namely, case (56). Let us return to these in the context of a somewhat different approach towards unifying NIC and SSC.

Consider again the basic structure of S, which we are assuming to be (66):

(66)   NP INFL VP, where INFL = [[$\pm$Tense], (AGR)]

Here AGR = PRO and is obligatory with [+Tense] and excluded with [−Tense].[59]

Suppose we were to consider AGR to be in some sense the "subject" when it is present, serving as a kind of antecedent to NP in (66). To avoid confusion, let us introduce the term "SUBJECT" having the following sense: the subject of an infinitive, an NP or a small clause (whether or not these are of the category A^i, etc., as suggested earlier) is a SUBJECT; AGR in (66) is a SUBJECT, but NP in (66) is not if INFL contains AGR. The notion SUBJECT accords with the idea that the subject is the "most prominent nominal element" in some sense, taking INFL to be the head of S. Thus we take the SUBJECT to be the capitalized element in (67):

(67)   (i)   John [$_{INFL}$ past AGR] win

(ii) he wants (very much) [for JOHN to win]
(iii) he believes [JOHN to be intelligent]
(iv) [JOHN's reading the book] surprised me
(v)   he considers [JOHN intelligent]

In cases (ii)–(v), the subject of the embedded phrase is the SUBJECT. In case (i), the subject is *John* and the SUBJECT is AGR. Furthermore AGR is the SUBJECT of the matrix clause in (ii)–(v).

Notice that on these assumptions, NIC reduces to SSC if we reformulate the SSC in terms of SUBJECT rather than subject. That is, *John* in (i) is in the domain of the SUBJECT and its position is therefore opaque in accordance with SSC. Recall that we are considering INFL to be a collection of features, so that AGR in (i) c-commands *John*.

Actually, it is not quite accurate to say that NIC in the sense of the OB-framework reduces to SSC; rather, what reduces to SSC is a version of the Propositional Island Condition (PIC: the predecessor to NIC) proposed by George and Kornfilt (1978), which takes the crucial element determining opacity to be agreement rather than tense (in the latter case, the Tensed-S Condition). In English, there is no distinction, since agreement is one-one correlated with tense. But this is not true in certain other languages. George and Kornfilt show that in Turkish, where tense and agreement are dissociated, it is agreement rather than tense that determines opacity. The same is true in Portuguese, as observed by Rouveret (see note 59). The inflected infinitive, containing the agreement element, assigns nominative Case to its subject, thus creating an opaque domain in the sense of the NIC or the George-Kornfilt version of the PIC.[60] We have tacitly been assuming the accuracy of the George-Kornfilt theory all along, taking AGR – the governor of the subject – to be the crucial element determining opacity. Now assuming AGR to be the SUBJECT, we have only one opaque domain: the domain of a SUBJECT. Thus NIC and SSC are unified, but along different lines than those we have so far discussed.

This approach has a conceptual advantage over the one presented above. Namely, it provides an answer to the question (55): why are NP and S the two governing categories? The answer now is that NP and S are the two categories containing SUBJECTS, and it is the SUBJECT that creates an opaque domain. In fact, we now have a somewhat different and more complex conclusion: S is a governing category for α in the former sense, because it always contains SUBJECT (cf. the discussion of 2.1.(25)), but NP is a governing category for α only when it contains a SUBJECT $\neq \alpha$, thus in (68) but not (69):

(68)   [$_{NP}$ John's story about α]
(69)   [$_{NP}$ a story about α]

Furthermore, other categories (e.g., adjective phrases) may also be governing categories if they contain subjects (hence SUBJECTS), as in the analysis of small clauses discussed in §§ 2.6, 3.2.1.

Clearly, then, we will have different answers in this theory to the question of how anaphors and pronouns behave in NP, the problematic case as we have seen. But this approach will reduce to the binding theory of the GB-framework for the case of arguments in clauses.

Both the binding theory reviewed earlier and this new alternative have attractive features. Let us therefore consider the possibility of amalgamating them, then turning to the problematic case of arguments within NP. We assume the binding theory proposed above (namely, (12)) without alteration, and the following two basic principles, where (II) replaces the definition (11) for "governing category":

(70)   (I) AGR is coindexed with the NP it governs

        (II) β is a *governing category for* α if and only if β is the minimal category containing α, a governor of α, and a SUBJECT accessible to α

It follows that β is a governing category only if it has a SUBJECT. Thus S is always a potential governing category, and NP is also a potential governing category when it has a subject, as is A^i, etc., under the theory of small clauses discussed earlier. The choice of governing categories now receives a rather natural characterization in terms of (70II), overcoming the conceptual problem (55). As we shall see, a number of empirical problems are also resolved. The question whether S or $\bar{S}$ should be selected as the governing category no longer arises.

It remains to explain the notion of accessibility in (70II). As for principle (70I), it expresses the phenomenon of agreement, given the more general condition that when NP and a pronominal (pronoun or PRO) are coindexed, they must share the appropriate features.[61] Thus (70I) reduces the phenomenon of obligatoriness of subject-verb agreement to general properties of proximate pronominals, including control.

The intuitive idea behind these constructions is that an anaphor or pronominal searches for the closest SUBJECT to which it can be linked, where linking involves coreference for an anaphor and disjoint reference for a pronoun. It cannot be linked to a more remote element. "Searching for a subject" is a standard device for anaphora in many languages, including those that appear to employ a somewhat different binding theory for certain anaphors.[62] The SSC and also the NIC (under this interpretation) thus may be thought of as constituting a "local version" of this device of searching for subject. Note however that the "locality" in question is to be sharply distinguished from subjacency, the bounding condition for trace. Cf. § 2.4.4.

We are assuming AGR to be identical to PRO, hence a noun. But it is not an NP. If it were an NP, and if its position is an A-position (which is not clear), then AGR would be a binder with respect to the binding theory, leading to violation of the principles of this theory. Thus, principle (C) would be violated by (71), since *John* would be A-bound by AGR; and we would expect to have such sentences as (72), since *each other* would be bound in its governing category:

(71)   John $[_{INFL}$ past, AGR$]$ win   (= (67i))
(72)   (i) each other won
        (ii) $[_S[_{NPi}$ each other$][_{INFL}[+$ Tense$]$, AGR $_i][_{VP}$ win$]]$

While AGR creates a governing category in which an anaphor must be bound and a pronominal must be free, AGR is not itself the binder; rather, binders are selected as before. If we restrict function chains to NP, as previously, then AGR does not enter into such chains.

Returning to the principles of (70), it remains to define "accessibility." The definition is given in (74) in terms of the well-formedness condition (73):[63]

(73)   *$[_\gamma \ldots \delta \ldots]$, where γ and δ bear the same index
(74) α is *accessible to* β if and only if β is in the c-command domain of α and assignment to β of the index of α would not violate (73)

Note that (74) refers to possible, not necessarily actual indexing of β. The condition (73) holds for a variety of constructions apart from those we are considering here, for example, those of (75):

(75)   (i) *$[_{NP_i}$ the friends of $[_i$ each other's$]$ parents$]$
        (ii) *There is $[_{NP_i}$ a picture of $[_{NP_i}$ itself$]]$ on the mantelpiece
        (iii) *$[_{NP_i}$ the owner of $[[_{NP_i}$ his$]$ boat$]]$
        (iv) *$[_{NP_i}$ the friends of $[[_{NP_i}$ their$]$ parents$]]$

The well-formedness condition (73) deserves further consideration. Perhaps it is too strong as it stands. In part, it may be reducible to other conditions; perhaps the A-over-A condition. Let us assume that it is basically correct and consider the notion of "accessibility" incorporating it. See notes 63, 64.

For the case of arguments within S, the new theory works in exactly the same way as the GB-theory just reviewed. The nominative subject of a clause has an accessible SUBJECT – namely, the AGR element of INFL, which also governs the subject. Hence the clause is a governing category and the nominative anaphor must be bound in this category (which is impossible) and pronominals must be free in this category (relevant only in the case of pronouns, since the position is governed by INFL). The governing categories in the other cases reviewed remain exactly as they were, since clauses must have subjects, hence SUBJECTS, and these are always accessible. So nothing further has to be said about this case.

In the case of arguments within NP (cf. (56ii)), the situation is rather different, however. Consider the example (76):

(76) $[_{NP*}$ stories about $\alpha]$ $[_{INFL}$ $[+$ Tense$]$, AGR$]$ disturb John

Here the subject NP* "stories about α" is coindexed with AGR, which governs it, by principle (I) of (70). Hence NP* is nominative and agrees with AGR, ultimately with the verb to which AGR is attached. AGR is accessible to NP*, so that the clause (76) is a governing category for NP*. If $\alpha = war$, we have the grammatical sentence (77):

(77)   stories about war disturb John

But AGR in (76) is not accessible to α because of the well-formedness condition (73), which would be violated if α were coindexed with AGR, hence with NP*, which is itself coindexed with AGR. Correspondingly, α does not enter into an agreement relation with AGR.[64]
     Consider the examples (78):

(78)   they heard $\left[_{NP}\left\{\begin{matrix}*my\\ the\\ \emptyset\end{matrix}\right\}\text{stories about each other}\right]$

The NP object contains a SUBJECT accessible to *each other* only when its specifier is *my* in (78). Therefore, just in this case the anaphor *each other* must be bound in this category, yielding the results indicated in (78).
     Consider next the examples (79):

(79)   (i)   they expected $[_{S*}$ me to hear $[_{NP*}$ stories about each other$]]$
         (ii) they expected that $[_{S*}[_{NP*}$ pictures of each other$]$ would be on sale$]$
         (iii) they expected that $\left[_{S*}\left[_{NP*}\left\{\begin{matrix}\text{PRO feeding each other}\\ \text{PRO to feed each other}\end{matrix}\right\}\right]\text{would}\right.$ be difficult$]$

In (i), NP* contains a governor of *each other* but no SUBJECT accessible to *each other*. Therefore, it is not a governing category for the anaphor. S*, however, does contain a SUBJECT accessible to *each other*, namely, its subject *me*. Therefore S* is the governing category for *each other*, which must be bound in this category; hence the ungrammaticalness of (i). Interchange of *I* and *they* in (i) would yield a grammatical sentence.
     Turning to case (ii) of (79), NP* contains a governor of *each other* but no SUBJECT accessible to it. Therefore it is not a governing category for *each other*. What about S*? The only candidate as an accessible SUBJECT is its agreement element AGR. But this element is coindexed with NP* by principle (I) of (70) and therefore is not accessible to *each other* because of condition (73). Therefore S* is not a governing category for *each other*.

The element AGR of the matrix clause is, however, accessible to *each other*. Therefore the matrix clause is the governing category for *each other*, which must be bound in this category. Thus (79ii) is grammatical with coindexing of *they* and *each other*. But (80) is ungrammatical, since *each other* is not bound in S*:

(80)   *they thought [$_{S*}$ I expected that pictures of each other would be on sale]

Case (iii) of (79) is similar. There is no problem about the anaphor *each other*, which must be bound in its governing category NP*, i.e., bound by PRO. What about PRO? As the binding theory requires, PRO is un-governed in (79iii) and can be coindexed in any manner consistent with the theory of control (cf. §2.4.3). Therefore (79iii) is grammatical, as is (81), in contrast to (80):[65]

(81)   they thought [$_{S*}$ I expected that$\begin{cases}\text{feeding each other}\\ \text{to feed each other}\end{cases}$would be difficult]

Consider next the examples (82), (83):

(82)   they think it is a pity that pictures of each other are hanging on the wall
(83)   *they think he said that pictures of each other are hanging on the wall

Example (82) is grammatical, while (83) is ungrammatical. The difference might be attributed to a phenomenon that has been frequently discussed in connection with the SSC, namely, that the nature of the subject that creates the opaque domain figures in determining the degree of violation of opacity, with agentive subjects inducing maximal violation and non-arguments minimal violation.[66] But other examples suggest a different approach.[67] Consider (84):

(84)   (i) *they think [it bothered *each other* that S]
        (ii) *he thinks [it bothered *himself* that S]
        (iii) he thinks [it bothered *him* that S]   (*him* proximate to *he*)

These differ in grammatical status, with (i) and (ii) ungrammatical and (iii) grammatical.[68] In (84), AGR in the embedded clause is a SUBJECT accessible to the italicized anaphor or pronominal and this clause is therefore the governing category for this element. The examples (84) therefore fall together with (83) and contrast with (82), indicating that the crucial distinction between (82) and (83) is not the agentivity (or some other property) of the subject *it*. We are left, then, with the problem of explaining the difference between (82) and (83), and explaining why (82) differs from (84).

The crucial difference between (82) and (84) is that in (82), the anaphor is internal to the extraposed clause associated with *it*, while in (84) it is external to that clause. Suppose that the association between *it* and the extraposed clause is given by the standard device of coindexing. Then (82) is of the form (85i), while the examples of (84) are of the form (85ii):

(85)　　(i)　they think $[_{S*}$ it$_i$ AGR$_i$ $[_{VP}$ is a pity$]$ $[_i$ that pictures of each other are hanging on the wall$]]$

　　　　(ii)　NP think(s) $[_{S*}$ it$_i$ AGR$_i$ $[_{VP}$ bother $\alpha]$ $[_i$ that S$]]$

In (85i), AGR of S* is not accessible to *each other,* since coindexing of the two would violate the well-formedness condition (73). Therefore S* is not the governing category for *each other.* Rather, the full clause is the governing category, since its AGR element is accessible to *each other.* But *each other* is bound in the full clause (namely, by its subject *they*), so that (85i) (= (82)) is grammatical. Note that in (85i), AGR is coindexed with *it* by (70I) and *it* is coindexed with the extraposed clause with which it is associated, accounting for the coindexing of AGR with the extraposed clause.

Consider (85ii). Here, AGR of S* is accessible to α, so that S* is its governing category. Therefore (84i,ii) are ungrammatical (cf. note 68) while (84iii) is grammatical in the intended interpretation. Example (83) falls together with (84), not with (82). The relevant distinction between (82) and (83) is not a property of the non-argument *it* as compared to *he,* but rather accessibility of the SUBJECT.

The element *there* should have the same effect as *it* in (82) (cf. §2.4.5), as in (86):

(86)　　(i)　they think there are $[$some letters for each other$]$ at the post office

　　　　(ii)　*they think he saw $[$some letters for each other$]$ at the post office

Example (86i) is analogous to (82), hence grammatical; (86ii) is analogous to (83), hence ungrammatical. Again, the differences in judgment seem to be in the predicted direction.[69]

The considerations just reviewed provide strong evidence that pleonastic *it* and *there* are coindexed with the post-verbal phrases associated with them: clauses and NPs, respectively. There is independent evidence to this effect in the case of *there*: namely, it must agree in number with this element (cf. §2.4.5). In the next chapter, we will see that this assumption yields additional consequences in the pro-drop languages.

Consider example (87):

(87)　　they found $[_{NP}$ some books $[_{\bar{S}}$ for each other to read$]]$.

The OB-system permits binding of *each other* by *they*, as does the version of the GB-system we are now considering; but the earlier version of the GB-system, not involving accessibility, rejects it as ungrammatical. The latter accords with my own judgment (cf. Chomsky (1979a)), but I have found in lectures and discussion that most speakers tend to regard it as grammatical, so perhaps this is not a problem for the version of GB-theory that we are now considering.

Compare the examples (88), (89):

(88)   I think it pleased them that pictures of each other are hanging on the wall

(89)   they think it pleased me that pictures of each other are hanging on the wall

Example (88), like (82), is grammatical. Judgments vary concerning (89), but it seems to me to be much better than (83). On our current assumptions, it is grammatical, and comparison with (83) supports this conclusion. Again, we see that it is an intervening (accessible) SUBJECT, not an intervening possible antecedent, that creates opacity, in accordance with the SSC, *me* being a possible antecedent in (89).

Amendment of the GB-theory to incorporate accessibility thus yields a variety of rather complex and desirable consequences. It is quite possible that the notion "accessibility" admits some degree of parametric variation, and that other factors intervene (e.g., the agentive character of the subject; cf. note 66). Furthermore, it may be that this entire discussion properly belongs to the theory of markedness rather than of core grammar, and that the phenomena we have been discussing reflect marked properties of English. If so, then the discussion may serve as an illustration for an observation in chapter 1, namely, that we do not expect to find chaos in the theory of markedness, but rather an organized and structured system, building on the theory of core grammar. This appears to be true in the present case. Cf. Chomsky (1979a) for some further discussion, along somewhat different lines.

Reviewing the basic points, we are now assuming a binding theory applying at S-structure and incorporating the binding principles (12) and principle (I) of (70), which is required in any theory, in some form. The notion "governing category" is defined as in (70II) in terms of "accessibility" as defined in (73), (74). This theory yields the positive results of the earlier version of the binding theory not involving accessibility and also accommodates a complex range of examples of anaphors as arguments in NP that contradict the earlier version. Of the examples involving anaphors discussed earlier, only one is not properly handled by the revised binding theory, namely, (90), which, as noted earlier, is also incorrectly marked grammatical by the OB-theory and our earlier version of binding theory:

(90)   *they preferred [$_{NP}$ each other's reading the book]   (= (62))

This is ungrammatical, though the anaphor is bound in its governing category in terms of the present theory. As noted earlier, however, it may be that (90) violates a different requirement of English, namely, the plurality condition discussed there.

With regard to examples such as (90), the revised binding theory nevertheless may constitute an improvement over the earlier version. Consider example (91):

(91)   *they thought $[_{S*}$ I preferred each other's reading the book$]$

In the earlier version, since *each other* lacks a governing category the binding theory does not prevent it from being bound by *they* in (91). But the revised version does prevent this, since *each other* does have a governing category S*, its AGR element being an accessible SUBJECT. Therefore (91) is ruled out apart from the plurality requirement. One might expect (91) to be still more unacceptable than (90), on these assumptions, which may be true, though one can hardly rely on such judgments. As noted earlier, comparative evidence should prove relevant.

It remains finally to consider pronouns in argument positions of NP; cf. (56). As we have seen, these raise various problems, the primary one being that their behavior is not consistent with that of anaphors. Let us reconsider again the examples (63)–(65), repeated here as (92):

(92)   (i) John saw $[_{NP*}$ my picture of him$]$
       (ii) *I saw $[_{NP*}$ John's picture of him$]$
       (iii) *$[_{S*}$ John saw $[_{NP}$ a picture of him$]]$
       (iv) John thought $[_{S*}$ I saw $[_{NP}$ a picture of him$]]$
       (v) $[_{S*}$ John read $[_{NP}$ his book$]]$
       (vi) John thought $[_{S*}$ I saw $[_{NP}$ his book$]]$
       (vii) (?) $[_{S*}$ John preferred $[_{NP}$ his reading the book$]$

Throughout, we are considering the case of *he* proximate to *John*; NP* and S* are the governing categories in the sense of the revised binding theory. In examples (i), (iv) and (vi), *he* is free in its governing category and the sentences are grammatical. In examples (ii) and (iii), *he* is bound in its governing category and the sentences are ungrammatical (cf. note 2). The status of (vii) is presumably determined by the Avoid Pronoun principle. This leaves only (v) as a problematic case. It is evident that either (92v) or (93) does not fall under the binding theory, since in these constructions the pronoun is not free where the anaphor is bound:

(93)   they read $[_{NP}$ each other's books$]$

We are assuming that (93) falls under the binding theory and that some other condition must permit (92v), overriding the requirements of the binding theory. It has sometimes been suggested that *his* in (92v) is an obligatory variant of *himself's,* which is in fact excluded in (92v) contrary to the prediction of the binding theory. Whether or not this is correct, it does focus attention on a phenomenon that is only partially captured by any of the approaches we have been investigating here, namely, the near complementary distribution between proximate pronouns and reflexives. Cf. notes 2, 68 and §5.2. For an account of such constructions as (92v) in different terms, see Fiengo and Higginbotham (1979). Comparative evidence suggests that something other than the binding theory is involved, given differences among languages as to whether the analogue of *his* in (92v) can be regarded as proximate to the matrix subject.

One problem left unresolved in the preceding discussion relates to the status of such examples as (94i-iv):

(94)   (i) there is a man in the room
        (ii) there arrived three men
        (iii) il est arrivé trois hommes   (= (94ii))
        (iv) NP* fu arrestato Giovanni
              ("Giovanni was arrested")
        (v) John is his worst enemy

In (i) and (ii), *there* is coindexed with the NP *a man, three men;* similarly, *il* is coindexed with *trois hommes* in (iii).[70] On the status of NP* in (iv), see §4.5; whatever it is, it is coindexed with *Giovanni,* as we shall see. In each of these cases, then, the post-verbal NP is coindexed with a c-commanding element in violation of principle (C) of the binding theory. This fact suggests that the coindexing in these cases is of a different nature than the coindexing relevant to the binding theory.[71] One possibility is that it is determined in the LF-component and is thus exempt from the binding theory, but this seems rather doubtful. It seems more natural to suppose that the coindexing, say in (i), is determined as part of the rule inserting *there,* or else "picked up" from the NP-trace relation if (i) is based on Move-α. Similarly in the other cases. Let us assume, then, that there is a different style of indexing in cases (i)–(iv) of (94); say, co-superscripting. The same, then, must be true of the closely analogous case involving *it* and a coindexed extraposed clause. In view of the interaction of this coindexing with that involving AGR and subject illustrated above, it is reasonable to assume that the subject-AGR relation established by (70I), which is also not a binding relation as we have seen, is co-superscripting rather than co-subscripting. I will henceforth adopt these assumptions, which will have certain consequences in the subsequent discussion.

Case (v) of (94) illustrates a different problem. There is at least a strong tendency to require *his own* in this case when *he* is taken as proximate to *John.* On this topic, see Edwards (1979), Higginbotham (1980).

The concept "anaphor" has been left rather vague in the preceding discussion; an anaphor has been characterized loosely as an NP with no intrinsic reference. As has often been observed, the cross-linguistic status of reflexives is particularly problematic; cf. note 62. It is worth noting that the opacity conditions seem to hold for certain elements that do not function as anaphors in the narrow sense that applies to NP-trace, *each other*, PRO, etc., but that fall under a somewhat looser characterization of the notion. For example, the trace of extraposition (cf. § 2.4.4) appears to meet the opacity conditions, as illustrated in (95):

(95) (i) *[John's novel t] arrived last week [that you ordered]
      (ii) [the books t] arrived last week [that you ordered]
      (iii) [a certain book t] arrived last week [that you ordered]
      (iv) [the fact t] is clear [that his arguments are invalid]

In case (i), the subject NP is a governing category for the trace of the extraposed clause, and the sentence is correspondingly ungrammatical, with a trace free in its governing category. Examples (ii)–(iv) suggest that it is not a specificity constraint that is involved, as it is in the case of *wh*-movement. The argument is not entirely straightforward, however, since relative clauses are less than perfect even in the non-extraposed case with possessive subjects. Still, (95i) seems much worse than its source (96), indicating that the effects of opacity may be involved:

(96) John's novel that you ordered arrived last week

Such examples again suggest that the notion "governing category" defined in terms of accessible SUBJECT is relevant, and that the concept "anaphor" should perhaps be extended to the trace of extraposition, so that (95) would fall under principle (A) of the binding theory.

Fiengo and Lasnik (1976) and Quicoli (1976) provide evidence suggesting that the relation of an NP to a displaced quantifier related to it (perhaps, the relation of the trace of the quantifier to the quantifier) is subject to opacity, though the conclusion is not unproblematic. The same idea is pursued in the GB-framework in Belletti (1980a). Cf. Jaeggli (1980b) for further discussion, including a wide range of examples and offering a principled basis for a generalization concerning floated quantifiers discussed in Baltin (1979). I will not pursue these interesting topics, which are also relevant to a proper understanding of the notion "anaphor."

A problem concerning anaphors noted by Luigi Rizzi is that anaphors may be governed but lack governing categories because there is no SUBJECT accessible to them, as in (97):

(97) [for each other to win] would be unfortunate

One might assume that (97) is barred by the fact that it has no interpretation, but this move will not resolve the problem properly, since it will prevent us from adopting the simplest rule for interpretation of *each other* (similarly, other anaphors): namely, apply the rule to any coindexed pair (NP, *each other*). This simplest rule would, in fact, incorrectly assign an interpretation if we were to extend (97) to (98):

(98)   [for [$_i$ each other] to win] would be unfortunate for them$_i$

The point is that the structural relation between the antecedent and the anaphor should be expressed in the binding theory, not by a (quite generally redundant) stipulation added to the rule of interpretation.

A simple way of overcoming this difficulty (suggested by Norbert Hornstein) is to adopt (99) as a principle of the theory of government:

(99)   A root sentence is a governing category for a governed element

The proposal is related to the prohibition of [$_\alpha$ e] discussed in §2.6. Adopting (99), both (97) and (98) are ruled ungrammatical by the binding theory, since they contain an anaphor free in its governing category.

Other questions arise that merit further consideration.[72] Recall the definition of "governing category" given as (70II):

(70II) β is a governing category for α if and only if β is the minimal category containing α, a governor of α, and a SUBJECT accessible to α

Suppose that we were to simplify this definition to (100), dropping the reference to government and introducing the obvious change in terminology:

(100) β is a *binding category for* α if and only if β is the minimal category containing α and a SUBJECT accessible to α

Correspondingly, we recast principles (A) and (B) of the binding theory as (101), and restate (99) as (102):

(101)   (A) An anaphor is bound in its binding category
         (B) A pronominal is free in its binding category
(102)   A root sentence is a binding category for a governed element

These modifications clearly have no effects for elements that are governed, since for such elements the governor will always be contained in the binding category. Hence there is no effect for NP-trace, which is always governed, by virtue of 2.4.1.(2i), a principle concerning trace-government that we have been assuming throughout and to which we return in the next chapter. In the case of overt elements, the only ungoverned position, we have assumed, is that of subject of gerunds, as in (103):

(103)   (i) they preferred [each other's reading the book]   (= (90))
         (ii) John preferred [his reading the book (himself)]   (= (92vii))

We have already discussed the problematic status of (i). It remains problematic under this revision of binding theory, even more so, perhaps, in that we now lack an account even of (91); but it is doubtful that this is a serious problem, since whatever principle bars (103i) will also bar (91), presumably. As for (103ii), we have attributed its questionable status with proximate *his* to the Avoid Pronoun principle. Putting the effects of this principle to the side, the status of (103ii) differs under the present and former theory. In the former theory, (103ii) was admitted since *his* lacks a governing category; under the revision, it is barred since *his* has a binding category (namely, the full clause) and is bound in this category, violating (101B). But again, it is doubtful that this is a meaningful difference, since as we have seen, other considerations must apply in any event in the case of possessive pronouns; see the discussion of (92v).

In summary, there seem to be no meaningful consequences to the proposed revision in the case of overt elements or NP-trace. This leaves only the case of PRO. The basic property of PRO is that it is ungoverned. This property is a consequence of the former theory, since PRO, as a pronominal anaphor, must lack a governing category by principles (A) and (B) of the binding theory. But this result no longer follows under the revision to (101). The only consequence that follows from (101) is that PRO lacks a binding category, which does not imply that it must be ungoverned. But the conclusion that PRO is ungoverned nevertheless follows under the revised theory, namely, from (101) in conjunction with (102), which, as we saw, was also required in the former theory. If PRO is governed, then by (102) it always has a binding category in which it must be both free and bound by (101); hence PRO is ungoverned.

It seems, then, that the former binding theory can be simplified, with (70II) replaced by (100). There remains, however, one problem, illustrated by (104):

(104)   (i) John expected [him to win]
         (ii) John tried [[PRO to win]]
         (iii) John knows [how [PRO to win]]

In (i), *him* cannot be coindexed with *John* or (101B) will be violated. But exactly the same argument shows that PRO cannot be coindexed with *John* in (ii), (iii), an incorrect result. Replacement of "binding category" by "governing category" gives the correct results, in this case. It therefore appears to be necessary to introduce a crucial reference to government in the binding theory, as in (70II), though its effects are so narrow as to suggest that an error may be lurking somewhere.

While there are a number of remaining problems,[73] in general the GB approach to the theory of binding seems quite successful in overcoming the empirical and conceptual problems that arose in the OB-framework, while extending empirical coverage. Of the problems raised in § 3.1, those involving PRO are resolved in quite a natural way, and of the conceptual problems, we have reached plausible answers to (1), (2) and (6): namely,

(1) the problem of redundancies between Case and binding theory, now resolved in terms of their common component, the theory of government; (2) the problem of explaining why the two unrelated domains subject-of-AGR and domain-of-subject should be opaque; (6) the problem of finding a more natural account of disjoint reference (but see note 39). Three of the problems raised in § 3.1 remain to be discussed: (3) the RES(NIC) phenomena; (4) the problem of deriving the *[that-t] filter from more reasonable assumptions and relating it to RES(NIC); (5) the problem of simplifying the indexing conventions of the OB-framework, reducing them if possible to random assignment of referential indices. As for (5), I have been assuming that the reduction is possible, thus taking the problem to be solved, but there are serious difficulties to which I will return in § 5.1; for the present, let us continue with the assumption for expository purposes. Problems (3) and (4) will be the topic of chapter 4.

Notes

1.   One might appeal to the Avoid Pronoun principle 2.4.2.(5) to account for this case, since PRO is permitted in the position of the pronoun. But the same phenomenon can be observed even where PRO is (for whatever reason) not acceptable: e.g., "John would hate it [for him to win]," *"John would hate it [to win]." Furthermore, the Avoid Pronoun principle generally seems to assign preferential readings, at least in English (but cf. Jaeggli (1980b), where a stronger interpretation is suggested in the Romance languages), whereas in the example (4vi) disjoint reference is obligatory; and with *everyone* as antecedent, the interpretation as "for all x, x would prefer for x to win" is completely excluded.

2.   For some reason, disjoint reference seems less than obligatory in many such cases, and reflexives can marginally appear, when the matrix subject is, e.g., *John*; though when the matrix subject is *everyone*, *he* in (xii) cannot be in its scope; that is, (xii) cannot be interpreted as "for all x, x heard some stories about x." Cf. Chomsky (1977a, chapter 3), where there is an appeal to the A/A principle to explain the marginal properties of these constructions.

3.   The assumption here is that while (5) is grammatical, (i) is not:

(i)   they thought I said that pictures of each other were on sale

Judgments in the case of such examples as (i) are not very solid, but I think that there is a difference of judgment in the assumed direction. I will return to the question of long distance binding for overt anaphors in § 3.2.3.

There are unresolved problems in this connection. Thus in English, (ii) is ungrammatical, by virtue of SSC, but in Dutch the equivalent is grammatical:

(ii)   they forced me to read each other's books

Recall that there is no long distance binding for trace because of the subjacency principle; cf. § 2.4.4.

4.   Cf. Koster (1978b,c), (1980); Kayne (1979c, 1980a).

5.   In fact, there is also a third component to the *wh*-island condition, as in such forms as *"who did John wonder how well t to do the work," where the ungrammaticalness appears still more extreme than in (11). We will suggest in § 3.2.2 that such examples are barred by the fact that the variable lacks Case and θ-role.

6.   Cf. Vergnaud (1974), who presents arguments to the effect that indirect object *a*-NP phrases in French are NPs; some interesting consequences of this and related assump-

tions in French and Spanish are developed in Jaeggli (1980b), to which we return. We might think of *of* in English as a similar element, in effect, a Case-marker.

7.   Cf. Kayne (1980d,e), Vergnaud and Zubizarretta (1980).

8.   Jaeggli (1980b) distinguishes s-government (namely, government by a subcategorization feature) from c-government (namely, by category). He points out that the limitations on s-government just noted might be overcome if we assume that the Exceptional Case-marker (*for, believe*) is subcategorized for a clause and that s-government of the clause percolates to its NP subject.

9.   But as we have seen in chapter 2, there are other reasons why raising verbs tend to be intransitive. Cf. 2.6.(38)–(39), 2.7.(24).

10.   The gerund might be analyzed as containing a clause internal to the NP. We put this question aside here, as irrelevant to the point at issue.

11.   Containment in (12) need not be proper containment; thus β is contained in $[_\alpha\ \beta]$. The same holds for domination. α^i is α with i bars.

12.   Compare "I want [the vase broken]," with obligatory $\overline{S}$-deletion in the complement position of a verb, excluding PRO and requiring a phonetically-realized NP subject for the small clause as discussed in §2.6.

13.   Hence there can be no possible Exceptional Case-marking in such structures as

(i)   NP V NP$[_{\overline{S}}[_S$ NP′ ...$]]$

Suppose there is $\overline{S}$-deletion in (i). Then inherent Case must be assigned to NP′, which is impossible, if inherent Case is linked as suggested to θ-role. This seems not unreasonable. See chapter 2, note 89.

14.   Cf. van Riemsdijk (1980) for a more general discussion, and Vergnaud (forthcoming) for a more fully developed theory. On Case-assignment by nouns in the Semitic languages, see Aoun (1979b), Borer (1979). See also Carlson (1978), Babby (1980).

15.   Cf. Bresnan and Grimshaw (1978), Groos and van Riemsdijk (1979), Fehri (1980), for varying approaches.

16.   See Aoun (1980b) for relevant discussion; also Borer (1979, 1980) for discussion of examples that appear to violate the assumption here that variables must have Case.

17.   Compare the argument by Kayne and Pollock (1978) that stylistic inversion is possible in French only after a *wh*-phrase or its trace. See also Kayne (1979a). Note that it is not important in this context to distinguish a theory of *wh*-movement from an alternative in which the *wh*-phrase is generated in its S-structure position or moved to this position in one step, with traces (or some equivalent) in the COMP position of successive-cyclic movement, as proposed, e.g., in Bresnan and Grimshaw (1978). Cf. §2.4.6.

18.   This is not the only possibility. We return in chapter 4 to the possibility that the complementizer *that* in English takes on properties of the relative pronoun, in which case it might be assumed that it too must pass the Case Filter. But even so, the same problem would arise when *that* too is deleted.

19.   Cf. May (1977) and work reviewed there, along with many subsequent studies. Note that the example (20) with the LF-representation (21) is presumably not excluded on any independent semantic grounds. Similar examples are grammatical in dialects that permit *for*-clause complements to *try*. Cf. Chomsky and Lasnik (1977).

20.   Note that this condition would not be operative in the case of a variable in a non-θ-position, as in application of *wh*-movement to an element in the italicized position of (i):

(i)   (a) they took *advantage* of John
        (b) *it* is raining

But such possibilities are presumably excluded by the requirement that variables, as R-expressions, require a θ-role. There remain problematic cases, for example, (ii) (compare "I can't make anything of that suggestion") and (iii):

(ii)   what do you make of that suggestion?
(iii)   how much advantage did you take of John?

We return to such examples as (ii) in chapter 6. Example (iii) is perhaps marginal, but as Roger Higgins has observed, it is far more acceptable than (iv), indicating that once restructuring has applied by an idiom rule, the complex phrase created and presumably assigned a lexical category by this rule is immune to further operations:

(iv)   *how much advantage was John taken of?

The exact status of the variable in such examples as (iii) or (v), etc., remains an open question in the system we are developing here:

(v)   how much food did they eat?

21.   See also Couquaux (1980, forthcoming); Burzio (1981).
22.   Recall that these cases may fall together if INFL is taken as the head of S.
23.   More precisely, the A-function chain of t is ($[NP,S]$, $[NP,[+V]^i]$), where i is the right number of bars for the maximal projection, under the assumptions discussed earlier A more precise formulation will be given in chapter 6.
24.   Recall Aoun's proposal that the PF-component pays no attention to NP lacking Case, while the LF-component disregards NP lacking θ-role, Case and θ-role playing analogous roles in the two components; see the last paragraph of §2.6.
25.   The facts of liaison are difficult to establish, in part because the relevant cases are somewhat artificial and perhaps taught. As for the semi-auxiliaries, which differ significantly among themselves, while there are arguments showing that some resemble raising verbs, there are others indicating the contrary (e.g., "John seems not to be interested," *"John has not to be interested"). On Longobardi's filter, see also van Riemsdijk and Williams (1980), Aoun, Sportiche, Vergnaud, Zubizurreta (1980).
26.   Cf. Kayne (1978), Jaeggli (1980a), Chomsky (1980b, chapter 4, note 24).
27.   Cf. Fiengo (1974, 1979), Burzio (1981).
28.   Cf. Jaeggli (1978, 1980b), Aoun (1979b), Vergnaud (forthcoming). A problem in this approach is that Case must sometimes be assigned to NPs with no lexical N as head, as in gerunds. Cf. §§2.3 and 4.5.
29.   Note that we may exclude cases of extraposition from this discussion, since they do not enter into binding theory, the trace not being an NP-trace; but see the discussion of 3.2.3.(95). We may also exclude from consideration cases of rightward NP-movement by adjunction, since in this case I am assuming that we never have a trace remaining at LF; the trace is filled either by a pronominal element (perhaps PRO; cf. §4.5) or by a pleonastic element such as *there*. A possible exception is French stylistic inversion (cf. Kayne and Pollock (1978), Kayne (1979a), Jaeggli (1980b)). We restrict attention in this discussion to movement-to-COMP (or adjunction to S or S̄; see chapter 2, note 33) and structure-preserving movement-to-NP.
30.   Unless we invoke the operator "for x = NP," as in Chomsky (1975) or Kayne (1979a) (in the latter, real use is made of this possibility).
31.   Cf. §2.4.3. on some questions that arise as to whether the c-command requirement is too strong.
32.   In unpublished work, Riny Huybregts suggests a definition of this sort for the notion "variable" (specifically, taking the local binder to be an element bearing an Ā-GF, not necessarily an operator of some sort), and explores the consequences on the assumption that clitics bind trace so that the bound trace is a variable.
33.   In the Pisa lectures themselves and some subsequent work of mine and by others, (11) was given as the definition of "minimal governing category." A governing category for β was defined as a category containing β and a governor of β, and a minimal governing category as a governing category contained in all governing categories. Note the tacit

assumption that governing categories are nested. I am now using only the notion "minimal governing category" of the Pisa lectures, now called "governing category". Note also similarities to the concepts of Rouveret and Vergnaud (1980), particularly their Case Island Condition. I return below to the choice of governing categories.

34.   This was the assumption in OB and in the Pisa lectures, but I will later suggest that it is incorrect and that the binding theory applies at S-structure. The discussion that follows is independent of this question, except where noted.

35.   To eliminate any ambiguity in (12), understand it in the following more explicit form:

Let β be a governing category for α. Then

(A)   if α is an anaphor, it is bound in β
(B)   if α is a pronominal, it is free in β
(C)   if α is an R-expression, it is free

Thus it is not presupposed that α has a governing category, an important matter, as we shall see.

In the lectures in Pisa on which this text is based, I gave the binding theory in a somewhat different form. Since it has been discussed in this form in subsequent literature, I will give this alternative version for reference:

(A)   If α is an anaphor or lacks a phonetic matrix, then (i) α is a variable or (ii) α is bound in every governing category
(B)   If α is Case-marked, then (i) α is an anaphor or (ii) α is free in every governing category
(C)   If α is a pronominal, then it is free in every minimal governing category

In this formulation, the terms "governing category" and "minimal governing category" are used in the sense of note 33, and the term "anaphor" is used only for overt anaphors such as *each other*, excluding trace.

Consider $[_{NP} \, e]$ with Case in this theory. Since it lacks a phonetic matrix, it is subject to (A), and since it is Case-marked, it is subject to (B). Therefore, since it is not an anaphor by definition, it is a variable and is free in every governing category. Thus principle 3.2.2.(16) follows from right to left; Case-marked trace is a variable. Since it plausibly holds from left to right, as we have seen in the preceding section, the principle holds in full generality in this system.

36.   As noted several times, the entire GB-theory must be extended to other cases: e.g., left dislocated items and topics, predicate nominals, heads of relatives. Another construction to be considered is the AUX-to-COMP case with nominative subject studied in Rizzi (1979b). As Rizzi notes, its island properties follow from the NIC. But they do not follow from the GB-theory unless there is some sense in which the construction is a governing category for the subject, with, perhaps, the NP subject governed by Aux in COMP, as Rizzi suggests. But problems arise in the improved version of the binding theory to which we will turn below, involving accessibility of subject. Cf. Chomsky (1981).

The remark in the text has one exception: empty NP in COMP. We assumed in § 2.6 that elements in COMP (i.e., operator-like elements) receive no θ-role. Let us assume further that they are not subject to the binding theory. Little turns on these decisions.

37.   Consider such examples as (i), (ii):

(i)   I spoke to the men about each other
(ii)   *I spoke about the men to each other

The order of the two PPs is free, with a preference for the *to*-phrase preceding ("we spoke to Bill about John," "we spoke about John to Bill"). But only in case (i) can the NP of the first PP be the antecedent of the anaphor. Case (ii) follows from the binding theory, since *each other* is not bound by *the men*, which does not c-command it. Case (i) might be the result of a reanalysis rule applying to *speak to*, thus permitting c-command in this case. If this is correct, we would expect (iii) to be preferable to (iv), and we would expect disjoint reference to be more easily violable in (vi) than in (v):

(iii)   the men were spoken to about the new regulation
(iv)   the new regulation was spoken about to the men
(v)   we spoke to John about him
(vi)   we spoke about John to him

On the same assumptions, the *to*-phrase should be like the *about*-phrase when the reanalysis is inapplicable. Thus (vii) should be as bad as (ii), and (viii) should be preferable to (ix):

(vii)   I spoke angrily to the men about each other
(viii)   (a) I spoke to John and Bill about each other
          (b) which men did you speak to about each other
(ix)   (a) I spoke to John and to Bill about each other
          (b) to which men did you speak about each other

Some of these consequences seem plausible, though judgments are uncertain. Others are wrong, specifically (vii). It is not clear whether this approach is on the right track.
38.   Recall that we are assuming a rather idiosyncratic rule of *for*-deletion in immediate postverbal position for certain verbs, with some dialectal variation. Cf. §2.4.2.
     My own judgment about (14iii,iv) is that they are marginal at best, but I have found that many speakers find them quite acceptable. In any event, they surely do not have the status of true binding theory violations such as (i):

(i)   *they would be happy if each other won

The internal structure of the complement of the matrix verb in (14iv) is not entirely clear. Suppose it were argued that it is an NP of the form *it-S̄*. Then the example would fall under the discussion of binding into NP to which I will turn shortly.
39.   Note that the examples given below are restricted to distinct reference. On disjoint reference more generally, see § 5.1.
40.   This example is noted in Bach (1977), along with (19) and (16vi).
41.   We actually derive the possibly stronger principle that PRO lacks a governing category. Given the definition (11) of "governing category," the two principles are equivalent, but one might explore a broader notion of governing category that takes β to be a governing category for α if β is the minimal category relevant to Case-assignment, i.e., in which Case is assigned or checked, whether α is governed in β or not. Cf. Belletti and Rizzi (1980), Jaeggli (1980b). With this broader notion – call it "governing category*" – including this case as the well as the case defined in (11), it follows from the binding theory as stated that PRO lacks Case. The point may not be inconsequential. Suppose, for example, that nominative Case in some language is assigned (or checked) by agreement with the verb rather than government by INFL, as is suggested for pro-drop languages such as Italian and Spanish in the references cited. Suppose further that the empty subject in such languages is PRO, as Jaeggli proposes. It is still crucially required that (20) hold in the old sense, though PRO now has a governing category*.
42.   Perhaps extending to [$_{NP}$ *e*] in COMP; cf. the discussion of 2.6.(44ii). We return to this question directly, and conclude finally in chapter 6 that no such extension is necessary.
43.   I am indebted to an anonymous reviewer for *Linguistic Inquiry* for this observation.
44.   Another case treated as PRO-movement in OB which, as noted there, excludes arbitrary interpretation, is the case of movement-to-COMP. Cf. the discussion of 2.6 (44ii) and note 115, chapter 2. See chapter 6 for a possible explanation.

45.   There are further ramifications, in particular, when stress varies, but they do not seem to me to bear directly on the questions now at issue.

For the subsequent discussion, the crucial cases of principle (C) are those in which an R-expression is not permitted to be bound by a pronominal, as in (i) or (ii):

(i)   *he$_i$ said that Mary kissed John$_i$
(ii)   *who$_i$ did he$_i$ say Mary kissed t$_i$

For our purposes, we could restrict principle (C) to this case, hence to (25i) but not (25ii).

Though the question is peripheral, let us consider the status of principle (C) as given: R-expressions are free. Clearly, this is the simplest and most general principle accounting for such cases as (i), (ii), (25i). Therefore, we will adopt this principle unless there is relevant empirical evidence to the contrary. Superficially, there appears to be such evidence: it is possible to contrive contexts in which such structures as (25ii) are acceptable (cf. Evans (1980)). But it is not clear that such contexts provide counter-evidence to principle (C), despite appearances. The reason is that there appears to be a general discourse principle of the rough form (iii), with the corollary (iv):

(iii)   Avoid repetition of R-expressions, except when conditions warrant
(iv)   When conditions warrant, repeat

Suppose that some general discourse condition of the form (iii), hence (iv), accounts for the contexts that permit (25ii). Then these contexts do not constitute counterevidence to principle (C); rather, they indicate that principle (C) may be overridden by some condition on discourse, not a very startling fact. By the same token, the judgment that (25ii) is ungrammatical does not constitute positive evidence for principle (C) (though it follows from this principle), since it falls under (iii).

Similar considerations apply in the case of alleged counter-evidence involving precedence conditions to the principles governing pronominal binding.

It may be that there is evidence to show that principle (C), as stated, is too strong, but to establish this is not as simple as is sometimes assumed.

Principles (iii) and (iv) quite possibly fall together with the Avoid Pronoun principle, the principles governing gapping, and various left-to-right precedence conditions as principles that interact with grammar but do not strictly speaking constitute part of a distinct language faculty, or at least, are specific realizations in the language faculty of much more general principles involving "least effort" and temporal sequence. Still, interactions with grammar may be very close, as is particularly clear in the case of the Avoid Pronoun principle.

46.   Say, those of Higginbotham (1979a) within the OB-framework or Higginbotham (1979c) within the GB-framework.

47.   But not in other respects, specifically, not in contexts of weak crossover in Wasow's sense, as in examples (34) below. For discussion, see Chomsky (1977a, chapter 4; 1980b, chapter 4), and the references of the preceding note.

48.   The same is true of weak crossover, and the similarity extends to the variable left by focal stress. See the references of the last two notes and (34), below.

49.   In this case, I am assuming a rule of LF-movement for the embedded *wh*-phrase *which book*, along the lines of Chomsky (1977a, chapter 3); Aoun, Hornstein and Sportiche (1980). We return to this topic in the next chapter.

50.   Examples such as (i), (ii) are cited by Brody (1979) in support of the conclusion that the binding theory holds at S-structure. Example (iv) is suggested by Dominique Sportiche.

51.   This problem was pointed out to me by Robert Freidin.

52.   We have restricted the theory of control to choice of antecedent (if any) for PRO. Therefore, technically the statement in the text is correct only if we accept the option $\alpha =$ PRO in (39). But it is reasonable to assume that if $\alpha = e$, then it is an extension of the theory of control that determines the coindexing of *a book* and $[_{NP} \, \alpha]$ in COMP in (41), given the ways in which θ-roles enter into determining the antecedent in purposive constructions. Let us therefore assume such an extension of the theory of control, in case $\alpha = e$. This issue

disappears under the reinterpretation of the notion "empty category" to which we return in chapter 6, where, in fact, we will suggest a somewhat different analysis but one that does not crucially affect the discussion here.

53.   I assume here the analyses proposed in Chomsky (1977b), which are analogous to the analysis of purposive constructions in OB, assumed throughout. I have put aside the question of the status of *for* in (48ii,iii). The conclusion that the *for*-phrase is in the matrix clause in (48ii) is based on considerations discussed in Chomsky (1977b) and references cited there. If the *for*-clause is regarded as internal to the embedded clause in (48ii), then this example reduces to (48i). On structures of the form (48ii), see § 5.4.

54.   One might suggest a different principle to account for examples (48i,ii), namely, that an anaphor cannot serve as an antecedent. This would also exclude such examples as (i), with *them* taken as proximate to *they*; and also (ii), (iii) and (iv):

(i)   they expected each other to get Bill to like them
(ii)   they expected each other to like each other
(iii)   they expected each other to hurt themselves
(iv)   they persuaded each other to enter the competition

Case (iv) is certainly grammatical, indicating that the proposed principle cannot be given in this general form. Examples of the type (i)–(iii) have been discussed in the literature on reciprocals. They seem to me rather marginal, but do not seem to constitute violations at all as clear-cut as those I have been discussing.

Note that the examples just discussed provide an argument, independent of those of Chomsky (1977b) and OB, for movement-to-COMP leaving a variable in such constructions as purposives and complex adjectival constructions such as (47). Namely, such movement is required to form the S-structures that will yield the proper interpretation of PRO under the binding theory.

55.   I am indebted to Jan Koster for several of these examples.

56.   One question for which I have no solution arises in connection with examples such as (39i). Here, $[_{NP}\ \alpha]$ in COMP does not c-command the variable t_i because of the presence of *for*; yet it binds t_i. We will see in the next chapter that there is some merit in the proposal that at least one type of government does not hold in similar structures. We might overcome the problem by redefining "variable," replacing "Ā-bound" by "coindexed with an operator in a c-commanding COMP." Cf. chapter 2, note 30. Pending further insights, I will leave the matter in this unsatisfactory state.

57.   But the analogue to (61) is grammatical in Dutch; cf. note 3. There is further variation among languages that should be explored. In English, *each other* often imposes a kind of plurality requirement elsewhere in the sentence, as in (i)–(iii):

(i)   *they read each other's book
(ii)   *they saw a picture of each other
(iii)   *they turned the child against each other

These become grammatical if *book, picture* and *child* are plural (and ambiguous, in case (iii)). In Finnish and Norwegian, this condition does not hold; the equivalents of (i), for example, are grammatical (Lauri Carlson and Tarald Taraldsen, personal communication). The situation with regard to such cases as (iii) in English is obscure. Thus (iv) seems more acceptable, as pointed out by Dominique Sportiche:

(iv)   they kicked the ball towards each other

Further investigation is necessary to determine the character and parameters of these constructions. Cf. § 5.2 for further comment.

58.   On the behavior of pronouns in NP, see Fiengo and Higginbotham (1979).

59.   I have assumed that this is the unmarked case, and that inflected infinitives, as in

Portuguese, constitute a marked exception. On the latter, see Rouveret (1979, 1980), Zubizarreta (1980).

60.   Recall that there are important advantages to the NIC over the PIC or Tensed-S Condition, for example, in the case of long-distance construal as in (i), (ii), which are admitted by the NIC but excluded by the PIC or Tensed-S condition without ad hoc stipulations:

(i)   they expected [$_{\bar{S}}$ that [pictures of each other] would be on sale]

(ii)   they expected [$_{\bar{S}}$ that [$\left\{\begin{array}{l}\text{PRO feeding each other}\\ \text{PRO to feed each other}\end{array}\right\}$] would be difficult]

In both cases, $\bar{S}$ is tensed (inflected for agreement) and hence would block construal of *each other* in (i) and PRO in (ii) with *they*, given the PIC or Tensed-S Condition, though both are admitted by the NIC. Cf. also note 36, for a problem in the GB-system.

61.   There is, plainly, more to be said about agreement. I will assume here that agreement of determiners and adjectives results by percolation from NP, AP and VP, where VP absorbs the features of INFL in a manner to which we turn in § 4.5. For more developed and somewhat different approaches, see Williams (1980), Manzini (1980).

62.   For example, in Japanese, Korean and many other languages, the element translated as reflexive in English does not observe the binding theory sketched above, but rather can be linked to a subject that c-commands it. It has been argued that such elements (in some languages, at least) can be subject to pragmatic control, i.e., without antecedents. In other respects, these languages seem to have a binding theory in some ways similar to the one outlined here, though there are numerous open questions. See Kim (1976), Oshima (1979), Farmer (1980), Mohanan (1980), and many other sources.

63.   Perhaps we should add to (73) the condition (i):

(i)   unless δ is coindexed with the head of γ

This unless-condition will accommodate relative clauses, permitting percolation of an index to the NP head of a relative clause, if the correct analysis of relatives is (ii):

(ii)   [$_{NP_i}$ NP$_i$ $\bar{S}$]

For example, (iii) is excluded from (73) by (i) and is thus grammatical:

(iii)   [$_{NP_i}$[$_{NP_i}$ the man] [$_{\bar{S}}$ [$_i$ who] [$_S$ t$_i$ saw [$_{NP_i}$ himself]]]]

As we will see directly, the only subcase of (73) that actually plays a role in this discussion is (iv):

(iv)   *[$\ldots \alpha_i \ldots [\beta_i \ldots \gamma_i \ldots] \ldots \alpha_i \ldots$]

where α_i appears either to the left or the right of the embedded configuration of (73) and γ_i is not the head of β_i. Therefore if (73) proves to be too strong as stated, we could replace it by (iv) in the definition of "accessibility."

64.   Note that this consequence is surely correct, and is all that we need to pursue the binding theory. The question that may be raised is whether this property – that is, (iv) of the preceding footnote – is "isolated" or rather follows from a more far-reaching principle such as (73), which may itself derive from some other principle.

If α in (76) is an anaphor, it may sometimes be bound by the object of *disturb*, yielding such constructions as 2.4.3.(18), despite the failure of c-command. Such cases are not accommodated by any of the theories reviewed here and may require a slight modification of binding theory, relaxing the notion of c-command. I have put this question aside here, throughout.

65.   While the judgments are less than crystal clear, the contrast between (80) and (81) seems to me correct. Cf. note 3.

66.   Cf. Chomsky (1977a, chapter 3), based on observations by Richard Kayne and Ivonne Bordelois. See also Koster (1978b).

67.   The following discussion is based on suggestions by Tim Stowell and Dominique Sportiche.

68.   Some speakers judge (84i) to be more acceptable than the same sentence with reflexive (*themselves*) in place of the reciprocal. If so, the reason may be that there is an alternative in the case of the reflexive, namely, a pronoun (in this case, *them*), whereas there is no alternative construction in the case of the reciprocal.

69.   Examples similar to (82), (86) are discussed in Postal (1974), and elsewhere in the literature.

70.   Cf. Jaeggli (1980b) for discussion of the status of *il* and similar elements, based on ideas of Kayne (1972).

71.   Note that we cannot restrict binders to arguments; non-arguments are regularly binders for NP-trace, for example, invoking principle (A) of the binding theory.

72.   The following discussion is suggested by some observations by Dominique Sportiche.

73.   For example, I have said nothing about subjunctives, a somewhat marginal construction in English that behaves in the manner of tensed clauses with regard to binding, though there is no overt AGR element. For the present, we must simply stipulate that there is a null AGR in English subjunctives. Many other questions arise when we turn to other languages, even closely related ones.

Chapter 4

Specification of empty categories

4.1. NIC and RES(NIC)

From the binding theory, it follows that a variable, while Ā-bound by definition, is A-free and thus exempt from any effect of the NIC or SSC, these being virtually theorems of binding theory – "virtually," because what in fact is derivable in this theory differs somewhat from the NIC and SSC as formulated elsewhere. Variables are therefore similar to names with regard to the binding theory, a natural result though not a necessary one.[1]

We have come across several respects in which variables do not satisfy the binding conditions (A) and (B) for anaphors and pronominals, which yield the NIC and SSC. Rizzi pointed out that *wh*-movement in Italian violates the SSC, a fact also illustrated in strong crossover. Freidin and Lasnik extended this observation to NIC. Strong crossover, purposives, and other constructions studied in 3.2.3 illustrate that variables observe principle (C) of the binding theory rather than principles (A) or (B).

As we have seen, the conclusion that variables do not obey the NIC raises problems, because in other respects they do seem to obey this condition. The structure (1) is excluded if . . . is non-null, where t is nominative and is the variable bound by α, which may be a *wh*-phrase or its trace in COMP:

(1)   *$[_{\bar{S}} \alpha \ldots [_S t \text{ INFL VP}]]$

This seems, *prima facie*, to be a violation of the NIC. Examples include indirect questions, *that*-trace effects, *if*-trace effects (which I will henceforth disregard subsuming them under categories (i) and (ii)), and the superiority condition, as in (2):

(2)   (i) *who do you wonder $[_{\bar{S}}$ how $[_S t$ solved the problem$]]$
       (ii) *who do you think $[_{\bar{S}}$ that $[_S t$ saw Bill$]]$
       (iii) *who do you wonder $[_{\bar{S}}$ if $[_S t$ solved the problem$]]$
       (iv) *it is unclear $[_{\bar{S}}$ what $[_S$ who saw t$]]$

In (i), the trace t is bound by *who*, and in (ii) it is bound by *who* or perhaps by a trace in the embedded COMP $[t \ that]$. Similarly in (iii). Hence these cases

232 Lectures on government and binding: the Pisa lectures

fall under (1). Example (iv) illustrates the same phenomenon, if we assume that a movement rule in the LF-component adjoins *who* to its COMP, giving the LF-representation (3), which contrasts with the grammatical example (4) with the LF-representation (4ii):

(3)   it is unclear $[_{\bar{S}} [_{COMP}$ who$_i [_{COMP}$ what$_j]] [_S t_i$ saw $t_j]]$
(4)   (i) it is unclear $[_{\bar{S}}$ who$_i [_S t_i$ saw what$]]$
         (ii) it is unclear $[_{\bar{S}} [_{COMP}$ what$_j [_{COMP}$ who$_i]] [_S t_i$ saw $t_j]]$

Cf. 3.2.3. (35 iii).

The examples of (2), then, are cases of (1), and appear to show that variables are indeed subject to NIC, a fact that motivated the work by Taraldsen, Kayne and Pesetsky cited above that aimed to derive the *[*that-t*] filter from NIC or some similar condition.[2]

The examples just illustrated yield something close to a contradiction in the OB-framework. It is only a near contradiction, since one might assume that the NIC holds only for the referential indices of variables but not their anaphoric indices (the case of crossover), or that NIC does not hold in the crossover cases for some other reason. I am skeptical about any attempt to avoid the problem along these lines, since the conclusion that variables are not subject to the NIC seems right on other grounds, in view of the conceptual relation between names and variables, which, if valid and relevant, would exclude variables from the NIC in principle, a conclusion supported by the general applicability of principle (C) of the binding theory to variables. Note further that any such attempt would exclude the superiority condition from the complex of cases illustrated in (2), since the relevant form (4ii) appears only at the level of LF-representation while the binding theory holds at S-structure. One might ask further why variables should be subject to the NIC while exempt from the SSC, rather than conversely. Furthermore, we know that pro-drop languages such as Italian and Spanish are not subject to the *that*-trace effects, so that variables in these languages do not appear to be subject to NIC. Why, then, do we not find languages that exempt variables solely from the SSC?

Such considerations as these suggest that the phenomenon illustrated in (2), while similar to the NIC effects, is really a separate phenomenon – what I have called "RES(NIC)" – and that the generalization with NIC is a spurious one. Some other principle is involved in RES(NIC), a phenomenon that holds at the level of LF-representation rather than S-structure, if (2iv) does belong to this complex. Looking ahead, I will suggest that the relevant principle is that traces are governed in some manner at LF. We have observed this property with regard to NP-traces (cf. §2.4), as illustrated in (5):

(5)   (i)   *John was asked [how [t to solve the problem]]
         (ii) *John was known [how [t to solve the problem]]
         (iii) *John was preferred [[t to win]]
         (iv) *John is illegal [[t to participate]]

Example (i) is an impossible S-structure,[3] and the sentences (ii)–(iv) are ungrammatical. We saw in § 2.4.1 that these results follow from the requirement that traces must be governed, and that this requirement is independent of other properties of empty categories. Extending the principle from NP-trace, as in (5), to all traces, we may hope to derive RES(NIC) as illustrated in (2). If this line of argument is correct, then RES(NIC) is not related to NIC or to the binding theory at all, but rather to a different principle of the theory of government, still to be formulated properly, namely, the principle that traces must in some sense be governed at LF. It is this approach that I would now like to pursue. For the moment, I will use the term "RES(NIC)" somewhat vaguely to refer to phenomena of the type (1), deferring the analysis until later.

4.2. Basic Properties of RES(NIC)

What are the properties of RES(NIC)? We can sharpen the question by looking at languages for which it does not appear to hold, e.g., Italian. Thus the Italian example (1) appears to be a straightforward violation of RES(NIC), contrasting with (2) in English:[4]

(1)   l'uomo [$wh\text{-}_i$ che [mi domando [$\text{chi}_j[\, t_k$ abbia visto $t_l\,]]]]$
(2)   *the man [$\text{who}_i[\,$ I wonder [$\text{who}_j[\, t_k$ saw $t_l\,]]]]$

In English, example (2) is excluded by the wh-island condition if $i = l$ and $j = k$, and is much more severely excluded by RES(NIC) if $i = k$ and $j = l$ (cf. 3.1.(9)–(14); 3.2.3.(30)–(31)). In Italian, (1) is grammatical with $l = i$ and $j = k$ (since the wh-island condition does not hold in such cases; see Rizzi (1978b)), and also with $i = k$ and $j = l$, violating RES(NIC).[5] Nevertheless, though RES(NIC) appears not to be operating in Italian, the NIC does hold in full generality elsewhere, as illustrated in (3):

(3)   (i) *NP sembra [che t Tense VP]
        (ii) NP crede [che pronominal Tense VP]

In (i), with the matrix verb *sembra* (*seems*), raising is impossible. In (ii), with the matrix verb *crede* (*believes*), the pronominal in the embedded clause need not be disjoint in reference from NP. These examples illustrate the NIC. The trace and the pronoun are free in their governing categories (the embedded tensed clause), so that (i) is ungrammatical, and (ii) is grammatical whether or not the pronominal is coindexed with NP, by principles (A) and (B) of the binding theory, respectively. In contrast, (1) is grammatical with the interpretation $i = k$, illustrating again that RES(NIC) seems to be a different phenomenon than NIC, since the former but not the latter is inoperable in Italian, as in other pro-drop languages. It appears, then, that RES(NIC) holds of trace, whether wh-trace as in (2) or NP-trace as in 4.1.(5), but not of pronominals. At least, so things appear at the level of superficial data arrangement.

Does RES(NIC) hold of all variables or only of *wh*-trace? If the latter, then we would expect it to be a principle operating at S-structure or in the PF-component. If it holds of all variables, including those formed by rules of the LF-component, then it is a principle holding in the LF-component after the operation of rules yielding these variables – say, as a condition on LF-representation. We have already seen some reason to suspect that RES(NIC) holds of all variables at the LF-level; namely, the similarity between the superiority condition and the other RES(NIC) phenomena (cf. 4.1.(2)). Let us now look at this question more closely.

Kayne (1979c) provided direct evidence that what we are now calling "RES(NIC)" holds of variables formed by LF-rules, hence at the level of LF-representation. He cites such examples as the following in French:

(4)   (i) je n'ai exigé qu'ils arrêtent personne
        (ii) *je n'ai exigé que personne soit arrêté
        (iii) j'ai exigé que personne ne soit arrêté

The corresponding LF-representations are (5):

(5)   (i) [for no x], j'ai exigé qu'ils arrêtent x
            ("for no x, I demanded that they arrest x")
        (ii) [for no x], j'ai exigé que x soit arrêté
            ("for no x, I demanded that x be arrested")
        (iii) j'ai exigé que, [for no x], x soit arrêté
            ("I demanded that for no x, x be arrested")

Example (4i), while slightly marginal, is much better than the ungrammatical (ii), while (iii) is unproblematic. The LF-representations are derived on the following assumptions:

(6)   (i) The particle *ne* is a scope indicator, determining the scope of *personne*
        (ii) *personne* undergoes the quantifier-movement rule in the LF-component

We can explain this array of data if we assume that RES(NIC) holds at LF. The ungrammatical example (4ii)–(5ii) illustrates a *that*-trace effect, exactly as in 4.1.(2ii), and thus falls under 4.1.(1). Let us assume, then, that RES(NIC) holds at the level of LF-representation, for all variables.

If this is correct, we should expect to find some indication of RES(NIC) applying to variables not bound by *wh*- in English as well. Kayne suggests examples of the following type:

(7)   in all these weeks, he's suggested that
        (i) they see no one
        (ii) they write not a single term paper

(iii) no one see them

(iv) not a single term paper be written

In cases (i) and (ii), the negated NP can have wide scope interpretation, but not in (iii) and (iv). The examples of (7) are somewhat more subtle than their French counterparts – presumably, Kayne suggests, because there is no overt scope marker in English to force the intended interpretations. But I think that Kayne's judgments are correct. If so, then RES(NIC) holds in English too at the level of LF-representation.

Kayne suggests further that the same phenomenon can be observed in connection with multiple *wh*-questions of the sort studied by Baker (1970). Consider the sentence (8):

(8)   who remembers where we bought which book

There is a narrow scope interpretation of *which book* as in (9i) with the possible answer (9ii), and a wide scope interpretation as in (10i) with the possible answer (10ii):

(9)   (i) for which person x, x remembers for which place z and which book y, we bought y at z

        (ii) John remembers where we bought which book

(10)   (i) for which person x and which book y, x remembers for which place z, we bought y at z

        (ii) John remembers where we bought the physics book and Bill remembers where we bought the novel

Assuming as in our earlier discussion the analysis in Chomsky (1977a, chapter 3), a rule of the LF-component moves the *wh*-phrase *which book* to COMP, giving either (9i) or (10i). A condition on this rule is that it moves the *wh*-phrase to a COMP containing an overt *wh*-phrase. Presumably, then, the rule is a "one-step" movement rule, not a successive cyclic movement rule such as syntactic *wh*-movement or raising. If so, it should not observe the standard island conditions that follow from subjacency.[6]

Judgments are not entirely clear, but it seems that this rule violates most conditions. It is immediately obvious that it violates the *wh*-island condition; cf. (10i). Similarly, violation of the complex NP-constraint seems quite tolerable:

(11)   I wonder who heard the claim that John had seen what

The rule also violates the specificity constraint that blocks (12); compare (13i), with the LF-representation (13ii):[7]

(12)   *what did you hear⎰John's⎱stories about
                          ⎱those ⎰

(13)   (i) I wonder who heard John's stories about what
         (ii) I wonder for which person x and which thing y, x heard John's
         stories about y

Note that the specificity constraint is a constraint on movement, not
interpretation; compare (14), which is grammatical; also 3.2.3.(57iv) and
other similar examples cited earlier:

(14)   they had the habit of feeding themselves (each other)

Nevertheless, it appears that the *wh*-movement rule of the LF-component
does not observe the constraint, which suggests that the constraint holds
only of bounded movement rules (rules of the syntax and quantifier-movement; cf. May (1977)) rather than being an "output constraint" at LF.

   In general, then, it seems that the rule in question does not observe the
usual conditions on bounded movement rules.[8] We therefore conclude that
it is indeed a "one-step" movement rule to a position filled by an overt
wh-phrase in COMP. Since the rule applies in the LF-component, it is
immune to the doubly-filled COMP filter of the PF-component. Let us
assume that exactly like the overt *wh*-movement rule, this LF-component
rule adjoins the *wh*-phrase to the left, say, to the left of COMP. Crucially,
in "long movement," there is no trace left in COMP immediately preceding
a moved subject, since the rule is not successive-cyclic.

   There seems to be a marked difference, however, between applications
of the rule that lead to the RES(NIC) violation 4.1.(1) and paired examples
that do not, as Kayne suggests:[9]

(15)   (i)(a) who remembers where John bought what
         (b) *who remembers where who bought that book
         (ii)(a) it is unclear who thinks (that) we saw whom
         (b) *it is unclear who thinks (that) who saw us
         (iii)(a) I know perfectly well who thinks (that) he is in love with
         whom
         (b) *I know perfectly well who thinks (that) who is in love with
         him
         (iv)(a) I don't know who would be happy for whom to win the
         prize
         (b) *I don't know who would be happy if who won the prize
         (c) *I don't know who would be happy that who win the
         prize
         (v)(a) I don't remember who believes him to have read what
         (b) I don't remember who believes whom to have read the
         book
         (c) *I don't remember who believes (that) who read the book

In all of these examples, one must be careful to exclude the echo-question interpretation, which is always possible. While the judgments are not perfectly sharp, they seem to me to go in the direction indicated; that they are not sharp is again hardly surprising, given that there is no overt indication of the intended interpretation. The starred examples are all of the form 4.1.(1) at LF, given that the *wh*-movement rule is not successive-cyclic, confirming Kayne's conclusion that the principle RES(NIC) holds at the level of LF-representation.

Assuming the distinctions marked in (15) to be valid, what is their significance? The starred examples are all of the form 4.1.(1), or more generally, of the form (16), where ... is non-null, t is nominative and is the variable locally bound by α, and α may be an operator (not necessarily a *wh*-phrase) or its trace in COMP:

(16) $\quad *[\alpha \ldots [_S t \text{ INFL VP}]]$

Examples (i) illustrate the superiority condition (cf. 4.1.(2iv)). The sets (iv) and (v) show that the phenomenon in question holds of nominative subjects but not subjects of infinitivals, and the other examples show that it holds only of subjects. The starred examples of (ii)–(v) in effect exhibit the *that*-trace effect (cf. 4.2.(2ii)). They again illustrate that syntactic movement is not a crucial element of this effect, and furthermore that the presence of the complementizer is immaterial. Thus the phenomenon captured by the *[*that-t*] filter or other devices that have been proposed does not crucially involve either the complementizer or overt movement. Rather, the effect is subsumed under a more general condition, RES(NIC), which holds at LF, including (16) as one class of cases and NP-trace examples such as 4.1.(5) as another class.

While this conclusion seems to me generally persuasive, it faces a number of problems. The most serious of these arises in connection with the pro-drop parameter. Assuming the modification in Chomsky and Lasnik (1977) of Perlmutter's generalization, the *that*-trace effect should be found with languages that do not allow "missing subjects" and only these: thus, French and English, but not Italian and Spanish, for example.[10] The *[*that-t*] subcase of RES(NIC) appears to be void for Spanish and Italian, as expected, but Rizzi (1979a) points out that the application of RES(NIC) to variables formed in the LF-component holds for Italian and Spanish as well, contrary to what is predicted. In particular, the French examples (4) are duplicated in Italian and Spanish. Consider the following examples in Italian:[11]

(17) (i) non voglio che tu parli con nessuno
        ("for no x, I want that you speak with x")
      (ii) *non voglio che nessuno venga
        ("for no x, I want that x come")
     (iii) voglio che nessuno venga
        ("I want that for no x, x come")

The examples (i)–(iii) are exactly parallel to the French examples (4i–iii), respectively. Thus it appears that RES(NIC) holds for variables formed by rules of the LF-component in Italian and Spanish (which is the same in this respect; cf. Jaeggli (1980b)), but not for variables formed by *wh*-movement. We are thus faced with an apparent contradiction: RES(NIC) holds of variables, by Kayne's argument, but does not hold of variables, as the preceding examples show. For the moment, let us put this problem aside, returning later to a solution based on Rizzi's work.

There are a number of other problems that arise in connection with the assumption that a condition of LF-representation is involved in RES(NIC). For one thing, the multiple *wh*-examples are much more acceptable when a *wh*-phrase appears throughout, as in (18), or (19i) as compared with (19ii):

(18)   it is unclear who thinks that who did what

(19)   (i) John wonders what who bought where
        (ii) *John wonders what who bought at the store

It is not obvious why this should be so. The rational assumption seems to be that RES(NIC) does hold for variables at LF, as Kayne suggests, and that some other factor accounts for the improved status of examples with *wh*-phrases throughout.[12]

Another problem has to do with the rule of FOCUS discussed in Chomsky (1977a, chapter 4). Applied to the sentences (20), this gives the representation of (21), where capitalization indicates heavy stress:

(20)   (i) 1 don't think that JOHN will win
        (ii) I wonder how JOHN solved the problem
(21)   (i) for x = John, I don't think that x will win
        (ii) for x = John, I wonder how x solved the problem

There is good evidence for such a rule on the basis of weak crossover phenomena, but it leads to an apparent violation of RES(NIC) in the examples (20), (21). A possible solution, suggested by Dominique Sportiche, is that the representations of (21) are incorrect and that in fact the specification of the variable should be internal to the embedded clause, as in (22):

(22)   (i) I don't think that, for x = John, x will win
        (ii) I wonder how, for x = John, x solved the problem

Then RES(NIC), as expressed in the configuration (16), will not be violated. Problems arise in the case of multiple focus. Jaeggli (1980b) observes that some facts concerning focus in Spanish noted by Contreras might be relevant in this connection. Certain matrix verbs (e.g., *sentir* – "regret") do not permit such structures as (20), while others (e.g., *decir* – "say") do permit them. The former class, then, observe RES(NIC) in the case of focal stress, a fact that might be explained on the grounds that they do not permit an "internal" analysis of focus as in (22) for some reason.[13]

A related problem has to do with broad scope interpretation of quantifiers, which will lead to a violation of RES(NIC) when the quantified expression is in subject position, as in (23):

(23) (i)   everyone expected that *some of the talks* (*certain talks*) would
            be too difficult for the audience to follow
      (ii) he told me what *everyone* said at the conference
      (iii) he told me what *everyone* did last summer
      (iv) I wonder how *anyone* understood that talk
      (v)   no one knows how well *any of us* did in the exam
      (vi) they couldn't tell me how *any of us* did in the exam
      (vii) I wonder how many problems *anyone here* has solved

If wide scope interpretation is possible for the italicized quantified expressions in such cases as these, then there is an apparent violation of RES(NIC). Perhaps one might argue that wide scope interpretation is a marked option, outside of core grammar, in some of these cases. Or it might be that the quantifier is not subject to quantifier movement, but is used in the quasi-referential sense studied by Higginbotham in forthcoming work; in this case, one would expect that substitution of *none of the talks* for *some of the talks* in (i) would prevent wide scope interpretation, which appears to be the case.

With regard to *any*, there is evidence that in some cases it is interpreted as a narrow-scope existential quantifier (cf. Linebarger (1980) for a review), though this does not seem to be an option in (23). My suspicion is that *any* should never be regarded as a wide-scope universal quantifier but rather in the manner of a free variable in a system of natural deduction, hence name-like, with corresponding "wide scope." Cf. Aoun, Hornstein and Sportiche (1980). In forthcoming work, Hornstein develops an interpretation in terms of substitutional quantification that has similar effects and many interesting consequences. Among many other examples, he points out that wide-scope universal quantifier interpretation cannot be the correct analysis for *any* in such discourses as: "Pick any number – if it is odd, then ... "

Examples of the sort just reviewed raise problems that must be overcome if the proposal that RES(NIC) is an LF-property is to be sustained. None of them appear to be insuperable, but clearly they require further thought and analysis.

In summary, we have some strong evidence that RES(NIC) extends beyond *wh*-trace to variables in general and thus is a principle applying in the LF-component, presumably, as a condition on LF-representation; and we have a number of residual problems that arise in areas that are not very well-understood, including one major problem concerning pro-drop languages, to which I will return. Let us leave these problems to the side and turn to some further properties of RES(NIC).

4.3. The pro-drop parameter (1)

The most interesting topic in connection with RES(NIC) is the clustering of properties related to the pro-drop parameter, whatever this turns out to be. In pro-drop languages (e.g., Italian), we tend to find among others the following clustering of properties:[14]

(1)　　(i) missing subject
　　　　(ii) free inversion in simple sentences
　　　　(iii) "long *wh*-movement" of subject
　　　　(iv) empty resumptive pronouns in embedded clause
　　　　(v) apparent violations of the *[*that-t*] filter

Non-pro-drop languages (e.g., French and English) lack all of these properties, characteristically. Examples of (1) in Italian are as in (2):

(2)　　(i) ho trovato il libro
　　　　　　("I found the book")
　　　　(ii) ha mangiato Giovanni
　　　　　　("Giovanni ate")
　　　　(iii) l'uomo [che mi domando [chi abbia visto]]
　　　　　　(with the interpretation: "the man x such that I wonder who x saw")
　　　　(iv) ecco la ragazza [che mi domando [chi crede [che possa VP]]]
　　　　　　("this is the girl who I wonder who thinks that she may VP")
　　　　(v) chi credi [che partirà]
　　　　　　("who do you think [(that) will leave]")

In (i), Italian has no overt subject, as distinct from French or English. Let us tentatively assume the subject to be [$_{NP}e$]. In (ii), the subject is inverted, an option that is open in French but only under highly restricted conditions.[15] The interpretation indicated in (iii) is excluded in French and English. In case (iv), taken from Taraldsen (1978b), we know that the missing subject of *possa* is not the trace of *wh*-movement (since this would violate subjacency), so it must be an empty resumptive pronoun, base-generated, in accordance with the resumptive pronoun strategy that operates in Italian (perhaps, non-standard); again, there is no analogue in French or English. We may assume that this resumptive pronoun too is [$_{NP}e$], for present purposes. Case (v) illustrates the *[*that-t*] phenomenon, already discussed.

For the case of inversion, let us assume that the post-verbal NP is coindexed with the empty category in subject position, though in a form distinct from the indexing relevant to binding; see the discussion of 3.2.3.(94). We might think of Case-assignment and θ-role assignment in this construction as an instance of assignment to the index or function chain, in the manner described in § 3.2.2; we return to a sharper formulation below and in chapter 6. Note that this discussion is so far independent of the question of the configuration in which post-verbal NPs appear (within VP or adjoined to VP), and of whether the post-verbal NP is moved by an inversion rule or base-generated in place. We return to these questions.

The optimal assumption, hence the assumption that we will assume to be correct pending evidence to the contrary, is that there is a single parameter of core grammar – the "pro-drop parameter" – that distinguishes Italian-type from French-type languages. When this parameter is set one way or another, the clustering of properties should follow. The language learner equipped with the theory of UG as a part of the initial state requires evidence to fix the parameter and then knows the other properties of the language that follow from this choice of value.

To begin with, let us assume – following Taraldsen (1978b) – that the parameter involves the inflectional element INFL, or more precisely, the agreement element AGR (= PRO) that is the crucial component of INFL with respect to government and binding. The intuitive idea is that where there is overt agreement, the subject can be dropped, since the deletion is recoverable. In Italian-type languages, with a richer inflectional system, the element AGR permits subject-drop while in French-type languages it does not. A language might have a mixed system, permitting subject drop in some constructions but not in others, a property that we might expect to find varying as inflection is or is not overt; Taraldsen gives examples from Irish; Hebrew is another case. The correlation with overt inflection need not be exact. We expect at most a tendency in this direction. The idea is, then, that there is some abstract property of AGR, correlated more or less with overt morphology, that distinguishes pro-drop from non-pro-drop languages, from which the clustering of properties in (1) follows.

There are various ways to realize this leading idea. Several will be considered as we proceed. For the moment, let us simply say that in Italian-type languages AGR is able to control the subject in some sense, whereas in French-type languages it is not. We continue to assume, then, that all of these languages have the basic core structure (3):

(3)   S→NP INFL VP, where INFL = $\left[\left[\pm\text{Tense}\right], (\text{AGR})\right]$
$$(\text{AGR} = \text{PRO})$$

We may now tentatively reformulate RES(NIC) as in (4):

(4) $\left[_{NP} e\right]$ must be locally controlled

The notion "local control" must be made precise. One case of "local control" will be agreement in pro-drop languages. Recall that the element AGR is coindexed with the subject that it governs. We have assumed this coindexing to be distinct from that of the binding theory, say, co-super-scripting; see the discussion of 3.2.3.(94). In the pro-drop languages, we take such coindexing to serve as "local control" in the required sense. A second case of "local control" is coindexing with an adjacent *wh*-phrase or trace of a *wh*-phrase in COMP, as in (5):

(5)   (i) I wonder $[\bar{s}$ who$_i]$s t$_i$ will be there$]]$
        (ii) who$_i$ did you think $[\bar{s}$ t$_i[$ s t$_i$ would be there$]]$

Let us tentatively assume co-superscripting to be assigned automatically in this case. We will modify this principle and try to determine its status more closely as we proceed. For the moment, let us simply assume it. Principle (4) is a variant of the idea, which has appeared in several contexts in the course of this discussion, that trace must be governed. See 2.9.(4).

This assumption immediately yields properties (i)–(iv) of the complex (1). In a pro-drop language, the subject $[_{NP} e]$ is locally controlled by AGR in tensed sentences. Therefore the subject may be missing (i.e., may be $[_{NP} e]$; property (i)); free inversion leaving the trace $[_{NP} e]$ is permitted (property (ii)); long-*wh*-movement is a free option (property (iii)); and an empty resumptive pronoun may appear in an embedded clause (property (iv)). In each case, the element $[_{NP} e]$ in subject position is locally controlled by AGR. In a non-pro-drop language, none of these options exists, since $[_{NP} e]$ will not be locally controlled. Short *wh*-movement, as in (5), is permissible, however, since the subject trace is then locally controlled from COMP. The analogous remarks hold of other variables if principle (4) is a condition on LF-representation. Note that principle (4) does not affect the status of infinitives (cf. 4.2.(15)). Thus all cases of (6) are barred:

(6)   (i) *Giovanni pensava di [Maria venire]
        (ii) *Giovanni pensava di $[[_{NP} e]$ venire$]]$
        (iii) *Giovanni pensava di $[[_{NP} e]$ venire Maria$]]$
        ("Giovanni thought Maria to come")

Cases (i) and (iii) are excluded by the Case Filter, since *Maria* lacks Case; and (ii) and (iii) are barred by principle (4), since there is no AGR to locally control the empty subject. The surface structure corresponding to (ii) is, of course, generated as a control structure with PRO instead of trace as the embedded subject. We will return to the case of raising verbs below.[16] These examples, then, are similar to 4.1.(5).

It remains to consider property (v) of the complex (1), the *that*-trace effects. Recall that we have dissociated the former NIC into two distinct categories, as illustrated in (7) and (8):

(7)   (i) *they think that each other are here
        (ii) *they think that PRO are here
        (iii) they think that they are here (with the proximate interpretation for the two occurrences of *they*)
(8)   RES(NIC), which applies to variables

Category (7) falls under the binding theory, which applies at S-structure. NIC must apply at S-structure or in the LF-component because of the cases of (7) (we concluded in § 3.2.3 that it holds at S-structure), but RES(NIC), now dissociated from NIC, might be in the LF- or PF-component or at S-structure.

Suppose, contrary to what we have been assuming so far, that RES(NIC) is in the PF-component, let us say, as a filter following deletion. In this case, one way to incorporate the *[*that-t*] filter into RES(NIC), now stated as (4), is to adopt an idea of Pesetsky (1978b), and to relate the *[*that-t*] filter to the filter (9), which bars doubly-filled COMP, as in (10):

(9)   *[$_{COMP}\alpha\beta$]

(10)   *... [the man [$_{\bar{S}}$ [$_{COMP}$ who that] [$_S$ you met t]]]

In (10), either *who* or *that* or both must drop, by virtue of (9). Assume that (9) holds as well for α = trace. Consider, then, a typical example of the *[*that-t*] effect such as the S-structure (11):

(11)   who do you think [$_{\bar{S}}$ [$_{COMP}$ t that] [$_S$ t left]]

If neither *t* nor *that* deletes,[17] we have a violation of (9). If only *t* deletes, we have no violation of (9) but we have a violation of RES(NIC) (= (4)) since the trace in subject position in (11) is not locally controlled. If *that* deletes and *t* remains, the structure is grammatical, exactly as in (5). In the pro-drop languages, however, the analogue to *that* need not (and does not) delete, since the trace in the embedded S is in any event locally controlled by AGR in INFL, so that RES(NIC) is not violated. Thus the *[*that-t*] filter, holding only for non-pro-drop languages, is derived from the doubly-filled COMP filter (9) and RES(NIC) (= (4)). Note that it follows that in languages that do not have the restriction against doubly-filled COMP, the *[*that-t*] effect should not be observed. Pesetsky gives supporting evidence; counter-evidence is presented in Bennis (1980).

A variant of this idea, suggested independently by Rizzi and Kayne, is that quite apart from the doubly-filled COMP filter, the trace is not locally controlled if *that* remains because its potential controller in COMP does not c-command it. Thus assume that *wh*-movement is adjunction to COMP, as proposed above, so that the embedded COMP in (11) is (12):

(12)   [$_{COMP}$ t [$_{COMP}$ that]]

Then if *that* is present, *t* does not c-command the subject trace in the embedded S of (11) and RES(NIC) is violated, if local control requires c-command.

On these assumptions, RES(NIC) will apply only to *wh*-traces, not to variables in general, since it is in the PF-component. Thus we fail to accommodate Kayne's observations discussed above or the superiority condition, though we do not face the problems raised in connection with the proposal that RES(NIC) apply to all variables.

Assuming that these problems can be overcome, we want RES(NIC) to apply in the LF-component. The clustering of properties (1) follows in much the same way. This is obvious in the case of properties (i)–(iv). Consider then property (v), the *[*that-t*] effects. Let us now explicitly assume, as in earlier discussion, that there is no *that*-deletion rule but rather the option of selecting or not selecting *that* in the base rules. Thus the base rule for COMP is something like (13), where as usual, none of the options may be chosen, leaving [COMPe]:

$$(13) \qquad \text{COMP} \rightarrow \begin{Bmatrix} [\pm \text{WH}] \\ \text{for} \end{Bmatrix}$$

If *that* ($= [-\text{WH}]$) is not selected, then the analogue of (11) without *that* is grammatical, since the trace in COMP locally controls the subject trace of the embedded S, assuming that empty COMP is deleted (or "invisible") by convention. If *that* is selected, we have a violation of RES(NIC) in the non-pro-drop languages either directly, if we assume with Rizzi and Kayne that local control requires c-command, or by virtue of the doubly-filled COMP filter, if we do not make this assumption.[18]

To run through the relevant cases, consider the S-structure representations (14):

(14)   (i)   who does John think [t that][t' left]
        (ii) who does John think [t][t' left]
        (iii) who does John think [t that][Bill saw t']
        (iv) who does John think [t][Bill saw t']

In case (i), if t is deleted at S-structure, we have a violation of RES(NIC) at LF since t' is not locally controlled; if it is not deleted we have a violation of the doubly-filled COMP filter (9) or of the c-command requirement for local control. In any case, (i) is ungrammatical. In case (ii), we have a violation of RES(NIC) at LF if *t* is deleted at S-structure but a grammatical structure if it is not. In case (iii), if *t* is not deleted we have a violation of the doubly-filled COMP filter (assuming Pesetsky's theory) but no violation if it is deleted. Case (iv) is grammatical whether or not *t* is deleted. Thus examples (iii) and (iv) are grammatical. In pro-drop languages, the analogues are grammatical throughout.

Thus we achieve the same results with respect to the *[*that-t*] filter whether RES(NIC) applies in the PF- or LF-component. The choice depends on the issues discussed above, in connection with Kayne's observation about variables and the superiority condition. I will assume that RES(NIC) does apply in the LF-component and that the problems noted above can be overcome. Then we may think of RES(NIC), now in the form of (4), as a condition on LF-representation.

Summarizing so far, we assume that pro-drop languages allow AGR to be a local controller while non-pro-drop languages do not, and that RES(NIC) applies to LF-representation. We have the option of (i) taking local control to require c-command or (ii) weakening this condition and appealing to the doubly-filled COMP filter (in which case we must assume the option of deleting non-Case-marked trace at S-structure, before the branching of the two interpretive components, while excluding trace deletion from the PF-component; cf. note 18). The *that*-trace effects follow on either option, and we derive the clustering of properties associated with the pro-drop parameter.

RES(NIC) is hardly acceptable in the form (4), since the notion "local control" seems so *ad hoc*. We have also noted certain problems, the most important of which is the apparent contradiction concerning variables in subject position in pro-drop languages.

Before turning to the latter problem and the status of RES(NIC), let us consider some further issues that arise in connection with the *[that-t]* case of RES(NIC). It is well-known that there are several structures in which the filter appears to be violated in non-pro-drop languages, specifically, in relatives and clefts, as in the examples (15):

(15)   (i) the book [that [t was on the table]]
        (ii) [a book] was lost [that [t was on the table]]
        (iii) it is the book [that [t was on the table]]

At S-structure, the embedded COMP in each case is something like (16):[19]

(16)   [COMP *wh*-phrase that]

Assuming now that RES(NIC) is a condition on LF-representation, then, as Kayne has observed, these problems do not arise at all if we derive the *[that-t]* filter from the doubly-filled COMP filter. The *wh*-phrase is present at LF, so that RES(NIC) is satisfied, and will be deleted in the PF-component, satisfying the doubly-filled COMP filter. Suppose, however, that we adopt the other option, dispensing with reference to the doubly-filled COMP filter and requiring c-command for local control. Then although the *wh*-phrase is present in COMP at LF, it will not locally control the embedded subject trace. We might deal with this problem by adopting another idea of Pesetsky (1978b), assuming that the complementizer *that* in (16) takes on the index of the *wh*-phrase which deletes at S-structure prior to the bifurcation of the two interpretive components.[20] This is rather natural, in view of the fact that the complementizer *that* in relative clauses has quasi-pronominal properties, being preferable with (or, for some speakers, limited to) inanimate antecedents, e.g., *book* but not *boy* in (15). The *that* in (15) will locally control the embedded subject trace, satisfying RES(NIC). The same approach is possible if, contrary to our present assumptions, RES(NIC) is located in the PF-component. Pesetsky's suggestion that the index on the *wh*-phrase or its trace is absorbed by the complementizer is, as he notes, well-motivated in French by the *que-qui* alternation that provides an "escape" from the effects of the *[*that-t*] filter, as in (17):

(17)   la fille que je crois qui est arrivée la première
        ("the girl who I think that [= *qui*] had arrived first")

Here *qui* may be regarded as a form of the complementizer *que* which is pronominal in that it has absorbed the index of the trace of the (ultimately deleted) relative pronoun, thus serving as a local controller.[21]

Consider some further observations of Kayne (1980a) on the *that*-trace effects and related matters. He notes certain differences between transitive verbs, on the one hand, and intransitive verbs and adjectives, on the other, as matrix elements in constructions related to RES(NIC). Consider his examples (18), (19):

(18)   (i) John, who it's essential [she talk to t]
        (ii) John, who it is essential [t talk to her]
        (iii) John, who it is essential that she talk to t
        (iv) John, who it is essential [that t talk to her]
(19)   (i) French, which it doesn't seem [Mary knows t at all well]
        (ii) Mary, who it doesn't seem [t knows French at all well]
        (iii) French, which it doesn't seem [that Mary knows t at all well]
        (iv) Mary, who it doesn't seem [that t knows French at all well]

The examples (iii) of (18) and (19) are grammatical and the examples (iv) ungrammatical as expected. The crucial cases are (i) and (ii). Kayne's judgments are that examples (i) of (18) and (19) are more acceptable than (ii), and he suggests drawing the line between grammatical and ungrammatical so as to distinguish (18i,iii), (19i,iii) as grammatical from (18ii,iv), (19ii,iv) as ungrammatical. Suppose we do so. Then (18i,iii) and (19i,iii) fall together with (14ii), while (18ii,iv) and (19ii,iv) fall together with (14i). Kayne suggests unifying these cases in terms of "case-binding." Rephrasing his proposal in our terms here, the local controller of *t* in COMP position must have Case for (4) to be satisfied. Assume that a transitive verb can assign Case in the COMP position of its complement, though not to the trace in a doubly-filled COMP. Then the grammatical examples are those in which the local controller in COMP has Case, and the ungrammatical ones are those in which it does not.

My own conclusion differs. It seems to me that the primary distinction is between (iv) of (18)–(19), the ungrammatical case, and (i), (ii), (iii), which are all grammatical (along with (14ii,iv)). I think that Kayne is correct in noting a subtle distinction between (i) and (ii) of (18) and (19) (though for me, (18i) is more acceptable with *that* as embedded complementizer). But I think this is a secondary effect. Consider the sets (20), (21):

(20)   (i) who does it seem to you [that John will visit t]
          (ii) who does it seem to you [John will visit t]
          (iii) who does it seem to you [t will visit John]
          (iv) who does it seem to you [that t will visit John]
(21)   (i) who is it essential [that John see t]
          (ii) who is it essential [John see t]
          (iii) who is it essential [t see John]
          (iv) who is it essential [that t see John]

My judgments are that the essential difference is between (iv) of (20)–(21), which are ungrammatical, and the other cases, which are all grammatical though varying in acceptability. Cases (i) of (20)–(21) seem to me completely acceptable, and cases (ii) and (iii) more marginal. Furthermore, as Kayne notes, for many adjectives there seems to be no difference between cases (ii) and (iii); the same is true with nominal heads, which also cannot Case-mark into COMP. Consider (22) and (23):

(22)   John, I am not certain (sure, convinced)
          (i) [t will ever win the election]
          (ii) [Bill will ever like t]
          (iii) [that t will like this book]
(23)   John, I don't have the impression
          (i) [t will like this book]
          (ii) [Bill will like t]
          (iii) [that t will like this book]

Again, the examples (iii) of (22), (23) are ungrammatical, violating the *[that-t] requirement; but examples (i) and (ii) seem to me on a par with regard to acceptability, and are surely radically different in status from (iii).

It seems to me, then, that the primary phenomenon to be explained is the difference in status of (iii) as opposed (i)–(ii) in (22)–(23); and correspondingly, the difference between (iv) and the other examples in (18)–(21).

The primary distinction is given by RES(NIC). The secondary, and much more subtle distinction, might be traced to other causes. It might be related to the slight preference for retaining the complementizer *that* in cases (i) and (ii) of (18)–(21), which somehow affects the judgment of (18ii), (19ii), (20iii), (21iii). Or, one might pursue a different approach, related to the one Kayne proposes (but now regarding it as a secondary phenomenon rather than the explanation for the RES(NIC) phenomena). Suppose that a kind of Exceptional Case-marking applies to trace in COMP, thus preventing trace-deletion in (14ii, iv) but not (14iii). Then with a transitive matrix verb, a structure will be grammatical under every option (since the trace in COMP can never be deleted), but with an intransitive verb or an adjective (as in (18ii), (19ii), (20iii), (21iii)), the structure will be grammatical only if the trace does not delete (one of the two options); thus (14ii,iv) are grammatical along more optional paths than (18ii), (19ii), (20iii), (21iii), which may account for the more marginal character of the latter set.

I am skeptical, then, about the attempt to account for the RES(NIC) phenomena on the basis of Case-marking of trace in COMP. Nevertheless, the latter property may hold. Apart from the evidence Kayne has adduced in the cited paper and elsewhere, there is additional support for the assumption, some of which we have cited earlier (cf. 3.2.2.(13), concerning Hungarian). Free relatives also exhibit this phenomenon, whatever the mechanisms may be Groos and van Riemsdijk (1979) give evidence that the head may be in COMP, while its Case may be that of the verb that governs the free relative. We return to other possible examples in § 5.2.

4.4. The empty category principle (ECP)

Let us now turn finally to the status of RES(NIC), which we have tentatively given in the form (1), a condition on LF-representation:

(1) $[_{NP} e]$ must be locally controlled   (= 4.3.(4))

There are a number of conceptual problems that arise in connection with this formulation:

(2)   (i) What is the notion of "local control" that appears in RES(NIC)?
        (ii) Why is there an asymmetry between subject of verb and object of verb?
       (iii) Why does RES(NIC) hold of nominatives, but not subjects of infinitives?
       (iv) How does RES(NIC) relate to recoverability of deletion and what is the character of the empty subject in the pro-drop languages?
        (v) Is there a connection between the NP-AGR relation assumed for the pro-drop languages and the relation of clitics to the positions in the verbal complement associated with them?

Problems (i) and (ii) are obvious. As concerns (iii), in dialects of English that lack the *[for-to] filter, RES(NIC) does not appear to hold for *for*-infinitivals in the case of overt movement (the question is untestable where the *[for-to] filter holds), so that we have such examples as (3):

(3)   who did you try $[_{\bar{S}}$ for $[_S$ t to VP$]]$

Cf. Chomsky and Lasnik (1977). Recall also examples 4.1.(15iv–v), such as (4), (5):

(4)   (i) I don't know who would be happy for whom to win the prize
       (ii) I don't remember who believes whom to have read the book
(5)   (i) *I don't know who would be happy if who won the prize
       (ii) *I don't remember who believes (that) who read the book

These examples too show that RES(NIC) is void for subjects of infinitives.

With regard to (2iv), the intuitive account of the pro-drop parameter given earlier suggests a relation to the principle of recoverability of deletion, and one might hope that this principle, at least in the case of pronouns, might follow in part from a proper formulation of RES(NIC). Question (2v) I will defer to § 4.6.

In addition to the conceptual problems of (2), there is one major empirical problem: namely, the problem of variables in pro-drop languages. There are also several other empirical problems, noted above, which I will ignore, since I have no useful ideas concerning them beyond what was mentioned.

Consider first problem (i) of (2). The major examples relevant to RES(NIC) have involved such configurations as (6):

(6) $[_{\alpha}[_{S}[_{NP}\beta]\,\text{AGR}\ldots]]$

We have so far assumed that β is e throughout this class of cases, as it is when it is the trace of a moved element: NP, a *wh*-phrase or a quantifier phrase. The element AGR may or may not be co-superscripted with the empty subject. I have so far assumed that this option constitutes the pro-drop parameter. The element α may be a *wh*-phrase or its trace or a quantifier phrase moved in the LF-component, co-superscripted with the empty subject. The elements α and AGR "locally control" the empty subject when they are co-superscripted with it. These are the only cases of "local control."

We already have a notion very similar to "local control" in this sense, namely, the notion of government, which has been central to this entire discussion. As a first approximation to an answer to (2i), then, let us simply take "local control" to be a subcase of government – as, in fact, has been assumed since § 2.4. Then RES(NIC) is reformulated as (7):

(7) $[_{NP}e]$ must be governed (in some sense)

Let us now turn to problem (ii) of (2). Why should there be an asymmetry in RES(NIC) between subjects and objects? We can relate this fact to the asymmetry of government. A verb governs its object but does not govern its subjects. Rather, INFL governs the subject, or something in COMP or in the matrix sentence governs the subject as in the case of *for*-infinitivals, Exceptional Case-marking, and raising verbs and adjectives. The asymmetry of subject and object thus follows without stipulation. Similarly, we have an answer to question (2iii): subjects of infinitives are ungoverned in the unmarked case and thus are excluded from the collection of phenomena related to RES(NIC). In the marked cases (3) and (4), the subject of the infinitive is governed so that (7) is satisfied; we return to case (3) and (4i), i.e., the case of *for*-clauses.[22]

The pro-drop parameter relates to the sense in which AGR governs subjects in the pro-drop languages. Principle (7) might be called "the empty NP principle." We have discussed such a principle a number of times already, beginning with § 2.4.1 where it was observed that trace must be governed. Though relevant evidence is sparse, I will tentatively assume that the empty NP principle extends to trace in general.[23] Thus we have the following principle of the theory of government:

(8)   The Empty Category Principle (ECP): $[_\alpha\, e]$ must be governed (in some sense)

Recall that this is one part of the more general principle 2.9.(4) holding of PRO as well.

In what sense must the empty category be governed? To clarify this notion, we must first extend our notion of government. In chapter 3, governors were restricted to elements of the form X^0 of the X-bar system: i.e., $[\pm N, \pm V]^0$. But we are now assuming that a coindexed NP in COMP may be a governor for ECP. Suppose then that we modify the definition of "governor" given in chapter 3 (namely, 3.2.1.(11)),[24] extending the class of governors:

(9)   Consider the structure (i):

(i) $[_\beta \ldots \gamma \ldots \alpha \ldots \gamma \ldots]$, where
     (a) $\alpha = X^0$ or is coindexed with γ
     (b) where ϕ is a maximal projection, if ϕ dominates γ then ϕ dominates α
     (c) α c-commands γ
     In this case, α *governs* γ

Recall that "c-command" is used in the extended sense of 3.2.1.(12).

We now tentatively define "proper government" as in (10), and reformulate the ECP as in (11):

(10) α *properly governs* β if and only if α governs β $[$and $\alpha \neq$ AGR$]$
(11)   ECP: $[_\alpha\, e]$ must be properly governed

The bracketed phrase in (10) is the pro-drop parameter. The notion of proper government for pro-drop languages excludes this condition, while it is retained for non-pro-drop languages. This notion replaces the device of co-superscripting introduced in the earlier exposition. Now AGR as α

in (10) governs as an instance of X^0 in (9ia), and an element in COMP is coindexed in the usual way.

Our discussion so far has been concerned with two categories of problems raised in chapter 3 in connection with the OB-framework: namely, the RES(NIC) phenomena and the problem of deriving the *[*that-t*] filter from more reasonable assumptions and relating it to RES(NIC) (problems (3) and (4) of § 3.1, final paragraph). The ECP offers an appropriate answer to these problems, if we can clear up the remaining open questions. It subsumes quite a wide range of phenomena, including NP-trace, *wh*-trace, and variables formed within the LF-component. It also subsumes the phenomena connected to the *[*that-t*] filter, which now simply appears to be an unnaturally selected subcase. The more general phenomenon does not crucially involve COMP or overt movement. Furthermore ECP is a rather natural principle, as distinct from the *[*that-t*] filter or any of the alternatives to it that have been suggested in the literature, quite apart from its considerably wider scope. That is, it is not unreasonable that UG should require that the presence of an empty category be signalled in some manner by elements that are overtly present (in this case, the relevant governor, or where the governor is a trace in COMP, its antecedent). Finally, ECP suggests a plausible approach to the pro-drop parameter and the clustering of properties related to it. I will turn in § 4.5–6 to problems (2iv,v): namely, the relation between ECP and the principle of recoverability of deletion, the relation of agreement to cliticization, and the precise character of the empty subject in pro-drop languages, which we have so far assumed to be [$_{NP}e$].

A few comments are in order before we proceed with the outstanding problems. Note first that the ECP as formulated in (11) covers trace but not PRO, since PRO has features and thus is not an instance of [$_{NP}e$]. Thus the ECP does not block such examples as (12):

(12)   I don't know [what [PRO to do t]]

Here the trace is properly governed by the verb *do*, but PRO is not. Thus ECP is satisfied, as is the principle of the binding theory that PRO is ungoverned.

Secondly, consider the example (13):

(13)   I know [$_{\bar{S}}$ what$_i$[$_S$ NP$_j$ saw t$_i$]]

By binding theory, the variable t_i bound by *what* must be A-free; hence $i \neq j$. Thus there is no possibility that *what* governs NPj in such a case.

Thirdly, the examples discussed in this chapter so far are restricted to traces as variables, but as we have seen in earlier discussion, ECP is independently motivated in the case of NP-trace. Cf. 4.1.(5). In short, ECP is not restricted to variables and is independently motivated quite apart from RES(NIC), which it properly subsumes. Our earlier discussion of the characteristics of trace and PRO (cf. §2.4) now falls into place under the theory of government, including ECP and the theory of binding, with its derivative principles concerning PRO. Other recent work (specifically, Kayne (1980b) and other papers, some of them briefly discussed in chapter 5), indicates that the scope of ECP is in fact still broader than the considerations of this chapter indicate. There is, then, good reason to believe that some version of ECP is a central principle of the theory of government.

Finally, consider again verbs of the *want*-type taking *for*-complements. In §2.4.2 (cf. 2.4.2.(18)–(19)), we concluded that verbs of this category do not permit S̄-deletion with infinitival complements; rather, the complementizer *for* may delete (with dialectal variation) in immediate post-verbal position in the PF-component. Consider again the examples (14):

(14)   (i) Bill was believed to have seen Tom
        (ii) *Bill was preferred (for) to have seen Tom
        (iii) *Bill was wanted to have seen Tom

The corresponding forms at the level of S-structure are (15):

(15)   (i) Bill was believed [$_S$ t to have seen Tom]
        (ii) *Bill was preferred [$_{\bar{S}}$ for [$_S$ t to have seen Tom]]
        (iii) *Bill was wanted [$_{\bar{S}}$ for [$_S$ t to have seen Tom]]

Example (i) is unproblematic. The embedded subject trace is properly governed by *believed* and is not assigned Case. The sentence satisfies the binding theory and ECP. Examples (ii) and (iii), however, raise interesting questions for the theory we have been developing here. In these examples, the trace is governed and, presumably, assigned Case by the governor *for*, as we see from such examples as (16):

(16)   (i) they'd prefer [$_{\bar{S}}$ for [$_S$ Bill to leave]]
        (ii) they want very much [$_{\bar{S}}$ for [$_S$ Bill to leave]]
        (iii) [$_{\bar{S}}$ for [$_S$ Bill to leave]] would be a mistake

Why exactly are these examples ungrammatical?

There are several possible ways to approach this problem.[25] What it seems to me we should say is that examples (15ii,iii) are comparable to 4.1.(5), that is, ruled out by ECP. We can maintain this conclusion if we exclude *for* from the class of proper governors though it evidently is a governor. The simplest way to achieve this result is to exclude prepositions entirely from the category of proper governors, thus restricting proper governors to lexical categories in the sense of §2.3, i.e., to categories with the features [+N] or [+V]. This proposal has far-reaching effects. Thus, if we were to regard AGR as not "lexical" in the appropriate sense, it would eliminate the possibility of having AGR serve as a proper governor, thus undermining our approach to the pro-drop parameter; I will suggest in the next section that this conclusion is correct, for other reasons. Another consequence of this proposal is to rule out preposition stranding, since the trace left behind will not be properly governed. Preposition stranding will only be possible, then, if some marked process applies. I will return to this topic in § 5.2, basically adopting this idea, and considering further problems that arise in connection with verbs that take *for*-complementizers.

4.5. The pro-drop parameter (2)

Let us now return to the major empirical problem raised earlier. According to Kayne's theory, which we have adopted in essence, ECP is a principle of the LF-component, applying to variables formed in the LF-component as well as to the trace of *wh*-movement and trace more generally, thus subsuming the superiority condition and the examples discussed in § 4.2. One case of ECP – namely, the case of *that*-trace and long-movement phenomena – is inapplicable in the case of the pro-drop languages, because the subject is properly governed by AGR so that it is immaterial whether a proper governor appears in COMP. We therefore predict that variables with wide scope should also appear in subject position in the pro-drop languages, contrasting with the situation in French and English. But this is false, as we have seen. The facts are as illustrated in (1) (= 4.2.(17)):

(1) (i) non voglio che tu parli con nessuno
     (ii) *non voglio che nessuno venga (where *nessuno* is interpreted with wide scope)
     (iii) voglio che nessuno venga

We therefore face an internal contradiction in the theory so far outlined.

A solution to this problem is suggested by Rizzi (1979a), who points out that in Italian and Spanish, there is a fourth option in the set (1), namely, (2):

(2) non voglio che venga nessuno
     ("for no *x*, I want that *x* come")

Thus while (1ii) is barred, its sense can be expressed by (2), in which the subject follows the verb. Example (2), of course, does not violate the ECP any more than (1i) does. As we have seen, one element of the cluster of properties connected with the pro-drop parameter is the fact that the pro-drop languages permit inversion quite freely (cf. 4.3.(1ii)). As Rizzi observes, these facts suggest that we rethink the structure of the cluster of properties (3) (= 4.3.(1)) that are characteristic of the pro-drop languages:

(3) (i) missing subject
     (ii) free inversion in simple sentences

(iii) "long *wh*-movement" of subject
(iv) empty resumptive pronouns in embedded clause
(v) apparent violations of the *[*that-t*] filter

Perhaps only properties (i) and (ii) properly belong to this cluster, and the pro-drop languages actually observe the constraint that blocks long *wh*-movement of subject, empty resumptive pronouns, and violations of the *[*that-t*] filter, exactly as the non-pro-drop languages do. If so, the apparent examples to the contrary illustrated in 4.3.(2iii–v) are spurious; what in fact is happening is that movement in these cases is not from the subject position but from the post-verbal position in which subjects may appear by virtue of (3ii); it is now natural to assimilate the case of resumptive pronouns to case (3i). Specifically, *wh*-movement of the subject in pro-drop languages, which appears to violate the *[*that-t*] filter, is actually from the post-verbal rather than the subject position, and, contrary to appearances, *wh*-movement does observe the *[*that-t*] filter in pro-drop languages. The underlying structure for (4), then, is (5) rather than (6):

(4)   chi pensi che verrà
       ("who do you think (that) will come")
(5)   pensi [₅ che [ₛα verrà chi]]
(6)   pensi [₅ che [ₛ chi verrà]]

Thus, *wh*-movement does not violate the *[*that-t*] filter. Assuming, then, that we somehow select α in (5) so that there is no violation of the filter in the "inversion" cases,[26] we may assume that the *[*that-t*] filter brooks no exceptions, that long *wh*-movement from subject position is always impossible, and that empty resumptive pronouns are now simply a special case of empty subjects, without exception. Crucially, it now follows that there is no contradiction between the apparent violations of the *[*that-t*] filter in the pro-drop languages and the assumption that ECP (from which the filter derives) holds of variables quite generally, as a property of LF-representation. Thus the major empirical problem that we faced is overcome. It remains to study the "inverted structures" more carefully, and to revise the pro-drop parameter in accordance with the analysis just outlined.

Rizzi's argument significantly modifies earlier assumptions concerning the pro-drop parameter. In Chomsky and Lasnik (1977), it was assumed that the rule of pro-drop eliminates the subject trace, thus voiding the effects of the *[*that-t*] filter and, incidentally, permitting free inversion (though the latter structures were not discussed there). Similarly, in the version of the ECP just outlined,[27] it is assumed that the pro-drop languages permit proper government of the subject position by AGR, thus permitting free inversion and voiding the effects of the *[*that-t*] filter. Rizzi argues, in contrast, that the fundamental property of the pro-drop languages is that they permit free inversion, leading to apparent (though not real) violations of the *$[that-t]$ filter (as well as apparent but not real long *wh*-movement from subject based on the inverted configurations).

Rizzi presents further evidence that *wh*-movement of subjects in Italian is from post-verbal position, arguing on the basis of possibilities of *ne*-cliticization from the *wh*-moved subject, a matter that goes beyond the scope of these remarks, though I will return to the phenomenon. What is important for us here is that his argument overcomes a contradiction concerning RES(NIC), hence ECP, in the case of the pro-drop languages.[28]

Before turning to the analysis of inversion and the status of α in (5), let us consider some independent evidence noted by Jaeggli (1980b) in support of · Rizzi's basic conclusion. Recall that among the instances of RES(NIC) (hence ECP) discussed earlier are those that fall under the superiority condition, for example, (7) (= 4.1.(2iv)) as contrasted with (8)(= 4.1.(4)):

(7)   *it is unclear $[_\bar{s}$ what$_j[_s$ who said t$_j]]$
(8)   it is unclear $[_\bar{s}$ who$_i[_s$ t$_i$ said what$]]$

The rule of the LF-component raising the embedded *wh*-phrase produces a violation of ECP in the case of (7) but not in the case of (8). Jaeggli observes that the analogue of (7) should not be ungrammatical in a pro-drop language if we accept Rizzi's analysis, which assumes that the subject is extracted from the post-verbal position; thus the effects of the superiority condition should be voided in these languages. One cannot check the prediction directly in Italian, because, for some reason, multiple *wh*-constructions seem in general to be unacceptable (cf. Rizzi (1978b)). But, Jaeggli points out, the prediction is verified in Spanish, where we have such examples as (9):[29]

(9)   (i) quién compro qué
            ("who bought what")
         (ii) qué compro quién
            ("what did who buy")
        (iii) Juan sabe qué dijo quién
            ("Juan knows what who said")
         (iv) Juan sabe quién dijo qué
            ("Juan knows who said what")

Thus we have confirming evidence that the essential properties of the pro-drop languages are (3i,ii): the possibility of dropping the subject and of free inversion. Apart from these, ECP applies in these languages as it does in the non-pro-drop languages. The examples (9), incidentally, indicate that it was correct to assimilate the superiority condition to the complex of properties associated with the pro-drop parameter. It follows that RES(NIC) (hence ECP) is a principle of the LF-component, thus offering independent confirmation for Kayne's theory discussed in § 4.2.

We must now revise ECP and the pro-drop parameter to accord with Rizzi's analysis. The basic problem is to determine the nature of α in the structures of (10), where α is missing in surface structure:

(10)   (i) α VP   (*mangia,* "he is eating")
        (ii) α V NP   (*arriva Giovanni,* "Giovanni is coming"; *ha mangiato Giovanni,* "Giovanni ate")

In our first attempt to formulate the ECP and the pro-drop parameter in the preceding section, we took α to be $[_{NP} \, e]$. But that will not do, since this assumption does not distinguish cases (i) and (ii) of (10)(which are examples of cases (i) and (ii), respectively, of the cluster of properties (3)) from the case of *wh*-movement, and in general, the other properties of the cluster (3). But this distinction is what we now have to establish.

The obvious suggestion is that α is PRO, the second of our empty categories.[30] The pro-drop languages will differ from the non-pro-drop languages in that PRO may appear instead of a pronoun in subject position. We might say, in accordance with the Avoid Pronoun Principle (cf. 2.4.2.(5)) that every language tries to use PRO instead of a full pronoun in this position (in fact, in every position), but the pro-drop languages have some property that makes this possible while other languages do not. What is this property? More generally, what is the property that prevents recourse to the Avoid Pronoun principle to drop a pronoun, say, in object position in English? We have assumed that the property is that PRO must be ungoverned, a conclusion that follows in a principled way from the binding theory and is supported by substantial empirical evidence. Extending the principle to the present case, we are naturally led to the conclusion that in the pro-drop languages the subject position may be ungoverned, thus accepting PRO, while in the non-pro-drop languages, this position is invariably governed. Our assumption until now has been that the subject position is governed by the AGR element in INFL. Assuming so, it follows that in the pro-drop languages the subject may fail to be governed by AGR. We still follow Taraldsen's basic intuition that a property of AGR determines the pro-drop parameter, but now inverting the logic, so that AGR in the pro-drop languages is a "weaker" rather than a "stronger" governor for the subject position. Pursuing the intuition that the pro-drop parameter is related to overt inflection, we might say that in the pro-drop languages the element AGR is more closely connected with the verbal element with which it is morphologically manifested, and thus need not govern the subject position.

There are various ways to execute this idea. To select one, let's focus on the fact that while INFL is a constituent of S outside of VP at S-structure, its elements – specifically, AGR – appear within VP in verbal morphology in surface structure. Therefore there is a rule – call it R – which assigns the elements of INFL to the initial verbal element of VP. Assume R to be, in effect, a rule of Affix-movement. If R applies in the PF-component, then

AGR governs the subject position at S-structure and at LF. If R applies in the syntax, then the resulting S-structure is (11):

(11)   NP $[_{VP}$ V-INFL ...$]$

In (11), AGR (in INFL) does not govern the subject position at S-structure or LF. Therefore PRO may appear in this position.

Suppose that we now take the pro-drop parameter to be (12):

(12) R may apply in the syntax

The pro-drop languages accept this option; R applies either in the syntax, yielding (11), or in the PF-component, as in the non-pro-drop languages. The non-pro-drop languages reject the option (12), so that R applies only in the PF-component and the subject is always governed by AGR at S-structure and at LF.

Before proceeding, let us settle a minor technical issue. The rule R is a local rule in the sense of Emonds (1976). It does not share the basic properties of the general transformational rule Move-α, but is more similar to morphological rules; in fact, in the non-pro-drop languages, or whenever R applies in the PF-component, then R is a rule of the morphology. As noted earlier, there is no reason to believe that rules of the PF-component leave trace, and we might assume that even when the rule R applies in the syntactic component, it does not leave trace; then the S-structure will indeed be (11), rather than an analogous structure containing $[_{INFL} e]$, the trace left by application of the rule R. We might say that in general, only rules moving some major category – e.g., NP or $\bar{S}$ – leave trace, or we might restrict trace in some other way to rules that are not simply local rules with a morphological character. Suppose, in contrast, that we permit R to leave trace when it applies in the syntactic component. Then this trace is technically a governor as we have defined this notion, establishing a governing category for the subject NP of (11) and excluding PRO, contrary to what we intend. We might avoid this consequence by an appeal to the reasoning of § 3.2.2. There, we developed a version of Aoun's proposal that to be "visible" in the interpretive components an element must have appropriate features: the features of a lexical item or of PRO (in the LF-component), or Case (in either the PF- or LF-components). Suppose that we now extend this notion to government; specifically, to qualify as a governor, an element must have such features. Then even if R leaves a trace it will not be a governor.

We therefore adopt one of the following conventions:

(13)   (i) Local rules such as R do not leave trace
        (ii) If $[_{\beta} \alpha]$ is a governor, then α has appropriate features

We will see in chapter 6 that (i) is the better of the two alternatives. It is also simpler and, I think, more natural. Let us therefore continue to adopt it here. Thus application of rule R yields (11), whether R applies in the syntactic component or in the PF-component.

For expository purposes, I will henceforth omit reference to features of INFL apart from AGR. I will also assume that after adjunction of INFL to V by R, both V and AGR govern whatever was governed by V prior to application of R, omitting technical details.

Returning to the main theme, the idea that we are now trying to establish is expressed in (14):

(14)   The subject of a finite clause is PRO if and only if R has applied in the syntax

Suppose that the subject of a finite clause is PRO. Then the binding theory requires that the NP subject PRO lacks a governing category; specifically, it is not governed by AGR. Therefore, R must have applied prior to the application of the binding theory; hence in the syntax, on the assumptions of chapter 3, where we concluded that the binding theory applies at S-structure. Therefore, (14) holds from left to right.

Let us now consider (14) from right to left. Suppose that R has applied in the syntax. The NP subject of (11) now *may* be PRO, but we must ensure that it *must* be PRO. We do not, for example, want to permit nonpronominal anaphors in this position. See the discussion of (38), below. We need not be concerned with NP-trace; this cannot appear in the subject position, by ECP, since the position is ungoverned at LF by virtue of (13). It suffices, then, to ensure that Case is not assigned to the subject in (11). This will exclude overt elements by the Case Filter, and will exclude variables by the requirement that variables must have Case (cf. § 3.2.2).

The only Case that can be assigned in the subject position is nominative Case, which is assigned under government by AGR, the mechanism being that of 3.2.3.(70I). AGR is coindexed with the NP that it governs (namely, the subject), assigning it nominative Case and sharing its grammatical features. But Case is assigned (or checked) at S-structure. Suppose, then, that R has applied in the syntax. Then the subject in (11) cannot receive nominative Case since it is no longer governed by AGR. Therefore, the subject in (11) cannot be an element that requires Case: a phonetically-realized NP or a variable. Since NP-trace is excluded from this position by ECP, it follows that only PRO may appear as the subject in (11). Therefore, (14) holds in both directions.

There is a gap in the argument showing that (14) holds from right to left. The argument shows that Case cannot be assigned *directly* by AGR to the subject of a finite clause after R has applied, but, as we have seen, the NP subject might still "inherit" Case from a coindexed NP with Case. The only circumstance under which this is possible is after inversion. Suppose, then, that R has applied in the syntax in a finite clause and the NP subject is inverted to the post-verbal position, leaving a coindexed trace t. But ECP is now violated by t unless t moves to COMP leaving a variable governed by the operator t in COMP. The latter configuration is impossible, however, for several independent reasons. The θ-criterion is violated, since the post-verbal subject and the variable have the same θ-role; the structure has no interpretation given that the clause is tensed; principle (C) of the binding theory is violated since the post-verbal NP is A-bound by the variable, which cannot serve as an impersonal element co-superscripted with it. Hence (14) does hold from right to left. Furthermore, we see that *wh*-movement is impossible from the vacated position after NP-inversion. Note that we have not excluded the possibility that PRO may appear in the subject position of a finite clause to which R has applied, inheriting Case from some coindexed NP. In fact, this situation arises, as we shall see.

Note that not only NP-trace, but any trace is excluded from the subject position in (11). This means, in effect, that the *that*-trace phenomena and related matters are independent of whether the language is or is not a pro-drop language.

The option (12) requires that we be a bit more precise about the mechanism for assigning nominative Case under agreement. This mechanism actually has two components:

(15)   (i) AGR is coindexed with the NP it governs   ($= 3.2.3.(70I)$)
        (ii) nominative Case is assigned to (or checked for) the NP governed by AGR

Condition (15i) expresses the phenomenon of agreement. We have assumed the coindexing in question to be co-superscripting; see the discussion of 3.2.3.(94). As for (15ii), it expresses the assumption that nominative Case-assignment (or checking) falls together with other major types of Case-determination in that it requires government; see the discussion of 3.2.2.(1i), below 3.2.2.(7), and note 41 of chapter 3. Clearly, (15ii) holds at S-structure. Prior to consideration of (12), there was no need to distinguish the two components of (15). Now, however, we must determine where (15i) applies. In fact, it must apply at D-structure, prior to the rule that forms (11). Let us therefore stipulate that this is the case:

(16)   Principle (15i) applies at D-structure

To see why this condition is required, consider the S-structure (17):

(17)   *NP sembra $[_S$ Giovanni leggere i libri$]$
        ("NP seems $[$Giovanni to read the books$]$")

The structure (17) is ungrammatical. But if R applies in the syntax, then *sembra* contains AGR at S-structure so that AGR will govern *Giovanni* in (17). If AGR could be coindexed with *Giovanni* by (15i), then both conditions for nominative Case assignment would be fulfilled: *Giovanni* would receive nominative Case in (17) and raising of the embedded subject would not be obligatory. But if the agreement phenomenon is determined at D-structure, then the structure (17) is barred as required.[31] Rather, AGR is coindexed at D-structure with the empty NP matrix subject, and it governs *Giovanni* after raising assigning it nominative Case, if R does not apply; we return to the question of what happens if R does apply, triggering inversion after raising.

The conclusion that (15i) applies at D-structure is also required, on our assumptions, to account for cases in which proximate PRO is the subject of a tensed embedded clause, as Howard Lasnik points out. In such a case PRO will share all features with its antecedent. But it will also have to agree with AGR in its clause (i.e., to agree with its verb), guaranteeing agreement between its antecedent and the verb of which it is subject, though at S-structure AGR no longer governs it, rule R having applied in the syntax to permit PRO subject.

Let us turn now to the assignment of θ-role and Case when the subject is post-verbal and the element α in the subject position of (10ii) is PRO. For convenience of exposition, I will henceforth refer to an NP drawn from the lexicon as "lexical" if it is not PRO, noting that this is a bit misleading in that PRO too is drawn from the lexicon.

In case (i) of (10) – the case of simple missing subject – we assume that PRO is base-generated in subject position just as a lexical pronoun would be generated in this position in a non-pro-drop language.[32] Then R must apply in the syntax, for if R were to apply in the PF-component, PRO would be excluded by the binding theory, being governed. In contrast, if R does not apply in the syntax, then a lexical NP must appear, by (14). With regard to *wh*-movement, or quantifier movement in the LF-component, such a lexical subject behaves exactly as in the non-pro-drop languages.[33]

Turning to case (ii) of (10), we have such examples as (18):

(18)   (i) telefonano molti studenti
         ("many students telephone")
        (ii) arrivano molti studenti
         ("many students arrive")

There is strong evidence that the structures differ in the two cases. In case (i), we have the adjoined structure (19i); in case (ii), the VP-internal structure (19ii):

(19)   (i) $[_{VP}[_{VP}$ telefonano$]$ $[_{NP}$ molti studenti$]]$
        (ii) $[_{VP}$ arrivano $[_{NP}$ molti studenti$]]$

One type of evidence supporting this conclusion is the fact that *ne*-cliticization is possible in (ii) but not (i), giving (20):

(20)   (i) *ne telefonano molti
         ("of-them many telephone")

    (ii) ne arrivano molti
       ("of-them many arrive")

Assuming that the relation between *ne* and its trace requires c-command,[34] the facts are explained by assuming the structures (19). Burzio (1981) presents substantial evidence supporting the analysis (19), specifically, the conclusion that in case (i) a rule of inversion from subject position has applied – an adjunction rule, adjoining the subject *molti studenti* (or *molti ne*) to the VP – whereas in case (ii) the subject *molti studenti* (or *molti ne*) is base-generated in the object position of the VP – his "ergative verbs."[35] Let us assume that his conclusions are correct. Then in case (i), the PRO that we assume to appear in subject position in the full structure (21) is inserted after the application of Move-α adjoining the subject to the VP:

(21) $[_S PRO [_{VP}[_{VP}$ telefon-AGR $][_{NP}$ molti studenti $]]]$

It is reasonable to adopt the same conclusion in the case of the base-generated form (19ii) in the light of the θ-criterion, which stipulates that D-structure is a representation of GF-θ –thematically relevant grammatical functions. It is the overt argument *molti studenti* in the full structure (22) that has the θ-role assigned to the subject, not the inserted element PRO:

(22) $[_S PRO[_{VP}$ arriv-AGR $[_{NP}$ molti studenti $]]]$

If so, then PRO must be inserted in this case as well in the course of the syntactic derivation. The question is delicate, however, given the conclusion in chapter 3 that θ-role assignment is to A-function chains, thus in effect to indices. We return to this topic. However the question is resolved, I will assume that a rule of PRO-insertion inserts PRO in (22), as must be the case in (21) on the assumption that an inversion rule has applied in the latter case.[36]

One fundamental property of ergative verbs in Burzio's sense is that they do not assign (or participate in assigning) a θ-role to subject position, but only to object position (cf. note 35). The rule of PRO-insertion for pro-drop languages is analogous to the rule of *there*-insertion in English or *il*-insertion in French, as in (23):[37]

(23)   (i) there arrived three men
        (ii) il est arrivé trois hommes   (= (i))

Again, pro-drop languages, by virtue of the parameter (12), adopt the Avoid Pronoun strategy in these cases.

Note that PRO cannot be inserted in place of the trace left by movement from any governed position or the binding theory will be violated. In this connection, consider again the pair of examples (24) (= 4.2.(3)):

(24)   (i) *NP sembra [che Tense VP]
        (ii) NP crede [che pronominal Tense VP]

Examples are (25i,ii):

(25)   (i) *gli amici sembrano [che partiranno]
           ("the friends seem that they will leave")
        (ii) gli amici credono [che partiranno]
           ("the friends believe that they will leave")

We are now assuming that in case (ii), the embedded subject is PRO. Notice, however, that (ii) is not a control structure. The PRO here is simply a base-generated uncontrolled pronominal which can be PRO rather than lexical in Italian because the pro-drop parameter permits the subject position to be ungoverned. Thus, PRO in (ii) may refer to the friends or to someone else, as in the case of a lexical pronoun in English or French. Note that when PRO in (ii) refers to someone other than the friends, it is not arbitrary in reference, as PRO is in a structure such as "it is unclear [what [PRO to do]]" or "John doesn't know [how [PRO to behave oneself in public]]" or their Italian equivalents. Rather, PRO in (ii) or in (10i), etc., refers to some specific persons like its overt pronoun analogue in a non-pro-drop language (cf. note 32). In general, PRO coindexed with AGR is not subject to control, hence cannot be arbitrary in reference. Similarly, PRO inserted by the PRO-insertion rule, which is coindexed with the post-verbal NP, is not subject to control. In general, then, PRO bearing a superscript is not subject to control. PRO may therefore be arbitrary in reference only in the position of subject of an infinitive or gerund, i.e., in a position that is assigned neither agreement with AGR or Case (assuming the analysis of Case-assignment to which we turn directly). See note 115 of chapter 2. On the status of Case on controlled PRO in Russian, see Schein (1980).

Consider now case (i) of (25). By the θ-criterion, the subject of the embedded clause must be trace; otherwise the matrix subject lacks a θ-role. But trace is impossible in this position. If the rule R has applied in the syntax in the embedded clause, the position is ungoverned and ECP is violated if trace appears in it. If the rule R applies in the PF-component in the embedded clause, then the binding theory is violated since the trace is governed but is an anaphor free in its governing category; redundantly, ECP is violated since the trace is not properly governed (see below). Therefore, (i) is ungrammatical.

Once again, we have a direct contrast between trace and PRO. Note that PRO in the embedded subject position of (25i) is not inconsistent with the binding theory, since this position may be ungoverned because of the pro-drop parameter. But the θ-criterion excludes this possibility.

In our earlier discussion of *there*-insertion, we assumed that *there* is coindexed with the post-verbal NP and shares features with it, specifically, number. Note that number-sharing is not true for French (cf. (23ii)), and thus represents parametric variation. Applying the same assumptions to post-verbal subjects in pro-drop languages, we assume that the inserted PRO is coindexed with *molti studenti* in (21), (22) and shares all of its features with the post-verbal NP. But recall that the coindexing of *there* or *il* with the post-verbal NP is distinct from the indexing relevant to the binding theory. Therefore, a different style of indexing is required in this case, reflecting a different kind of association, distinct from binding; we assumed it to be co-superscripting, as in (15i). The same must be true for the inserted PRO, which, like impersonal *it* or impersonal *il*, is a non-argument lacking an independent θ-role.

We now have to settle the question of assignment of nominative Case to the post-verbal NP and its agreement with the verb. There are two possibilities:

(26)   (i) Case-assignment is to the post-verbal NP
        (ii) Case-assignment is to the pre-verbal NP subject and is then "inherited" by the post-verbal NP from the co-superscripted PRO in the pre-verbal subject position

The S-structures relevant to this discussion are those of (27):

(27)   (i) $PRO^i [_{VP}[_{VP} V\text{-}AGR^i] NP^i]$ (= (19i))
        (ii) $PRO^i [_{VP} V\text{-}AGR^i NP^i]$ (= (19ii))

The co-superscripting of PRO and the post-verbal NP expresses the relation of the impersonal pronoun to the associated NP, as just discussed. Recall also that PRO is co-superscripted with AGR by the agreement rule (15i), since PRO is inserted into the position governed by AGR at D-structure. Therefore PRO, AGR and the post-verbal NP are co-superscripted. In (27i), PRO and the post-verbal NP are furthermore co-subscripted by the movement rule; we might assume conventions to ensure that these modes of association are correlated, a straightforward matter that I will ignore.

Suppose now that we adopt (26i). In each of the S-structures of (27), AGR governs the post-verbal NP and is coindexed with it. Therefore nominative Case is assigned to this NP.

Suppose we adopt (26ii), thus dropping the government requirement for nominative Case-assignment.[38] This approach too is tenable, if we now rely on the idea that Case is assigned to an index and then realized optionally on an NP with this index, with qualifications to which we return, this being a way to realize the informal notion "inheritance," cf. § 3.2.2. Principle (26ii) does raise a problem, however, in that we have been led to assume that Case cannot be assigned directly to the subject position in (27), a crucial step in establishing (14). To maintain (26ii), then, we would have to modify our framework somehow so as to permit Case-assignment directly to the PRO subject but not to other subjects in a structure to which the rule R of (12) has applied. But this in effect undermines the proposal.

The two options of (26) reflect the two possibilities for nominative Case-assignment that we have been considering all along. Option (i) expresses the idea that government is a crucial factor in determining nominative Case-assignment (alongside of agreement) as in other major instances of Case-assignment. Option (ii) expresses the idea that agreement alone suffices. Option (i) is preferable if it is sustainable in that it avoids the problem noted in the preceding paragraph and in that it unifies nominative Case-assignment with other instances under the theory of government. It also leads to a more natural concept of "governing category," along the lines discussed in the preceding chapter; cf. chapter 3, note 41; and chapter 5, note 23. Let us tentatively assume, then, that option (i) is correct and explore its consequences.

We now understand the Case-marking rules for nominative Case-assignment under agreement as (28):

(28)   At S-structure, assign nominative Case to NP co-superscripted with and governed by AGR

Recall that the co-superscripting of AGR and the NP it governs is determined at D-structure. The formulation (28) leaves open the possibility that nominative Case may appear in other constructions. It can easily be reformulated if Case-marking is to be interpreted as Case-checking rather than Case-assignment, as we will in fact assume below.

We are now concerned with derivations in which the rule R has applied, moving INFL into the VP, converting the D-structure (29) to the S-structure (30i) or (30ii):

(29) $\alpha [_{INFL} AGR] [_{VP} V \ldots]$

(30)   (i) $\beta [_{VP} V\text{-}AGR \ldots]$
          (ii) $\beta [_{VP} [_{VP} V\text{-}AGR \ldots] NP]$

We derive (30ii) when not only R but also NP-inversion has applied.

Suppose first that (29) is an ergative construction in Burzio's sense. Then $\alpha = [_{NP} e]$ and is co-superscripted with AGR at D-structure. We derive (30i) by application of R and the rule of PRO-insertion that co-superscripts the inserted PRO with the post-verbal NP in ... of (29), (30i). In the S-structure (30i), then, $\beta =$ PRO co-superscripted with AGR and with the post-verbal NP. Since the latter two are co-superscripted and AGR governs the post-verbal NP, nominative Case is assigned to this NP under (28)—or, we might assume, assigned to its index, so that β also bears nominative Case, by "inheritance."

Suppose now that (29) is not an ergative construction. Then α of (29) is drawn from the lexicon. Suppose that α is a lexical NP. Then α is co-superscripted with AGR at D-structure and the rule R applies, yielding one of the two forms of (30). It is in fact necessary for NP-inversion to apply, yielding (30ii) rather than (30i); for if it does not, then Case will not be assigned to $\beta = \alpha$ and the Case Filter will be violated. After NP-inversion and PRO-insertion we have (30ii), with $\beta =$ PRO co-superscripted with post-verbal NP to which nominative Case is assigned by (28).

Suppose that in (29) $\alpha =$ PRO, inserted from the lexicon in D-structure as the subject pronominal, as in (10i), the case of simple missing subject. Again, α is co-superscripted with AGR, and R applies yielding one of the two forms of (30), either (31) of the form (30i) or (32) of the form (30ii):

(31)   PRO $[_{VP}$ mangi-AGR$]$ $(= (10i), \ mangia)$

(32)   PRO $[_{VP}[_{VP}$ mangi-AGR$]]$ PRO

Either (31) or (32) is derived from the D-structure (33) by application of the rule R:

(33) $\alpha [_{INFL}$ AGR$]$ mangi- $(= (29))$

In (31), PRO $(= \alpha)$ is the subject pronominal inserted from the lexicon. As distinct from the case in which α of (29) is lexical, NP-inversion is not required here since PRO is not subject to the Case Filter. In (31) PRO is ungoverned, and the structure is grammatical. In (32), the PRO in the post-verbal position is α of (33), and the PRO in subject position is the inserted impersonal PRO co-superscripted with it and with AGR. By (28), nominative Case is assigned to the post-verbal NP (or its index), as before. However, as matters now stand (32) is barred by the fact that PRO in post-verbal position is governed by AGR. Therefore, when $\alpha =$ PRO in the D-structure (33), NP-inversion is not possible. If the rule R applies to the D-structure (33), then NP-inversion applies if and only if α is lexical.

I will assume in subsequent discussion that the foregoing analysis is correct, but before proceeding let us consider the possibility that NP-inversion is possible in case $\alpha =$ PRO in (33). This would require that the inverted PRO in (32) be regarded as a non-anaphor, so that it may have a governing category in which it is free, as is any pronominal. Assuming some such modification of the binding theory, NP-inversion may optionally apply to (33) yielding (32). A possible argument in favor of this approach would be that it allows us to take (28) to be an obligatory rule, as Case-marking rules are in general.[39] In contrast, if we proceed with the earlier analysis, then (28) must be regarded as an optional rule, so as to admit the S-structure (31). If, in fact, we were to take (28) to be obligatory, then NP-inversion would not only be permissible with the D-structure (33), but would be obligatory even with $\alpha =$ PRO in (33), as it is obligatory when α is lexical.

The interpretation of (28) as obligatory receives a rather natural formulation if we reconstruct the process of Case-assignment in terms of Case-checking. Suppose we assume that each noun drawn from the lexicon, whether a lexical noun or PRO, may have one or another Case, and that by convention an NP receives the Case of its head noun. We now restate (28) as (34):

(34)   In S containing AGR, there is a nominative NP co-superscripted with and governed by AGR

Principle (34), like (28), applies at S-structure. The requirement that (34) holds at S-structure is equivalent to principle (28), now interpreted as an obligatory rule. Some elaboration is necessary to deal with variables and NP without an N head, e.g., gerunds; a version of this idea will be developed in chapter 6, in a different context.

If we were to adopt (34) (or equivalently, obligatoriness of (28)), then we would derive two conclusions. First, if the rule R applies in the syntax, then the S-structure must have a post-verbal subject: either it is an ergative construction, or NP-inversion must have applied whatever the choice of α of (33) in a non-ergative construction. Second, case (10i) (namely, simple "missing subject") reduces in effect to case (10ii) (namely, free inversion). This line of argument extends Rizzi's proposal that free inversion is the basic property of the pro-drop languages. Following Rizzi, we have argued that in the cluster of properties (3) characteristic of pro-drop languages, all elements apart from (i) and (ii) (namely, (10i) and (10ii)) reduce to free inversion, which would now remain as the sole independent element of the cluster of properties (3).

I will not, however, pursue these possibilities or the modifications of GB-theory that they would entail.

Let us now return to the assumption that the rule (28) of nominative Case assignment is optional, so that only (31), not (32), is derivable from (33) where α = PRO. Consider now the class of examples illustrated in (35):[40]

(35)   (i) sembrano intervenirne molti
        (ii) PRO_i sembrano $[_S t_i[_{VP}$ intervenir-ne$_j[_{NP}$ molti t$_j]]]$
             ("seem (plural) to intervene of-them many"; "many of them seem to intervene")

Cliticization of *ne* shows that we have a structure of the form (27ii), with an embedded ergative clause, so that the S-structure is (35ii). Here, PRO_i has been raised from the position of t_i. The matrix verb *sembrano* agrees with PRO_i, which in turn agrees with the post-verbal NP *molti* of the embedded clause. Thus we have the curious phenomenon that the matrix verb agrees with the embedded post-verbal NP.

Note that we find essentially the same phenomenon in the English counterpart (36):

(36)   there seem $[_S$ t to be several options$]$

Here the matrix verb also agrees with the embedded post-verbal NP *several options*. The reason is that *there* (which is co-superscripted with *several options* in the embedded clause) matches *several options* in number, and retains this property under raising, requiring that the matrix verb be plural. The analysis should be similar in the corresponding Italian case, where we have PRO instead of *there*.

How, then, is Case assigned to the post-verbal NP in (35), so as to satisfy the Case Filter? It cannot receive Case within the embedded clause, since there is no AGR element in this infinitival construction. Nor can it receive Case from the matrix AGR, since the latter does not govern it. Therefore, it must "inherit" Case from some element that is Case-marked by (28). Which element? The element assigned Case by AGR must be co-superscripted with and governed by AGR. The only element with this dual property is t_i. Since AGR is associated with *sembrano* by application of rule R, it does govern t_i. Furthermore, it is co-superscripted with t_i, assuming the natural convention that superscripts, like subscripts, are retained under movement (i.e., the rule Move-α maintains coindexing for all indices) and that there can be no superscript conflict. PRO_i is co-superscripted with AGR by virtue of the fact that it occupies the position governed by AGR at D-structure. Furthermore, PRO_i is co-superscripted with the post-verbal NP *molti* as a result of the PRO-insertion rule for ergatives applying prior to raising of PRO_i. It follows that PRO_i, t_i, $[_{NP} molti \, t_j]$, and AGR of the matrix clause are all co-superscripted. In particular, t_i is co-superscripted with the matrix AGR that governs it, so that nominative Case is assigned to the index of t_i and "inherited" by the post-verbal co-superscripted lexical NP, which is therefore nominative and passes the Case Filter.

Example (36) is basically similar, except that in this case rule R has not applied in the syntax, so that the post-verbal NP inherits its Case from the matrix subject, which is governed by and co-superscripted with AGR at S-structure.

Note that in both the Italian and English case, we must assume that the post-verbal NP cannot be moved to the position of the embedded trace after raising, a possibility not ruled out now by the Case Filter. We might appeal here to the principle of the strict cycle, or to deeper assumptions from which it may follow (cf. Freidin, 1978).

Essentially the same analysis would hold under the rejected option that (28) is obligatory (equivalently, (34)), so that PRO-inversion in the matrix clause is also obligatory.

The analysis of (35ii) has some unusual properties that are worth noting. One is that nominative Case is assigned to t_i, which is the trace of NP-movement, hence an anaphor rather than a variable. This result is inconsistent with a narrow interpretation of principle 3.2.2.(16), which identifies variables and Case-marked traces, though it is not inconsistent with this principle if we assume, as in § 3.2.2 and since, that Case is assigned to an index and then optionally assumed by an element of the function chain with this index. Recall, however, that we have made no use of the subpart of 3.2.2.(16) to which this question is relevant, namely, the subpart which states that a Case-marked trace is a variable. Therefore, it is not clear whether this question is of any real significance. A further property of (35ii) is that the trace t_i with nominative Case is an anaphor that is not bound in the minimal S that contains it, a situation that arises with objective Case under Exceptional Case-marking but that does not arise elsewhere with nominative Case in the range of material we have discussed. The trace is, however, bound in its governing category – the matrix clause in (35ii) – as required by the binding theory.

We see, then, that the assumptions we are now considering lead to the Case-assignment principle (37) or a Case-checking variant of it:

(37)   Case is assigned to an index and inherited by lexical NP with this
          index

In § 3.2.2 we saw that inheritance could be upward to a c-commanding element in the case of *wh*-movement. Here, we have seen that it can be downward to a c-commanded element. We return in chapter 6 to a more careful formulation of the principle (37), introducing the required quali-fications that have so far been tacitly assumed.

Assuming, then, that the problems of Case-assignment in structures with post-verbal NP in (27) can be handled in this way, we must next con-sider the problem of θ-role assignment in these structures. The general line of argument in § 3.2.2 can be adopted in the inversion cases, with θ-roles assigned to appropriate function chains. In the ergative case, θ-role is assigned directly to the post-verbal NP. I will delay a more careful account until chapter 6, where the question of empty categories will be reconsidered in a somewhat different light.

Consider now such examples as (38):

(38)   *Giovanni crede [che se stesso ha mangiato le mele]
          ("Giovanni believes [that himself ate the apples]")

Suppose that R applies in the PF-component. Then at S-structure, the embedded clause is the governing category for the anaphor *se stesso*, which is governed by AGR. Example (38) is then barred by principle (A) of the binding theory. Suppose that R has applied in the syntax. Then the sentence is barred by the Case Filter, since *se stesso* cannot be assigned nominative Case; or in the Case-checking variant, because principle (34) is violated.

Let us turn to some further examples of a type similar to those discussed above. Burzio points out the contrast between (35) and (39):

(39)   (i) *sembrano [$_S$ molti studenti intervenire]
          (ii) *Giovanni pensava di [$_S$ venire Maria]
              ("Giovanni thought [Maria to come]")

Example (i) is barred in a straightforward way by the Case Filter, as is generally true with lexical subjects of infinitives apart from Exceptional Case-marking. Recall that fronting of *molti studenti* after raising is impossible, by the strict cycle. Example (ii) has the S-structure (40i), contrasting with (40ii):

(40)   (i) *Giovanni pensava di [$_S$ PRO venire Maria]
        (ii) PRO sembrano [$_S$ t intervenirne molti] (= (35ii))

PRO in (i) contrasts directly with trace in (ii), still another distinction between trace and PRO. Example (i) is ungrammatical by the Case Filter, since *Maria* lacks Case. This would be true even if PRO in (i) were coindexed with *Giovanni*; Case could not be inherited downwards to *Maria*, since the intervening PRO breaks the function chain; cf. chapter 6 for a more precise formulation of this tacit assumption throughout. But furthermore, PRO in (i) cannot be coindexed with *Giovanni*. If it were, then (i) would be a control structure; but PRO in (i) is impersonal PRO with a superscript, co-superscripted with *Maria*, and this element is not subject to control.[41] It is not an argument and has no reference, either determined by control or arbitrary.

Consider the examples (41):

(41)   (i) [$_{NP}$ e] is known [how [Bill to solve this problem]]
        (ii) [$_{NP}$ e] gli fu suggerito [di PRO tentare]
            ("it to-him was suggested [to try]"; "it was suggested to him to try")
        (iii) *Giovanni gli fu suggerito di tentare
            ("it was suggested to him that Giovanni try")
        (iv) gli fu suggerito che tentasse Giovanni
            ("it was suggested to him that Giovanni try")
        (v) è facile capire
            ("it is easy to understand," in the sense of "to understand is easy")
        (vi) *Giovanni è facile capire
            ("it is easy for Giovanni to understand")
        (vii) è facile che capisca Giovanni
            ("it is easy that Giovanni understand")

Example (i) satisfies the properties of D-structure, but *Bill* must be raised to satisfy the Case Filter. This is impossible, however, since the trace left by movement will then be ungoverned (cf. 2.4.1.(10iii)). The examples (ii)–(vii) illustrate the same phenomenon in Italian, but on the basis of slightly different mechanisms. Example (ii) is grammatical, with impersonal PRO (the equivalent of English *it*) inserted in the matrix subject position, co-superscripted with the extraposed infinitival clause, presumably. Suppose that (iii) were derived from a similar structure by raising *Giovanni* from the position of subject of *tentare*. Again, the sentence is barred by ECP. But suppose that the inversion option is taken in the embedded clause, as is possible; compare the grammatical example (iv). Then if *Giovanni* is raised from the inverted position, its trace is properly governed by *tentare*; recall that *wh*-movement is possible after NP-inversion. But (iii) is still barred, now by the binding theory. The impersonal subject PRO of the embedded infinitival, inserted after inversion, is an accessible SUBJECT in the sense of the binding theory, so that the trace left after movement would be free in its governing category, violating principle (A). Suppose that after NP-inversion in the embedded clause, the inverted NP were *wh*-moved to COMP, leaving a trace which is a variable. Then the binding theory does not apply, but this operation is still impossible since the variable would not have Case and would therefore lack a θ-role (cf. § 3.2.2). The examples (v)–(vii) illustrate the same phenomena in the case of an adjectival construction that does not assign a θ-role to the subject, thus not blocking NP-movement to the subject directly by the θ-criterion.

Consider again the impersonal constructions discussed briefly in § § 2.4.1, 2.7.[42] There are three basic cases to be considered:

(42)   (i) si mangia le mele
        (ii) le mele si mangiano
        (iii) si mangiano le mele
        ("the apples are being eaten")

In each case, *le mele* is understood as the direct object of *mangiare* at LF. By the projection principle and the assumption that the lexicon is maximally simple, we conclude that there is a common base form, namely (43), underlying all the examples of (42):

(43) $[_{NP}e]$ si mangia $[_{NP}$le mele$]$

Case (42iii) is unproblematic; we can reduce it to case (ii), taking it to derive from (ii) by the inversion process characteristic of pro-drop languages: Move-α followed by insertion of impersonal PRO co-superscripted with the NP adjoined to VP. See 6.(31)–(33) for details.

Turning to (42i), let us assume (following Rizzi (1976)) that *si* is a clitic related to the subject; furthermore, that it is in INFL in D-structure.[43] Then if the rule R of (12) applies in the syntax, *si* along with AGR will be in VP at S-structure and LF, whereas if R applies in the PF-component, *si* will remain in INFL governing the subject at S-structure and LF. On these assumptions, (42i) has the S-structure (44), R having applied in the syntax:

(44)   PRO $[_{VP}$si-mangia le mele$]$

Here PRO is coindexed with *si* and ungoverned, as required.

Assume further that *si*, like passive morphology, can "absorb" the objective Case-marking of a transitive verb (cf. §2.7). If this happens, then NP-movement from object position is obligatory by virtue of the Case Filter, converting (43) to (42ii), which is interpreted as an impersonal passive. The impersonal passives have the two basic properties of passive discussed in §2.7: Case is absorbed by some element other than the object, and the subject position [NP,S] lacks a θ-role, though *si* retains the θ-role of subject, thus, incidentally, excluding agent phrases in these constructions.

The S-structures of (42), then, are (45):

(45) (i) PRO [$_{VP}$ si-mangia le mele] (= (44))
      (ii) le mele [$_{INFL}$ Tense, AGR, si] [$_{VP}$ mangi- t]
      (iii) PRO [$_{VP}$ si-mangiano le mele]

Furthermore, the VPs of (i) and (iii) differ in internal structure, with *le mele* in the object position in (i) and adjoined to an internal VP in (iii).

It follows, then, that in a non-pro-drop language such as French, we should find only the analogue to (ii). This is indeed the case.[44]

Assuming the analyses in (45), how are Case and θ-role assigned? In (i), the object *le mele* receives objective Case in the normal way; assume then that *si* is marked nominative. The θ-roles of object and subject are assigned to *le mele* and *si*, respectively. The properties of (ii) and (iii) then follow from the properties of Move-α and PRO-insertion, as already discussed, though there are some refinements necessary, some of which we will discuss in chapter 6, when the relevant notions are made more precise.

Belletti notes further that *si* has the inherent feature [+plural], as indicated by such sentences as (46):

(46) (in questo paese) si vive sempre nervosi
      ("(in this country) one (*si*) always lives nervous (pl.)")

We thus have the curious situation that the verb is singular in (45i) with a plural subject (*si*). Belletti argues that *si* is not only in INFL, but is in fact the realization of AGR in these cases, so that *mangia* in (45i) and *vive* in (46) are unmarked stems. I omit here the required execution.

In short, we are assuming that in the D-structure (43), *si* may be assigned nominative Case, yielding the active sentence (42i); or it absorbs objective Case, triggering NP-movement and yielding the impersonal passive (42ii), which may then be converted to (42iii) by the normal inversion process. Questions of execution have been left open, and only one of several possible alternatives has been considered. But it seems that the construction fits rather naturally in the present framework.[45]

In note 14, we mentioned Longobardi's observation that agreement to the right in copular constructions appears to be another property associated with the complex of properties (3) of pro-drop languages. This conclusion follows quite naturally from our present assumptions. Compare the copular constructions (47) in Italian and French (or English):

(47)   (i) sono io
        (ii) c'est moi
        ("it's me")

The corresponding S-structures are (48):

(48)   (i) $[_S \text{NP}^* [_{VP} \text{copula-AGR NP}]]$
        (ii) $[_S \text{NP}^* \text{AGR} [_{VP} \text{copula NP}]]$

In (i), the rule R of (12) has applied. Therefore, the subject NP* is impersonal PRO co-superscripted with the NP predicate *io*. AGR governs and assigns nominative Case to *io*. Since NP and AGR are co-superscripted and are pronominals, they must agree in all features. Therefore, the copula agrees with the post-verbal nominative NP; *sono* is first person singular in (47i).

In (ii), in contrast, R has not applied so that NP* is governed and cannot be PRO. NP* must therefore be a third person impersonal element (*ce* in French, *it* in English), which is Case-marked by and agrees with AGR. The copula is therefore third person, and it assigns objective Case to NP.

There are further properties of these constructions that require discussion; cf. the references of note 14. Longobardi points out that a trace in the post-copular position appears to violate ECP; e.g., this position is not in general subject to relativization, as in *"the man who John is left yesterday." This might be accounted for by extending the observations on proper government in the final remarks of §4.4. Suppose that only lexical categories can be proper governors. Then it might be that the copula is not a lexical category in the required sense in such constructions as (47); it can govern, but not properly govern.

It is possible that other conditions should be imposed on proper government, for example, some kind of adjacency condition. Such a condition would, for example, offer an independent means for ruling out such structures as (49):

(49)   (i) ... $[_{VP} \text{V NP} [\text{t to VP}]]$
        (ii) *John was persuaded Bill $[\text{t to win}]$
        (iii) *who did John persuade Bill $[\text{t to win}]$

If there is no $\bar{S}$-deletion in the embedded clausal complement, then the structures of (49) are excluded by ECP. If $\bar{S}$-deletion has taken place, then ECP would not be violated if proper government does not require adjacency. These considerations do not, however, provide a motivation for an adjacency requirement for proper government. Recall the discussion of 2.6.(19)–(22) which showed that such examples as (49) are ruled out on independent grounds. In fact, we have seen some direct evidence conflicting with such an adjacency requirement, specifically, (50):

(50)   John impressed me [t as intelligent]   (= 2.6.(28i))

An adjacency condition on government is proposed in OB. It would require a "small verb phrase" analysis for such structures as "John [gave Bill] a book," "John [persuaded Bill] [PRO to leave]," etc. But it is not required by anything we have considered, and would call for adjustments that do not appear to be motivated.

This discussion barely scratches the surface of a collection of intricate and important problems, several of which are discussed more extensively in the references cited. It must also be regarded as quite tentative. The selection of options explored represents only one possible path among several that seem reasonable; see the references of note 30. But this suffices for present purposes. Returning to (10), repeated here as (51), we take α to be PRO, inserted by a rule of PRO-insertion in (ii) and base-generated in place in the D-structure (i) in accordance with the Avoid Pronoun principle, which is operative in pro-drop languages given the parameter (52):

(51)   (i) α VP
        (ii) α V NP
(52)   *R* may apply in the syntax   (= (12))

PRO in (i) is a true referential pronominal; in (ii) it is an impersonal pronominal, analogous to pleonastic *it*, *there*, *il*. PRO in (i) can have an antecedent, as a referential pronoun can; but it cannot be arbitrary in reference. PRO in (ii) is not an argument and cannot be controlled or arbitrary in reference. The post-verbal NP in (51ii) is assigned Case by AGR in constructions that do not involve raising, and inherits its Case from the trace of the co-superscripted PRO in the case of raising.

This analysis, which follows directly from independent assumptions for the most part, restricting parametric variation and stipulation of options to a minimum, yields the required conclusions concerning the pro-drop parameter and the cluster of properties associated with it. The principle ECP is maintained as (53) (= 4.4.(11)), but the definition of "proper government" is now reformulated as either (54) or (55) (the latter, if the final remarks of § 4.4 and the suggestion concerning (48) are correct), no longer incorporating the pro-drop parameter:

(53)   ECP: [$_\alpha$ e] must be properly governed
(54) α *properly governs* β if and only if α governs β and $\alpha \neq$ AGR
(55) α *properly governs* β if and only if α governs β and α is lexical

As between (54) and (55), the latter is preferable if tenable. The definition of "government" remains as in 4.4.(9), including the case of government by a category X^0 and the case of coindexing; the latter case applies only for an element in COMP governing an embedded subject, analogous to government in *for*-infinitivals and, at a step removed, Exceptional Case-marking structures and raising predicates. Case-assignment is contingent on government, and governing categories are those that contain governors.

It may be that still more restrictive conditions should be placed on the notion "proper government." In § 3.2.1 we saw that in the configuration (56), the head of β governs but does not properly govern NP*, where α and β are categories of the same type (though perhaps with different number of bars); cf. 3.2.1.(7)–(9), (18):

(56) $[_\alpha \text{NP*} \, \beta]$

To determine more precisely the property of "proper government" that is involved, recall that V properly governs NP* in (57) and that A properly governs NP* in (58):

(57) $[_{VP}[_{VP} \text{V} \ldots] \text{NP*}]$
(58) $[_{AP}[_{\bar{A}} \text{quite A}][_S \text{NP* to} \ldots]]$

Thus, *wh*-movement is possible from the position of NP* in (57) and NP-movement is possible from the position of NP* in (58). The crucial difference between (56) on the one hand and (57)–(58) on the other appears to be that in (56), NP* is in the specifier of α in the sense of X-bar theory, whereas in (57)–(58) it is in the complement of the head V or A (in a somewhat extended, though natural sense of "complement" in (57)). If COMP is taken to be the head of $\bar{S}$ with S as its complement, then the coindexing cases of proper government fall together with (57)–(58) rather than (56), as required. A natural, if tentative conclusion, then, is that α properly governs β only if β is in the complement of α. The precise formulation of this notion is straightforward.

The examples reviewed determine a highly specific notion of "proper government," but enough questions arise about the scope and representative character of these examples to suggest that a good deal of further work is necessary before an exact definition can be proposed with any security.

For further discussion of conditions on "proper government," along somewhat different lines, see Kayne (1980b).

In § 2.4.1, we gave a tentative formulation of the general principle of government for empty categories: namely, that trace is governed and PRO ungoverned (cf. 2.4.1.(13), restated as 2.9.(4)). The first part of this principle is now slightly modified, as ECP; the second part follows from the binding theory. We have also found reasons, deriving from considerations of θ-theory, for assuming that variables are Case-marked. Putting these observations together, we have the principle (59):

(59)   *Generalized ECP:* If α is an empty category, then

(i) α is PRO if and only if it is ungoverned

(ii) α is trace if and only if it is properly governed

(iii) α is a variable only if it is Case-marked

We have found no reason to strengthen (iii) to "if and only if," and the considerations just reviewed concerning impersonal PRO argue against doing so. The status of (59) will be further clarified in chapter 6.

4.6. Recoverability and clitics

We have now discussed the first three conceptual problems that arise in connection with RES(NIC), namely, 4.4.(2i–iii): the problem of determining the nature of "local control," of explaining the asymmetry between subject and object, and of explaining the distinction between nominative and subject of infinitive. We have also discussed in some detail the central part of 4.4.(2iv), namely, the question of the character of the empty subject in the pro-drop languages. It remains to consider the residual question of 4.4.(2iv) and 4.4.(2v), namely, the relation of ECP to recoverability of deletion and the relation between the pair (NP, AGR) and the pair (clitic, post-verbal empty position).

Actually, we have already dealt with one aspect of the relation of ECP to recoverability, namely, with regard to subjects. Following Taraldsen's basic idea as modified by Jaeggli, the option of permitting PRO as subject is related to overt manifestation of AGR in verbal morphology, a relation that is not precise in detail but reflects a strong tendency. The residual problems, then, concern the matter of cliticization. Again, there are a number of ways to pursue these questions. I will develop one possibility, extending the ideas just outlined.

We distinguish two types of cliticization: (i) cliticization of PP, as in the case of Italian *ne* or French *y*, *en*; (ii) cliticization of direct or indirect objects. I will put aside case (i), assuming that it involves a movement rule operating in the manner briefly discussed above and in more detail in the references cited. We are now concerned with case (ii). Note that the cliticization option is independent of the pro-drop parameter. Thus, French is like Italian and Spanish and different from English in that it has clitics, but it is like English and unlike Italian and Spanish with regard to the pro-drop parameter. We want to show, if possible, that French, Italian and Spanish are basically alike with regard to cliticization,[46] and that they differ minimally from English-type languages in this regard. Let us assume that the basic distinction lies at the level of D-structure: languages may have either the base form (1) or (2):

(1)   NP INFL $[_{VP}$ cl-V NP$]$

(2)   NP INFL $[_{VP}$ V NP$]$

This property of D-structure might derive from the lexicon or from the categorial component. INFL includes AGR where it is $[+$Tense$]$. The relation of AGR to the subject NP seems quite similar to that of the clitic *cl* to the object. The Avoid Pronoun principle operates uniformly, permitting empty subjects where the element AGR is sufficiently "strong" to allow recoverability (only a tendency, as noted). Correspondingly, this principle will allow the NP associated with the clitic to be empty, but not an NP associated with no clitic, as in (2). In this manner, we might hope to incorporate a fairly general principle of recoverability within the present theory, dealing with problem 4.4.(2iv).[47]

Let us now consider more carefully the problem of developing such an approach within our present framework. Consider the French example (3), which we now assume to have the D-structure (4) and, presumably, the LF-representation (5):[48]

(3)   Pierre le voit
       ("Pierre sees him")
(4)   Pierre $[_{VP}$ le voit NP$]$
(5)   Pierre $[_{VP}$ voit $[_{NP} \alpha]]$

Assuming D- and S-structure to be as in (4), the projection principle is satisfied as regards subcategorization, and will also be satisfied as regards θ-marking if we ensure that NP in (4) receives a θ-role. What is the character of the NP object in (4) and the character of α in (5), and what are the relations among the verb, the clitic, and the object?

The obvious conclusion, pursuing the line of thinking in the preceding section, is that the NP in (4) and α in (5) are PRO. If so, then the object position must be ungoverned. Let us assume that the clitic "absorbs" government in a manner to be clarified. Thus the object, which we will naturally assume to be coindexed with the clitic, is ungoverned, hence PRO. The coindexing must be distinct from that relevant to the binding theory. Suppose, then, we again take it to be co-superscripting, as in earlier cases of the same sort.

We have related subcategorization and θ-marking throughout to government. But we are now assuming that the object position in (4), (5) is not governed by the verb, though it must be subcategorized by the verb and the NP occupying it must be θ-marked by the verb to satisfy the projection principle and the θ-criterion. The simplest move seems to be to continue to hold that α θ-marks the position that it governs – the clitic position in (4) – and to extend slightly the notions of subcategorization and θ-marking defined in § 2.2. Recall that β is θ-marked by α if β or its trace is in a position θ-marked by α. Suppose we now add that β is θ-marked by α if a co-superscripted element (in this case, a clitic) is in the position θ-marked by α, extending the notion of subcategorization in the same way. Then the object position in (4) and (5) is subcategorized by the verb; the NP that occupies this position is θ-marked by the verb, although the verb does not govern or θ-mark this position; the properties of subcategorization and θ-marking are "inherited" from the co-superscripted clitic. We are now supposing the clitic position to be governed by the verb, and accordingly, to be Case-marked by the verb.[49] The clitic, however, is not an argument; rather, the co-superscripted NP object is the argument.[50]

There is variation with regard to clitic doubling, as in standard Spanish (6) and River Plate Spanish (7):

(6)   lo vimos a él
          ("we saw him")
(7)   lo vimos a Juan
          ("we saw Juan")

Case (7) is excluded in standard Spanish, and the analogues of both (6) and (7) are ungrammatical in French and (standard) Italian. In all Spanish dialects, (8) is ungrammatical:

(8)   *lo vimos Juan

These facts illustrate an important observation of Kayne's: where there is clitic-doubling, there must be some device to assign Case to the NP that appears in the position associated with (co-superscripted with) the clitic. In Spanish, the device employed is insertion of a preposition, as in English *of*-insertion. We continue to assume, then, that the "doubled" NP is ungoverned by the verb in (6), (7). The *a*-insertion rule of Spanish is required to assign it Case, so that the Case Filter is not violated.

There are no examples of clitic doubling in the case of PP-clitics. This follows from the assumption that we have actual movement rather than base-generation of these clitics, which are not subcategorized by the verb.

The discussion of clitics relates to the ECP in interesting ways. Consider the case of Spanish (cf. Jaeggli (1980b)). In the case of clitic-doubling, the post-verbal NP is ungoverned (though it has Case). Therefore it should be impossible, by ECP, for a variable to appear in the position of the postverbal NP, whether the variable is produced by *wh*-movement or by a quantifier-movement rule of the LF-component, if the preceding discussion of ECP is correct. Consider the base structures (9) in Spanish:

(9)   (i)   lo viste a quién
              ("whom did you see?")
      (ii) viste a quién
              ("whom did you see?")
      (iii) las vi a todas las mujeres
              ("I saw all the women")
      (iv) vi a todas les mujeres
              ("I saw all the women")

In cases (i) and (iii), the D-structure is generated with a clitic; in case (ii) and (iv), with no clitic. The *wh*-phrase may be moved, yielding (10i,ii) corresponding to (9i,ii); or it may be left in place, so that the S-structures are (9i,ii):

(10)   (i) a quién lo viste t
        (ii) a quién viste t

In (10), the trace becomes a variable at LF-representation. In the examples of (9), a rule of the LF-component moves the *wh*-phrase of (i), (ii) and the quantified phrase of (iii), (iv), leaving a variable in the vacated position. According to the ECP, examples (9i,iii) and (10i) should be ungrammatical, because government is absorbed by the clitic so that we have an ungoverned variable at LF-representation; but (9ii,iv) and (10ii) should be grammatical, because the variable is governed by the verb, thus satisfying ECP. Exactly this is the case, Jaeggli points out.

Jaeggli also points out that the familiar definiteness requirement for clitic-doubling (namely, that the post-verbal NP must be definite) follows from the same assumptions, if we regard indefinite NPs as quantified expressions, hence subject to the rule of quantifier-movement (cf. May (1977)). He also notes that indirect objects differ from the examples cited above, in that *wh*-movement with cliticization is possible, from which he concludes that ECP should be restricted to NPs, the assumption being that the rule of *a*-insertion creates an NP of the form $[_{NP}a\,NP]$ in contrast to the true preposition *a* of the base, which appears in the construction $[_{PP}a\,NP]$. Cf. Jaeggli (1980b) for elaboration of this idea, based in part on observations by Vergnaud (1974).

While there is obviously much more to say about the topic of cliticization,[51] this brief discussion illustrates one approach that seems quite plausible and that fits naturally into the framework we have been considering. A close relation is established between clitic-NP pairs and subject-verb agreement, and the condition of recoverability of deletion for pronouns is to a considerable extent accommodated within the GB-theory. Furthermore, a relation to ECP is established with regard to cliticization.

The conceptual problems concerning RES(NIC) appear to be resolved in a reasonably satisfactory way in terms of the principle ECP of the binding theory and two basic parameters, which are independent: the pro-drop parameter and the option of having clitics, the latter admitting of various subcases. ECP forms part of the Generalized ECP 4.5.(59), the residue falling under the binding theory and θ-theory. Throughout, the concept of government plays a central role, as it does in Case theory and θ-theory.

Notes

1.   Recall that there are also differences between variables and names, specifically, with regard to weak crossover. Cf. notes 46–8 of chapter 3. Recall also that if the binding theory applies at S-structure, as we assumed finally, then in the strong crossover cases we

have quantifier phrases rather than variables in the position comparable to that of the variable in *wh*-movement at the point where the binding theory applies.

2.   The superiority condition in the sense of Chomsky (1977a, chapter 3), as illustrated in (2iv), (3), (4), has not generally been considered in this context, but this phenomenon does seem to fall together naturally with the other examples of RES(NIC). For other interpretations of this condition, see Fiengo (1979), George (1980).

Note that while the LF-representation (3) is blocked by (1) and the LF-representation (4ii) is permitted by (1), thus accounting for the distinction between the ungrammatical (2iv) and the grammatical (4), nevertheless a problem remains concerning (4): namely, we want to say that in (4ii) *who* governs t_i, for reasons that will become clear later on, whereas *who* does not govern t_i in (3) (or at least, does not "properly govern" it, in the sense to which we return). But *who* does not c-command t_i in either case. The problem is similar to one noted in chapter 3, note 56. We might deal with it in several ways. One possibility is to assume that COMP takes the index of its head, thus j in (3) and i in (4ii), and that it is COMP that is (derivatively) the governor (cf. Aoun, Hornstein and Sportiche (1980)). Another, suggested by Aoun, is to suppose that the *wh*-movement rule of the LF-component is in fact a rule of adjunction to $\bar{S}$ with a *wh*-phrase in COMP, which will give the desired results. Still another possibility would be to take $\bar{S}$ to be a projection of COMP, slightly modifying the notion of "c-command" presented in 3.2.1.(12), restricting c-command in a "chain" of categories with the same features to its head, thus *who* in (4ii) but not in (3). Pending further clarification, I will leave the question open, assuming in the subsequent discussion that the problem receives a solution, perhaps in one of these ways.

3.   The surface structure (5i) is irrelevantly possible with the different S-structure (i):

(i)   John was asked t[how [PRO to solve the problem]]

4.   Assume *wh-i* in (1) to be the moved *wh*-phrase which does not appear in surface structure.

5.   Later, we will see that there is good reason to suppose that RES(NIC) does exclude this configuration in Italian, with this interpretation of (1) deriving from a different source. But for the moment, let us put this possibility aside and continue to take (1) to be the correct analysis.

6.   Huang (1980) argues that in Chinese, where there is no overt movement in normal *wh*-phrases, clefts, and similar constructions, there is nevertheless a movement rule in the LF-component analogous to the quantifier-movement rule or the *wh*-movement rule we are now considering, yielding effects that he describes. But he concludes that the *wh*-movement rule of the LF-component violates such constraints as the complex NP constraint though not the specificity constraint.

7.   Cf. Chomsky (1977b), OB, Fiengo and Higginbotham (1979). The basic observations concerning specificity discussed in Chomsky (1977b) are due to George Horn (cited in Hornstein (1977)) and Robert May (1977).

8.   Violations of the coordinate structure constraint seem impossible, however:

(i)   *I wonder who wrote which textbook and that novel

Perhaps a parallelism constraint of the sort studied in George (1980) is involved.

9.   The examples (v) are due to Leland George, who had noted this phenomenon independently. Similar examples were noted independently by Jane Grimshaw.

10.   The generalization is not unproblematic, and there has been much discussion, which I will not review here, of apparent counterexamples. I will tentatively assume that the generalization is a valid one, and that either a sharper formulation of it or reanalysis of the languages that appear to provide counterexamples will overcome apparent problems, as in the case of Hungarian discussed in § 3.2.2; cf. 3.2.2.(13). It should be emphasized that this is a strong assumption, which may prove false.

11.   Irrelevantly, (ii) may have the reading: "not (I want that for no x, x come)".

12.   See Kayne (1979c) for a suggestion as to what this factor might be.
13.   The English equivalents allow (20), hence the internal analysis if Sportiche is correct, in all cases. The same is true of Chinese, Huang (1980) observes. Many other questions arise concerning constructions with focal stress. Cf. Rochemont (1978).
14.   Giuseppe Longobardi suggests that another property related to this complex is agreement to the right in copular constructions, as in (i) contrasting with (ii):

(i)   sono io
(ii)   c'est moi
         ("it's me")

In (i), *sono* is first person singular; in (ii), third person singular. In work in progress, he explores many interesting consequences of RES(NIC) for predicate positions, and also offers an interpretation of the pro-drop parameter that differs from the one I will develop here, again exploring a variety of consequences. On copular constructions, see also Edwards (1979), Higginbotham (1980).
        There are other properties that appear to be associated with this complex; e.g., restructuring in the sense of Rizzi (1978a). I will omit this and other related problems discussed in the literature. Cf. Burzio (1981).
15.   Cf. Kayne and Pollock (1978), Kayne (1979a). Jaeggli (1980b) suggests that this rule is "stylistic," i.e., in the PF-component.
16.   For a much more extensive treatment of these and related questions, based on somewhat different assumptions than those developed here, see Burzio (1981), from which elements will be borrowed below, as indicated.
17.   Alternatively, if *t* does not delete and *that* is present, assuming (as above) that we have no rule of *that*-deletion, but rather the option of base-generation of *that*.
18.   Suppose we assume the doubly-filled COMP filter to be operative, as in Pesetsky's theory. Then we must ensure that trace in COMP not be deleted in the PF-component prior to the application of the filter, or (14i) will incorrectly be marked grammatical. But trace must be deletable in COMP, to permit (14iii) to pass the filter. Therefore trace must be optionally deletable at S-structure but not in the PF-component prior to the filter.
        If we rely rather on the assumption that local control requires c-command (with Rizzi and Kayne), then we may assume as in chapters 2, 3 that non-Case-marked trace is "invisible" in the PF-component, hence invisible specifically to the filter.
19.   For (15iii), I assume the analysis of clefts in Chomsky (1977b), which is quite well-motivated in terms of its explanatory force and also in view of the fact that overt *wh*-phrases can appear in the COMP position of clefts, as in "it is John to whom I spoke."
20.   If we assume that there is no *wh*-deletion but rather movement of an empty category as discussed earlier, then we must assume that the empty category (say, PRO) and *that* are "absorbed" into a single quasi-relative pronoun with the features of *that* and the index (and perhaps other features) of PRO at S-structure. Another possibility, suggested by Aoun, is that the element *that*, lacking a semantic function, is "invisible" in the LF-component just as Case-free trace is invisible in the PF-component, a possibility that should be explored in the more general context developed in Aoun (1979b). Cf. the final remarks of §2.6. For a variant of Pesetsky's proposal along somewhat different lines, see Aoun, Hornstein and Sportiche (1980).
21.   Cf. Pesetsky (1978b). Also Chomsky and Lasnik (1977). See Kayne (1980a) for extensive further discussion of this and related matters.
22.   There are other relevant examples in the category of infinitivals, for example, those discussed in Rizzi (1979b). I will not pursue these topics, however. Cf. Rizzi (1980c), Chomsky (1981).
23.   Should the ECP in fact be extended beyond NPs, as assumed here without relevant evidence? That the answer may be negative is suggested by interesting evidence adduced by Jaeggli (1980b), to which I return briefly in §4.6.
        The ECP might be related to the principle discussed in §2.6 and §3.2.3 that categories of the form $[_\alpha \; e]$ must have some sort of antecedent. I will not pursue this question, however.

24.   Recall that 3.2.(11) was one of a series of proposals for defining "government." An analogous modification is required if one of the alternatives is selected.

25.   For example, we might add the stipulation, which we have been considering from various points of view throughout this discussion, that Case-marked trace is a variable, so that (15ii,iii) are blocked by principle (C) of the binding theory, since the trace is an A-bound variable. But we would hope to derive this stipulation from the theory, insofar as it is correct, rather than relying on it as an independent principle. A second possibility is to appeal to the *[*for-to*] filter assuming now that *for*-deletion in post-verbal position follows the filter. This makes the prediction that in such dialects as Ozark English that lack the filter such sentences as (15ii,iii) should be grammatical. I have not been able to determine satisfactorily whether this is the case, but I doubt it.

Note that neither of these proposals – or any others, to my knowledge – give a satisfactory answer to one problem discussed inconclusively in Chomsky and Lasnik (1977), namely, the marginally acceptable character of (i):

(i)   who do you want most of all (very much) t to win

26.   Recall that we have left open the question of how the structures with post-verbal subjects are generated.

27.   Which is, in essence, the version I presented at the GLOW workshop in Pisa in April 1979, where the empirical problem we have now been discussing was noted on the basis of Rizzi's observations but left unresolved.

28.   Perhaps a methodological aside is warranted at this point. It is, I think, generally valid to say that proposals concerning generative grammar in the 1950s and 1960s were rarely faced with direct counter-evidence, the usual problem being that the proposals lacked explanatory depth or could only be applied to some range of phenomena in a clumsy and unenlightening way. In more recent years, the situation has changed. Much more restrictive theories with a considerably more articulated internal structure have been proposed and, correspondingly, a great deal of apparent counter-evidence has been put forth. Often it is unclear what to make of such evidence. As has often been noted, principles of UG cannot be directly confirmed or refuted by linguistic data, but only by grammars; and unanalyzed data generally are uninformative with regard to the grammar from which they derive. A datum does not wear its explanation on its sleeve. In some cases, the counter-evidence seemed real, in that the grammatical rules that appeared to be implicated did conflict with the proposals concerning UG. In many cases, the counter-evidence has indeed proven real, leading to modification of theory or simply standing unresolved.

In linguistics, as in the other "human sciences," a badly-misunderstood "Popperian methodology" has often been proposed which requires that a theory be abandoned in the face of (apparent) counter-evidence, as in the case of ECP just discussed. Very commonly, it has proven to be a wise move to persist in maintaining principles of UG that had significant explanatory power in some domain, even when they were faced with what appeared to be counter-evidence. Quite often, it has turned out that the phenomena were misanalyzed or misunderstood or that the basic ideas of the partially successful theory were sound, though some change in perspective or in the precise form of principles was required. To cite one case, it was noted in Chomsky (1977a, chapter 3; dating from 1970) that pronouns directly refuted the binding conditions proposed there; in essence, the SSC and NIC. It became obvious shortly after that this was the result of a mistaken way of looking at the behavior of pronouns. A number of other examples have been mentioned above, and the literature contains a host of others. The example of ECP, just discussed, is a case in point.

As theoretical work advances and proposals become more significant, we expect – in fact, hope – that serious empirical and conceptual problems will arise. That is what makes progress possible. The methodological principle just mentioned, which is familiar in linguistics and similar fields, has one certain consequence: it will block any progress in understanding, since there is much too much that is simply not understood. The rational conclusion is not to dismiss counter-evidence, contradictions, and conceptual problems raised in connection with ideas that have explanatory force in some domain, nor is it, surely, to abandon these ideas when there is no more successful alternative. Rather, the rational approach is to pursue these ideas as intensively as possible, always considering the possibility of reshaping them to overcome outstanding problems, or to reconsider the character of the alleged problems, or to abandon them in the face of some alternative of still greater explanatory power. The greater the explanatory force of the ideas in question, the more rational it is to persist in developing them in the face of apparent counter-evidence.

Needless to say, these remarks are obvious to the point of truism in any developed science.

29.   These are Jaeggli's examples (4.105). As he notes, the ungrammatical status of (i) is irrelevant here; (i), like (ii) lacking a *wh*-phrase subject, is ungrammatical because obligatory inversion has not taken place:

(i)   *qué quién compró
(ii)   *qué Juan compró

30.   The basic line of argument in this paragraph derives from Jaeggli (1980b), who develops the idea somewhat differently, however. For different and quite plausible approaches to the questions we are now considering, see Rizzi (1980a, 1980c), Burzio (1981), and forthcoming work by Longobardi.

31.   The string (17) may be marginally acceptable after raising and inversion, but not with the structure (17). Since the argument presented here relies on a property of D-structure, it provides empirical support for a theory based on Move-α as a syntactic rule with a postulated D-structure as compared with a variant that assumes base-generation of S-structure with new interpretive rules with exactly the properties of Move-α. As noted in §2.4.6, it is extremely difficult, if indeed it is ultimately possible, to find empirical differences between these theories. Hence it is not surprising that this argument, like others to the same effect that have appeared earlier, is highly theory-internal. It seems likely than any empirical argument distinguishing these virtually identical alternatives would have to be of this character, as we have observed several times.

32.   Notice that recourse to the Avoid Pronoun principle for subjects is permitted in pro-drop languages, by virtue of the option (12). We may assume that the principle holds generally, but it is applicable only in the pro-drop languages. The conditions under which lexical pronouns may or must appear in Italian and Spanish seem rather complex. I will not pursue the issue, which I do not fully understand.

33.   Whether this assumption is fully tenable is not clear. Rizzi (1979a) argues that even "short *wh*-movement" within a clause from subject position is excluded in Italian. If this is the case, we might assume that application of the rule R in the syntax is obligatory when the subject is empty, including variables as well as PRO, inversion being obligatory in all other cases. Appearance of subjects in pre-verbal position, which is of course possible, might be the result of topicalization or of a rule of the PF-component moving the inverted NP into subject position. Or, as Aoun suggests, there might be an abstract complementizer in COMP that prevents c-command of the trace in subject position by the *wh*-element in COMP, blocking "short *wh*-movement" from subject position. The latter option might be preferable, as Aoun observes, in the light of the fact that quantifier movement is possible from pre-verbal subject position, though it is not possible from topicalized position. I will put these questions aside, noting that a problem may exist.

34.   We adopt the assumption of Kayne (1975) that there is clitic-movement in these cases. On *ne*-cliticization, see Belletti and Rizzi (1980). See the discussion of 3.2.1.(12), concerning the relevant notion of c-command.

35.   Burzio's discussion, based in part on ideas of David Perlmutter, extends far beyond the questions we are considering here. Ergative verbs, in Burzio's sense, have the property that they do not assign Case to their direct object but do assign it θ-role (presumably, theme). In accordance with 2.6.(40), these verbs do not assign θ-role in subject position.

36.   Burzio presents independent evidence that we have PRO-insertion rather than base-generation of PRO in these cases. He notes the observation in Kayne (1975) that the

reflexive clitic can only be associated with a base-generated NP in (pre-verbal) subject position; for example, the surface subject of a passive cannot be reflexivized. But reflexivization is impossible in the case of post-verbal subject as well, implying that PRO is inserted rather than base-generated in this case. Cf. note 31.

37.   Following Stowell (1978), Burzio argues that all cases of *there*-insertion are base-generated in the form (i):

(i). $[_{NP} e]$ be NP . . .

See also Couquaux (1980, forthcoming). On the behavior of French pronominal subjects, see Jaeggli (1980b), developing ideas of Kayne (1972).

38.   See Belletti and Rizzi (1980) for argument in support of option (ii). Cf. § 5.3.

39.   The analysis of (30) as (32) with α = PRO in (33), with NP-inversion, merits skepticism, but one familiar type of argument that might be levelled against it seems to me to lack force: namely, that the analysis involves too complex a derivation for such a simple sentence. If we consider, say, the kind of analysis carried out by the visual system in identifying a rotating plane figure or a cube moving through space, the automatism proposed here for the analysis of (32) seems trivial indeed. There is a tendency in the study of language and psychology of language to assume that analytic steps (say, steps in derivations) are "costly" in time, effort, etc., in comparison with look-up of items in memory, which is essentially "free." Conceivably this is true, but on the basis of the extremely limited amount known about human mental operations, the assumption appears to be quite unwarranted. One might just as readily draw the opposite conclusion – with just as little conviction. For example, successful chess-playing programs generally exploit vast memory and limited analytic resources, in contrast to human chess masters who appear to rely on extensive analysis and limited memory – not that much can be concluded from this fact. Furthermore, any contrast between "look-up" and "computation" is misleading from the start, in that "look-up" of course involves computation, of what nature and complexity, no one really knows.

On this matter, see Weinberg and Berwick (forthcoming). They discuss the fact that in the investigation of motor control, as well as visual and auditory processing, while early approaches tended to assume large amounts of "table look-up" in place of rapid, deep processing, subsequent discoveries concerning both neuropsychology and the theory of computation have reversed the emphasis. They also show that currently available psycholinguistic results leave the question of the role of look-up versus computation quite open, contrary to what has often been assumed. One common fallacy is to assume that if some experimental result provides counter-evidence to a theory of processing that includes a grammatical theory *T* and a parsing procedure *P* (say, a procedure that assumes that operations are serial and additive, in that each operation adds a fixed "cost"), then it is *T* that is challenged and must be changed. The conclusion is particularly unreasonable in the light of the fact that in general there is independent (so-called "linguistic") evidence in support of *T* while there is no reason at all to believe that *P* is true. On these matters, see also forthcoming work by E. Barton. Clearly, one should be very wary of a priori judgments on these matters. See chapter 2, note 139.

Studies of language processing certainly might prove valuable in principle in providing insight into the nature of grammar, at least if we adopt the normal "realist" assumptions of inquiry, but the arguments will have to be rather skillfully crafted. See, e.g., Forster (1979); Fodor et al. (1980).

40.   From Burzio (1981), whose analysis I follow in part. The importance of structures illustrating the agreement phenomenon of (35) was pointed out by Giuseppe Longobardi, who suggests a rather different interpretation of them in forthcoming work.

41.   We might also argue that (40i) violates the binding theory, under certain assumptions about transitivity of coindexing. Then if *Giovanni* is coindexed with PRO by control and PRO is co-superscripted (hence coindexed) with *Maria*, it would follow that *Maria* is coindexed with *Giovanni*, violating principle (c) of the binding theory. Since *Maria* is not

co-superscripted with *Giovanni*, it is not exempt from this condition as is the pair (PRO, *M aria*). The point would have to be made with more precision, but the direction is clear.
42.   The following remarks are modelled on the analysis in Belletti (1980b), where further consequences are outlined; see the references of chapter 2, note 123.
43.   In the next section, it will be suggested that nominal clitics are base-generated in place and receive Case and θ-role.
44.   Why do we not have *il*-insertion in French analogues to(42i,iii)? Perhaps because *il* itself is a subject clitic, as argued in Jaeggli (1980b), following Kayne.
45.   Cf. note 43, chapter 2. Note that the analysis presented here accords with the proposal in this footnote that the PRO subject of the impersonal construction is not subject to control. CF. Burzio (1981) for an analysis along somewhat different lines.
46.   There are, however, subsidiary differences, a few of which we will discuss. See Jaeggli (1980b) for a much more extensive discussion, based on assumptions rather similar to those outlined here, which are, as noted, in part borrowed from Jaeggli's modifications of the proposals presented in the Pisa lectures themselves, and on work by Kayne, Quicoli, Rizzi, Strozer, Rivas and others whom Jaeggli cites.
47.   The principle suggested is fairly general, but does not apply to such languages as Japanese in which pronouns can be missing much more freely.
48.   The analysis of verbal clitics seems to extend without problem to adjectival clitics, as in French "il lui est cher," related to "il est cher a lui (a lui-même)" ("it is dear to him"). Cf. 2.7.(4).
49.   This conclusion is reached for different reasons by Jaeggli (1980b), modifying some ideas of Aoun (1979a). The analysis proposed in the original Pisa lectures was somewhat different, and did not accord with the projection principle. Forthcoming work by Hagit Borer suggests that it may have been on the right track, however, in preference to the approach briefly outlined here, and that it can be adapted to the present framework.
50.   We could not assume that the θ-role of the object is determined by assigning θ-role to the index in the manner we have discussed; cf. § 3.2.2. There are two reasons. First, this would permit Case to be "inherited" by the NP object, thus permitting clitic-doubling freely, contrary to fact. Second, the actual mechanism for assigning Case or θ-role to an index (cf. 3.2.2.(32) and related discussion) bars this approach – correctly, as we see – since the NP object is the sole member of the A-function chain to which Case or θ-role would be assigned, the clitic not being a member of this chain since it is not in an A-position.
51.   Note that I am putting aside here important questions related to clitic climbing, as in the case of restructuring in the sense of Rizzi (1978a) and causatives (cf. Burzio (1978, 1981), Rouveret and Vergnaud (1980), for recent discussion), or when the verbal auxiliary attracts the clitic. Furthermore, Jaeggli's observations just reviewed do not appear to generalize to other languages with clitics. The latter topic is investigated in forthcoming work by Borer, Aoun and others. There are, needless to say, numerous other questions relating to clitics that I have not mentioned at all.

Chapter 5

Some Related Topics

Before turning to some concluding remarks in chapter 6, I would like to mention a few related topics and to make some comments about them. These remarks will be rather unsystematic, some simply noting problems for further study, others extending earlier discussion, and still others referring to some of the work that has been done since the April 1979 workshop in Pisa where many of the basic ideas outlined here were presented and discussed.

5.1. The theory of indexing

I have been assuming a very simple indexing theory: there are no anaphoric indices in the sense of OB, but only referential indices, and these are assigned either by movement or freely. But this approach is too simple as it stands.[1] I have so far restricted myself to examples of coreference and distinct reference, avoiding problems of disjoint reference more generally and of "scattered antecedents."[2] But such examples raise problems for the very simple theory of indexing I have been using so far. Consider the examples of (1):

(1)   (i) John$_i$ told Bill$_j$ that they$_k$ should leave
       (ii) *we lost my way
       (iii) we expected me to like John

In (i), *John* and *Bill* are indexed differently, and *they* cannot be coindexed with either *John* or *Bill*, in accordance with the indexing conventions presented above. Thus i, j, k are three distinct indices. Compare, in contrast, sentence (2):

(2)   John$_i$ told Bill$_j$ that he$_k$ should leave

Here k can be identical to either i or j (or neither). Therefore, the behavior of *he* as proximate or obviative is captured within the theory of free indexing in (2), but the analogous property – namely, that *they* can refer to John and Bill, or to neither, or to one or the other with some other people – is not captured in case (1i). This seems a questionable result, though it leads to no internal contradiction. Note that the same question arises in the more complex OB-framework.

Examples (1i) and (2) can be brought together in one of two ways: by abandoning the interpretation of proximate and obviative pronouns in terms of indexing in case (2), or by extending the theory of indexing to use of more complex indices in obvious ways in case (1). The former approach seems wrong, since the behavior of pronominals captured by the indexing convention is so closely analogous to that of anaphors with respect to the theory of binding. The latter approach therefore seems called for, if indeed these cases are to be brought together, as it seems reasonable to assume.

Examples (1ii) and (1iii) raise questions of a different sort. In case (ii), the idiom requires coindexing of *we* and *my*, as in (3):

(3)   (i) I lost my way
        (ii) *I lost his way

The question is: how do we interpret coindexing of *we* and *my* in (1ii)? The example indicates that we must take coindexed elements to be strictly coreferential, not merely overlapping in reference, so as to assign to (1ii) its proper status as ungrammatical.

Making this assumption, let us turn to cases of disjoint reference, as in (1iii), which clearly contrasts in status with (4), as noted originally by Paul Postal:[3]

(4)   we expected John to like me

We have only two options in the present theory of indexing for such examples as (1iii) and (4): the two pronouns may be coindexed or differently indexed. If they are coindexed, then (1iii) is barred and (4) admitted by the binding theory, as required. But this decision entails that in (4), the pronoun *me* is understood as overlapping in reference with *we* under coindexing, which is inconsistent with the analysis of (1ii). If, on the other hand, we take the index of the singular pronoun to differ from that of the plural pronoun in both (1iii) and (4), consistent with the analysis of (1ii), then the binding theory fails to explain the difference of status of (1iii) and (4), which is surely an incorrect result. Note that this problem does not arise in the more complex indexing theory of the OB-framework. In that theory, the referential indices of the pronouns will differ, and the anaphoric indices will indicate the required properties of overlapping and disjoint reference in the case of (1ii,iii) and (4).

Clearly, then, the theory of indexing we have been using here is defective, and something more complex is required. The theory of anaphoric indices in the OB-framework overcomes these problems, with the exception of (1i) and (2). In § 3.1, I cited the complexity of this theory as one of the problems to be addressed in improving the OB-framework, and in the exposition above I have avoided all of these problems, but only by restricting myself to too narrow a class of examples. This problem, along with several others relating to the theory of indexing, therefore still stands, in contrast to the other problems raised, which receive a natural solution in the GB-framework.

Let us put aside these questions (which are not slight), and still assume the theory of free indexing with no anaphoric indices. Consider examples in which we have a quantifier and a pronoun as in (5), where order is irrelevant and *he* stands for *he* or *him*:

(5)   ... everyone ... he ...

After the application of the LF-rule of quantifier-movement, we have (6):

(6)   for every person x, ... x ... he ...

The conditions under which x and *he* may be coindexed are given by the binding theory, apart from the conditions of weak crossover that are stated at the LF-level. Coindexing is possible at S-structure only in case a name in place of x can be coindexed with *he*. Where the variable and *he* are coindexed, we interpret (6) as (7):

(7)   for every person x, ... x ... x ...

This is the basic principle discussed by Higginbotham (1979a): a pronoun can be interpreted as a variable bound by a quantifier only if replacement of the quantifier by a name gives a possible case of non-disjoint reference. Thus the pronoun can be so interpreted in (8) but not (9), just as it can be proximate to *John* in (10) but not (11):

(8)   everyone expected that he would win
(9)   everyone expected him to win
(10)   John expected that he would win
(11)   John expected him to win

The "only if" of this principle cannot be extended to "if and only if" because the pronoun must be within the scope of the quantifier for this interpretation to be possible (furthermore, because of weak crossover). Thus the pronoun is not in the scope of the quantifier in (12) and correspondingly cannot be interpreted as a variable bound by the quantifier, though the pronoun can be proximate to *John* in (13):

(12)   the man who everyone likes saw him
(13)   the man who John likes saw him

While significant problems remain, the principle seems close to correct.[4]

Higginbotham obtains this result by means of a reindexing rule that assigns to a pronoun the referential index of a variable to its left except in a certain configuration designed to handle the weak crossover cases: call it the configuration K. He shows further that reindexing may apply either before or after the quantifier-movement rule of the LF-component. In the approach assumed here, there is no reindexing rule. We might say, then, that a derivation of (6) with the index i assigned to both x and *he* is permissible only if at some stage x is to the left of *he* and K does not hold. Thus, Higginbotham's theory is reinterpreted as a theory of proper derivations in the LF-component. Alternatively, the condition may be formulated directly on LF, with interesting results, as shown in Higginbotham (1979c).

Suppose now that a derivation meeting the reindexing convention (however stated) yields the LF-representations (14), (15) for (8), (9), respectively:

(14)   for every person x_i, x_i expected that he$_i$ would win
(15)   for every person x_i, x_i expected he$_i$ to win

Then *he$_i$* is interpreted as x_i. Case (15) is ruled out by principle (B) of the binding theory at S-structure, but case (14) is grammatical.

In Higginbotham (1979a), where the OB system of anaphoric indices is adopted, the pronoun *he* will have the index (i, null) in (14) and the index $(i, \{i\})$ in (15), where the second term of the index is the anaphoric index, the set of referential indices of elements to which *he* is disjoint in reference. The index $(i, \{i\})$ is "contradictory" in that it appears to indicate that *he* is disjoint in reference from itself. But here some care is necessary. Why precisely is (16) contradictory?:

(16) $[_{\text{NP}(i, \{i\})} \text{he}]$

Presumably, because of some principle that says that by virtue of its anaphoric index, *he* cannot be coreferential with an NP elsewhere bearing the index i; but by virtue of its referential index, *he* must be coreferential with such an NP. Hence, a contradiction. But suppose the NP in question is a variable. Then the principle could be interpreted as saying that *he* cannot refer to any value of the variable. But this interpretation is too strong, as we see from the examples of note 3. Consider the examples (17):

(17)   (i) Carter voted for every Democrat
        (ii) someone in Plains, Georgia, voted for Carter
        (iii) who voted for Carter?
        (iv) who did Carter vote for?

From (i), it does not follow that Carter did not vote for himself, and (ii) is consistent with the assumption that Carter is the only person in Plains, Georgia, who voted for Carter. Similarly, "Carter" is a perfectly good answer to (iii) or (iv). Therefore, we cannot maintain without further argument that the index $(i, \{i\})$ on *he* in (15) yields an absurdity. An apparent advantage of the OB-framework therefore appears to be illusory.

5.2. Prepositional phrases

I have assumed that the governing categories are those with accessible SUBJECTs – S when its SUBJECT is accessible, NP and other maximal projections when they have SUBJECTs that are accessible.[5] But there is some evidence that PP might also serve as a governing category. For example, a problem for the binding theory sketched in chapter 3 (noted by Jean-Yves Pollock) is that in the Romance languages, pronouns in PP can regularly be coindexed with NP antecedents in the same clause, as in (1):

(1)   Jean m'a parlé de lui
        ("John spoke to me about himself")

According to the binding theory of chapter 3, *lui* is bound in its governing category, the full clause, if it is coindexed with *Jean* in (1), violating principle (B). The problem would be overcome if the PP in which *lui* appears serves as a governing category.

It seems unlikely, however, that this is the correct approach. In the first place, theory-internal considerations argue against it. In general, governing categories have SUBJECTs, indeed, accessible SUBJECTs, and there seems little reason to assume that PP in Romance has a SUBJECT whereas its analogue in languages like English does not. It seems more reasonable to try to relate these differences to other differences between the language types in question.

It is possible that this matter is related to limitations on the distribution of reflexives. There is (near) complementary distribution between reflexives and proximate pronouns, a fact that motivated earlier transformational theories of pronominalization, but that is not captured directly in the current framework.[6] But it is unlikely that this is the correct approach either. It seems more plausible to relate this matter to the option of cliticization.

As has been commonly observed, clitics in the Romance languages do behave in the manner of English pronouns with regard to disjoint reference. This observation suggests that it is clitics rather than full pronouns which fall under principle (B) of the binding theory in languages that allow cliticization. Quite generally, full pronouns in these languages do not observe principle (B) (e.g., such examples as "Giovanni fu arrestato lui"; cf. chapter 2, note 122). Perhaps full pronouns in languages with the clitic option should be regarded as somehow emphatic, thus immune to principle (B) of the binding theory. It might be that the question of when pronouns are used in the subject position in pro-drop languages is also relevant in this connection.

In English too there are well-known examples similar to (1), e.g., (2), (3):[7]

(2)   (i) John always keeps his wits about him (*himself, *Bill)
       (ii) the melody has a haunting character to it (*itself, *Bill)
       (iii) John likes to take his work home with him (*himself, *Bill)
(3)   (i) John pushed the book away from him
       (ii) John drew the book towards him
       (iii) John turned his friends against him
       (iv) John saw a snake near him

In the examples (2), a proximate pronoun is obligatory; in (3), it is optional. Judgments tend to waver as to whether a proximate pronoun or a reciprocal should be used in some of the examples of type (3), and obscure factors enter into preference one way or another (e.g., there is a strong preference, perhaps necessity, for a pronoun in (3iv)). Thus, compare (3iii) with (4):

(4)   John turned the argument against himself (**him*, where the reference is to John)

One might argue that in the cases where reflexives are excluded, PP is a governing category. If this is correct, then reciprocals also should be excluded. Judgments again are often unclear, though in some cases the correlation is reasonably straightforward: compare (3iii), (4) with (5i,ii), where we consider only the interpretation with *each other* bound by the subject:[8]

(5)   (i) *they turned their friends against each other
       (ii) they turned the arguments against each other

A proper theory dealing with these matters should explain the choice of elements and also the haziness of the judgments concerning them in many cases.

It is tempting to suppose that such examples as (3), at least, should be treated as analogous to (6):

(6)   (i) John considers Mary angry at him (*himself, *her, herself)
       (ii) John strikes Mary as angry at himself (*him, her, *herself)

Again, we consider only the proximate interpretation of the pronoun. In these cases, it is reasonable to assume that there is an embedded clause at LF-representation (and, assuming the projection principle, at every level of representation). The representations are then of the form (7), as we have assumed earlier:[9]

(7)   (i) John considers [Mary angry at him]
        (ii) John $_i$ strikes Mary [t $_i$ as angry at himself]

Correspondingly, one might argue that in case (3iv), the representation at LF is something like (8), where *John* controls PRO, which is the subject of the predication *near him*:

(8)   John saw a snake [$_S$ PRO near him]

The idea might be worked out in various ways.

    While not implausible in the case of (8), this idea seems quite inappropriate in the other cases illustrated in (2), (3), which suggests that it is on the wrong track, at least as an attempt at a general account of the phenomenon under review. Manzini (1980) shows on the basis of comparative evidence that the plausibility in case (8) is also perhaps illusory. Consider the Italian analogues to (6i), (3iv)–(9) and (10), respectively:

(9)   Gianni considera Maria arrabbiata con lui (*se, *se stesso)
(10)   Gianni vide un serpente vicino a lui (se, *se stesso)

Italian has two reflexive elements, *se* and *se stesso*, corresponding roughly to the English element *X-self*. Manzini observes that the distribution of *se stesso* is a subclass of that of *se* and that the restrictions on the former do not relate to the theory of binding. She suggests further that the English form *X-self* corresponds more closely to *se stesso* than to *se*, and that the same irrelevant reasons that bar occurrence of *se stesso* in (10) bar *himself* in (3iv), even though reflexive is structurally permitted in this case as (10) illustrates. In contrast, reflexive is barred in (9), hence also (6i) (correspondingly, (6ii)), by the binding theory. Examples (9) and (10) argue against a unified treatment of (3iv) and (6); the apparent similarities may be an artifact based on peculiarities of English reflexivization. It is highly doubtful, then, that such facts as (3iv) should be used as the basis for any structural argument.

    Manzini suggests that PP, like other categories, has a kind of PRO subject functioning as an agreement element, and that PP is a governing category, allowing pronouns and anaphors accordingly, a suggestion with implications that she explores. It follows, then, that (11) should be possible in English, with the reciprocal bound by the subject:

(11)   they saw snakes near each other

Again, judgments tend to be uncertain, as throughout this category of examples, quite commonly. In any event, it is doubtful that (3iv) is to be treated as a case of control, with the binding theory invoked in the manner of (7).[10]

Another problem concerning prepositional phrases, which has given rise to much productive work in recent years, is the problem of preposition stranding, as in (12), (13):

(12)   (i) who did John speak to
        (ii) who did John give the book to
        (iii) *which meal did John speak to Bill after
(13)   (i) Tom was spoken to
        (ii) *Tom was given the book to
        (iii) *the meal was spoken to Bill after

In a review of comparative evidence, van Riemsdijk (1978b) observes that preposition stranding is a relatively rare and presumably marked phenomenon, and that stranding after NP-movement, as in (13), is a subcase of stranding after *wh*-movement, as in (12); a fact illustrated in (12)–(13). He develops an analysis of the phenomenon on the assumption that certain PPs have a COMP position that serves as an "escape hatch" for movement, an assumption that has overt correlates in Dutch and more marginally in English. Weinberg and Hornstein (1978), basing themselves in part on work by B.E. Dresher, note that stranding is restricted to PPs that are within the VP, as in (12i,ii) as contrasted with (12iii). They propose that a reanalysis rule within the VP creates a complex verb including the preposition, the NP object of the preposition becoming the object of the complex derived verb, hence accessible to movement in the normal way; movement of the object of a preposition that is not reanalyzed in this way (in particular, in a PP that is outside the VP, hence not accessible to reanalysis) is excluded by a filter that blocks empty oblique elements, assuming that P assigns oblique Case while verbs assign objective Case (cf. OB). They argue in forthcoming work that no phrasal reanalysis is required; rather, the relation of the verb to the object of a preposition in a PP within the VP may be treated as an instance of "thematic raising" along the lines of Rouveret and Vergnaud (1980). NP-movement from a prepositional phrase is further constrained by a requirement that the remaining phrase be a possible predicate, as in (13i) but not (13ii,iii). Cf. Davison (1980) for extensive discussion of the range of examples in English.

The possibility of analyzing preposition stranding within the framework of the theories of Case, government and binding has been explored in several papers by Kayne. In Kayne (1979b) an approach to preposition stranding is outlined in terms of Case theory. Suppose we assume (in accordance with OB) that "inherent Case," including now the Case assigned by prepositions, is assigned at D-structure and that "structural Case," including the Case assigned by verbs in the unmarked case, is assigned at S-structure.[11] Suppose further that English has lost the inherent Case system; thus prepositions do not assign inherent oblique Case but rather structural objective Case, as do verbs. In French, Italian, and other languages that do not allow preposition stranding,[12] prepositions assign oblique Case. The marked character of preposition stranding would then follow from the presumably marked loss of oblique Case-assignment.

On these assumptions, consider preposition stranding in, say, French and Italian, in the case of *wh*-movement. Assuming that Case is carried along (as are all features) under *wh*-movement, then the remaining trace will lack Case. It will also not be assigned structural Case, and hence will lack Case at S-structure and LF. If variables must have Case (cf. § 3.2.2), then the structures are barred. In English, in contrast, structural Case will be assigned to the NP governed by a preposition, so that stranding is possible.

To accommodate Weinberg and Hornstein's observation, we may modify Kayne's suggestion slightly, assuming that the Case system is lost in English only within VP, whereas PPs that are immediate constituents of S have inherent Case-marking, accounting for the distinction between (12i,ii) and (12iii).

Kayne extends this analysis to preposition stranding in passives on the basis of the following assumptions:

(14)　(i) Case-marked trace must be bound by an operator such as a *wh*-phrase

　　　(ii) NP-movement is N^3-movement in the sense of Siegel (1974) (hence leaving Case behind on the trace) as distinct from *wh*-movement, which is N^4-movement, taking Case with it

　　　(iii) Reanalysis follows inherent Case-assignment

Assumption (i), along with the assumption that the trace of *wh*- (along with other variables) must have Case, amounts to identifying Case-marked trace as a variable. Cf. § 3.2.2. Assumption (ii) is defended in Siegel (1974); one consequence is Emonds' structure-preserving hypothesis for NP-movement, by virtue of the Case Filter, since NP-movement that is not structure-preserving will yield NP without Case in S-structure.[13] Assumption (iii) lacks independent motivation, but is not unreasonable.

Given these assumptions, suppose that a preposition assigns oblique Case in the base, as in French and Italian and, in general, the unmarked case. Then NP-movement, by virtue of (14ii), will leave trace with Case, which is impossible by (14i). Furthermore, by virtue of (14iii), even reanalysis of (15i) as (15ii) (as in English "*speak to* NP," "*take advantage of* NP"; also in French, for reasons that Kayne discusses) will not permit NP-movement, since it follows inherent Case-assignment:

(15)　(i) $V \ldots [_{PP} P \ NP]$

　　　(ii) $[_V V \ldots P] NP$

But in English, lacking inherent Case-assignment in VP, reanalysis will permit passive, since no structural Case is assigned by the passive participle

(16), for the usual reasons:

(16) $\left[\left[_{+V} \right] \text{en-V} \ldots P \right]$

Kayne extends the analysis to other languages, and notes that this approach assumes minimal parametric variation among languages and deals appropriately with marked constructions.

Assumption (14ii) can be given in a somewhat more natural form. Suppose, following Siegel, that NP is analyzed as $N^i + $ CASE ($i = 3$ in Siegel's theory, and NP $= N^4$), where CASE is an unfilled category of the base provided with its content by the Case-assignment rules. The rule Move-α can insert α only in the position of N^3, where the latter is empty in the base. If N^4 is moved into this position, then we derive (17), which we may take to be an impossible structure:

(17) $\left[_{N^4} N^3 \text{ CASE CASE} \right]$

Therefore, only N^3 can be moved to this position, leaving (18):

(18) $\left[_{N^4} \text{t Case} \right]$

As for *wh*-movement, if Move-α were to move the *wh*-phrase N^3 leaving CASE behind, then the *wh*-phrase will necessarily lack Case and will be blocked by the Case Filter (assuming that the problems concerning deletion of the *wh*-phrase can be overcome). Therefore, this is impossible, and *wh*-movement must move N^4. There is no need, then, to stipulate that NP-movement and *wh*-movement differ in this respect; their differences follow from Case theory.

Kayne (1980c) develops an interesting extension and modification of these ideas. Here he accepts in essence the Weinberg-Hornstein idea of reanalysis,[14] while retaining the assumption that P and V govern and assign Case in different ways in French, but in the same way in English. Specifically, V in general and P in English govern in the structural sense of the preceding discussion, assigning structural Case, while P in French (and in general in languages that lack preposition stranding) governs and Case-marks an NP inherently, say, at D-structure, but only when the NP is subcategorized by the preposition.

Why, then, does French lack the V . . . P reanalysis rule (however stated) that permits preposition stranding in English? As Kayne observes, French does have other reanalysis rules, e.g., V–V reanalysis as in causatives. He suggests the general principle that reanalysis involving two lexical categories is possible only if they govern in the same way. Thus, V–V reanalysis is possible in French and V . . . P reanalysis is possible in English, but V . . . P reanalysis is not possible in French.

Kayne then extends the same ideas to what appears to be quite a different class of distinctions between French and English, namely, those involving Exceptional Case-marking, e.g., (19):

(19)   (i) I believe [John to be the most intelligent of all]
        (ii) *je crois [Jean être le plus intelligent de tous]

In contrast to English, French requires that the embedded subject be PRO. There is, however, one exception, namely, (20):

(20)   quel garçon crois-tu [t être le plus intelligent de tous]
        ("which boy do you believe to be the most intelligent of all"]

Thus *croire* and similar verbs in French have the property that " . . V NP VP" is ungrammatical if NP is lexical and remains in place, but is grammatical if NP is a *wh*-phrase and is moved.[15] Crucially, Kayne notes, these facts distinguish the post-verbal NP here from the NP in other V-NP-X constructions, which never require that the NP be moved; e.g., normal transitives, or such structures as (21):

(21)   je crois Jean intelligent
        ("I believe John intelligent")

By the projection principle, (21) should have the form (22):

(22)   je crois [$_S$ Jean intelligent]

$\overline{S}$-deletion permits the embedded subject to remain, Case-marked by the matrix verb, and excludes PRO. But it then follows that there is no $\overline{S}$-deletion in the corresponding expressions (19ii), (20). As Kayne points out, "the odd property of 'V NP VP' illustrated by (19ii) vs. (20) is doomed to remain inexplicable if that NP is analyzed as the true object of V,"[16] that is, if the structure is (23):

(23)   [$_{VP}$ V NP VP]

Thus we have additional evidence for the projection principle, and for the analysis of (19) with the clausal bracketing as indicated.
    This leaves two questions:

(24)   (i) What is the explanation for (20):
        (ii) What is the nature of the brackets in (19)?

As for the bracketing of (19ii) and (20), it must be $\overline{S}$, as noted. I have been assuming that in the English example (19i), $\overline{S}$-deletion has taken place, a marked property of English *believe* and similar verbs. Kayne assumes, in contrast, that there is no $\overline{S}$-deletion in these cases, but rather a zero complementizer $\emptyset$, which is prepositional and both governs and assigns Case, a complementizer analogous to *for* – essentially, the analysis of Chomsky and Lasnik (1977), as Kayne notes. Let us assume this to be so. Then French and English do not differ in the structures assigned to (19): in each case, there is a $\emptyset$-complementizer. Our two problems (24) are now rephrased as (25):

(25)   (i) What is the explanation for (20)?
       (ii) Why does the $\emptyset$-complementizer in (19) govern and assign Case in English (19i) but not in French (19ii)?

Kayne proposes that the basic difference between French and English is, once again, that in English the preposition (in this case, $\emptyset$) governs and assigns Case in the same structural manner as a verb, whereas in French a preposition governs and assigns Case only inherently to an NP in its subcategorization frame, so that $\emptyset$ neither governs nor assigns Case to the subject of the infinitival construction in (19ii). Hence question (25ii) reduces to the same principle that accounts for preposition stranding; a single distinction between French and English accounts for their differing behavior with regard to preposition stranding and Exceptional Case-marking. There is no difference between English *believe* and French *croire*, but rather a difference in the way prepositions govern in English and French.

This leaves question (25i): what is the explanation for (20)? Note that under the theory of successive-cyclic *wh*-movement, the S-structure of (20) is actually (26):

(26)   quel garçon crois-tu $[_{\bar{S}}$ t $\emptyset[_{S}$ t' être le plus intelligent de tous$]]$

The position of t' is the D-structure position of *quel garçon*, which is moved to the position of t and then to its S-structure position in the COMP of the matrix sentence. Suppose that we now revise the notion of government (hence, Case-assignment) slightly, allowing V (and other categories) to govern across one S-type boundary but not two such boundaries. Then *croire* in (26) governs and assigns Case to the trace t in COMP in (26).[17] Thus *quel garçon* in (26) receives Case by inheritance from its trace and the Case Filter is satisfied. Therefore, (20) is grammatical but not (19ii), answering question (25i).

Recall that we had been led earlier to assume that a trace can assume (rather than transmit) a θ-role only if it has Case. Cf. § 3.2.2. In (26), however, t' lacks Case but must assume a θ-role. Once again, we are led to the conclusion that Case is assigned to an index, then optionally assumed by an element with that index; cf. §§ 3.2.2, 4.5.[18] Then t' can inherit Case from t, and we can retain the idea that a trace is "visible" in the LF-component only if it has Case, one way of dealing with the idea that variables are in effect Case-marked traces.

Compare (26) with (27), derived by cyclic *wh*-movement:

(27) (i) *who did you try $[_\bar{S}$ t $[_S$ t' to win$]]$
  (ii) *the man $[$(who) you tried $[_\bar{S}$ t $[_S$ t' to win$]]$

Assuming that *try* (like *seem*, but unlike *believe, croire*) is intransitive, the trace *t* in the COMP position of (27), while governed, will not receive Case. Therefore *t'* will not inherit Case so that the θ-criterion is violated. The same would be true, for example, in (28), since the adjective *certain* is not a Case-assigner:

(28) (i) *who is it certain $[_\bar{S}$ t $[_S$ t' to win$]]$
  (ii) *the man $[$(who)$]$ it is certain $[_\bar{S}$ t $[_S$ t' to win$]]$

This analysis of (19), (20) naturally raises the question whether French has an infinitival complementizer analogous to English *for*. Kayne argues that the elements *de, di* in French and Italian, respectively, are complementizers analogous to English *for*, taking infinitival complements. But, once again, English *for* differs from French *de* (or Italian *di*) in that it governs and assigns Case to the subject of its infinitival complement. Thus we have the situation illustrated in (29), (30):[19]

(29) (i) it would be a pity $[_\bar{S}$ for $[_S$ something to happen to him$]]$
  (ii) *ce serait dommage $[_\bar{S}$ de $[_S$ quelque chose lui arriver$]]$
(30) (i) *it would be a pity $[_\bar{S}$ for $[_S$ PRO to leave now$]]$
  (ii) ce serait dommage $[_\bar{S}$ de $[_S$ PRO partir maintenant$]]$

In (29i), *for* governs and assigns Case to *something*, satisfying the Case Filter. But the Case Filter is violated in (29ii), since *de* does not assign Case to *quelque chose*. In contrast, (30i) is excluded since PRO is governed by *for*, whereas (30ii) is grammatical since PRO is ungoverned.

Again, the difference between English and French (or Italian) illustrated by (29), (30) reduces to the same distinction in the behavior of prepositions that accounts for preposition stranding and Exceptional Case-marking. Kayne's analysis thus shows how a single parameter of UG accounts for a variety of properties of the two language types, while providing further evidence for the projection principle, successive cyclic movement and several other principles.

The proposed analysis of Exceptional Case-marking raises certain problems, however. One problem arises in connection with such examples as (31):

(31) (i) *him to be here is hard to believe
  (ii) *what is hard to believe is him to be here

In the framework of Chomsky and Lasnik (1977), examples (31) are blocked by the *[NP-*to*-VP] filter, but the latter has now been eliminated in favor of the Case Filter. If the $\emptyset$-complementizer assigns Case, there is no obvious explanation for (31). A second problem is raised by the examples (32):

(32)   (i) who did you believe Bill to have seen
    (ii) who would you prefer for Bill to have seen
    (iii) who did you want Bill to have seen

At S-structure, the analyses are, in each case, of the form (33):

(33)   who did you V $[_{\bar{S}} [_{COMP} t \; \alpha] [_{S}$ Bill to have seen t$]]$

In (32i), $\alpha = \emptyset$; in (32ii), $\alpha = for$; in (32iii), $\alpha = for$, subject to later deletion in the PF-component, or $\alpha = \emptyset$, an optional alternative to *for* for such verbs. In each case, α governs and assigns Case to *Bill*.

But consider again the passives corresponding to (32), namely, (34):

(34)   (i) Bill was believed to have seen Tom
    (ii) *Bill was preferred for to have seen Tom
    (iii) *Bill was wanted to have seen Tom

In § 4.4 we suggested dealing with this class of cases by assuming that *for* is not a proper governor, perhaps as a special case of the principle that the only proper governors are the lexical categories (cf. 4.5.(54)–(55). Then the examples (34ii,iii) are barred by ECP while (34i) is admitted because of $\bar{S}$-deletion. To accommodate this proposal in Kayne's framework, we would have to assume that while *for* is not a proper governor (and perhaps, no preposition is a proper governor), still $\emptyset$ is a proper governor. To account for (31), we would have to stipulate further that $\emptyset$ is a Case-assigner only in immediate post-verbal position. This virtually amounts to accepting the $\bar{S}$-deletion hypothesis for Exceptional Case-marking and raises some doubts as to whether an analysis assuming a $\emptyset$-complementizer is really the correct one. Kayne's approach to unifying preposition stranding and Exceptional Case-marking is, however, sufficiently attractive so that an attempt to resolve the remaining difficulties surely seems in order.

If we were to adopt the proposal in § § 4.4–5 that prepositions are not proper governors, then preposition stranding would be excluded in general. It would be permitted only in case a marked rule were to allow proper government by V. This line of thought leads us back to the Weinberg-Hornstein hypothesis that a rule R associating the verbal head of a VP and the prepositional head of a PP within this VP is responsible for the phenomenon of preposition stranding; R in effect permits the preposition to "transmit" proper government from the verbal head. Suppose we were to accept as well Kayne's suggestion that there is indeed a $\emptyset$-complementizer in the bare infinitival cases, and that $\emptyset$ is a governor in English so that the reanalysis is possible in accordance with his principle that reanalysis (the rule R) is associated with same style of government. But suppose we assume that $\emptyset$, while a governor, is not a Case-assigner. Case-assignment with a $\emptyset$-complementizer is possible, then, only when the rule R applies. This assumption will permit (32i) while barring (31), overcoming part of the problem.

It remains to account for (34). Suppose we were to assume that the reanalysis rule R in fact is applicable in both of the conditions of (35):

(35) (i) believe $[_{\bar{S}} \emptyset [_S \text{NP} \dots]]$
      (ii) want $[_{\bar{S}} \text{for} [_S \text{NP} \dots]]$

Then the position of NP is properly governed by the matrix verb in both cases. In the case of *wh*-movement, we derive (36):

(36) (i) who did John believe $[_{\bar{S}} \emptyset [_S t \text{ to have won}]]$
      (ii) who did John want $[_{\bar{S}} \text{for} [_S t \text{ to have won}]]$

Example (36i) is grammatical; the status of (36ii) depends on presence or absence of the *[for-to]* filter in the dialect in question. In dialects in which it is operative, (36ii) is replaced by the corresponding form with *for* deleted in the PF-component in immediate post-verbal position.

Turning to (34), recall that applicability of the rule R does not suffice to permit NP-movement under the assumptions we are now considering; some additional condition is also required. Thus we have such contrasts as (37):

(37) (i) who did you give the book to
      (ii) *John was given a book to

Weinberg and Hornstein assume that some notion of "possible predicate" is involved over and above proper government to permit passivization. Whether this is correct or not, it is clear that some further condition is required, since the NP-movement cases constitute a proper subcase of the *wh*-movement cases with preposition stranding. We might suppose that it is this extra condition that permits (34i) while assigning to (34ii,iii) the status of (37ii). It might be, for example, that *for*-deletion, which is in any event restricted to post-verbal context, does not apply in post-participle context, and that the presence of the overt complementizer suffices to invoke the condition that blocks passivization in (37ii). Perhaps some such approach is feasible.

There are a few additional problems to consider in this connection, for example, the status of (38):

(38) (i) I don't know who would be happy for whom to win the prize
          (= 4.1.(15iva))
      (ii) I don't know who would prefer for whom to win the race

In accordance with the discussion in chapter 4, the embedded *whom* must be properly governed in both (i) and (ii). Perhaps this results again from application of the rule *R* of reanalysis, so that the examples of (38) are, in effect, instances of preposition stranding to which the *[*for-to*] filter does not apply since the filter is in the PF-component.[20]

A final question has to do with the status of (39) in dialects such as Ozark English that lack the *[*for-to*] filter:

(39)   I'd prefer $[_\alpha$ for $[_\beta$ PRO to do it myself$]]$

Here PRO must be ungoverned, though in (36ii) the corresponding position of trace is governed. It may be that these dialects preserve an option in which α = PP and β = NP in (39), as proposed for earlier stages of the language in Lightfoot (1979). Lightfoot (1980) suggests rather that α = $\overline{S}$ and β = S in these cases, as in (36). If so, we are led to assume that the *for*-complementizer is optionally a governor.

5.3 Modifications of the ECP

Since the Pisa workshop of April 1979, there has been much productive study of the principle ECP of the theory of government, some of it incorporated into the preceding discussion. In the course of this work, a number of modifications have been proposed and the principle, in one or another form, has been brought to bear on a considerable range of phenomena. See particularly Kayne (1980b) and Jaeggli (1980b).

I have briefly discussed Kayne's proposal that verbs can govern a COMP across an $\overline{S}$ boundary. Suppose that we were to regard COMP as the head of $\overline{S}$, as is perhaps not unnatural if INFL is regarded as the head of S. The well-known COMP-INFL relations are then head-head relations, as is standard. Then the proposal is that a verb governs the head of the clause it governs. Suppose that we generalize this proposal to all categories. Then in place of our earlier assumption that maximal projections – in particular, NP and $\overline{S}$ – are absolute barriers to government, we have the principle (1):

(1)   The head of a maximal projection is accessible to an external governor but peripheral positions[21] are not

This formulation is proposed in Belletti and Rizzi (1980), where consequences are investigated with regard to the theory of government, and in relation to properties of bounding (subjacency).[22] In particular, it follows that the matrix verb governs the COMP of the embedded $\overline{S}$, as in the examples previously discussed, and also that a verb governs the nominal head of an NP that it governs. Belletti and Rizzi exploit this idea to deal with a variety of cases of subject vs. object asymmetry, including cases that had been discussed by Belletti in terms of the binding theory of the OB-framework. They take the basic asymmetry to be one of government: elements in the VP are governed by V, while the pre-verbal subject position is ungoverned.[23]

From these two assumptions – namely, that verbal complements but not pre-verbal subjects are governed, and (1) – a number of interesting consequences follow. Belletti and Rizzi consider the paradigms (2) and (3):

(2) (i) tre settimane passano rapidamente
       ("three weeks pass rapidly")
     (ii) tre passano rapidamente
       ("three pass rapidly")
     (iii) *tre ne passano rapidamente
       ("three of-them pass rapidly")
(3) (i) Gianni passerà tre settimane a Milano
       ("Gianni will spend three weeks in Milan")
     (ii) *Gianni passerà tre a Milano
       ("Gianni will spend three in Milan")
     (iii) Gianni ne passerà tre a Milano
       ("Gianni of-them will spend three in Milan")

Thus, *ne*-cliticization is permitted from the object position (3iii) but not the subject position (2iii); in contrast, zero-pronominalization is possible in the subject position (2ii) but not the object position (3ii).

These observations follow at once from the two assumptions, given the framework so far established. In (2ii), the subject is (4), where the nominal head is PRO (following Kayne (1980b)), and in (2iii) the subject is (5), where the nominal head is the trace of *ne*-cliticization, a movement rule:

(4) $[_{NP} \text{tre PRO}]$
(5) $[_{NP} \text{tre t}]$

Given that the subject is ungoverned, PRO and trace are ungoverned in (4) and (5) even though by assumption (1) they are accessible to external government. Therefore, (4) is possible in (2ii) but (5) is impossible in (2iii), by the binding theory and ECP, respectively.[24] In (3ii), the object is (4), and in (3iii) it is (5). Since the nominal head is governed by the verb in accordance with assumption (1), (4) is inadmissible in (3ii) by the binding theory since PRO would be governed, but (5) is acceptable in (3iii) since it is in a properly governed position so that ECP is satisfied.

These examples again illustrate the contrast between trace and PRO discussed in § 2.4.1 and subsequently.

Belletti and Rizzi show that these results extend to other constructions: where NP is ungoverned, (4) is possible, and where it is governed, it is impossible. Thus we have (6), where (4) is in Topic position, and (7), where the subject is governed by Aux in COMP (cf. Rizzi (1979b)):

(6)   (di libri), $[_{TOP}[_{NP}$ tre PRO$]]$, credo che li leggerò domani
       ("(of books), three, I think that I will read them tomorrow")

(7)   *(di libri), $[_{\bar{S}}[_{COMP}$ essendo$]$ $[_S$ $[_{NP}$ tre PRO$]$ usciti l'anno
       scorso$]]$, . . .
       ("of books), three having come out last year, . . . ")

The principle (1) subsumes Kayne's principle that government can cross one S-type boundary but not two such boundaries. In fact, α may govern β in (8) but not in (9), in accordance with (1), whether or not γ is null:

(8)   (i) $\alpha [_S \beta \ldots]$
       (ii) $\alpha [_{\bar{S}} \beta [_S \ldots]]$
(9) $\alpha [_{\bar{S}} \gamma [_S \beta \ldots]]$

Thus in (10), the trace t in COMP is governed by *try* on these assumptions, but PRO is not:

(10)   what did you try $[_{\bar{S}} t [_S$ PRO to do $t']]$

As we saw in the preceding section, t is not assigned Case by *try* in (10). We face certain problems in connection with such examples as (11):

(11)   who did you believe Bill to have seen

Assuming Kayne's proposal discussed in the preceding section, the S-structure of (11) is (12):

(12)   who did you believe $[_{\bar{S}}[_{COMP} t \emptyset][_S$ Bill to have seen $t]]$

The representation is analogous to that of (13):

(13)   (i) who would you prefer for Bill to have seen
       (ii) who would you prefer $[_{\bar{S}} [_{COMP} t$ for$] [_S$ Bill to have seen $t]]$

In (12), we must assume that Case is assigned to the trace in COMP, in accordance with Kayne's analysis of 5.2.(26). But then it would seem to follow that Case must also be assigned to the trace in COMP in (13), so that trace is not deletable by convention (or is not "invisible" to PF-component rules, under a different convention). This conclusion raises a variety of problems. In the first place, it is inconsistent with the analysis of contraction suggested by Kayne and others and adopted earlier (cf. § 3.2.2. (36)–(40)). Secondly, both $\emptyset$ and *for* must govern and assign Case to the embedded subject *Bill* in (12), (13), though they will not c-command it if the trace in COMP is not deleted. These observations suggest that the trace in COMP is not assigned Case in (12), (13). If so, then the question raised in 5.2.(25i) remains unanswered. Perhaps the point is that Case-assignment into COMP is a secondary phenomenon as suggested at the end of §4.3, and that such structures as 5.2.(20) have a status similar to those of 4.3.(18)–(23).

Example (13ii) raises a question (noted by Howard Lasnik) concerning the subjacency condition. If the trace is deleted at S-structure, then subjacency cannot be an output condition as suggested by Freidin (1978) and Koster (1978b), but rather must be a condition on the movement rules themselves. It remains a possibility to regard subjacency as a condition on S-structure representation applying before trace-deletion, if stylistic rules in the PF-component and movement rules in the LF-component are not subject to this condition. Alternatively, the presence of trace must not block government by *for* in (13ii).

Consider the status of trace in COMP with regard to ECP, as in (14):

(14)   who do you think $[_{\bar{S}} t \, [_{S} t' \text{ saw Bill}]]$

Is t subject to ECP? One might answer in the negative, on the assumption that ECP holds only for trace in A-positions. But let us suppose that the answer is positive. Then it is necessary to eliminate the $\bar{S}$ boundary in (14) if, as we have now assumed tentatively, we do not have government into COMP in the unmarked case. Suppose, then, that there is an optional rule replacing an $\bar{S}$-boundary by an S-boundary, so that if this option is taken, (14) becomes (15):

(15)   who do you think $[_{S} t \, [_{S} t' \text{ saw Bill}]]$

Note that the $\bar{S}$-to-S rule subsumes $\bar{S}$-deletion. That is, if $\bar{S}$ is replaced by S and COMP is missing we have (16), which reduces to (17) in the restrictive theory of Lasnik and Kupin (1977):

(16) $\ldots [_{S} [_{S} \ldots]] \ldots$
(17) $\ldots [_{S} \ldots] \ldots$

If the $\bar{S}$-to-S rule applies to (14), giving (15), then t is properly governed, satisfying ECP. If the rule does not apply, then (14) is ill-formed, assuming that trace in non-argument position is subject to ECP.

An obvious question is whether the phenomenon of bridge verbs in the sense of Erteschik (1973) is accommodated in these terms on the assumption that certain matrix verbs permit the $\bar{S}$-to-S rule while others do not. Those that do permit $\bar{S}$-to-S allow successive-cyclic movement satisfying ECP. Verbs with infinitival complements are invariably bridge verbs; thus the $\bar{S}$-to-S rule is always an option in these cases. Whatever the factors and language differences may be in connection with the possibility of successive-cyclic movement, it seems that the phenomenon might be described in these terms.

Consider the implications of these assumptions for control verbs such as *try*. To permit the sentence (10) we must apply the $\bar{S}$-to-S rule, giving the S-structure (18):

(18)   what did you try $\left[_{S} t \left[_{S} \text{PRO to do } t' \right]\right]$

If t deletes at S-structure, then (18) presumably reduces to (19), which is illegitimate since PRO is now governed by *try*:

(19)   what did you try $\left[_{S} \text{PRO to do } t' \right]$

Therefore t must remain in (18).[25] In (18) no maximal projection intervenes between *try* and PRO, raising the question why *try* does not govern PRO thus barring the sentence. We might invoke Kayne's principle that government cannot cross two S-type boundaries, or, we might once again build the notion "minimal c-command" into the definition of government; cf. § 3.2.1. Then *try* does not govern PRO because PRO is c-commanded by t. The latter move is also suggested by cases of apparent multiple government under this analysis of their bridge verb phenomenon. Consider (20), after the application of the $\bar{S}$-to-S rule:

(20)   NP V $\left[_{S} \text{NP}' \text{ INFL VP} \right]$

Here NP' is multiply governed if INFL contains AGR, but clearly it is only the government by INFL that is relevant to Case assignment. Again, the problem would be overcome by introducing a minimality requirement into the concept of government.

Suppose that contrary to the assumptions above we take trace-deletion in COMP to be obligatory in such structures as (18). Then the $\bar{S}$-to-S rule cannot apply to yield (18) or we will derive (19) in which PRO is governed. Continuing to maintain the assumption that trace in COMP must be governed (and accounting for the bridge phenomenon in these terms), we must therefore assume that the S-structure corresponding to (19) is formed by a single "long movement" of *what* from the position of t', crossing the internal boundary $\left[_{\bar{S}} \right._{S}$. Therefore the sentence (19) should have the acceptability status of a *wh*-island violation, which it certainly does not.

The problem would be resolved if we were to look at the matter of subjacency in a slightly different way. Suppose that we replace the base rule (21i), which we have so far been assuming, by (21ii):

(21)   (i) $\bar{S} \rightarrow \text{COMP S}$
        (ii) $\bar{S} \rightarrow (\text{COMP}) \text{ S}$

We retain the same rules as before for analysis of COMP: COMP may be $[\pm WH]$, where $[-WH] = that$ in English, or it may be *for* (or French *de*, Italian *di*, if Kayne's analysis discussed in § 5.2 is correct), presumably a marked option. In addition we have rules relating COMP and INFL, in part presupposed though not explicitly given in our earlier discussion:

(22)   (i) INFL is $[+ \text{Tense}]$ only if $\bar{S}$ contains COMP
        (ii) INFL is $[+ \text{Tense}]$ if COMP is $[-WH]$
        (iii) INFL is $[- \text{Tense}]$ if COMP is *for*

Let us now characterize bounding nodes as follows:[26]

(23)   (i) $\bar{S}$ is a bounding node if and only if it is in the context: $-[\pm WH]$
        (ii) S is a bounding node if and only if it is in the context: $[\pm WH]-$

Thus in (24), both $\bar{S}$ and S are bounding nodes, but in (25), neither is a bounding node:

(24) $[_{\bar{S}}[\pm WH][_S \ldots]]$
(25)   (i) $[_{\bar{S}}[_S \ldots]]$
        (ii) $[_{\bar{S}} \text{for} [_S \ldots]]$

We might assume (23i) to be general, while (23ii) is an option for certain varieties of English.

    Returning to the problematic example (19), we can now accommodate the bridge character of the matrix verb without resort to the $\bar{S}$-to-S rule. At D-structure, (19) has the form (26), yielding the S-structure (27) after *wh*-movement:

(26)   you tried $[_{\bar{S}}[_S \text{PRO to do what}]]$
(27)   what did you try $[_{\bar{S}}[_S \text{PRO to do t}]]$

Since neither $\bar{S}$ nor S is a bounding category in accordance with (23), one-step *wh*-movement is consistent with the subjacency condition and there is no trace in the embedded COMP at any stage. Since $\bar{S}$ is still present in (27), *try* does not govern PRO. On the same assumptions, we derive such S-structures as (28):[27]

(28)   (i) who did John expect $[_S \text{Bill to see t}]$
        (ii) who did John want $[_{\bar{S}}[_S \text{PRO to see t}]]$

In (28i), *expect* governs *Bill*, but in (28ii), *want* does not govern PRO and contraction is possible.

    Consider (29):

(29)   *who did you try $[_{\bar{S}}[_S \text{t to leave}]]$

This is not a subjacency violation, but it violates ECP, which therefore guarantees that variables have Case in such structures. Note that the S-structure (30) is now excluded by ECP applying to t:

(30)   who did you try $[_{\bar{S}} t [_S \ldots t' \ldots]]$

An approach of this sort might be workable, tying together a number of phenomena.

In § 2.4.1, we noted that the status of such sentences as (31) is apparently determined by the subjacency condition:

(31)   *John seems $[_{\bar{S}}$ that $[_S$ it is certain $[_S t$ to like ice cream $]]]$
         (=2.4.1.(9vii))

As noted there, the conclusion raises problems. In English dialects with S as a bounding node, (31) is a subjacency violation, though even in this case the conclusion is problematic since its status is plainly less acceptable than many *wh*-island violations that involve S as a bounding node. And in Italian, or English dialects lacking S as a bounding node, (31) does not count as a subjacency violation on our present assumptions. Suppose we were to try to deal with the problem by modifying (23ii), now requiring that S be a bounding node invariably in the context (32i), but allowing parametric variation in the context (32ii) (this being the parameter determining the *wh*-island condition):

(32)   (i) $[-WH] -$
         (ii) $[+WH] -$

Then (31) is a subjacency violation independently of the status of the embedded S boundary.

These assumptions, however, are unacceptable, for consider (33):

(33)   *John$_i$ is clear $[_{\bar{S}}$ to whom $[_S$ it seems $[_S t_i$ to like ice cream $]]]$

Where S is not a bounding node (e.g., in Italian, according to Rizzi's analysis, which we have been assuming throughout), structures such as (33) should then be grammatical, which is false. The problem is to distinguish between (33) and (34), which is permissible in a language that does not observe *wh*-island violations, with t the trace of *what* and t' the trace of *to whom*:

(34)   what does John know $[_{\bar{S}}$ to whom $[_S$ Bill gave t $t']]$

We would have to assume that the structure (35) is an absolute barrier to NP-movement into an A-position (as in (33)), but not an absolute barrier to *wh*-movement to COMP (as in (34)):

(35) $[_{\bar{S}}$ to whom $[_{S}$

This seems hardly plausible.

The obvious alternative seems to be that it really is the embedded S boundary that counts as a bounding node in (31), irrespective of the *wh*-island phenomenon. This conclusion suggests that we replace (23) by (36):

(36) (i) $\bar{S}$ is a bounding node in the context:$-[\ \pm WH\ ]$
    (ii) S is a bounding node in the context: $[\pm WH\ ]-$
    (iii) S is a bounding node when governed

Case (iii) distinguishes between raising and control, assuming $\bar{S}$-deletion for raising predicates. The *wh*-island parameter now involves (36ii). Where (36ii) holds, we have *wh*-island violations.[28]

In accordance with (36), (33) and (34) differ crucially because of the presence of the most deeply embedded clause (governed by *seem*) in (33); and (31) and (33) are barred irrespective of the status of *wh*-island violations.

This suggestion has numerous ramifications. Consider, for example, the D-structure (37) in Italian:

(37) i libri che sai $[_{\bar{S}} [_{COMP} [+ WH]] [_{S} [_{NP} e]$ pareva $[$a quanta gente$]$
    $[_{\bar{S}} COMP [_{S}$ Piero aver prestato *wh-*$]]]]$
    ("the books that you know $[_{\bar{S}} [_{COMP} [+ WH]] [_{S} [_{NP} e]$ seemed
    [to how many people] $[_{\bar{S}} COMP [_{S}$ Piero to have lent *wh-*$]]]]$")

With *wh*-movement of *a quanta gente* to the $[+ WH]$ COMP, NP-movement of *Piero* to $[_{NP} e]$, and *wh*-movement of *wh-* to the COMP position of *che*, we derive (38):

(38) i libri che sai $[_{\bar{S}}$ a quanta gente $[_{S}$ Piero pareva t $[_{\bar{S}}$ COMP $[_{S}$ t' aver
    prestato t''$]]]]$
    ("the books that you know to how many people Piero seemed to have lent")

In (38), *t* is the trace of *a quanta gente*, *t'* is the trace of *Piero*, and *t''* is the trace of the relative. If the *wh*-island phenomenon is related to the status of S as a bounding node, then (38) should presumably be grammatical, since after $\bar{S}$-deletion in the most deeply embedded clause, the only bounding node is the $\bar{S}$ following *sai*. If (36) is correct, however, then (37) should be ungrammatical irrespective of the *wh*-island phenomenon since the most deeply embedded S is a bounding node after $\bar{S}$-deletion by virtue of (36iii). In fact, (38) should have the same status as (39):

(39) i libri che sai a quanta gente Piero diceva di aver prestato

("the books that you know to how many people Piero said to have lent")

In the latter case, the subject of *aver prestato* is PRO; (39) is a control structure as compared with the raising structure (38). Both (38) and (39) should be ungrammatical, on the assumption that relative movement is in a single step.

Suppose, however, that relative movement is successive cyclic in these cases. According to the theory of Rizzi (1978b), (39) is still ungrammatical, since movement from the *di*-clause to the matrix position (which must be in a single step because of the internal *wh*-movement to COMP in the medial clause with a $[+\text{WH}]$ COMP) is blocked by the two intervening $\bar{\text{S}}$-nodes. But it might be argued that (38) should be grammatical, with the following derivation: first, the element *wh-* in (37) moves to the most deeply embedded COMP; second, the $\bar{\text{S}}$-to-S rule applies after *pareva*; third, the *wh*-element moves in a single step to the matrix COMP of the relative clause, now crossing only a single $\bar{\text{S}}$-node. Then even if $[_{\bar{\text{S}}}\text{-}t\text{-}[_{\text{S}}$ collapses to $[_{\text{S}}$ in the most deeply embedded clause, making it a bounding node in the sense of (36iii), this will not affect the derivation.

I am not sure what the facts are in such cases in Italian – or in French, where the same situation should obtain – so I will leave the matter in this inconclusive state.

Consider finally such examples as (40):

(40)   in which room did you say that John saw Bill t

What is the status of the trace of *in which room*, with regard to ECP? One possibility is that the underlying structure is (41), so that V properly governs the trace in accordance with one of the definitions of "government" considered in § 3.2.1:

(41)   NP INFL $[_{\overline{\text{VP}}}[_{\text{VP}} \text{V} \dots]$ in which room$]$

Another possibility is that ECP holds only of NP, as suggested by Jaeggli (1980b); cf. § 4.6.

As should be obvious, these remarks are intended to be at most suggestive. Various proposals have been considered that are not mutually consistent, and none has been worked out in requisite detail or with sufficient attention to consequences. Furthermore, the range of relevant phenomena has barely been sampled. My intention has been only to review a number of options that might be further explored.

5.4. Complex adjectival constructions

Since the origins of work in generative grammar, considerable attention has been given to such constructions as (1):

(1)   (i) John is easy to please
       (ii) John is an easy person to please

Nevertheless, they still pose unresolved problems. Let's ask what form some of these problems take in the context of the GB-theory.

I will assume here the approach to these constructions outlined in Chomsky (1977b), where they are included among those that exhibit the basic properties of *wh*-movement. It is particularly natural to assume in this case that the embedded phrase *to please* in (1) is a residue of a clause that has undergone something like *wh*-movement, since the *wh*-phrase may in fact be overt in constructions of the form (1ii), e.g., (2):

(2)   (i) this is an easy violin on which to play sonatas
       (ii) this is a pleasant room in which to work

Assuming that the constructions (1i) and (1ii) are related – perhaps, by extraposition of the residual clause *to please* of (1ii) from the adjectival phrase *easy to please* (similarly in (2)) – it follows that the underlying structure of the complement of the adjective *easy*, *pleasant*, etc., is a clause with a moved element in the COMP position leaving a trace as variable. In accordance with earlier discussion, let us assume that in (1i) the embedded clause has been subject to movement of PRO from the base structure (3i), giving the S-structure (3ii):

(3)   (i) John is $[_{AP}$ easy $[_{\bar{S}}$ COMP $[_S$ PRO to please PRO$]]]$
       (ii) John is $[_{AP}$ easy $[_{\bar{S}}$ PRO$_i$ $[_S$ PRO to please t$_i]]]$

The embedded subject PRO is arbitrary in reference, with an index distinct from i, by the binding theory. The embedded trace is a variable since it is $\bar{A}$-bound. PRO in COMP is coindexed with *John*.

Pursuing the analysis of (1), we reach a paradox of θ-theory. There is good evidence that the matrix subject *John* is lexically-inserted into its S-structure position.[29] The matrix subject position must, therefore, be a θ-position, as is the position of the variable t_i in (3ii). We therefore expect it to be resistant to idiom chunks and other non-arguments, as illustrated in (4), as compared with (5) (*t* the trace of the subject throughout):

(4)   (i) *good care is hard to take t of the orphans
       (ii) *too much is hard to make t of that suggestion
       (iii) *there is hard to believe t to have been a crime committed[30]
(5)   (i) good care seems t to have been taken t of the orphans
       (ii) too much seems t to have been made t of that suggestion
       (iii) there is believed t to have been a crime committed t

In short, examples such as (1i) are not formed by movement from the embedded clause to the matrix subject position, and the latter is a θ-position.

But adjectives of the *easy*-category also take clausal complements that prevent the matrix subject position from being a θ-position, as in (6):

(6)   (i)   it is hard [to like John]
        (ii) it is pleasant for the rich [for the poor to do the hard work]

Therefore we have to assume a dual lexical categorization for these adjectives with clausal complements: the subject is a θ-position if and only if the complement does not undergo internal movement.[31] We are assuming that lexical properties are "checked" at the LF-level, though lexical items are inserted at the base. Therefore, there is no contradiction in the assumption of dual lexical entries, though it seems questionable and is a departure from the optimality assumptions that we have so far found to be tenable in discussing the projection principle and the θ-criterion. This is the first of several problems that arise in connection with constructions of the form (1).

Since movement-to-COMP takes place in the clausal complement to the adjective in (1i), the construction is an island for further movement under the subjacency condition, assuming S to be a bounding category for English or under the alternative approach suggested in § 5.3. Thus it is, in effect, a *wh*-island. We have such familiar examples as (7i,ii), formed by *wh*-movement from (8i,ii), respectively, where *t* is the trace of the *wh*-phrase in the matrix COMP:

(7)   (i)   *which sonatas are the violins easy [to play t on]
        (ii) *which people are the books easy [to convince t [to read]]
(8)   (i)   the violins are easy [to play the sonatas on]
        (ii) the books are easy [to convince people [to read]]

The examples of (7), then, are analogous to (9), (10):[32]

(9)   (i)   *who$_i$did you ask [what$_j$John had given t$_j$to t$_i$]
        (ii) you asked [what$_j$John had given t$_j$to him]
(10)   (i)   *what$_i$did you ask [who$_j$John had given t$_i$to t$_j$]
        (ii) you asked [who$_j$ John had given the books to t$_j$]

Again, some problems arise. Examples such as (7) are sometimes judged to be more unacceptable than corresponding *wh*-island violations, though the question is fairly murky. Another problem, exactly the contrary one, is that *wh*-movement of "peripheral phrases" is sometimes more acceptable than corresponding *wh*-island violations, as in (11):

(11)   which violins are the sonatas [easy to play on t]

Thus extraction of an "internal phrase" from a complex adjective construction seems to be too severe a violation, while extraction of a "peripheral phrase" is not a severe enough violation.

Complicating the situation further is the fact that "peripheral" *wh*-movement is sometimes far less acceptable than (11), as in (12), or completely ungrammatical, as in (13):

(12)   (i) which table is the book easy [to put on t]
       (ii) which garage is the car easy [to keep in t]
(13)   (i) *how intelligent is John possible [to consider (to be) t]
       (ii) *how intelligent is John possible [to think of (regard) as t]

The problem with (13) is not that the phrase *how intelligent* cannot be *wh*-moved from the embedded clause; compare (13) with (14), which, while hardly elegant, seem considerably more acceptable:

(14)   (i) how intelligent is it possible to consider John (to be)
       (ii) how intelligent is it possible to think of (regard) John as

It seems, then, that the complex adjective-complement construction raises further barriers to *wh*-extraction, over and above those that may assign a degree of unacceptability to (14). Examples (12), as contrasted with the more acceptable (11), illustrate that *wh*-movement of a "peripheral" clause is more unacceptable to the extent that the phrase is, in some sense, closely related to the verb.

We might unite these facts (which, again, are hardly crystal clear, though the phenomena appear to be real) by assuming that in examples such as (12) and (13) there is in the underlying structure a complex verb (15):

(15)   (i) [$_V$ V – [$_{PP}$ P NP]]   ("put – on the table,"
                                              "keep – in the garage")

       (ii) [$_V$ V – (. . .) adjective]   ("consider – (to be) intel-
                                              ligent," "think of (regard) –
                                              as intelligent")

The structures underlying (12) and (13), then, are as in (16), where *t* here is the trace ultimately associated with the matrix subject:

(16)   (i) the book is easy [to [$_V$ put on the table] t]
       (ii) John is easy [to [$_V$ consider intelligent] t]

These are analogous to (17):

(17)   (i) it is easy [to put on the table a book written by Tom]
       (ii) it is easy [to consider intelligent a person like Tom]

The assumption, then, is that *put on the table, consider intelligent* are reanalyzed in the base as complex verbs assigning Case to their objects *a book written by Tom, a person like Tom*, respectively.[33] This reanalysis is obligatory in such cases as (13), and is adopted with varying degrees of obligatoriness in such cases as (12), as the connection between the verb and its PP-complement varies. Then *wh*-extraction in (13) and (12) (with varying force) is a case of "internal" extraction like (7) rather than "peripheral" extraction like (11).

Summarizing, "internal" *wh*-extraction tends to be less acceptable than corresponding *wh*-island violations, while "peripheral" extraction tends to be more acceptable. A possible solution to the question of "peripheral" *wh*-extraction is suggested in Chomsky (1977b).

Still another problem is that adjective-complement constructions with matrix argument subject are impossible for the case analogous to (6ii); i.e., (18i) as contrasted with (18ii):

(18)   (i) *the hard work is pleasant for the rich [for the poor to do]
        (ii) the hard work is pleasant for the rich [to do][34]

An approach to this complex of problems that might be explored is one based on the assumption that the adjective-complement phrase in (1) is subject to reanalysis, with *easy-to-please* (etc.) taken as a complex adjective. Thus (3ii) becomes (19):

(19)   John is $[_{AP}[_A$ easy to please$]$ $t_i]$

Compare "how easy to please" is John. The trace t_i, no longer $\bar{A}$-bound, is not a variable but rather an anaphor after reanalysis; it also lacks Case. If it is coindexed with *John*, as is an option under the free indexing convention, the sentence is grammatical. We now assume that there is no rule of control relating *John* and PRO in COMP in (3ii); rather, there is an antecedent-anaphor relation relating *John* and t_i.

Turning now to the problems noted, consider first the matter of dual lexical representation for the adjective-complement constructions. Since the trace in (19) is in a θ-position, we may assume that it transmits its θ-role to its antecedent in the usual way. Therefore, we need no longer assume that the matrix subject position is a θ-position. Correspondingly, there is no need for a dual lexical representation. Adjectives of the *easy*-category never assign a θ-role to their matrix subject when they have clausal complements; the matrix subject assumes the θ-role of its coindexed trace, exactly as in the case of movement.

Constructions of the form (1) are analogous to constructions formed by the rule Move-α in the way that θ-roles are assigned, but different in the way they are generated, accounting for the fact that idiom chunks and other non-arguments cannot appear in the matrix subject position as they can under application of Move-α.[35] In earlier work, these constructions were analyzed as involving movement to matrix subject position or as involving base-generation of the matrix subject (as in Lasnik and Fiengo (1974), an analysis adopted in Chomsky (1977b)). Under the approach we are now considering, each of these ideas is regarded as correct in a particular sense, and the paradox of θ-theory is resolved.

Now, however, we have a new problem of θ-theory. If the matrix subject is lexically inserted in the D-structure, then the projection principle requires that its position be a θ-position, contrary to what we have just assumed. It therefore follows that the matrix subject is not inserted at D-structure, but is also not moved to the matrix subject position. The only resolution to this paradox, in our terms, is to assume that lexical insertion of the matrix subject is at S-structure in this case. In other cases, however, the projection principle requires that lexical insertion be at D-structure, so that θ-positions will be filled by arguments at D-structure. We are therefore led to the conclusion that lexical insertion can take place freely either at D-structure or at S-structure. The projection principle determines which option is adopted. In fact, the only possibility for lexical insertion at S-structure will be in the construction we are discussing here (or others with the same essential properties), namely, in a non-θ-position assigned an appropriate function chain by reanalysis so that a θ-role can be inherited from a trace, where this trace results from movement of an argument that is base-generated in the position it occupies to satisfy the projection principle. In short, if we simplify the theory of lexical insertion, permitting it to apply freely either at D- or S-structure, we see that the complex adjectival constructions we are now considering fill a gap in the pattern of possibilities.

Turning now to the problems of *wh*-extraction, the relatively high degree of unacceptability of such examples as (7) results from the fact that extraction is from within a category formed by reanalysis – in effect, a lexical category. The acceptability of *wh*-extraction of "peripheral elements," as in (11), results from the fact that there is no subjacency violation, since the structure underlying (11) after reanalysis is (20):

(20)   the sonatas are $[_{AP}[_A$ easy to play$]$ t_i on $[_{wh-}$ violins$]]$

Reanalysis as a complex adjective may be assumed to be more difficult to the extent that it separates closely related items, placing one within the derived lexical category and the other outside it, accounting for the status of such examples as (12), (13). Thus (12i), for example, would have to derive from (21), in which *put* is separated from its complement *on the table*:

(21) $[_{NP_i}$ the book$]$ is $[_{AP}[_A$ easy to put$]$ t_i on the table$]$

The sentence "the book is easy to put on the table" would then derive from the form (16i).

As for the final problem, the ungrammaticality of (18i), we may assume that reanalysis is barred by the presence of the embedded subject, the reanalysis rule requiring adjacency of the matrix adjective *easy* (*for NP*) with the embedded infinitive. On the same grounds, one might hope to account for the familiar fact that constructions such as (1) tend to be more acceptable with embedded infinitivals rather than tensed clauses, though the latter are sometimes more or less acceptable, as in (22):

(22)   (i) this book is difficult [to convince people [to read t]]
        (ii) this book is difficult [to convince people (anyone) [that they ought to read t]]

Tensed embedded clauses may be more resistant to reanalysis than infinitivals.

Consider the example (23):

(23)   *John is easy [t to like Mary]

On the earlier analysis, this example is blocked for the same reason as (24), with a non-Case-marked variable unable to assume a θ-role:

(24)   *who is it easy [t to like Bill]

On the alternative analysis we are now considering, (23) is blocked by the impossibility of reanalysis, as in (18i).

It seems, then, that an approach to these constructions based on some notion of reanalysis is worth exploring more carefully, and that it might be worthwhile to inquire further into its implications for the related constructions discussed in Chomsky (1977b).

Notes

1.   For the following observations, I am indebted to Howard Lasnik. The promissory note in Chomsky (1979a) is not fulfilled, in this respect.

2.   Recall that we are not considering the problems of the theory of reference in this connection, but are concerned rather with properties of LF-representation that enter into interpretations of sentences in terms of intended coreference and intended distinct (disjoint) reference, where the "reference" in question does not carry ontological commitment. The question of how to interpret properly the indexing of names and pronouns is taken up by James Higginbotham in work in preparation. Cf. also Evans (1980), and other recent work.

3.   The existence of the phenomenon of disjoint reference has occasionally been denied on the basis of constructed situations in which such expressions as (1iii) are relatively acceptable. But these examples are beside the point, which is that (1iii) and (4) are clearly different in status – no analogous situations have to be contrived with regard to (4) – and crucially, that this difference in status mirrors the behavior of anaphors with regard to the binding theory.

The same crucial fact rules out as completely implausible the proposal of Katz (1980) that the phenomenon belongs to pragmatics rather than grammar; if this were so, why should the phenomenon reflect so closely the properties of binding theory in cases that clearly belong to grammar in anyone's sense, e.g., the range of interpretation for such sentences as (i) and (ii)?:

(i)   everyone expected him to like John
(ii)   everyone expected John to like him

In a sense, this criticism of Katz's proposal is beside the point, since his critique of other work (specifically, mine) is vitiated throughout by the fallacy of equivocation: he uses the term "grammar" in a radically different sense from the one adopted in the work he criticizes. For Katz, the scope of what he calls "grammar" is delimited by certain *a priori* considerations, for example, the problem of formalizing certain patterns of inference. In the work he criticizes, no such criterion is adopted: the domain of what is called "grammar" is an empirical question, to be determined in ways that have frequently been described. A similar equivocation undermines Katz's critique of conclusions concerning the level of LF-representation. He is simply using the term "logical form" in a sense quite different from that of the work he criticizes. Katz's fallacy is clear, for example, when he criticizes grammatical studies for assigning to LF phenomena that he regards as belonging to pragmatics. If he is correct in the latter contention, that simply shows that some elements that relate to pragmatics belong to the level of LF-representation, as certainly might be the case. Katz's criticisms could be recast as an argument that the term "LF" should be rephrased by some other phrase, but this question is surely too insignificant to merit discussion, particularly, since the work he criticizes has always been quite clear about the issue. Cf. Chomsky (1980b, chapter 4; 1980c) for further discussion of these and related fallacies. Also chapter 6, below.

With regard to disjoint reference, some of the examples that have been put forth in criticism of the notion in fact support it, e.g., such examples as "I dreamed that I was Jesus Christ and that I forgave me for my sins." In a proper theory of the interpretation of indexing, a different "referent" will presumably be assigned to *I* and *me* in the "constructed world" of the dream. The development of such a theory is a matter of interest, but does not affect the point at issue. Similarly, such examples as (iii) have been adduced (e.g., by Katz) to reject the phenomenon of disjoint reference, on the grounds that (iii) does not entail that Carter did not vote for himself:

(iii)   everyone in Plains, Georgia, voted for Carter

But again this simply misses the point. Assuming the proper LF-representation to be something like (iv), where x and Carter are differently indexed as required by binding theory, the proper interpretation of variables in LF does not exclude the possibility that Carter is a value of x:

(iv)   for every person x in Plains, Georgia, x voted for Carter

But this observation, to which we return, does not impugn the obvious distinction between, say, (i) versus (ii), (v):

(v)   everyone expected (that) he would like John

In (ii) or (v), the pronoun may be identified with the variable bound by *everyone* at LF, giving (vi) and (vii) as possible representations of (ii) and (v), respectively; but (viii) is not a possible representation of (i):

(vi)   for every person x, x expected John to like x
(vii)   for every person x, x expected (that) x would like John
(viii)   for every person x, x expected x to like John

In other words, *he* can be coindexed with x under the binding theory in (ii) and (v) but not in (i), by the disjoint reference principle, such coindexing being interpreted as sameness of variable (say, by the device of reindexing of Higginbotham (1979a)). The fact that Carter may be a value of x in (iv) has no bearing on the legitimacy of the notion of disjoint reference, though it is relevant to the question of interpretation of LF-representations.

4.   Among the more difficult problems is Peter Geach's example (i), where the pronoun is understood as somehow within the scope of the quantifier though it is not formally within its scope:

(i)   the woman every Englishman admires most is his mother

5.   See the discussion of §§ 2.6, 3.2.1, on the possibility that other categories too may have subjects, in fact, accessible SUBJECTs in the sense of chapter 3.

6.   Nor is this the only such case. It is worth noting that as theories of grammar have become more restrictive over the years, thus enhancing explanatory depth in some domains, certain topics that had received a suggestive and sometimes illuminating analysis in terms of less constrained theories have in effect been abandoned. For example, in a theory with generalized transformations such as that of Chomsky (1955), there are possibilities for accounting for the ambiguity of the bracketed expressions in such structures as (i)–(iii) in terms of transformational mapping from D-structures that express GF-θ in a natural way:

(i)   [the shooting of the hunters] disturbed me
(ii)   I was disturbed by [John's driving]
(iii)   [visiting relatives] can be a nuisance

More recent work has in effect abandoned the attempt to give a principled account of such cases (which were a staple of earlier work), resorting to lexical rules that are hardly more than descriptive statements of the problem to be solved. It may be that these steps are warranted – that this is the way language works, so that there is nothing of interest to say about such examples as these. But one should, I think, bear in mind the more interesting possibilities explored in earlier work. In some cases, a move towards lexical analysis is well-motivated empirically; e.g., the case of derived nominals discussed in Chomsky (1972, chapters 1,3), (1974), and much other work. In some cases, the move is dictated by the success of more constrained theories in other domains and the valid methodological principle that guides the search for such theories. These reasons should be kept distinct, with an eye towards the possibility of recapturing earlier explanatory options that may express genuine insights that have been lost.

7.   Cf. chapter 2, note 109.

8.   Recall that there is an obscure plurality condition invoked in the case of English reciprocals. Thus (ii) becomes ungrammatical in the intended interpretation when *arguments* is replaced by *argument*. Cf. chapter 3, note 57.

In general, reciprocals often seem marginal in prepositional phrases, except under reanalysis, though not always. Compare the marginal examples (i) with the more acceptable (ii) (under reanalysis) and (iii):

(i)   (a) they left with each other
           (b) they are easy for each other to talk to
(ii)   (a) they spoke to each other
           (b) they are sorry for each other
(iii)   (a) they told Mary about each other
           (b) they told Mary stories about each other

It may be that the somewhat marginal status of (iv) is to be explained on similar grounds:

(iv)   they were happy for each other to leave

Cf. chapter 3, note 38.

9.   See the discussion of 2.6.(28).

10.   On the behavior of English reflexive as compared with comparable elements in Dutch, see Koster (1978b) and Huybregts (1979).

11.   Cf. Lightfoot (1980) on further implications of this assumption.

12.   Whether there are cases of preposition stranding in these languages in certain cases is an open question; in any event, if the phenomenon exists, it is far more restricted. Cf. Vinet (1979).

13.   The status of the second part of assumption (ii) is rather questionable. It serves here only to block *wh*-movement with inherent Case-marking; assignment of structural Case to the variable in any event follows *wh*-movement, so that in the grammatical cases, NP- and *wh*-movement are indistinguishable. Thus unless independently motivated, the assumption amounts to the stipulation that *wh*-phrases cannot bind an oblique variable, although other operations – e.g., those formed by quantifier movement in the LF-component – may do so. It might be argued that (14ii) is nevertheless more natural than this *ad hoc* stipulation; see below for an argument to this effect.

14.   But instead of their Empty Oblique Filter, Kayne proposes an explanation in terms of government, in accordance with Kayne (1980a).

15.   There is an attempt to explain this in OB in the framework proposed there, based on the assumption that clitic-movement is analogous to *wh*-movement in this respect. But Kayne observes that the phenomenon is restricted to *wh*-movement, contrary to the factual assumptions of OB, referring to the detailed analysis of this topic in Rizzi (1978c).

16.   I have replaced his numbering – (64) vs. (65) – by numbering consistent with the sequence of examples here.

17.   Recall the discussion of assignment of Case to an element in COMP in § 3.2.2 (cf. the discussion of 3.2.2.(13)) and of free relatives.

18.   But a modification of the mechanism proposed in § 3.2.2 is required, since the trace *t* that is assigned Case in (26) is not part of the A-function chain including *t'*, as defined in § 3.2.2. This modification, which may not be straightforward, accords with the conception of Case-assignment into COMP.

19.   Examples from Kayne (1980c).

20.   There are further problems. One, noted by Josef Aoun and Hagit Borer, concerns multiple *wh*-constructions, as in (i), (ii):

(i)   it is unclear who read which book
(ii)   it is unclear who left the book near what

According to the theory outlined in chapter 4, the embedded *wh*-phrase should be permissible only in a position that is properly governed. Assuming the theory just sketched, such positions in PP are restricted to those in which the PP is within VP, hence not in case (ii), a case that does not permit preposition stranding. Case (i) exhibits the same problem in simpler form; *which* is not in a properly governed position. Perhaps in both cases the answer is that the LF-rule of *wh*-movement involves pied-piping. There are numerous ramifications that I will not attempt to explore here.

21.   Specifiers and complements, in the terminology of *X*-bar theory. Kayne (1980b) generalizes the proposal that COMP is accessible to external government in a quite different way.

22.   With regard to the theory of bounding, Belletti and Rizzi propose a revision of subjacency to deal with the fact that something analogous to government by a verb seems to be a requirement for movement, not only in the case of preposition stranding (as noted by Weinberg and Hornstein; cf. § 5.2) but more generally. Thus, adverbial constructions that are outside of VP are always islands. Similar questions have been explored by Marantz (1979b), Kayne (1980b) and Stowell (1980b), who develop somewhat different approaches.

23.   Note that this assumption differs from that of the preceding chapter, where it was assumed that INFL may optionally govern the pre-verbal subject in Italian. Belletti and

Rizzi modify the notion "governing category" to assure that pre-verbal lexical subjects have governing categories (see chapter 3, note 41; and the discussion of 4.5.(26ii)). Thus a governing category need not contain a governor, if Case is assigned to it. There is a proliferation of consequences with regard to the topics discussed in chapter 4. See the following footnote.

24.   As Belletti and Rizzi observe, *ne*-cliticization in (2iii) is independently blocked by the binding theory, since the trace of *ne* is unbound, *ne* being inside the VP and hence not c-commanding its trace. Thus there are two possibilities for explaining the ungrammatical status of (2iii). If Jaeggli is correct in restricting ECP to NPs (see § 4.6), then the violation of c-command is what is involved. Note that in that case the apparent satisfaction of ECP in (3iii) is not relevant.

Suppose that INFL is optionally a governor of subject in Italian, as proposed in chapter 4. Then (2i) is grammatical if the option is not exercised, while (2iii) is blocked by the c-command requirement. The examples (3) are unaffected. Therefore these examples are consistent with the theory of chapter 4, apart from (2ii), for which we must assume that AGR is not able to govern the head of the subject NP. In forthcoming work, Aoun relates this to the well-formedness condition 3.2.3.(73).

25.   To deal with the case of *want-to* contraction we must therefore assume, as in the discussion of 3.2.2.(36)–(40), that non-Case-marked trace is "invisible" to rules of the PF-component, a special case, perhaps, of the more general property discussed there: that elements must have appropriate features to be "visible" in the interpretive components.

26.   Perhaps one might deal with some of the rather complex phenomena involving infinitival clauses and subjacency in Italian, discussed by Rizzi (1978b), in these terms.

27.   Assuming here that S̄-deletion is the device responsible for Exceptional Case-marking.

28.   I have been considering only the case of $[+\text{WH}]$ in (36ii). The case of $[-\text{WH}]$ bears on the question of *wh*-movement from NP. This is a complex matter that I will not try to enter into here. Cf. Chomsky (1977b), Rizzi (1978b), Cinque (1979), Steriade (1980).

29.   On this and other assumptions, see Chomsky (1977b) and references cited there. Cf. Nanni (1978) for a more comprehensive discussion of many properties of these constructions.

30.   Compare "it is hard to believe there to have been a crime committed," hardly felicitous, but surely far more acceptable than (iii). Note that the problem with (ii) is not that *there* is too deeply embedded for extraction: compare "John is hard[to believe[t to be an accomplice in such crimes]]," again infelicitous but far more acceptable than (iii). In the case of (i), (ii), one should expect some variability in judgment insofar as idiom chunks vary in the degree to which they are regarded as independent elements, but the crucial point is the clear contrast between (4i,ii) and (5i,ii).

31.   External movement, as in "whom is it hard to like," from (6i), is irrelevant here.

32.   It has frequently been suggested that the status of (7) is the result of a constraint – perhaps a processing constraint – against multiple gap constructions that are not nested. Thus in (7) we have the non-nested structures (i):

(i)   (a) [$_i$ which sonates] are [$_j$ the violins] easy to play t_i on t_j
       (b) [$_i$ which people] are [$_j$ the books] easy to convince t_i to read t_j

But no satisfactory formulation of this principle has been offered. Thus, it would appear to be satisfied in (9), which is ungrammatical in the dialects considered here, and it is violated in many other constructions that have been discussed – for example, it is violated freely in Italian, where the *wh*-island constraint does not hold. It is difficult to suppose that processing constraints vary from language to language, unless the variation is somehow triggered by relevant structural differences, which does not appear to be the case here. Similarly, consider examples of the following type, noted by Tim Stowell:

(ii)   the cake took you all day to help John bake (in that oven)

(iii)   *which oven did the cake take you all day to help John bake in
(iv)   which oven did it take you all day to help John bake the cake in

These constructions share essential properties of the *easy*-complement class. In (iii), the antecedent-gap pairs are nested, yet the sentence is far less acceptable than (iv). But (iii) and (iv) do differ in terms of the *wh*-island condition, i.e., subjacency with S as a bounding node.

Nevertheless, there may be an effect relating to nesting. But even if such a condition is operative, it seems that it is only a peripheral part of the story, and that the *wh*-island condition (traced ultimately to subjacency) operates independently. See also examples (11)–(13) below, in which the nesting condition is uniformly observed but the sentences are of varying degrees of unacceptability.

Cf. Reinhart (1979b) for a plausible version of a nesting constraint. On reasons for such a constraint, see Miller and Chomsky (1963) and references cited there, particularly, Chomsky (1959). Also Chomsky (1965, chapter 1).

33.   The analysis in this respect would be similar to the analysis of such constructions in Chomsky (1955). See chapter 2, note 120.

34.   On the status of the phrase *for the rich*, see Chomsky (1977b).

35.   The analysis is similar in some respects to the resumptive pronoun strategy for relatives, or to the examples discussed by Taraldsen (1979), in which a base-generated trace acts as a variable.

Empty categories and the rule move-α

A major preoccupation throughout this discussion has been the status of categories that have no intrinsic phonetic content. Two types of such empty categories have been considered: trace and PRO. Each of these has a certain cluster of properties: trace is properly governed and bounded by subjacency, and it transmits rather than retains its θ-role (i.e., its antecedent has no independent θ-role); PRO is ungoverned and not necessarily bounded, and does not transmit θ-role (i.e., its antecedent, if it has one, has an independent θ-role). Within the category of trace, a distinction has emerged between variables and other traces. Let us now restrict attention to NP, the focus of our concern throughout apart from § 2.4.4. Then we have two types of trace: variables and NP-trace. Each of these too is associated with a certain cluster of properties: specifically, variables are R-expressions and NP-traces are anaphors, with consequences that follow from binding theory.

In § 2.9, it was observed that the three types of empty category – PRO, variable, NP-trace – partition the class of possible positions of NP. We have since seen that this conclusion is not exactly correct, though it is close to true. NP is either governed or ungoverned. If ungoverned, an empty category is PRO; if governed, it can only be trace, but the further requirement of proper government must be met for trace to be admissible. Thus in positions that are governed but not properly governed we can have neither trace nor PRO, leading to consequences discussed in § § 2.6, 3.2.1: In positions that are properly governed, trace may or may not receive Case. Suppose we assume principle 3.2.2.(16) characterizing variables as case-marked traces to be valid, though in fact we have only grounded and utilized it from left to right. Then a trace is a variable if it is Case-marked and it is an NP-trace if it is not Case-marked. Excluding positions that are governed but not properly governed, the remaining distribution is in fact divided into three exhaustive and exclusive categories: PRO, variable, NP-trace.

If the three empty categories partition a certain distribution – in this case, virtually the distribution of NP – then it is reasonable to presume that in fact there is only one basic empty category α; each occurrence of α has one of three clusters of properties. This assumption will explain the partitioning, which otherwise remains mysterious. Our discussion so far has been concerned primarily with the clustering of properties. Let us now assume that this clustering is established, and look more carefully at the question of the internal constitution of the elements that manifest this clustering.

We have been assuming that PRO, variable and NP-trace are distinguished by their internal constitution. PRO has the features person, number and gender, while trace lacks these features though it may have others, specifically, Case, and perhaps the feature [*wh-*] that signals movement-to-COMP. Furthermore, NP-trace and variable are distinguished by the feature Case, if 3.2.2.(16) is valid. Therefore, rules that distinguish among the three types of empty category can do so merely by inspecting their internal constitution: an occurrence of an empty category is PRO, or a variable, or NP-trace depending on its internal properties. This has been a useful expository device, but it is no necessary requirement of the theory we have been developing. For the rules of this theory to operate properly, it is only necessary that each occurrence of an empty category can somehow be identified as PRO, variable, or NP-trace. Difference of internal constitution is sufficient for this purpose, but it is not necessary. For example, we can determine whether an occurrence of [NP *e*] is a variable or an NP-trace by asking whether it is locally Ā-bound (hence a variable) or not (hence an NP-trace). While it may be true that variable and NP-trace are in fact distinguished by internal constitution – presence or absence of Case – the rules, say, of the binding theory would apply just as well and in exactly the same way if they were not so distinguished.

Consider now trace and PRO. We have been assuming that PRO has the features person, number and gender, as is quite reasonable. PRO enters into typical agreement phenomena, as in (1):

(1)   (i) John tried [PRO to help himself]
        (ii) they tried [PRO to become doctors]
        (iii) they tried [PRO to be happy]

In (i), PRO has the feature [masculine] and in (ii) the feature [plural], triggering agreement, just as an overt pronoun would in a comparable position. In a language with inflected adjectives, the analogue of *happy* in (iii) would be plural. Furthermore, arbitrary PRO may be inherently either singular or plural, a parameter distinguishing related languages, as we have seen. So it makes good sense to think of PRO as having these features, exactly as pronouns do. It was such considerations that led us to define the category of pronominals – PRO or overt pronoun – in terms of possession of just these features, with perhaps an optional phonological matrix, the option distinguishing PRO from pronoun.

However, we have so far been glossing over similar arguments that show that trace should have these features as well. Thus consider (2):

(2)   (i) who did John think [t would help herself]

    (ii) they seem [t to be doctors]
    (iii) they seem [t to be happy]

The same considerations that suggest that PRO has the features in question apply in (2) (and their analogues in more inflected languages) to indicate that trace also has these features, so that there will be no internal difference in the constitution of trace and PRO. Further evidence to this effect is provided by the possibility that trace may be "spelled out" as a pronoun, as in the case of emphatic pronouns in Italian (cf. chapter 2, note 122). Assuming the trace to have the relevant features, this possibility would simply amount to allowing a certain rule of morphology to associate with this collection of features its corresponding phonological matrix.

We therefore have both conceptual and empirical reasons to suppose that there is really only one basic empty category, which may have the grammatical features person, number, gender, Case, [*wh-*], and perhaps others, as determined by its derivation and context. If these grammatical features – specifically, person, number and gender – are base-generated without a corresponding phonological matrix, we have PRO. If they are "left behind" by a movement rule, then we have trace. If the trace is locally Ā-bound, then it is a variable; otherwise not. If 3.2.2.(16) is valid, then if the trace has Case it is a variable; otherwise not.[1]

The conceptual reason for assuming that there is only a single empty category is that a distribution which is virtually that of NP is partitioned by the empty categories, a fact explained if they are variants of a single basic element, but otherwise unexplained. The empirical reasons are those just indicated, involving agreement.

We see that we can distinguish occurrences of the empty category – assuming now that there is only one – as PRO, NP-trace, or variable in terms of the derivation. Can we also identify occurrences as PRO, NP-trace or variable in terms of properties of the structure in which they appear, whether LF, S-structure or D-structure? As noted, variables are identified by the fact that they, and they alone, are locally Ā-bound. The only problem, then, is to distinguish NP-trace from PRO.

Since §2.4.1, we have been assuming that the fundamental distinction between NP-trace and PRO lies in θ-theory. Movement is possible to a non-θ-position only, so that the antecedent of trace is always in such a position. If the antecedent of PRO is an argument, then it is in a θ-position. Thus we can determine whether α is NP-trace or PRO by inspection of its antecedent, i.e., its local A-binder β, if it has one. If α is free or β is in a θ-position, then α is PRO; if α is bound and β is in a non-θ-position, then α is NP-trace.[2]

This method works only if bound PRO always has an argument as its binder. Quite generally, this is true; thus, pleonastic *it* or *there* (as in "it seems that ...," "there are three men ...") never binds PRO. But consider (3):

(3)   it sometimes rains after $[\,\alpha$ snowing $]$

Here, α must be PRO, since it is ungoverned; but its controller is "weather *it*." Controlled PRO normally assumes the referential properties of its antecedent, but the antecedent in this case is non-referential. Or to put it differently, weather-*it* behaves as though it were referential, but it can have no referent.

The latter property is not as strange as it sounds; in fact, it is not uncharacteristic of what are often considered "referential expressions." If I say "the flaw in the argument is obvious, but it escaped John's attention," I am not committed to the absurd view that among the things in the world are flaws, one of them in the argument in question. Nevertheless, the NP *the flaw in the argument* behaves in all relevant respects in the manner of the truly referential expression *the coat in the closet* – for example, it can be the antecedent of *it* and serves as an argument, taking a θ-role. Suppose now that we make a rather conventional move, and assume that one step in the interpretation of LF is to posit a domain D of individuals that serve as values of variables and as denotata. Among these individuals are specific flaws that can appear in arguments (cf. "the same flaw appears in both arguments"), John's lack of talent, and so on. Then we might also assume that weather-*it* denotes a designated member of D, and is thus "referential" in the sense required for our discussion.

Note that this step in the process of interpretation is not to be confused with what might be called "real semantics," that is, the study of the relation between language or language use and the world.[3] Rather, it should be considered to be in effect an extension of syntax, the construction of another level of mental representation beyond LF, a level at which arguments at LF are paired with entities of mental representation, this further level then entering into "real semantic interpretation." But let us put the details and appropriate qualifications aside and adopt the assumption that there is a domain D of individuals associated with arguments at LF as values of variables, denotata of names, etc. It is not excluded, then, that among these individuals is an element of D denoted by weather-*it*.

But while this step is not ruled out in principle, there is reason to believe that it is not correct. To see why, let us consider a little more closely the behavior of variable-like elements of LF.

There are two such elements: what we have called "variables," that is, locally $\bar{A}$-bound empty categories; and PRO with arbitrary reference. Consider sentences in which these appear, e.g., (4):

(4)   (i)   who hit Bill   (for which person x, x hit Bill)

      (ii)   it is possible to roll down the hill   (it is possible for PRO to roll down the hill)

      (iii) *what rains   (for which x, x rains)

In case (i), an individual of D can serve as a value of x if its properties place it within the domain of the restricted quantification; thus, the answer to (i) can be "John hit Bill" but not "the rock hit Bill." An analysis of (ii) which is crude but sufficient for our purposes takes PRO to be a variable bound by some operator. But the domain of this variable is restricted: (ii) may be taken as referring to people rolling down the hill, but hardly to rocks, though the properties of "roll down the hill" permit either subject and there is no general restriction of PRO to humans in D. The natural explanation for the ungrammatical status of (iii) is, then, that as a matter of grammatical principle, no element of D meets the requirements imposed by the predicate *rains* on its subject. Then weather-*it* denotes no element of D.

Note that there may be other considerations, factual or conceptual, that constrain D; for example, perhaps it does not or cannot include thinking rocks, so that the sentence "which rock thinks" is also ungrammatical. But the principle in the case of weather-verbs is of quite a different type.

It seems, then, that weather-*it* is similar to arguments in that it can control PRO but unlike them in that it denotes no member of D, as a matter of grammatical principle. Let us then distinguish two classes of arguments: *true arguments* with potentially referential function – apart from conceptual constraints (e.g., those that may bar thinking rocks) there may be elements of D that they take as values or denotata – and *quasi-arguments* that lack any such function as a matter of grammatical principle. Let us assume, correspondingly, that one of the possible θ-roles is that of quasi-argument.

The pronoun *it* can be a true argument ("it is on the table"), a quasi-argument ("it is raining"), or a non-argument ("it seems that John is here"). The same is true of PRO: it can be a true argument ((4ii) or "he tried [PRO to roll down the hill]"), a quasi-argument ((3) or the base-generated subject of a weather-verb in a pro-drop language), or a non-argument (the impersonal pronominal of a pro-drop language; cf. §4.5).

In part, the argument status of PRO is determined by its form. It follows from the θ-criterion that PRO is a non-argument if it is co-superscripted with a post-verbal argument; this is implicit in the informal discussion of "inheritance" of θ-roles above and will be made explicit directly. Recall that there are two types of superscripted arguments in post-verbal position: NPs and clauses, the latter, as in "it seems that S." Recall also that there was strong reason to suppose that in the latter case, the pronominal non-argument subject is coindexed with the post-verbal clause (cf. 3.2.3.(82-5)). Let us continue to assume that this coindexing is co-superscripting, as is natural given the close analogy to *there*-constructions. Then PRO is a non-argument if it is co-superscripted with a post-verbal argument, this case arising only in a pro-drop language. In the theory developed in chapter 4, if superscripted PRO is not co-superscripted with a post-verbal argument, then it is an argument, the analogue of a pronoun in a non-pro-drop language. In either case PRO is co-superscripted with some AGR, as are lexical arguments in subject position. Therefore, PRO^i is a non-argument if and only if it is co-superscripted with a post-verbal argument, an NP or a clause.

Suppose that PRO ^{i} is an argument. Then it functions with respect to D in exactly the manner of an overt pronoun in a non-pro-drop language. Specifically, it is not interpretable as arbitrary in reference, any more than *he* is so interpretable in "he is eating." Rather, we may assume that in each utterance, it is a true argument associated with some element of D of the appropriate sort or it is a quasi-argument functioning in the manner of weather-*it*. Suppose that PRO ^{i} is a non-argument. Again, it cannot be interpreted as arbitrary in reference, since there is no element of D that can satisfy it. Nor can it be bound by an antecedent in this case, since PRO is bound by an antecedent only if it is an argument, either a true or quasi-argument. In short, PRO ^{i} cannot appear in what we intuitively think of as a "control structure." In a non-pro-drop language, PRO cannot appear with a superscript; therefore, all structures with PRO are "control structures," with PRO either arbitrary in reference or controlled by an antecedent, as determined by the theory of control. The same is true in pro-drop languages. It follows, then, that there is no need to stipulate which structures are "control structures." In fact, we can dispense with the notion, apart from expository purposes. PRO has a superscript if and only if its S-structure position is governed at D-structure.

We can reach the same conclusion from a slightly different point of view. Consider possible occurrences of PRO ^{i} in what would be taken as control structures in a non-pro-drop language, say, as subject of infinitive, as in (5):

(5)   (i) NP V $[$ PRO ^{i} venire Giovanni $]$ (ergative)
           (ii) NP V $[$ PRO ^{i} mangiare Giovanni $]$ (NP-inversion)
           (iii) NP V $[$ PRO ^{i} sembrare $[$ ^{i} che S $]$

     (e.g., "I want $[$ PRO to seem that S $]$"; "I want it to seem that S")

The structures (i) and (ii) are barred by the Case Filter, since the post-verbal NP receives no Case. Therefore, raising of PRO ^{i} is necessary. We will see directly that (iii) is also barred by a slight generalization of the argument that applies to (i) and (ii). It follows, then, that PRO co-super-scripted with a post-verbal argument can never appear in a construction that would be a control structure in a non-pro-drop language. To put it differently, the control structures are essentially the same whatever the value of the pro-drop parameter.

Given these conclusions, consider the sentences (6):

(6)   (i) (a) I want $[$ it to snow $]$
             (b) *I want $[$ PRO to snow $]$
         (ii) (a) $[$ for it to snow all day $]$ would be a nuisance
             (b) *$[$ PRO to snow all day $]$ would be a nuisance
        (iii) (a) $[$ its snowing all day $]$ would be a nuisance
             (b) *$[$ PRO snowing all day $]$ would be a nuisance

(iv) (a) [it having snowed all day], I decided to stay home
    (b) *[PRO having snowed all day], I decided to stay home
(v) (a) I believe [it to have snowed all day]
    (b) *I believe [PRO to have snowed all day]

For reasons discussed in § 2.1, we assume that all clausal structures – hence all the bracketed structures in (6) – must have subjects. But as these examples illustrate, the subject of a weather-verb cannot be PRO unless, as in (3), there is a quasi-argument controller. The explanation for (6) is that *snow* requires a quasi-argument as subject, but PRO in a control structure (i.e., any PRO in a non-pro-drop language) can be a quasi-argument only if it has a quasi-argument as an antecedent, as we have just seen. Redundantly, example (vb) is barred by the fact that PRO is governed.

Consider now the analogues to the sentences of (6) in a pro-drop language, say, Italian. There are no analogues to the (a) examples, and the (b) examples are barred in control structures, for example, (6ib). But PRO may appear in the control structures (e.g., (iv)). See Rizzi (1980c), Chomsky (1981).

Similar observations hold in the case of non-argument subjects (e.g., "for it to be clear that S would be a nuisance," *"PRO to be clear that S would be a nuisance," etc.). PRO is co-superscripted in this case with the extraposed clause. The argument (to which we return) that rules out (5iii), a generalization of the argument that rules out (5i,ii), excludes PRO subject co-superscripted with an extraposed clause in this case as well. The analogues in the pro-drop languages are again impossible in the control structures. See Rizzi (1980c), Chomsky (1981), for discussion of other cases.

Note that these facts provide an independent reason for assuming that weather-verbs and verbs lacking an argument subject actually do have subjects – namely, PRO – at every level of syntactic structure in the pro-drop languages, as we have been assuming throughout. For if they did not, there would be no reason not to expect the analogues of (6) or of the sentences with non-argument subjects to be grammatical throughout.

Like PRO, lexical pronouns have arguments as antecedents, if they have antecedents. We might say that (7i) is an exception, if the two occurrences of *it* are coindexed; or (7ii), where the idiom chunk is the antecedent of *it*:

(7)   (i) it sometimes rains before it snows
      (ii) care was taken of the orphans, but it was insufficient
      (iii) *what did you take of the orphans
      (iv) what did you make t of that suggestion

Example (i) illustrates again the quasi-argument status of weather-*it* and thus poses no problem. As for (ii), suppose we say that idiom chunks are also quasi-arguments appearing in base-generated θ-positions that require quasi-arguments. The quasi-argument status of the idiom chunk is illustrated in (iii) (cf. (4iii)), recalling that variables are true arguments. But (iv), on this assumption, indicates that some idiom chunks are true arguments, unless what undergoes *wh*-movement in this case is not an NP but rather a QP, as in "how much care did they take of the orphans." However this question is resolved, we can maintain the conclusion that all pronominals, pronouns or PRO, require arguments as antecedents, if they have antecedents.

While there is plainly more to say about these questions, let us put the topic aside and assume the foregoing. Let us now return to the problem of distinguishing NP-trace from PRO. We can do so in a straightforward way: a non-variable occurrence of the empty category is PRO if its local A-binder is in a θ-position or if it is free, and is NP-trace if it is locally A-bound by a category in a non-θ-position. This is basically the way in which we distinguished trace from PRO in studying their properties in §2.4.1 and subsequently.

While we can determine whether an empty category is NP-trace or PRO merely by inspecting S-structure along the lines just indicated, clearly this approach misses something important: namely, it merely stipulates that the antecedent of NP-trace is in a non-θ-position, whereas before we were able to show that the antecedent of NP-trace is in a non-θ-position, and more generally, that movement is always to a non-θ-position. This was an important property of the rule Move-α, whether it was employed to relate GF-θ to GF-$\bar{\theta}$ or to interpret idioms and non-arguments as in the case of NP-movement, or to associate *wh*-operators with the variables they bind, or to provide the interpretation of extraposed phrases – a property that followed from the projection principle. Surely, then, the principled way to proceed is by inspecting the pair (D-structure, S-structure). If α in S-structure has been derived by movement of β from the position occupied by α, then we will say that α is *the trace of* β and β is *the t-antecedent of* α. By the projection principle, the t-antecedent of α is in a non-θ-position; cf. 2.1.(17), 2.6.(35)-(37), 3.2.3.(44). We extend the definitions in the obvious way for successive movement. If α is locally $\bar{A}$-bound by a t-antecedent, then it is a variable. If α is locally A-bound by a t-antecedent, then it is NP-trace, a non-pronominal anaphor. In any other case, an empty category is PRO, a pronominal anaphor. It follows that if α is free or bound by a local A-binder in a θ-position, then it is PRO.

Though this approach is, I take it, the correct one, replacing a stipulation by an argument based on more fundamental principles, I will, for ease of exposition, assume the former analysis in the subsequent discussion, thus in effect assuming a consequence of the projection principle rather than tracing the discussion back to this principle at each point.

Notice one crucial property of the principled approach to identifying the empty category just outlined. Suppose that the NP β is moved to a position in which it does not c-command its trace α, as in NP-inversion (cf. §4.5). Then α is by definition the trace of β and β is the t-antecedent of α, but α is PRO by definition, since it is free. This is exactly the result we want, since the trace of NP left by NP-inversion is in fact PRO, not NP-trace, as we see from properties of government and binding. Thus the principled characterization of empty categories just outlined in fact incorporates what amounts to the rule of PRO-insertion stipulated in § 4.5; it follows by definition, from the most principled definitions, that the trace left by NP-inversion is PRO. Notice that there is no internal contradiction: it does not follow from the definitions just given that if α is the trace of β, then α is a trace, in particular, an NP-trace; i.e., "trace-of," as defined, is a relational notion, but "is a trace" is a monadic predicate, so there is no problem in the conclusion that an element α may be the trace of β and yet not be a trace but rather interpreted as PRO. Notice further that although the rule of PRO-insertion need no longer be stipulated, now simply following by definition, we must still stipulate the rule of co-superscripting of the inverted NP and its trace, which is (impersonal) PRO.

In chapters 2 and 3, we discussed the option of choosing PRO or trace as the element moved to COMP in purposives and other constructions that involve movement-to-COMP with no phonetic reflex; e.g., (8), where α is the empty category:

(8)   John gave Bill a book $[\alpha [\text{PRO to read t}]]$

From our present standpoint, this (rather inconclusive) discussion was vacuous; there was no option. The element α in (8) is simply an occurrence of the empty category. It is not NP-trace, since it is not locally A-bound by a t-antecedent. In fact, its local A-binder is in a θ-position, and is not its t-antecedent. Therefore α is (8) is PRO, this being the only other option. Similarly, in D-structure it is PRO, occupying a θ-position.

We have so far been assuming that α gains its referential properties from its binder, the phrase *a book* in (8). But as the preceding discussion makes clear, this assumption really makes no sense, because α is an operator of some sort and hence has no referential properties; it is not the kind of element that can denote an individual of D. The proper interpretation of (8) is that the variable *t* bound by α must select as its value the element of D denoted by the argument coindexed with it, namely, *a book* (as throughout this discussion, extensions are necessary to deal with plural antecedents, but we continue to put this aside). If there is no antecedent then (8) simply receives no interpretation; it is ungrammatical, since its operator lacks intrinsic content. It follows, then, that (8) will receive an interpretation and stand as a grammatical sentence only if α and *t* (which are coindexed by the rule Move-α) are coindexed with some argument of the matrix sentence; the theory of control requires that this argument be *a book* in (8). This analysis, following in essence a suggestion by Hagit Borer, eliminates the one basic outstanding problem that we faced in connection with such constructions as (8), namely, why α, taken as PRO, cannot be arbitrary in reference. Since this element has no reference at all, it cannot be arbitrary in reference. As we saw in § 3.2.3 (cf. 3.2.3.(45)), the subject PRO of the embedded purposive clause can be arbitrary in reference (though not in (8)), but the bound variable must take as its value some entity of D denoted by a coindexed expression of the matrix clause. Further questions arise: e.g., just what relations must there be between the purposive clause and the matrix clause for interpretation to be possible? These, however, go beyond the bounds of the present discussion, and do not seem to bear directly on the specific topics we have been concerned with.

Let us now proceed to make some of the notions discussed so far more precise. We continue to restrict attention to NP, except where indicated; extension to other cases is straightforward.

Let us begin by considering the notion "empty category." Assume that there is some set of grammatical features ϕ that characterize pronouns; i.e., pronouns are distinguished from overt anaphors and R-expressions in that the grammatical features of pronouns are drawn solely from ϕ, whereas overt anaphors and R-expressions have some other grammatical features as well. Thus *John* and *each other* each have some grammatical feature that identifies them as non-pronominal, i.e., some feature outside of the set ϕ. This assumption is unavoidable. There must, e.g., be some property of *John, each other,* etc., that indicates that they are not pronouns. The set ϕ includes person, number, gender, Case, and perhaps other features (e.g., perhaps [*wh*-]). We refer to the members of ϕ as ϕ-features.

We call α an *empty category* if $\alpha = [_{NP} F]$, where $F \subset \phi$, F non-null. If α is not an empty category, call it a *lexical category*. We now have the definition (9) and the principle (10):

(9) α is a *variable* if and only if it is locally $\bar{A}$-bound and in an A-position

(10)   If α is an empty category and not a variable, then it is an anaphor

Quite probably, (10) will follow from a more principled characterization of the notion "anaphor," perhaps along the lines sketched informally in § 3.2.3. We stipulate further that variables are either empty categories or pronouns, admitting the case of resumptive pronouns. The class of A-positions will be slightly modified directly.

The convention associated with the rule Move-α is that when α is moved by this rule it leaves behind the *trace* $[_{NP} F]$ coindexed with α, where F is the set of ϕ-features of α.

A pronominal has no grammatical features other than ϕ-features, and may or may not have a phonological matrix. Specifically, we have the definition (11), recapitulating our earlier discussion:

(11) α is a *pronominal* if and only if $\alpha = [_{NP} F, (P)]$, where P is a phonological matrix and $F \subset \phi$, and either (i) or (ii):
        (i) α is free
        (ii) α is locally A-bound by β with an independent θ-role

If $\alpha = [_{NP} F]$, it is PRO; otherwise, α is a pronoun. Since PRO meets (10) as well as (11), it is a pronominal anaphor, as required by the binding theory. If $[_{NP} F]$ is locally A-bound by β lacking an independent θ-role, it is not a pronominal but rather NP-trace, a non-pronominal anaphor.

Note that we are referring throughout to occurrences of a symbol in a string. Thus one occurrence of $[_{NP} F]$ in a string S might be a pronominal, while another is a non-pronominal anaphor and still another a variable, etc. Occurrences are identified as PRO, NP-trace or variable exactly as they were in our earlier discussion. Arguments are identified exactly as in earlier discussion, except that we now include quasi-arguments alongside of true arguments as arguments, along the lines discussed above.

At D-structure, we may have lexical or empty categories or the null category, lacking any features: the empty categories, by definition, have ϕ-features. Since there is no indexing at D-structure, hence no binding, an empty category is a pronominal by virtue of (11i). Depending on its position, it will be an argument, a quasi-argument or a non-argument. The last case is excluded if we take D-structure to be a "pure" representation of GF-θ. At S-structure, NPs not as yet indexed by application of Move-α are indexed, say, randomly.

Let us now turn to the notions of Case and θ-theory, recapitulating and somewhat sharpening our earlier proposals. I will put aside the problem of clitics, discussed briefly in §4.6. In §§2.6, 3.2.2-3, 4.5, we saw that to account for the "inheritance" of Case and θ-role, these properties should be assigned to indices, or more properly, to certain function chains. Let us now turn to this notion. The intuitive idea we want to capture is that of the projection into S-structure of a derivation from D- to S-structure by Move-α. Intuitively, a *chain* is a sequence of categories at S-structure coindexed by Move-α, each member except the first being a trace of the first member, which we will call the *head* of the chain. The function chain is simply the associated sequence of GFs, properties of which we have discussed. To deal with "inheritance" of Case and θ-role, we continue to assign Case and θ-role to certain function chains, or just as well, to certain chains.

We saw in §3.2.2 that the appropriate objects for θ-role assignment are chains with the head in an A-position (call them "A-chains"), but we assumed that Case could be assigned to (function) chains headed by a category in COMP, the only relevant case being that of a chain headed by a *wh*-phrase in COMP. The theory would be more uniform if this case were excluded, so that we could limit attention to A-chains throughout. In fact, we need not assume that Case-inheritance is possible for a *wh*-phrase in COMP.[4] Rather, we may assume Case to be an inherent feature of an item drawn from the lexicon, interpreting Case-assignment as Case-checking, in the manner discussed earlier. To implement this idea we assume (12):

(12)   (i)   The Case of an NP is derived from that of its head, or is assigned by a Case-assignment rule if the NP has no head (e.g., a gerund)

        (ii) Case is one of the ϕ-features "left behind" under movement

Then a *wh*-phrase in COMP has Case if it is drawn from the lexicon and inserted in its D-structure position with Case; the variable it leaves under movement-to-COMP retains this Case. If the *wh*-phrase is drawn from the lexicon without Case, the variable it leaves behind will be assigned Case by (12i) if it is in a position to which Case is assigned. The phrase moved to COMP will not have Case if it is PRO, as in purposives and similar constructions; we leave it as an open question whether these elements have the feature [*wh-*], i.e., are actually *wh*-phrases, a question raised but not settled in earlier discussion. A *wh*-phrase may be assigned Case in its S-structure position (as, e.g., in certain free relatives; cf. note 2). Our discussion of these topics has been so sketchy, considering so few examples, that it puts us in no position to make specific proposals at this point. I will therefore simply leave these questions open, and concentrate on NP within S.

Assuming these questions to be settled by refining in one or another way the approach just sketched, we can restrict attention to A-chains, excluding those with heads in COMP. We have considered two Ā-positions in the preceding discussion: (i) COMP, or in any event peripheral to S; (ii) the adjunction position created by NP-inversion. Type (ii) was a major topic of discussion in chapter 4. It is fairly clear from that discussion and from the earlier consideration of Case and θ-role inheritance that the relevant distinction we require is between A-positions and (ii) on the one hand, and positions peripheral to S on the other. The first type enter into chains relevant to Case and θ-role inheritance; the second type break such chains. Let us therefore slightly modify our earlier terminology and include the adjunction position (ii) among the A-positions, revising the notions "A-bind," etc., accordingly. We now restrict the term "chain" to A-chains in this sense, sharpening the notion as we proceed. Let us also restrict attention to chains that are maximal in the obvious sense, to be made precise.

Let us now consider more closely the properties of the chains required for Case-assignment and θ-role assignment. Suppose that $C = (\alpha_1, \ldots, \alpha_n)$ is one of these chains. We will call each pair (α_i, α_{i+1}) a *link* of the chain C. In the chains discussed in chapters 2 and 3, each link was a case of local binding; i.e., α_i locally binds α_{i+1}. We also saw that an element in COMP breaks a chain into two separate chains for the purpose of assignment of Case and θ-role. We may therefore assume that in each link (α_i, α_{i+1}), α_i locally A-binds α_{i+1}. The head of the chain C is a lexical category, PRO, or a variable, and each non-head is a trace coindexed with the head. We have been assuming all along that the head of a chain is an NP, as are its other elements. We will now assume explicitly that the head is an NP, leaving open the categorial status of other elements of the chain, assumptions with certain consequences, as we shall see.

In chapter 4, we extended these notions to chains $C = (\alpha_1, \ldots, \alpha_n)$ in which α_n is a post-verbal NP co-superscripted with α_{n-1}, which was impersonal PRO inserted by a rule of PRO-insertion (or its trace). Recall that we have either (13i) or (13ii), the former base-generated and the latter deriving from (14) by Move-α:

(13)   (i) $\beta \left[_\text{VP} \text{V NP} \right]$ (ergative constructions)
        (ii) $\beta \left[_\text{VP} [_\text{VP} \text{V} \ldots] \text{NP} \right]$ (NP-inversion)
(14) $\text{NP} \left[_\text{VP} \text{V} \ldots \right]$

We ignore INFL, which is within VP in (13) and is a sister to NP and VP in (14).

In (13), β and post-verbal NP are co-superscripted, i.e., coindexed by an indexing distinct from that involved in binding. Let us now define "BIND" (similarly, "X-BIND," "locally BIND," etc.) analogously to "bind" (etc.), but now including superscripting as well as subscripting. Thus, α BINDs β if α and β are coindexed and α c-commands β, where coindexing includes either co-superscripting or co-subscripting; similarly, for X-BIND, etc.

We may now define the notion "chain," meeting the conditions just outlined:

(15) $C = (\alpha_1, \ldots, \alpha_n)$ is a *chain* if and only if:
        (i) α_1 is an NP
        (ii) α_i locally A-BINDS α_{i+1}
        (iii) for $i > 1$, (a) α_i is a non-pronominal empty category, or (b) α_i is A-free
        (iv) C is maximal, i.e., is not a proper subsequence of a chain meeting (i-iii)

In case (iiib), since α_i is A-free but A-BOUND, it must be co-superscripted with α_{i-1}; that is, α_i is the post-verbal NP of (13) and α_{i-1} is β of (13), if α_i is an NP. Note that i need not be n in this case, since we have extended A-BINDing to include links (α_i, α_{i+1}) where α_i is the post-verbal subject of (13ii), this now being considered an A-position. And an element in this position c-commands elements of the VP to which it is adjoined. We return to such cases.

Every NP is in a chain; at least, a chain with $n = 1$. Though chains are maximal, it still does not follow that each NP is in exactly one chain. Thus, α can c-command β and γ though neither β nor γ c-commands the other. This is the case, for example, when a *wh*-phrase binds two variables that are not related by c-command. Such a case cannot arise by movement; see the discussion of 3.2.3.(44). But it might arise in other ways, for example, by the devices studied by Taraldsen (1979). It appears to be the case, however, that all such cases are excluded by other properties of the system when we restrict attention to A-positions (including our current extended sense of this notion). Assuming so, every NP is in one and only one chain. Let us assume this to be the case.

As in our earlier discussion, Case and θ-role are assigned to certain chains. Considering first Case, we have the principle (16) for Case-assignment and the Case Filter (17):

(16)   The chain $C = (\alpha_1, \ldots, \alpha_n)$ has the Case K if and only if for some i, α_i occupies a position assigned K by β

(17)   Every lexical NP is an element of a chain with Case

Recall that if $\beta = $ AGR, it assigns Case to α_i only if it is co-superscripted with α_i. Since we are assuming that Case may be a feature of a lexical category introduced into D-structure from the lexicon (hence a feature of the NP of which it is the head, by (12i)), we require the obvious conventions to bar instances of Case conflict under (16).

Other properties of the system require that no chain can be assigned Case by more than one category β.[5] Apart from configurations such as (13), it will always be the case that $i = 1$ in (16); see the discussion of 3.2.2.(33), and of 4.5.(35). θ-role assignment is determined by the principle (18):

(18)   Suppose that the position P is marked with the θ-role R and $C = (\alpha_1, \ldots, \alpha_n)$ is a chain. Then C is assigned R by P if and only if for some i, α_i is in position P and C has Case or is headed by PRO.

This condition restates 3.2.2.(32), differing only in that it includes the disjunction "has Case or is headed by PRO" instead of referring only to presence of "visible" features. But the preceding analysis shows that the apparent generalization obtained in the earlier formulation was spurious since the postulated difference in form between trace and PRO has proven groundless, and it was just this difference that made the generalization possible.

The intuitive sense of (18) is that θ-role is assigned to an element α in a θ-marked position P and is then inherited (upwards or downwards) by an argument in the chain containing α, but only if the chain has Case (which generally means that its head is in a Case-marked position) or the head is PRO. It follows that a variable must have Case,[6] and that *wh*-movement from a non-Case-marked position is impossible; cf. § 3.2.2.

Note that there is a redundancy in (18) in the case of a chain headed by PRO: if this PRO is co-superscripted with a post-verbal noun phrase, then the chain has Case, and falls under the first part of the disjunctive condition. To eliminate this redundancy, we might restate (18) so that a θ-role is assigned to C if C has Case or is headed by *argument* PRO, that is, PRO in a control structure or the "missing subject" in a pro-drop language. The formulation will then differ in coverage from (18) only in the case of PRO co-superscripted with a post-verbal argument. We return to the significance of this issue directly.

We can now formulate the θ-criterion as in (19):

(19)   *θ-criterion:* Given the structure S, there is a set K of chains, $K = \{C_i\}$, where $C_i = (\alpha^i_1, \ldots, \alpha^i_n)$, such that:

    (i) if α is an argument of S, then there is a $C_i \epsilon K$ such that $\alpha = \alpha^i_j$ and a θ-role is assigned to C_i by exactly one position P.

    (ii) if P is a position of S marked with the θ-role R, then there is a $C_i \epsilon K$ to which P assigns R, and exactly one α^i_j in C_i is an argument.

In case (i), α has the θ-role assigned by P.

We continue to assume the projection principle in the form 2.2.(6). The projection principle determines, on the basis of lexical properties, what are the configurations that appear at each syntactic level (LF, D-structure, S-structure); the θ-criterion determines the elements that appear in these configurations. More specifically, the projection principle guarantees that at each syntactic level, each lexical head appears in a configuration determined by its properties of θ-role assignment; the θ-criterion requires that arguments be distributed properly in the configurations that are jointly determined by the projection principle and by principles of the categorial component of the base, including those idiosyncratic properties that are stipulated by rule (e.g., order of major constituents) and those determined by general principle (e.g., presence of a subject in clausal phrases, consequences of the adjacency condition on Case-assignment where it holds). The θ-criterion must be met at LF, and by the projection principle, at D- and S-structure as well. The θ-criterion is satisfied in essentially the same way at S-structure and LF; the chains are essentially the same, apart from the internal structure of α^i_j if some rule of the LF-component has applied. But at D-structure, each chain has only one member, which must be in a θ-position if it is an argument. If we take D-structure to be a pure representation of GF-θ, then not only will arguments appear in every θ-position and nowhere else, but also only the null category (not to be confused with an empty category $[_{NP}F]$, $F \subset \emptyset$, F non-null) will appear in a non-θ-position, excluding other non-arguments.

The binding theory and ECP apply exactly as before to occurrences of empty or lexical categories. ECP is now stated so as to hold of trace rather than of $[_{NP} e]$. Each occurrence of an empty category is uniquely identified as PRO (a pronominal anaphor) or trace; and if as trace, then as NP-trace (a non-pronominal anaphor) or variable (an R-expression). Results outlined earlier follow as before.

Evidently, this is only the sketch of a true formalization. Further elaboration is necessary for full precision, and it is necessary to ensure that other properties of the system are so narrowly and specifically constrained that they do indeed entail the consequences outlined. But the basic properties of the system we have been developing are incorporated into this account, and it is fairly clear how to proceed to fill in the gaps. It is an open question whether full-scale formalization is a worthwhile endeavor at the moment as compared with the task of considering a broader class of phenomena or attempting to resolve problems within this framework; the usual question that arises with respect to formalization. My personal feeling is that the point has been reached where these further steps should be undertaken, that there is a sufficient depth and complexity of argument so that formalization will not merely be a pointless technical exercise but may bring to light errors or gaps and hidden assumptions, and may yield new theoretical insights and suggest new empirical problems for investigation. In the 1950s, formalization proved useful in exposing problems in then current theories, and it may be that it will now be similarly useful in the investigation of the richer theories of generative grammar that have been developed since.

In earlier discussion, we have seen that Case theory and θ-theory have a considerable overlap of consequences. In fact, the connections are still closer than what has been indicated. The basic principle of Case theory is the Case Filter (17). We are now able to derive (17) from the θ-criterion, an important step in unifying the system of principles we have been considering for two reasons, apart from the desirability of eliminating an independent principle: first, this will eliminate the redundancy between Case and θ-theory; second, while the θ-criterion is virtually a condition of adequacy at the level of LF, the Case Filter, while natural, seems highly specific to the internal structure of grammar. Let us see how such a derivation of the Case Filter would proceed.[7]

We restrict attention to lexical categories, since the Case Filter is stipulated only for these. The Case Filter states that each lexical NP must be a member of a chain with Case; it must either be in a Case-marking position or must inherit Case. Though we need not appeal to the fact in the following discussion, other properties of the system require that Case-inheritance, as distinct from θ-role inheritance, is only "downwards"; it applies only in the case of post-verbal NP of the configuration (13) as discussed in §4.5. Let us divide all lexical categories into three classes: (i) arguments that are not post-verbal superscripted NP as in (13); (ii) post-verbal superscripted NP; (iii) non-arguments. We want to show that for an element of each of these classes, the Case Filter follows from the θ-criterion.

Consider first class (i), i.e., an argument α that is not a post-verbal superscripted NP. Suppose that Case is not assigned to the chain C of α. Since $\alpha \neq$ PRO, no θ-role is assigned to C by (18) and the θ-criterion is violated. Therefore, for an argument that is not a post-verbal superscripted NP, we need not stipulate that the Case Filter holds.

Consider now a chain $C = (\alpha_1, \ldots, \alpha_n)$ where some α_i is a post-verbal superscripted NP. Recall that α_1 is in fact the non-argument co-superscripted with it: English *there*, French *il*, Italian impersonal PRO ($= \beta$ of (13)), etc. The θ-criterion requires that a θ-role be assigned to C, since α_i is always an argument. By (18), a θ-role is assigned to C only if C has Case or α_1 is PRO. In discussing (18), we suggested that PRO in (18) be taken as argument PRO to eliminate a redundancy in the formulation. In fact, this was the only relevant case in the original formulation of this condition in § 3.2.2. Let us therefore assume that (18) is to be understood in this way, eliminating the redundancy. Then a θ-role is assigned to C only if C has Case, since C is not headed by argument PRO. Therefore for class (ii), the Case Filter follows from the θ-criterion.

It remains to consider class (iii), i.e., non-argument *it* as in "it is clear that John will win," etc., and its analogues in other languages. We have been restricting attention in this chapter to NP arguments, but, as we have seen, the clause in the VP is an argument coindexed with impersonal *it* in these constructions and is in fact co-superscripted with *it*. The definition of "chain" permits a clausal argument as a member of the chain. Now this class reduces to class (ii). If $C = (\alpha_1, \ldots, \alpha_n)$ is a chain with α_i (in fact α_n) a clausal argument, the θ-criterion requires that C be assigned Case or be headed by argument PRO. Since the latter case is impossible, C must be assigned Case. Therefore the Case Filter also follows for class (iii). This is the missing argument referred to in the discussion concerning (5iii) and (6), above. For discussion of the analogous argument in the case of pro-drop languages, see Chomsky (1981).

The Case Filter therefore follows, *in toto*, from the θ-criterion, and it can therefore be eliminated as an independent principle of GB-theory.

A few comments are necessary, however, tempering this conclusion in part. First, recall that one motive for trying to reduce the Case Filter to the θ-criterion was that the Case Filter appeared to be a special, if not unnatural, property of grammar, as distinct from the θ-criterion which is virtually a criterion of adequacy for LF. But note that in the preceding argument we are still appealing to a special property of grammar, though a much narrower one than the Case Filter; namely, the formulation of (18), on which we relied, is motivated by the requirement that movement-to-COMP must be barred from a non-Case-marked position. In discussing this topic in § 3.2.2, we noted that Case identifies an empty category as "visible" for certain rules: θ-role assignment in the LF component and phonological rules. We are still appealing to this fact, embodied in (18). It is this assumption, along with the θ-criterion, that yields the Case Filter as a consequence. An obvious topic for inquiry, then, is to sharpen this notion of "visibility," perhaps along the lines discussed in § 3.2.2.

The second observation is more technical. Consider clausal arguments, as in (21), (22):

(21)   (i) it is clear [that Bill is intelligent]
        (ii) it is believed [that Bill is intelligent]
(22)   (i) I believe [that Bill is intelligent]
        (ii) my belief [that Bill is intelligent]
        (iii) John is believed [t to be intelligent]
        (iv) John seems [t to be intelligent]

In the examples of (22), the bracketed clause is an argument but does not belong to a chain. Therefore, the preceding discussion does not apply to it at all. Rather, in such cases as these we simply assume that the clausal argument is θ-marked in the position that it occupies. We might ask whether there is some more general approach that will not distinguish the two kinds of θ-role assignment as I have done.

Other considerations suggest that there is more to be learned in this connection. Note that the clausal arguments of (22) are excluded from chains by specific stipulation: namely, (15i). It was for this reason that attention was drawn to the assumption that chains are headed by NP. Note further that this move was not innocuous. Suppose, in fact, that we had allowed chains not headed by NP, so that the bracketed clausal arguments of (22) constitute single member chains. Then such chains would not be assigned a θ-role by (18) and the θ-criterion would be violated. The reason is that Case is not assigned to the bracketed clause, at least in examples (ii)-(iv).

Consideration of (21) suggests similar qualms. In case (i), the bracketed clause is perhaps not in a θ-marked position, so that we might want to assume that it inherits its θ-role from the position of the co-superscripted antecedent *it* through the chain (*it* ^{i}, [^{i}that Bill is intelligent]). We have assumed throughout, however, that at least in (21ii), the bracketed clause is in a θ-marked position, namely, the same position that it occupies in (22i); cf. § 2.7, where it is noted that the conclusion seems even more evident if we replace *believe* in (21ii) by verbs such as *hold, reason* that do not (for many speakers) permit the clausal subject to appear in pre-verbal position. But then we have another redundancy, since the post-verbal clause is the final member of a chain in these cases; indeed, this assumption is crucial if we are to be able to derive the Case Filter for non-arguments, in such cases as these. For the latter argument to go through, we must, in fact, assume that it is by virtue of their appearance in these chains that the post-verbal arguments assume their θ-roles. We seem to be led, then, to the conclusion that if an argument is in a chain, then it receives its θ-role only by virtue of its membership in the chain, not by virtue of the position that it occupies, as is the case in (22). This requires stipulation, again raising the suspicion that something has been missed.[8]

Though there is reason to believe that the reduction of the Case Filter to the θ-criterion has not really exhausted the issue, nevertheless it seems to be a step towards unification of theory and elimination of redundancy and special conditions; and there are also specific empirical consequences, as we saw in discussing (5iii) and (6). The partial success and the outstanding questions recall the discussion in chapter 1 as to whether it really is a valid methodological principle to adopt, in the study of grammar, the kinds of intuitive considerations of simplicity and the search for unification of principle that have proven so fruitful in the natural sciences for the past several hundred years and that are pursued with little question today. In the course of this discussion, we have seen that these rather vague but yet intelligible guidelines can yield interesting results. For example, the considerable improvement of the binding theory discussed in chapter 3 was largely motivated by problems of this sort; specifically, the redundancy of Case and binding theory, which led to the clarification of the central role of government in each; and the rather special nature of the two unrelated opacity conditions of the OB-framework. The attempts to overcome the very special character of the *$[that\text{-}t]$* filter reviewed in chapter 4 (specifically, the work of Taraldsen, Kayne and Pesetsky) constitute another example illustrating the productive character of these methodological guidelines. Other examples have appeared throughout. We now have another case: sharpening (18) to overcome a slight redundancy leads to reduction of the Case Filter to the θ-criterion and an independently required principle concerning the role of Case in making empty categories "visible" to rules, thus overcoming a substantial redundancy between Case and θ-theory. While the reservations of chapter 1 concerning these topics merit careful consideration, still it seems to me that the work of the past few years suggests that it makes a good deal of sense to pursue the working hypothesis that the theory of core grammar, for reasons that are not at all obvious, does have some of the properties of the systems studied in the more fundamental natural sciences, and that for some reason neural structures at least in this domain instantiate a perhaps surprisingly simple and unified system of principles.

Correspondingly, it seems reasonable to continue to adopt these guidelines and to search for a principled way to eliminate the stipulations noted in discussing the θ-criterion and the Case Filter, along with the many similar cases that have been noted in the course of this discussion, not to speak of those undiscussed or yet to be discovered.

Let us leave this topic, noting that we have achieved a degree of success while leaving some unresolved problems, and look a little more closely at the examples (13), (14), repeated as (23), (24):

(23) (i) $\beta[_{VP}V\ NP]$
      (ii) $\beta\ [_{VP}\ [_{VP}\ V \ldots]\ NP]$
(24) $NP\ [_{VP}\ V \ldots]$

Example (23i) is a base-generated ergative construction, and (23ii) is derived from the D-structure (24) by NP-inversion. What is β in (23)? Consider first (23ii), recalling our earlier discussion of the principled approach to identifying occurrences of empty categories (see the discussion above (8)). As we have seen, β in (23ii) is the trace of the post-verbal NP, which is its t-antecedent; but β is PRO, by definition. Recall that the principled definitions given in effect incorporate the rule of PRO-insertion of §4.5 in this case, though we must still stipulate that β is co-superscripted with the post-verbal NP, necessarily, of course, or the structure will be ruled out by the binding theory. Therefore this stipulation in effect states that the structure can exist. We continue to refer to β in (ii) as "impersonal

PRO." Its properties are exactly as discussed in chapter 4. The impersonal PRO β is a non-argument, so that the θ-criterion is satisfied. Being the trace of the post-verbal NP, $\beta = [_{NP} F]$, where F is the set of ϕ-features of this NP. If β is moved subsequent to formation of (23ii) by NP-inversion, then the element "left behind" is again $[_{NP} F]$, now by definition the trace of its t-antecedent PRO $= [_{NP} F]$, the two occurrences co-subscripted. In this case, the trace of PRO appearing in the position of β in (23ii) after subsequent movement is in fact a trace, since its t-antecedent is its local A-binder in a non-θ-position. The θ-criterion again is satisfied. The resulting form would be, for example, (25), where the matrix PRO agrees with the embedded post-verbal subject:

(25) $\quad$ PRO$_i^j$ sembr-AGR $[_S t_i^i [_{VP} [_{VP} \text{mangiare}] NP^i]]$
$\quad$ ("seem-AGR $[_S$ to eat NP $]$"; e.g., "the men seem to eat")

What about (23i)? Following Burzio (1981), as in the discussion in §4.5, we assume that the post-verbal position in VP is a θ-position, as is standard in ergative constructions in Burzio's sense. As before, we may assume β to be $[_{NP} e]$ in D-structure, so that D-structure is a "pure" representation of GF-θ. The ϕ-features of the post-verbal NP are then introduced into the position of β as a consequence of the syntactic rule of co-superscripting, given the general requirement that proximate elements have the ϕ-features of their antecedents. Alternatively, we might assume β to be $[_{NP} F]$ in D-structure, a non-argument analogous to impersonal *there* or *it*, where F is the set of ϕ-features of NP, as in general must be the case for proximate pronominals. In either case, the θ-criterion is satisfied. Again, β is PRO by definition, since it is unbound; but it is impersonal PRO, a non-argument. The same analysis applies if impersonal PRO is raised, as in (26):

(26) $\quad$ sembrano intervenirne molti (= 4.5.(35))

The analysis given informally in chapter 4 thus falls into place in a straightforward way.

Suppose that *wh*-movement applies to a structure such as (23). Consider, for example, the sentence (27) (from Rizzi (1979a):

(27) $\quad$ quanti credi che ne siano usciti (l'anno scorso)
$\quad$ ("how many do you think that of-them appeared (last year)";
$\quad$ "how many of them (e.g., of the books) do you think appeared (last year)")

Cliticization of *ne* shows that the structure to which *wh*-movement applies is (28), where α^i is β of (23i):

(28) $\quad$ credi $[_S$ che $[_S \alpha^i [_{VP} ne_j$ siano usciti $[_{NP}{}^i$ quanti $t_j]]]]$

After *wh*-movement, we have (29):[9]

(29) $[_{NP_k^i} \text{ quanti } t_j] \text{ credi } [\text{che } [_S \alpha^i [_{VP} \text{ne}_j \text{ siano usciti } t_k^i]]]$

The chain C for (29) is (30):

(30) (α^i, t_k^i)

Case and θ-role are assigned to C as required. INFL is in VP at S-structure and t_k^i retains the nominative Case base-generated in the NP *quanti-ne*.

What is the variable in (29)? By definition, a variable is an empty category that is locally $\bar{A}$-bound. Though t_k^i is BOUND by α^i, it is not bound by it, and therefore it is locally $\bar{A}$-bound by the NP *quanti* in COMP, which does not bind α^i. Therefore, t_k^i is the variable, corresponding to the intuitive sense. Note that the variable is A-free, as required by the binding theory. Not being bound, α^i is impersonal PRO, as required.

Consider another example involving the configuration (23), namely, the *si-* constructions 4.5. (42-5):

(31) (i) si mangia le mele
  (ii) le mele si mangiano
  (iii) si mangiano le mele

In particular, consider the derivation proposed in § 4.5 for (iii):

(32) (i) $[_{NP} e]$ si mangia $[_{NP} \text{ le mele}]$ (D-structure)
  (ii) $[_i \text{ le mele}]$ si mangia t_i (by Move-α)
  (iii) $\beta_i [_{VP} [_{VP} \text{ si mangia } t_i][_{NP_i} \text{ le mele}]]$ (by Move-α)
  (iv) $\beta_i^i [_{VP} [_{VP} \text{ si mangia } t_i][_{NP_i^i} \text{ le mele}]]$ (by co-superscripting)

I have omitted reference to INFL. From the D-structure (i), we derive (ii) by movement of the object *le mele* to the non-θ-position of subject. The derivation might have stopped at this point, yielding (31ii), with agreement of the verb and the derived subject, INFL remaining outside of VP at S-structure, as discussed in § 4.5. But we can proceed to apply NP-inversion, yielding (iii), with INFL moving into the VP as we have discussed. In (iii), β_i is the empty category of (23ii) with the ϕ-features of *le mele*, also shared by t_i. We derive (32iv) by co-superscripting. AGR of INFL, now in the VP, governs and is co-superscripted with the post-verbal NP *le mele*, to which it assigns nominative Case and with which it agrees, so that the verb is third person plural. The resulting chain is (33):

(33) $(\beta_i^i, [_{NP_i} \text{ le mele}], t_i)$

Nominative Case is assigned to the chain and a θ-role is assigned to the chain as well since it has Case and t_i is in a θ-position, namely, object of *mangia*. We thus derive the grammatical sentence (31iii). Recall that while t_i is in a θ-position, it is not assigned Case, the Case-assigning property of *mangia* having been "absorbed" by *si*, as discussed in § 4.5.

Note that the chain (33), while conforming to the definitions, is unusual in that its medial element is not an empty category. Furthermore, while the second element locally A-binds the third, under the extension of "A-bind" discussed earlier, and the third is the trace of the second, it is so only derivatively, as we see by inspecting the derivation (32). Thus in this case, the chain is not the "projection" of a derivation to S-structure. But the facts seem to fall into place, as required, with no stipulation.

There are many further questions to be considered, but the approach outlined in earlier chapters seems to be accommodated with no essential difficulty. Summarizing, we distinguish occurrences of PRO from occurrences of NP-trace, and distinguish both from trace which is a variable, but without requiring that these occurrences differ in internal constitution; in fact, they do not. The question of whether variables are Case-marked traces has essentially dissolved, though the essential property that variables are Case-marked remains in (18). The question whether the empty category in COMP is trace or PRO has dissolved entirely. The rule of PRO-insertion is unnecessary, its essential content following from principled definitions, though a residue remains as the process of co-superscripting in (32). The fact that empty categories are in complementary distribution follows without stipulation. Their combined distribution (virtually) exhausts the distribution of NP, again without stipulation; the theories of government and binding determine that every possibility is realized except for the case of positions that are governed but not properly governed. Agreement with trace or PRO follows as required. The clustering of properties that we have observed for empty categories follows as before from the theory of bounding and the theory of government, specifically, from the partial subtheories of the latter: ECP, θ-theory, and the theories of binding, Case and subcategorization, supplemented with the projection principle. These theories also determine the properties of lexical categories, including pronouns and overt anaphors. Like the overt pronoun *it*, PRO may appear as a quasi-argument or a non-argument. The Generalized ECP 4.5.(59) stands as a fundamental principle of government, in part reducible to the theory of binding, which itself is based on the concept of government.

The crucial difference between trace and PRO lies in the fact that trace is formed by the rule Move-α whereas PRO is base-generated, just like an overt pronoun, or derived by a rule of PRO-insertion which reduces to the rule of co-superscripting. The notion of grammatical transformation, now simplified to Move-α (perhaps with certain parameters), lies at the heart of the rule system, introducing the fundamental distinction between the two basic types of empty categories, each with its cluster of properties and roles. In accordance with the fundamental assumption of the Extended Standard Theory (EST), the "projection" of syntactic derivations in S-structure is what determines the functioning of the PF- and LF-components and of the theories of government and binding (but cf. (33)). D-structure constitutes a representation of GF-θ, one of the two components into which S-structure is "factored," the other being the rule Move-α. The crucial role of the notion of grammatical transformation now appears still more clearly than in the earlier exposition, since we have reduced trace and PRO to the single notion of empty category, returning, from a considerably different and much more refined point of view, to the conclusion of OB and earlier work. Recall that the conclusions extend to extraposition, and are to a large extent – though not completely – independent of whether we regard Move-α as a transformational rule of the syntax or as a special type of interpretive rule in the LF-component with exactly the properties of the transformational rule, these being crucially distinct from properties of rules of construal in the LF-component.

As has been noted several times, the basic notions that we have employed derive in each case from a core intuition which is then given a structural formulation that incorporates the core cases but generally is somewhat distinct in extension. For example, the core intuition lying behind the notion of government relates it to subcategorization, but the formal definition incorporating this intuition in structural terms extends to other cases (e.g., government of specifier and subject, raising and Exceptional Case-marking) and may in fact be narrower in certain cases (cf. the discussion of cliticization in §4.6). Similarly, the fundamental notion of chain at S-structure is based on the intuitive idea of projection of a derivation into S-structure, but when made precise, the notion differs in extension (cf. (33)). The same has been true throughout, and represents an important conclusion about the nature of language, if correct.

The θ-criterion and the projection principle impose narrow constraints on the form of grammar and lead to a wide variety of consequences. At the LF-level, the θ-criterion is virtually a definition of well-formedness, uncontroversial in its essentials, though the nature of the syntax of LF, hence the precise way in which the θ-criterion applies at this level, is an important if difficult empirical issue. The projection principle, in contrast, is not at all obviously correct. It is violated by most existing descriptive work, and it has some important consequences in several domains: internal to grammar, it serves to reduce the base rules to a very small number of parameters and to limit severely the variety of S-structures, and it enters into many specific arguments, as we have seen; beyond, it poses the problems of processing and acquisition in a decidedly different light, delimiting fairly narrowly the ways in which these problems should be pursued. It is, therefore, a principle that should be considered with caution; if correct, it is important.

The most fundamental level of representation is S-structure. Surface structure is relevant to phonology, but not to syntax except insofar as it has implications concerning S-structure. The arguments in favor of particular conclusions about S-structure are generally far stronger than arguments bearing on D-structure and LF, as we have seen throughout.[10] In fact, D-structure can be regarded as basically one factor in determining S-structure, along with the rule Move-α; in this sense, it is abstracted from S-structure. And the LF-representation differs only minimally from S-structure, given the projection principle, which, furthermore, assigns to the lexicon a central role in determining the nature of syntactic representations at every level.

The system that has been developed is highly modular, though there are some basic properties that appear in several of the components, in particular, the basic notions of the theory of government, which serves to unify the subtheories of grammar. While there is some significance to the analysis of the rule system as 1.(1), by far the most interesting questions concern the subsystems of principles 1.(2). Though the basic properties of each subsystem are quite simple in themselves, the interaction may be rather complex, and a change in a single parameter may have proliferating effects. These are the properties that we expect the theory of UG to have, for reasons discussed in chapter 1; though of course, the fact that the theory outlined has these properties to a certain extent does not show that it is the right theory. It does seem to me fair to say, however, that for the first time in the long and rich history of the study of language, we are now in a position to put forth theories that have some of the right properties, and that have significant explanatory power over a considerable range, as well as at least the beginnings of a deductive structure. There has, I think, been a qualitative change in this regard in the work of the past several years, some of which has been summarized and extended in the preceding discussion. Whatever the defects of current theories may be – and they are sure to be severe – recent developments seem to me to open up new and exciting prospects, and may point the way to new and deeper understanding of the nature of language, with non-trivial implications over a considerably broader range.

Notes

1.   But the subpart of 3.2.2.(16) that stipulated that if $[_{NP} e]$ is Case-marked then it is a variable would no longer be true if PRO can be Case-marked, if PRO and trace are not distinguished by internal features. Since we have made no use of this part of the principle and have suggested no reason why it should hold (and have suggested some reason why it should not; cf., e.g., the discussion of 3.2.3.(35)), no relevant consequences follow.

2.   Ken Safir observes that this account is not quite accurate because of such constructions as "after PRO reading, John was shot t," where *John* arguably A-binds PRO under the extended notion of c-command though it is in a non-θ-position, receiving its θ-role from *t*. Strictly speaking, then, we should replace "is (not) in a θ-position" by "has (lacks) an independent θ-role." I will ignore this refinement in expository passages.

3.   The same is true of descriptive work in model theoretic semantics for the most part, a fact often obscured by restriction of examples to avoid what Gilbert Ryle called "systematically misleading expressions," an important topic of discussion since the 18th century (cf. Chomsky (1965), chapter 1, note 12), and indeed much earlier. Note that this is quite a different matter from the issue of fictional or abstract entities such as Pegasus, justice, or the set of prime numbers; the flaw in the argument or John's lack of talent are neither fictional nor abstract entities. Similar comments apply, I believe, with regard to recent varieties of essentialism; cf. Chomsky (1975), pp. 46f. I think it is proper to regard this work as invoking a level of mental representation ("mentalese"), often mistakenly identified as a domain of individuals in the world. Empirical argument is required to justify the hypothesis, exactly as in the case of LF, thematic relations, etc.

4.   These notions are inadequate for Case-assignment to an element in COMP, as, e.g., in connection with the Hungarian example 3.2.2.(13) or the French example 5.2.(26), or free relatives with the head in COMP assigned Case by external government. Recall again that modifications and extensions are required for constructions that I have not been considering in this discussion, as noted throughout.

5.   We are, crucially, assuming that the derivation of (i) from (ii) is blocked by the θ-criterion:

(i)   NP V t
(ii)   [NP e] V NP

Cf. the discussion of 3.2.2.(41). A comment is necessary in connection with case (iii), discussed there:

(iii)   *advantage took t of John

We assumed this to be ruled out by the θ-criterion, on the assumption that *take* assigns a θ-role to its subject, hence to the non-argument *advantage*. We are now, however, regarding *advantage* as an argument, though a quasi-argument. Thus this case reduces to such cases as (iv):

(iv)   *John hit t

Recall that this analysis permits derivation of "ergatives" such as *the ship sank* from *NP sank the ship* (with base-generated null subject) only if appropriate conditions are established to ensure that such verbs do not assign θ-role to the subject position when they do not assign Case to the object position. Similar modifications are required if such expressions as *the book reads easily,* etc., are to be derived by Move-α, as suggested in the references cited earlier.

6.   In § 3.2.2. we noted a problematic class of cases in which variables appeared not to have Case, namely, cases in which a quantifier was in effect "lowered" to a non-Case-marked position, so that quantifier movement leaves a variable in this position (cf. the discussion of 3.2.2.(23-6)). Norbert Hornstein points out that this case might fall under the same principle of downward Case-inheritance that holds for post-verbal subjects, as discussed in § 4.5. This idea seems feasible. It relates, perhaps, to the question of "reconstruction rules" that in effect interpret an element in the position of a trace, discussed several times above. Pending further inquiry into this general problem, I will leave the question with no further comment.

7.   Recall that as throughout, our discussion is limited to certain construction types, and must be extended to a variety of others: topicalization, the question of heads of relative clauses, etc.

8.   I am indebted to Donca Steriade for raising some of these questions. See Marantz (1981) for a rather different approach to them.

9.   We are glossing over some questions about indexing that should be addressed in a more careful treatment.

10.   Arguments for the structure of LF, as distinct from S-structure, turn on the distinction between principles that hold of S-structure and principles that hold of LF. Thus, we have argued that the binding principles hold at S-structure but that ECP and the principle involved in weak crossover hold at LF. The rules relating S-structure and LF are of two types, only one of which we have exemplified: (I) rules extracting S-structure elements from S, such as the rule of quantifier-movement, the rule of focus, and the *wh*-movement rule for multiple *wh*-questions (or for normal questions in languages that do not require overt *wh*-movement); (II) reconstruction rules, which interpret a phrase in the position of a trace, not necessarily its trace. We have discussed several examples that may involve

rules of the type (II), e.g., such cases as (i), (ii):

(i)   pictures of each other are what they like to see
(ii)   his brother is the person whom everyone admires most

While such examples are perhaps marginal, they do not seem ungrammatical, and if not, some sort of reconstruction seems necessary, though the trace position in which the matrix subject phrase is somehow interpreted is not the position from which it moved. Cf. Burzio (1981) and forthcoming work by J. Higginbotham for discussion of these topics.

The existence of a level of D-structure, as distinct from S-structure, is supported by principles and arguments that are based on or refer to specific properties of this level, which is related to S-structure by the rule Move-α. This rule, as we have seen, plays other roles in the grammar as well. It is, in fact, not *a priori* obvious, hence important if true, that this rule relates the representation of GF-θ to S-structure. We have come across a number of cases where specific reference to properties of D-structure figures crucially in arguments:

(a)   asymmetric properties of idioms (cf. chapter 2, note 94)
(b)   movement only to non-θ-position (cf. 2.1.(17), 2.6.(36-7), and discussion above 6.(8) of the distinction between NP-trace and PRO)
(c)   restriction of an operator to a single variable (cf. 3.2.2.(44))
(d)   the requirement that AGR-subject coindexing be at D-structure, as distinct from government by AGR at S-structure, with its various consequences (cf. 4.5.(17))
(e)   the possibility of inserting lexical items either at D- or S-structure (cf. discussion following 5.4.(19))

As noted repeatedly, arguments bearing on the distinction between S-structure and either LF or D-structure are highly theory-internal. A theory that postulates a D-structure or LF level distinct from S-structure is only subtly different from one that does not, and it is not at all clear that the theories, when properly understood at the appropriate level of abstraction, will prove to be empirically distinguishable. Properties of the subsystems of principles are much more salient; the same is true of the distinction between the rule "Move-α" (however understood) and rules of construal, and of the questions relating to the projection principle, though in this case as well it is quite possible that alternative approaches that appear superficially to be quite different may fall together, when the proper level of abstraction is identified and clarified.

Bibliography

Aissen, J. and D. Perlmutter (1976), "Clause reduction in Spanish," Proceedings of the Second Annual Meeting of the Berkeley Linguistics Society.

Akmajian, A. (1975), "More evidence for an NP cycle," *Linguistic Inquiry* 6.1.

Akmajian, A., S. Steele and T. Wasow (1979), "The category Aux in universal grammar," *Linguistic Inquiry* 10.1.

Anderson, M. (1977), "Transformations in noun phrases," mimeographed, University of Connecticut.

Anderson, S. (1977), "Comment on Wasow (1977)," in Culicover, Wasow and Akmajian, eds.

Anderson, S. and P. Kiparsky (1973), *A Festschrift for Morris Halle*, Holt, Rinehart, and Winston.

Aoun, J. (1979a), "A short note on cliticization," mimeographed, MIT.

Aoun, J. (1979b), "On government, Case-marking, and clitic placement," mimeographed, MIT.

Aoun, J. (1979c), "Indexing and constituency," mimeographed, MIT.

Aoun, J. (1980a), "ECP, move α, and subjacency," mimeographed, MIT; to appear in *Linguistic Inquiry*.

Aoun, J. (1980b), "Feature transportation and the move α convention," mimeographed, MIT.

Aoun, J. (1980c), "Expletive PROs," mimeographed, MIT.

Aoun, J., N. Hornstein and D. Sportiche (1980), "Some aspects of wide scope quantification," mimeographed, MIT and Columbia.

Aoun J., D. Sportiche, J.-R. Vergnaud and M.-L. Zubizarreta (1980), "Reconstruction and logical form."

Babby, L. (1980), *Existential Sentences and Negation in Russian*, Karoma.

Bach, E. (1977), "The position of embedding transformation in a grammar revisited," in A. Zampolli, ed., *Linguistic Structures Processing*, North-Holland.

Bach, E. (1980), "In defense of passive," *Linguistics and Philosophy* 3.3.

Baker, C.L. (1970), "Notes on the description of English questions: the role of an abstract question morpheme," *Foundations of Language* 6.2.

Baker, C.L. (1979), "Syntactic theory and the projection problem," *Linguistic Inquiry* 10.4.

Baltin, M. (1978), *Toward a Theory of Movement Rules*, MIT PhD Dissertation.

Baltin, M. (1979), "A landing site theory of movement rules," mimeographed, NYU.

Baltin, M. (1980), "The structure of infinitival complements," mimeographed, NYU.

Barwise, J. (1979), "On branching quantifiers in English," *Journal of Philosophical Logic* 8.

Belletti, A. (1980a), "On the anaphoric status of the reciprocal construction in Italian," mimeographed, MIT and Scuola Normale Superiore.

Belletti, A. (1980b), "'Morphological' passive and pro-drop: a note on the impersonal construction in Italian," mimeographed, MIT and Scuola Normale Superiore.

Belletti, A., L. Brandi and L. Rizzi, eds. (forthcoming), *Theory of Markedness in Generative Grammar*, Proceedings of the 1979 GLOW conference, Pisa, Scuola Normale Superiore.

Belletti, A. and L. Rizzi (1980), "The syntax of 'ne': some theoretical implications," paper presented at the 1980 GLOW conference, Nijmegen, mimeographed, MIT and Scuola Normale Superiore.

Bennis, H. (1980), "Coindexing and complementizer-trace phenomena," paper presented at the 1980 GLOW conference, Nijmegen, mimeographed, Amsterdam.

Besten, H. den (1976), "Surface lexicalization and trace theory," in H. van Riemsdijk, ed., *Green Ideas Blown Up*, University of Amsterdam, Publikaties van het Instituut voor Algemene Taalwetenschap, no. 13.

Besten, H. den (1979), "A Case filter for passives," mimeographed, University of Amsterdam; to appear in Belletti, Brandi and Rizzi, eds.

Bochner, H. (1976), *On Complement Object Deletion*, B.S. Thesis, MIT.

Bordelois, I. (1974), *The Grammar of Spanish Causative Complements*, MIT Phd dissertation.

Borer, H. (1978), "Restrictive relative clauses in modern Hebrew," mimeographed, MIT.

Borer, H. (1979), "Empty subjects and constraints on thematic relations," paper presented at NELS X, Ottawa, mimeographed, MIT.

Borer, H. (1980), "On the definition of variables," mimeographed, MIT.

Brame, M. (1980), "Hope," *Linguistic Analysis* 6.3.

Bresnan, J. (1970), "On complementizers: toward a syntactic theory of complement types," *Foundations of Language* 6.3.

Bresnan, J. (1972), *Theory of Complementation in English Syntax*, MIT Phd dissertation.

Bresnan, J. (1976), "Nonarguments for raising," *Linguistic Inquiry* 7.3.

Bresnan, J. (1980), "The passive in lexical theory," mimeographed, MIT.

Bresnan, J. and J. Grimshaw (1978), "The syntax of free relatives in English," *Linguistic Inquiry* 9.3.

Brody, M. (1979), "Infinitivals, relative clauses and deletion," mimeographed, University of London.

Burzio, L. (1978), Italian causative constructions," *Journal of Italian Linguistics* 3.2.

Burzio, L. (1981), *Intransitive Verbs and Italian Auxiliaries*, MIT Phd dissertation.

Carlson, L. (1978), "Central problems in Finnish syntax," mimeographed, Academy of Finland.

Chomsky, N. (1951), "Morphophonemics of modern Hebrew," mimeographed, University of Pennsylvania; Garland, 1979.

Chomsky, N. (1955), *The Logical Structure of Linguistic Theory*, mimeographed, Harvard; Plenum, 1975 (in part).

Chomsky, N. (1959), "On certain formal properties of grammars," *Information and Control 2.*

Chomsky, N. (1965), *Aspects of the Theory of Syntax*, MIT.

Chomsky, N. (1972), *Studies on Semantics in Generative Grammar*, Mouton.

Chomsky, N. (1974), "The Amherst lectures," lectures given at the 1974 Linguistic Institute, University of Massachusetts, Amherst; Université de Paris VII, 1974.

Chomsky, N. (1975), *Reflections on Language*, Pantheon.

Chomsky, N. (1977a), *Essays on Form and Interpretation*, North-Holland.

Chomsky, N. (1977b), "On wh-movement," in Culicover, Wasow and Akmajian, eds.

Chomsky, N. (1978), "A naturalistic approach to language and cognition," mimeographed, MIT; to appear in *Cognition and Brain Theory* 4.1, 1981.

Chomsky, N. (1979a), "On markedness and core grammar"; to appear in Belletti, Brandi and Rizzi, eds.

Chomsky, N. (1979b), "Principles and parameters in syntactic theory," mimeographed, MIT; to appear in Hornstein and Lightfoot, eds.

Chomsky, N. (1980a), "On binding," *Linguistic Inquiry* 11.1.

Chomsky, N. (1980b), *Rules and Representations*, Columbia.

Chomsky, N. (1980c), "On the representation of form and function," mimeographed, MIT; to appear in Mehler, ed., and in *Linguistic Review.*

Chomsky, N. (1981), "A note on non-control PRO," to appear in the *Journal of Linguistic Research.*

Chomsky, N. and H. Lasnik (1977), "Filters and control," *Linguistic Inquiry* 8.3.

Cinque, G. (1978), "La sintassi dei pronomi relativi 'cui' e 'quale' nell'italiano moderno," *Rivista di Grammatica Generativa* 3.

Cinque, G. (1979), "On extraction from NP in Italian," mimeographed, Padua and MIT; to appear in *Journal of Italian Linguistics.*

Cinque, G. (1980), "On the theory of relative clauses and markedness," mimeographed, Padua, 1980.

Couquaux, D. (1980), *La transformation MONTEE en français,* thèse de doctorat d'Etat, Université de Paris VII.

Couquaux, D. (forthcoming) "French predication and linguistic theory," in J. Koster and R. May, eds.

Culicover, P., T. Wasow and A. Akmajian, eds. (1977), *Formal Syntax,* Academic press.

Cushing, S. (1979), "Semantic considerations in natural language," *Studies in Language* 3.

Davison, A. (1980), "Peculiar passives," *Language* 56.1.

Edwards, J. (1979), "Equatives: some preliminary considerations," mimeographed, Queens.

Emonds, J. (1976), *A Transformational Approach to English Syntax,* Academic Press.

Emonds, J. (1980), "Word order in generative grammar," *Journal of Linguistic Research* 1.1.

Engdahl, E. (1980), *The Syntax and Semantics of Questions in Swedish,* University of Massachusetts Phd dissertation.

Erteschik, N. (1973), *On the Nature of Island Constraints,* MIT Phd dissertation.

Evans, G. (1980), "Pronouns," *Linguistic Inquiry* 11.2.

Farmer, A. (1980), *On the Interaction of Morphology and Syntax,* Mit Phd dissertation.

Fehri, A. (1980), "Some complement phenomena in Arabic, lexical grammar, the complementizer phrase hypothesis and the non-accessibility condition," mimeographed, University of Rabat.

Fiengo, R. (1974), *Semantic Conditions on Surface Structure,* MIT Phd dissertation.

Fiengo, R. (1977), "On trace theory," *Linguistic Inquiry* 8.1.

Fiengo, R. (1979), *Surface Structure: the Interface of Autonomous Components,* mimeographed, Queens College – CUNY; to be published by Harvard University press.

Fiengo, R. and J. Higginbotham (1979), "Opacity in NP," mimeographed, Queens-CUNY and Columbia, 1979; to appear in *Linguistic Analysis.*

Fiengo, R. and H. Lasnik (1976), "Some issues in the theory of transformations," *Linguistic Inquiry* 7.1.

Fillmore, C. (1975), "The future of semantics," in R. Austerlitz, ed., *The Scope of American Linguistics,* Peter de Ridder press.

Fodor, J. (1975), *The Language of Thought,* Crowell.

Fodor, J., M. Garrett, E. Walker and C. H. Parkes (1980), "Against definitions," *Cognition* 8.

Forster, K. (1979), "Levels of processing and the structure of the language processor," in W. Cooper and E. Walker, eds., *Sentence Processing,* Erlbaum, 1979.

Freidin, R. (1978), "Cyclicity and the theory of grammar," *Linguistic Inquiry* 9.4.

Freidin, R. and H. Lasnik (1979a), "Disjoint reference and *wh*-trace," mimeographed, MIT and U. of Connecticut; to appear in *Linguistic Inquiry.*

Freidin, R. and H. Lasnik (1979b), "Core grammar, Case theory and markedness,"; to appear in Belletti, Brandi and Rizzi, eds.

George, L. (1980), *Analogical Generalizations of Natural Language Syntax,* MIT Phd dissertation.

George, L. and J. Kornfilt (1978), "Finiteness and boundedness in Turkish," mimeographed, MIT and Harvard.

Goodman, N. (1951), *The Structure of Appearance,* Harvard.

Grimshaw, J. (1979), "Complement selection and the lexicon," *Linguistic Inquiry* 10.2.

Grimshaw, J. (1980), "On the lexical representation of Romance reflexive clitics," Center for Cognitive Science, MIT, Occasional Paper #5.

Groos, A. and H. van Riemsdijk (1979), "Matching effects in free relatives," mimeographed, University of Amsterdam; to appear in Belletti, Brandi and Rizzi, eds.

Guéron, J. (1978), "The grammar of PP extraposition," mimeographed, Université de Paris VIII; to appear in *Linguistic Inquiry* 11.4.

Hale, K. (1973), "A note on subject-object inversion in Navajo," in B. Kachru et al., eds. *Issues in Linguistics: Papers in Honor of Henry and Renée Kahane*, Illinois.

Hale, K. (1978), "On the position of Walbiri in a typology of the base," mimeographed, MIT.

Hale, K., L. Jeanne and P. Platero (1977), "Three cases of overgeneration," in Culicover, Wasow and Akmajian, eds.

Hall, B. (1965), *Subject and Object in Modern English*, MIT Phd dissertation.

Hall, R. (1979), "Subjectless verbs and the primacy of the predicate in Romance and Latin," Amsterdam Studies in the Theory and History of Linguistic Science IV, *Current Issues in Linguistic Theory* vol. 11.

Halle, M. and J.-R. Vergnaud (1980), "Three dimensional phonology," *Journal of Linguistic Research* 1.1.

Helke, M. (1971), *The Grammar of English Reflexives*, MIT Phd dissertation.

Hendrick, R. (1980), "An essay on passive and core grammar," mimeographed, University of North Carolina.

Higginbotham, J. (1979a); "Pronouns and bound variables," mimeographed, Columbia; to appear in *Linguistic Inquiry* 11.4.

Higginbotham, J. (1979b), "Reciprocal interpretation," mimeographed, Columbia; to appear in *Journal of Linguistic Research*.

Higginbotham, J. (1979c), "Anaphora and GB: some preliminary remarks," mimeographed, Columbia; paper given at NELS X, Ottawa.

Higginbotham, J. (1980), "Crossover and control in equatives," mimeographed, MIT.

Higginbotham, J. and R. May (1979a), "Questions, quantifiers and crossing," mimeographed, Columbia and Rockefeller; to appear in *Linguistic Review*.

Higginbotham, J. and R. May (1979b), "Crossing, markedness, pragmatics," mimeographed, Columbia and Rockefeller; to appear in Belletti, Brandi and Rizzi, eds.

Higgins, R. (undated), "On the use of idioms as evidence for movement: a cautionary note," mimeographed.

Hintikka, J. (1974), "Quantifiers vs. quantification theory," *Linguistic Inquiry* 5.2.

Hoekstra, T., H. van der Hulst and M. Moortgat, eds. (1980), *Lexical Grammar*, Foris.

Hornstein, N. (1977), "S and $\overline{X}$ convention," *Linguistic Analysis* 3.2.

Hornstein, N. and D. Lightfoot, eds. (forthcoming), *Explanation in Linguistics*, Longmans.

Huang, C.-T. J. (1980), "Move WH in a language without *wh*-movement," mimeographed, MIT.

Huybregts, M. A. C. (1979), "On bound anaphora and the theory of government-binding," paper presented at NELS X, Ottawa.

Jackendoff, R. (1972), *Semantic Interpretation in Generative Grammar*, MIT.

Jackendoff, R. (1977), *$\overline{X}$-Syntax: A Study of Phrase Structure*, Linguistic Inquiry Monograph 2, MIT.

Jaeggli, O. (1978), "On abstract Case," mimeographed, MIT.

Jaeggli, O. (1980a), "Remarks on *to*-contraction," *Linguistic Inquiry* 11.1.

Jaeggli, O. (1980b), *On Some Phonologically-null Elements in Syntax*, MIT Phd dissertation.

Jaeggli, O. (1980c), "On the absence of passive morphology in agentive causatives," mimeographed, MIT.

Katz, J. (1980), "Chomsky on meaning," *Language* 56.1.

Kayne, R. (1972), "Subject inversion in French interrogatives," in J. Casagrande and B. Saciuk, eds., *Generative Studies in Romance Languages*, Newbury House.

Kayne, R. (1975), *French Syntax: the Transformational Cycle*, MIT.

Kayne, R. (1978), "Binding, clitic placement, and leftward quantifier movement," *Rivista di Grammatica Generativa* 3.2, (Italian translation).

Kayne, R. (1979a), "Rightward NP movement in French and English," *Linguistic Inquiry* 10.4.

Kayne, R. (1979b), "Case marking and LF," mimeographed, Université de Paris VIII.

Kayne, R. (1979c), "Two notes on the NIC," mimeographed, Université de Paris VIII; to appear in Belletti, Brandi and Rizzi, eds.

Kayne, R. (1979d), "Binding, quantifiers, clitics and control," mimeographed, Université de Paris VIII; to appear in F. Heny, ed., *Binding and Filtering*, Croom Helm.

Kayne, R. (1980a), "Extensions of binding and Case-marking," *Linguistic Inquiry* 11.1.

Kayne, R. (1980b), "ECP extensions," mimeographed, Université de Paris VIII; to appear in *Linguistic Inquiry* 12.1.

Kayne, R. (1980c), "On certain differences between French and English," mimeographed, Université de Paris VIII; to appear in *Linguistic Inquiry* 12.3.

Kayne, R. (1980d), "Comments on Chomsky (1980c)," mimeographed, Université de Paris VIII; to appear in Mehler, ed.

Kayne, R. (1980e), "Unambiguous paths," mimeographed, Université de Paris VIII; to appear in Koster and May, eds.

Kayne, R. and J.-Y. Pollock (1978), "Stylistic inversion, successive cyclicity, and Move NP in French," *Linguistic Inquiry* 9.4.

Kean, M.-L. (1975), *The Theory of Markedness in Generative Grammar*, MIT Phd dissertation.

Kean, M.-L. (1979), "On a theory of markedness: some general considerations and a case in point," *Social Sciences Research Reports*, 41, University of California, Irvine.

Keenan, E. (1979), "Passive: A case study in markedness," mimeographed, UCLA and Tel Aviv University; to appear in Belletti, Brandi and Rizzi, eds.

Keenan, E. (1980), "Passive is phrasal not (sentential or lexical)," in Hoekstra, van der Hulst and Moortgat, eds.

Keyser, S. J., ed. (1978), *Recent Transformational Studies in European Languages*, Linguistic Inquiry Monograph no. 3.

Kim, W.-C. (1976), *The Theory of Anaphora in Korean Syntax*, MIT Phd dissertation.

Koster, J. (1978a), "Why subject sentences don't exist," in Keyser, ed.

Koster, J. (1978b), *Locality Principles in Syntax*, Foris.

Koster, J. (1978c), "Conditions, empty nodes, and markedness," *Linguistic Inquiry* 9.4.

Koster, J. (1980), "Configurational grammar," mimeographed, Max-Planck-Institute, Nijmegen.

Koster, J. and R. May, eds. (to appear), *Levels of Syntactic Representation*, Foris.

Lapointe, S. (1979), *A Theory of Grammatical Agreement*, University of Massachusetts Phd dissertation.

Lapointe, S. (1980), "A lexical analysis of the English auxiliary verb system," in Hoekstra, van der Hulst and Moortgat, eds.

Lasnik, H. (1976), "Remarks on coreference," *Linguistic Analysis* 2.1.

Lasnik, H. (1979), "Restricting the theory of transformations," mimeographed, University of Connecticut; to appear in Hornstein and Lightfoot, eds.

Lasnik, H. (1980), "Learnability, restrictiveness, and the evaluation metric," mimeographed, University of Connecticut.

Lasnik, H. and R. Fiengo (1974), "Complement object deletion," *Linguistic Inquiry* 5.4.

Lasnik, H. and J. Kupin (1977), "A restrictive theory of transformational grammar," *Theoretical Linguistics* 4.3.

Levelt, W. J. M. (1974), *Formal Grammars in Linguistics and Psycholinguistics*, vol. 2, Mouton.

Lightfoot, D. (1979), *Principles of Diachronic Syntax*, Cambridge.

Lightfoot, D. (1980), "The history of NP movement," in Hoekstra, van der Hulst and Moortgat, eds.

Linebarger, M. (1980), *The Grammar of Negative Polarity*, MIT Phd dissertation.

Longobardi, G. (1978), "Double-Inf," *Rivista di Grammatica Generativa* 3.2 (revised and updated in *Journal of Italian Linguistics*, forthcoming.)

Longobardi, G. (forthcoming), "Super-raising and subjacency."

Manzini, M.-R. (1980), "On control," mimeographed, MIT.

Marantz, A. (1979a), "Assessing the X̄ Convention," mimeographed, MIT.

Marantz, A. (1979b), "Notes toward a revision of subjacency," mimeographed, MIT.

Marantz, A. (1981), *On the Nature of Grammatical Relations*, MIT Phd dissertation.

Matthews, P. (1980), "Review of Chomsky (1980b)," *Times Literary Supplement*, Nov. 21, 1980.

Matthews, R. (1979), "Are the grammatical sentences of a language a recursive set?," *Synthese* 40.
May, R. (1977), *The Grammar of Quantification*, MIT Phd dissertation.
May, R. (1979), "Must COMP-to-COMP movement be stipulated," *Linguistic Inquiry* 10.4.
May, R. (1980), "Quantifier and referential phrases at logical form," mimeographed, MIT.
McCarthy, J. (1976), "Passive," mimeographed, MIT.
Mehler, J., ed. (forthcoming), Proceedings of the June 1980 CNRS Conference on the Cognitive Sciences, Paris, forthcoming.
Miller, G. and N. Chomsky (1963), "Finitary Models of Language Users," in D. Luce, R. Bush and E. Galanter, eds., *Handbook of Mathematical Psychology*, vol. 2, Wiley.
Milner, J.-C. (1978), "Cyclicité successive, comparatives, et cross-over en français," *Linguistic Inquiry* 9.4.
Milner, J.-C. (1979), "Le système de la négation en français et l'opacité du sujet," *Langue Française* 44.
Milsark, G. (1974), *Existential Sentences in English*, MIT Phd dissertation.
Milsark, G. (1977), "Toward an explanation of certain peculiarities of the existential construction in English," *Linguistic Analysis* 3.1.
Milsark, G. (1980), "On markedness, vacuous rules, and the English auxiliary," mimeographed, Temple.
Mohanan, K. (1980), "Grammatical relations, case, and clause structure in Malayalam," mimeographed, MIT.
Moravcsik, J. (1980), "Comments," in *The Behavioral and Brain Sciences*, 3.1 (March, 1980).
Nanni, D. (1978), *The Easy Class of Adjectives in English*, University of Massachusetts Phd dissertation.
Nash, D. (1980), *Topics in Warlpiri Grammar*, MIT Phd dissertation.
Newmeyer, F. (1980), *Linguistic Theory in America*, Academic press.
Obenauer, H.-G. (1976), *Etudes de syntaxe interrogative du français*, Niemeyer.
Oshima, S. (1979), "Conditions on rules: anaphora in Japanese," in G. Bedell, E. Kobayashi and M. Muraki, eds., *Explorations in Linguistics: Essays in Honor of Kazuko Inoue*, Kenkyusha.
Otero, C. (1976), "The dictionary in a generative grammar," mimeographed, UCLA.
Otsu, Y. and A. Farmer, eds. (1980), *Theoretical Issues in Japanese Linguistics, MIT Working Papers in Linguistics*, vol. 2.
Pesetsky, D. (1978a), "Some conditions on bounding nodes," mimeographed, MIT.
Pesetsky, D. (1978b), "Complementizer-trace phenomena and the nominative island condition," mimeographed, MIT; to appear in *Linguistic Review*.
Peters, S. (1973), "On restricting deletion transformations," in M. Gross, M. Halle and M.-P. Schützenberger, eds., *The Formal Analysis of Natural Language*, Mouton.
Peters, S. and R. Ritchie (1973), "On the generative power of transformational grammars," *Information Sciences* 6.
Piattelli-Palmarini, M., ed. (1980), *Language and Learning*, Harvard.
Piera, C. (1979), "Some subject sentences," *Linguistic Inquiry* 10.4.
Pinker, S. (1979), "Formal models of language learning," *Cognition* 7.3.
Postal, P. (1971), *Cross-Over Phenomena*, Holt, Rinehart & Winston.
Postal, P. (1974), *On Raising*, MIT.
Postal, P. (1976), "Avoiding reference to subject," *Linguistic Inquiry* 7.1.
Postal, P. (1977a), "About a 'nonargument' for raising," *Linguistic Inquiry* 8.1.
Postal, P. (1977b), "Antipassive in French," *Lingvisticae Investigationes* 1.1.
Pulleyblank, D. (1980), "Some binding constructions in Yoruba," mimeographed, MIT.
Pullum, G. and D. Wilson (1977), "Autonomous syntax and the analysis of auxiliaries," *Language* 53.
Pullum, G. and P. Postal (1979), "On an inadequate defense of 'trace theory'," *Linguistic Inquiry* 10.4.
Quicoli, C. (1976), "Conditions on quantifier movement in French," *Linguistic Inquiry* 7.4.
Reinhart, T. (1976), *The Syntactic Domain of Anaphora*, MIT Phd dissertation.

Reinhart.T.. (1979a)"Syntactic domains for semantic rules," in F. Guenthner and S. Schmidt, eds., *Formal Semantics and Pragmatics for Natural Languages.*

Reinhart, T. (1979b), "A second COMP position," mimeographed, Tel Aviv University; to appear in Belletti, Brandi and Rizzi, eds.

Reuland, E. (1980), "Governing '-ing'," mimeographed, MIT and Rijksuniversiteit Groningen, 1980.

Riemsdijk, H. van (1978a), "On the diagnosis of *wh*-movement," in Keyser, ed.

Riemsdijk, H. van (1978b), *A Case Study in Syntactic Markedness,* Foris Publications, Dordrecht.

Riemsdijk, H. van (1980), "On theories of Case: the Case of German adjectives," mimeographed, Amsterdam and MIT.

Riemsdijk, H. van and E. Williams (1980), "NP-structure," to appear in: *The Linguistic Review* I, 3.

Rizzi, L. (1976), "La montée du sujet, le *si* impersonnel et une regle de restructuration dans la syntaxe Italienne," *Recherches Linguistiques* 4.

Rizzi, L. (1978a), "A restructuring rule in Italian syntax," in Keyser, ed.

Rizzi, L. (1978b), "Violations of the *wh*-island constraint in Italian and the subjacency condition," in C. Dubisson, D. Lightfoot and Y. C. Morin, eds., *Montreal Working Papers in Linguistics,* vol. 11.

Rizzi, L. (1978c), "Nominative marking in Italian infinitives and the nominative island constraint," mimeographed, Scuola Normale Superiore; to appear in F. Heny, ed., Proceedings of the 1978 GLOW conference, Amsterdam.

Rizzi, L. (1979a), "Remarks on variables, negation and *wh*-movement," mimeographed, Scuola Normale Superiore; to appear in Belletti, Brandi and Rizzi, eds.

Rizzi, L. (1979b), "'Aux to COMP' and the *wh*-island constraint," mimeographed, Scuola Normale Superiore.

Rizzi, L. (1980a), "Wh-movement, negation and the pro-drop parameter," mimeographed, Scuola Normale Superiore.

Rizzi, L. (1980b), "Comments on Chomsky (1980c)," mimeographed, Università della Calabria; to appear in Mehler, ed.

Rizzi, L. (1980c), "Negation, *WH*-movement and the null subject parameter," mimeographed, Università della Calabria.

Rochemont, M. (1978), *A Theory of Stylistic Rules in English,* University of Massachusetts Phd dissertation.

Rochette, A. (1980), "French infinitval complements," mimeographed, MIT; to appear in *MIT Working Papers in Linguistics,* vol. IV.

Ross, J. (1967), *Constraints on Variables in Syntax,* MIT Phd dissertation.

Rouveret, A. (1978), "Result clauses and conditions on rules," in Keyser, ed.

Rouveret, A. (1980a), "Sur la notion de proposition finie," *Recherces linguistiques* 9.

Rouveret, A. (forthcoming), "Sur la notion de proposition finie: gouvernement et inversion, *Langage* 60.

Rouveret, A. and J.-R. Vergnaud (1980), "Specifying reference to the Subject," *Linguistic Inquiry* 11.1, 1980.

Sag, I. (1976), *Deletion and Logical Form,* MIT Phd dissertation.

Schein, B., "Non-finite complements in Russian," mimeographed, MIT.

Selkirk, E. (1972), *The Phrase Phonology of English and French,* MIT Phd dissertation.

Siegel, D. (1974), *Topics in English Morphology,* MIT Phd dissertation.

Sjoblom, T. (1980), *Coordination,* MIT Phd dissertation.

Sportiche, D. (1979), "On bounding nodes in French," mimeographed, MIT.

Steriade, D. (1980), "On the derivation of genitival relatives in Romance," mimeographed, MIT.

Stowell, T. (1978) "What Was There Before There Was There", in D. Farkas et al, eds., Papers from the Fourteenth Regional Meeting, Chicago Linguistic Society, pp. 457–471.

Stowell, T. (1980a) "Subjects Across Categories", to appear in *The Linguistic Review.*

Stowell, T. (1980b) "Complementizers and the Empty Category Principle", presented at NELS XI, to appear in the proceedings of the conference.

Taraldsen, K. T. (1978a), "The scope of *wh* movement in Norwegian," *Linguistic Inquiry* 9.4.

Taraldsen, K. T. (1978b), "On the NIC, vacuous application and the *that-trace* filter," mimeographed, MIT; Indiana Linguistics Club, 1980.

Taraldsen, K. T. (1979), "The theoretical interpretation of a class of marked extractions," to appear in Belletti, Brandi, Rizzi, eds.

Thiersch, C. (1978), *Topics in German Syntax*, MIT Phd dissertation.

Vergnaud, J.-R. (1974), *French Relative Clauses*, MIT Phd dissertation.

Vergnaud, J.-R. (forthcoming), *Quelques éléments pour une théorie formelle des Cas.*

Vergnaud, J.-R. and M.-L. Zubizarreta (1980), "Mixed representations and virtual categories," mimeographed, University of Massachusetts and MIT; to appear in Mehler, ed.

Vinet, M.-T. (1979), "Core grammar and intransitive prepositions in one variety of French," mimeographed, McGill.

Wasow, T. (1972), *Anaphoric Relations in English*, MIT Phd dissertation.

Wasow, T. (1977), "Transformations and the lexicon," in Culicover, Wasow and Akmajian, eds.

Wasow, T. (1979), *Anaphora in Generative Grammar*, E. Story-Scientia Gent.

Weinberg, A. and R. Berwick (forthcoming), "The theory of parsing and the theory of grammar."

Weinberg, A. and N. Hornstein (1978), "Preposition stranding and Case-marking," mimeographed, MIT and Harvard; forthcoming in *Linguistic Inquiry*.

Wexler, K. and P. Culicover (1980), *Formal Principles of Language Acquisition*, MIT.

Wilkins, W. (1977), *The Variable Interpretation Convention*, UCLA Phd dissertation.

Wilkins, W. (1979), "Adjacency and variables in syntactic transformations," mimeographed, UCLA; to appear in *Linguistic Inquiry* 11.4.

Williams, E. (1974), *Rule Ordering in Syntax*, MIT Phd dissertation.

Williams, E. (1975), "Small clauses in English," in J. Kimball, ed., *Syntax and Semantics*, vol. 4, Academic press.

Williams, E. (1978), "Across-the-board rule application," *Linguistic Inquiry* 9.1.

Williams, E. (1980a), "Predication," *Linguistic Inquiry* 11.1.

Williams, E. (1980b), "Passive," mimeographed, University of Massachusetts.

Williams, E. (1980c), "Argument structure and morphology," mimeographed, University of Massachusetts and Max-Planck-Institute, Nijmegen, to appear in *The Linguistic Review.*

Witherspoon, G. (1977), *Language and Art in the Navajo Universe*, Michigan.

Zubizarreta, M.-L. (1980), "Remarks on Portuguese infinitives," mimeographed, MIT.

Index of Names

General Index

368   *General Index*

Recursiveness, 11 ff., 16 fn. 16
Reciprocal, 101 f., 209, 217, 228 fn. 54,
    228 fn. 57, 290 f., 316 fn. 8, see also
    Anaphor
Redundancy Rules, 31 f., 93
Reference, see also Coreference
    arbitrary, see arbitrary PRO
    disjoint, see Disjoint Reference
    free –, 65
    inherent –, 21, 188, 190 f., 218
    lack of independent –, 24
    overlapping –, 286
    potential –, 102
    of PRO, see under PRO
    of pronoun, 65
Referential Expression (R-expression), 101
    f., 115 f., 324
    and binding, 155, 188, 193
    features of –, 330
Reflexive, 44, 102, 217 f., 219, 222 fn. 2,
    229 fn. 62, 230 fn. 68, 283 fn. 36, 289
    ff., 317 fn. 10, see also Anaphor
    emphatic –, 99 ff, 142 fn. 45
Reindexing, 287 f., 316 fn. 3
regard, 109 f.
Relative, 54, 102, 140 fn. 31, 143 fn.
    66, 143 fn. 69, 149 fn. 115, 167 f.,
    175, 229 fn. 63, 245, 319 fn. 35, 345
    fn. 7, see also Relativization
    free –, 111, 173, 175, 180, 248, 317
    fn. 17, 332, 345 fn. 4
    Relative Clause Extraposition, 80 ff.,
    141 fn. 39, 219
Relativization, 7, 280 fn. 20
Representation, levels of, 4, 17 ff.,
Residue of the NIC (Res (NIC)), 160 f.,
    186, 195, 198 f., 222, **231 ff.**, **241 ff.**,
    248 ff., 255
    at LF, 232 ff., 242 ff., 255
    at PF, 243 ff.
Restructuring, 41, 139 fn. 19, 140 fn. 28,
    224 fn. 20
Rightward Movement, see rightward Move-
    ment
River Plate Spanish, 277
Romance Languages, 6, 28, 41, 84, 120,
    122, 132, 140 fn. 28, 142 f. fn. 58, 145
    fn. 84, 147 fn. 103, 171, 222, 289, see
    also French, Italian, Portuguese, *pro-
    drop* languages and Spanish
Root Sentence, 28, 220
Russian, 140 fn. 25, 147 fn. 106, 188, 262

S, see Sentence
S̄, see Sentence-bar

S̿, see Sentence-double-bar
Scope, 155, 201, 234 f., 287
    indicator, 234 f.
    narrow, 239
    wide, 144 fn. 79, 239, 253
seem, 27, 35, 40, 43, 55, 57 ff., 67 f.,
    79, 105 f., 110, 175, see also *Raising*
Select, 38
self-Deletion, 74, 170
Semantic,
    description, 35
    relation, 35
Semantics,
    model theoretic, 344 fn. 3
    real, 324
Semitic Languages, 27, 223 fn. 14
Sentence (S), see also Root Sentence
    head of –, 138 f. fn. 13, 140 fn. 20,
    140 fn. 24, 146 f. fn. 98, 162
    structure of –, 19, 24 ff., 32, 41, 96 ff.
Sentence-bar (S̄, S-bar), see also Clause
    S̄-*Deletion*, 66 ff., 93, 98 ff., 106 f.,
    146 fn. 92, 162 ff., 167, 169, 172,
    298, 303, 307
    S̄-to-S *Rule*, 303 f., 308
    structure of, 96 ff., 304
    transparacy, 173
Sentence-double-bar (S̿, S-double-bar),
    140 fn. 27
si (impersonal) (Italian), 62 ff., 122 f., 141
    f. fn. 43, 168, 270 f., 341, see also im-
    personal Passive
    features of –, 271
si (Reflexive) (Italian), 168
Small Clause, 33, 105 ff., 134, 167 ff., 210
    f., 290 f.
SOV Languages, 145 fn. 86
Spanish, 26, 28, 61, 145 fn. 83, 171 f.,
    174, 223, 226 fn. 41, 232, 237 f., 253,
    255, 275, 277, 282 fn. 32, see also
    River Plate Spanish
Specified Subject Condition (SSC), 14 f.,
    58, 72 f., 153 ff., 179, 187 ff., 194 f.,
    208 ff., 214, 216, 231 ff.
Specifity Constraint, 235 f., 279 fn. 6
Speech Communities, 8
S-structure, 4 f., 17 ff., 34, 41 f., 45, 183,
    196 ff., 245, 313, 331
    base generation of –, see existence of
    Deep-Structure
    without empty categories, 92
    factoring of –, 39, 43
Structural,
    change, 86
    description, 86